NATIONAL
GEOGRAPHIC

GUIDE TO THE

National
Historic Sites
of Canada

NATIONAL GEOGRAPHIC

GUIDE TO THE

National
Historic Sites
of Canada

NATIONAL GEOGRAPHIC
Washington, D.C.

TABLE OF CONTENTS

THE SOUL OF CANADA

Canadians share a rich and diverse heritage. The many people, places, and events that shaped our national identity can be found all across this great nation.

National historic sites are places of profound importance to Canada. Each one tells its own story, contributing a sense of time, identity, and place to our understanding of the country as a whole. They bear witness to Canada's defining moments and illustrate its human creativity and cultural traditions. They are the very soul of Canada.

Located in every province and territory, national historic sites are found in almost any setting—from rural and urban locales to wilderness environments. They may be sacred spaces, archaeological sites, battlefields, heritage buildings, or places of scientific discovery. They can recall moments of greatness or compel us to reflect on our sacrifices. They may also cause us to contemplate the complex and challenging times that helped define the Canadian values of today.

Each national historic site is a distinct and vibrant illustration of where Canada has come from, where it is today, where it is headed.

Parks Canada is proud to manage a system of 168 national historic sites, which includes six UNESCO World Heritage sites recognized for their outstanding universal value. These sites provide a wealth of opportunities to learn about our diverse heritage.

From the largest national historic site, Saoyú-ʔehdacho, commemorating an Indigenous landscape of great cultural and spiritual importance, to the Sahtúgot'įnę, to L'Anse aux Meadows,

Fort Anne, Canada's oldest national historic site

recalling a Viking settlement 1,000 years old, to the Fortifications of Québec that witnessed early colonial Canada, these sites represent thousands of years of human history and hundreds of years of nation building.

National historic sites tell the stories of who we are, including the history, cultures, and contributions of Indigenous Peoples. Parks Canada is proud to work with more than 300 Indigenous communities in conserving, restoring, and presenting Canada's natural and cultural heritage.

Parks Canada is committed to protecting the commemorative integrity and special cultural heritage of these places for all time.

Here you can journey the passes, trails, and waterways traditionally travelled by Indigenous Peoples and the early European explorers that followed, walk on battlefields that changed the course of history, or view original writings of beloved Canadian authors. Canadians and visitors from around the world can enjoy innovative programming that offers a living history, a feel for what Canada used to be and what it is today.

The year 2017 marks the 150th birthday of Canada. There is no better time to connect with these incredible national historic sites that celebrate our national diversity and at the same time unify Canada in a shared history and culture.

These moving and memorable reflections of Canada will provide you with incredible gateways to history and culture. If you have already discovered some of the national historic sites, this guide will encourage you to explore further. If you are thinking about visiting us for the first time, I can promise you incredible, lifetime memories.

Parks Canada looks forward to offering you a warm welcome. We invite you to enjoy some of the most interesting places on Earth.

—Daniel Watson
Chief Executive Officer, Parks Canada

Manoir Papineau in Québec, the 19th-century estate of luminary Louis-Joseph Papineau

EXPLORING CANADA'S HISTORY

In this guide you will read about many remarkable national historic sites in Canada. To be declared a national historic site, these important places must first be given consideration by the Historic Sites and Monuments Board of Canada (HSMBC).

Established in 1919, this distinguished board is composed of members from each province and territory, the Librarian and Archivist of Canada, along with senior representatives of the Canadian Museum of History and Parks Canada. They meet twice a year to review new subjects for commemoration. The board submits its recommendations to the minister responsible for Parks Canada, who makes the final decision on what merits a designation. Upon approval, places receive an official designation date and are recognized as national historic sites. All the sites in this guide went through this process.

WHAT MAKES A HISTORIC SITE?

To be eligible for designation, a building or site must be at least 40 years old, people must be deceased for over 25 years, and events need to have occurred more than 40 years ago. Citizens can nominate subjects for consideration. Parks Canada administers the National Program of Historical Commemoration and prepares the archaeological and historical reports that support the board's work. Canada has more than 2,000 designations of national historic significance—whether a structure, a building, a group of buildings, a district, a cultural landscape, or an archaeological site. At these sites, bronze plaques commemorate people, places, and events.

WHAT'S IN A NAME?

A national historic site's name is usually its historic name linked to its original use or given to it by its makers, whether by Indigenous Peoples, European settlers, or others. For example, Mnjikaning Fish Weirs National Historic Site, near Peterborough, Ontario, reflects its creation and use by the Mnjikaning First Nation. Historically other places often changed their names when they changed owners. For example, Fort Beauséjour, built by the French in 1750, became Fort Cumberland in 1755 after the English defeated the French. Today it is known by both names. Occasionally, a site's name becomes controversial over time. Typically, these are sites named after an individual who was once viewed as a heroic leader and who now may be understood as having acted in ways considered immoral today. As our values and views change, names might be challenged.

For more about the places, people, and events with historic designation, consult the online *Directory of Federal Heritage Designations* in French and English at *pc.gc.ca/apps/dfhd/ search-recherche_eng.aspx*.

USING THIS GUIDE

This guide features 236 of the most visited and celebrated sites. Each site's story extends well beyond the land and structures themselves. Many sites have interpreters who will guide you to see the integral part a place plays in Canada's colourful and complex heritage. Find out more

about each site's history at *historic places.ca*.

Each chapter begins with a map that features the historic sites in the province or region covered in that chapter. A mileage key gives you an idea of the sites' proximities, if you are planning to visit several during one excursion.

Coverage of each site begins with a portrait of its provincial setting and history, including stories of key people and events. We highlight the role of the Indigenous Peoples who first settled many areas where today's sites stand, as well as the sites inscribed on the UNESCO World Heritage List for their cultural value (emblem at right).

Besides a historic overview, all sites have contact information. For larger sites, you'll also find the following information:

HOW TO GET THERE

Find travel guidance and route recommendations. For more remote

Fort George overlooks the Niagara River in Ontario.

⊕ Country capital city

0 mi ⊢———┼———⊣ 400
0 km ⊢———┼———⊣ 400
                 400

UNITED STATES
CANADA

Yukon

Northwest Territories

N u n

FAR NORTH
332-345

BRITISH
COLUMBIA
302-331

Alberta

PRAIRIE PROVINCES
230-283

Manitoba

ROCKIES
284-301

Saskatchewan

CANADA
UNITED STATES

destinations, contact the site for guidance on how to get there.

WHEN TO GO

Many sites are open year-round. To avoid crowds, visit a popular site during off-peak months (April, May, or late August). Off-season facilities and programming may be limited.

INFORMATION & ACTIVITIES

This section offers detailed visitor information for each site, including:
• **Entrance Fees.** The prices listed in Canadian dollars in this book are average prices. The daily entrance fees at the time of printing range from $3.90 to $17.60 for adults and $9.80 to $44.10 for a family or group

gives unlimited access to nearly 100 park properties. The current cost is $67.70 for adults, $57.90 for seniors, $33.30 for youth, and $136.40 for a family/group.

• **Pets.** Check the individual site. Some have trails and nearby recreational areas, where dogs are welcome but must be leashed.

• **Accessible Services.** This section lists a site's accessibility to visitors with disabilities.

• **Special Advisories.** Take care when visiting sites with outdoor components, such as cliff-side trails. Accidents do occur. Most are caused by recklessness or failure to heed warnings.

ATLANTIC PROVINCES
12–89

Newfoundland and Labrador

QUÉBEC
90–161

Prince
Edward Island

ONTARIO
162–229

New
Brunswick

ATLANTIC
PROVINCES
12–89

Nova
Scotia

Ottawa

• **Campgrounds.** Find contact information for local campgrounds and RV parks. For sites near or in most national parks, the Campground Reservation Service (877-RESERVE, *reservation.pc.gc.ca*) handles reservations.

• **Hotels, Motels, & Inns.** The guide gives a sampling of accommodations as a service to readers. These do not imply endorsement by National Geographic or Parks Canada. The information can change without notice. Contact the site or local tourism centres for suggestions.

(up to seven people, with a maximum of two adults, visiting the site together). You can purchase daily entry passes at the site or at the Parks Canada website *(parkscanada.gc.ca)*. You can also purchase an annual Parks Canada Discovery Pass that

ATLANTIC
PROVINCES

Sunset "Taps" at the Fortress of Louisbourg *Page 12:* Visitor to the Alexander Graham Bell museum (top); guard at Halifax Citadel (middle); Castle Hill fortress (bottom) *Page 13:* Cape Spear Lighthouse National Historic Site

ATLANTIC PROVINCES

Prince Edward Island, Nova Scotia (which includes Cape Breton), New Brunswick, and Newfoundland and Labrador comprise Canada's four Atlantic provinces. The first three—collectively known as the Maritime Provinces—share a common political, cultural, and economic heritage.

The Mi'kmaq First Nation, whose range encompassed the Maritime Provinces for thousands of years, and other Indigenous Peoples of the region encountered Europeans in 1497, when John Cabot, an Italian explorer sailing for England, landed in North America and claimed the territory for his sponsor, King Henry VII. By 1605, the French had also arrived and established Acadia (Acadie in French), with its first capital at Port-Royal (present-day Annapolis Royal) in what is today Nova Scotia.

In the ensuing struggle between England and France for control of the region—and, more generally, for global empire—the Acadians, who by the end of the 17th century had become almost wholly self-reliant, tried to remain neutral. Nevertheless, their communities were scattered by the British in 1755, on the eve of the Seven Years' War (1756–1763). With the signing of the Treaty of Paris in 1763, France formally ceded its Canadian territories to the British. On July 1, 1867, Nova Scotia and New Brunswick joined the Province of Canada to form the Dominion of Canada. Prince Edward Island followed in 1873. Newfoundland and Labrador, which had initially rejected Confederation in 1869, finally joined in 1949. Today, the Atlantic provinces retain distinct cultures rooted in English, French, and Celtic traditions.

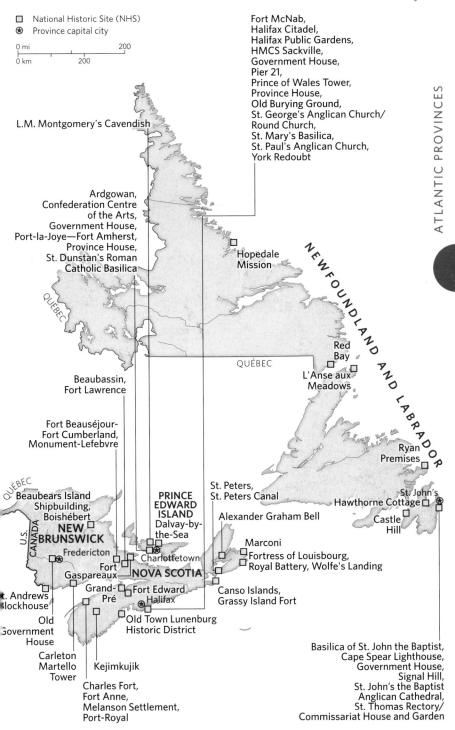

National Historic Site (NHS)
Province capital city

0 mi   200
0 km   200

Fort McNab,
Halifax Citadel,
Halifax Public Gardens,
HMCS Sackville,
Government House,
Pier 21,
Prince of Wales Tower,
Province House,
Old Burying Ground,
St. George's Anglican Church/
Round Church,
St. Mary's Basilica,
St. Paul's Anglican Church,
York Redoubt

ATLANTIC PROVINCES

L.M. Montgomery's Cavendish

Ardgowan,
Confederation Centre
of the Arts,
Government House,
Port-la-Joye—Fort Amherst,
Province House,
St. Dunstan's Roman
Catholic Basilica

QUÉBEC

Hopedale
Mission

NEWFOUNDLAND AND LABRADOR

QUÉBEC

Red
Bay

L'Anse aux
Meadows

Beaubassin,
Fort Lawrence

Ryan
Premises

Fort Beauséjour-
Fort Cumberland,
Monument-Lefebvre

QUÉBEC

St. Peters,
St. Peters Canal

St. John's

Beaubears Island
Shipbuilding,
Boishébert

PRINCE
EDWARD
ISLAND
Dalvay-by-
the-Sea

Alexander Graham Bell

Hawthorne Cottage

Castle
Hill

NEW
BRUNSWICK

Fredericton

Charlottetown

Marconi
Fortress of Louisbourg,
Royal Battery, Wolfe's Landing

U.S.
CANADA

Fort
Gaspareaux

NOVA SCOTIA

t. Andrews
lockhouse

Grand-
Pré

Fort Edward
Halifax

Canso Islands,
Grassy Island Fort

Old
Government
House

Old Town Lunenburg
Historic District

Carleton
Martello
Tower

Kejimkujik

Basilica of St. John the Baptist,
Cape Spear Lighthouse,
Government House,
Signal Hill,
St. John's the Baptist
Anglican Cathedral,
St. Thomas Rectory/
Commissariat House and Garden

Charles Fort,
Fort Anne,
Melanson Settlement,
Port-Royal

This Prince Edward Island home inspired author Lucy Maud Montgomery's *Anne of Green Gables*.

PRINCE EDWARD ISLAND

At just 224 km (139 mi) long, Prince Edward Island may be the nation's smallest province, but it looms large in the popular imagination—not least because of the wild, windswept beauty of its beaches and red-sand cliffs. Archaeological evidence suggests that Indigenous Peoples have lived here for at least 10,000 years. When the French arrived in the early 18th century, they named it Île Saint-Jean, changed by the British to Prince Edward Island in 1799. The Mi'kmaq continue to call it Abegweit, or "land cradled on the waves." In the late

19th century, this idyllic panorama
prompted one oil tycoon to erect a
lavish estate overlooking the sea,
Dalvay-by-the-Sea (see p. 22). The
island is also home to Anne Shirley,
beloved heroine of Lucy Maud Montgomery's *Anne of Green Gables* books.
Montgomery grew up on the north
shore and set her books in the pasto-
ral landscape that she herself called
home (see pp. 18–21). Other historic
sites pepper the island, particularly
in the provincial capital of Charlottetown, where the idea of Canada as a
Confederation was born in 1864.

A red-haired Anne Shirley reenactor greets guests.

▶ L. M. MONTGOMERY'S CAVENDISH

CAVENDISH, PE
Designated 2004

Perhaps no Canadian literary character is better known than Anne Shirley. Ever since the 1908 publication of *Anne of Green Gables,* the wilful, redheaded orphan has charmed readers with her tales of adventure in Avonlea—a stand-in for Cavendish, the Prince Edward Island community where Green Gables author Lucy Maud Montgomery grew up.

Each year, the enduring legacy of the books—which have spawned adaptations for film, stage, television, and radio—draws hundreds of thousands of visitors to Cavendish, an idyllic rural community that overlooks the Gulf of St. Lawrence on the north shore of Prince Edward Island. Wide, sandy beaches allow for swimming, sunbathing, and surfing. Rolling green fields and red cliffs stand in striking contrast to the blue skies and waterfront.

Cavendish is significant not only for the role it played in a beloved literary series but also for its role in the life of one of the country's best loved novelists. Within Cavendish, the national historic site comprises two separate but nearby locations: Green Gables Heritage Place and the site of Montgomery's Cavendish home. At Green Gables Heritage Place, visitors can access a short network of walking paths, including Haunted Wood Trail and Lover's Lane, that feature prominently in the Green Gables books.

The paths and places within the national historic site hold great significance in terms of Canada's contribution to the arts on a global scale. The immediate international success of *Anne of Green Gables* (and its seven follow-up books) means Cavendish has long been a pilgrimage site for fans from all over the globe.

Because of Montgomery's far-reaching influence, the government of Canada named her a national historic person in 1943. Her Ontario home has also been designated a national historic site.

GREEN GABLES HERITAGE PLACE

The original farm at Green Gables was built by David Macneill, Sr. The 52-ha (128 acres) farm was settled in 1831, and was eventually passed down to David Macneill, Jr., a cousin of Montgomery's grandfather. Today, much of that land is taken up by Green Gables Golf Club. Green Gables Heritage Place comprises roughly 10 ha (25 acres) of the site.

Montgomery never lived at Green Gables Heritage Place, but she visited often, travelling from the nearby Cavendish home of her maternal grandparents to spend time in the bucolic farm surroundings that went on to inspire her books. In fact, the vast majority of the more than 20 books she wrote in her lifetime were set on Prince Edward Island. Even after she moved to Ontario, she continued to write about the eastern landscape.

"Cavendish is to a great extent Avonlea," she said in her published journals. "Green Gables was drawn from David Macneill's house . . . , though not so much the house itself as the situation and scenery, and the truth of my description of it is attested by the fact that everyone has recognized it."

Green Gables has undergone changes since its initial establishment. Most notably, a fire in 1997 damaged portions of the house's first and second floors. In recent years, however, Parks Canada has worked to restore the home and surrounding outbuildings (including a barn, woodshed, and granary for animal feed) to be authentic to the late 1800s, when Montgomery's books were set.

For fans of Montgomery's book, a visit to Green Gables is the closest they can come to stepping inside the pages of their favourite book. Part of the magic is in walking in and among the buildings described in the Green Gables series. Wander the barns and the house, stroll the gardens and the well-maintained paths.

Exploring the house is even more of a thrill. Green Gables has been completely styled after the house in Montgomery's books, complete with real-life and fictional relics.

In the front hall, floral-papered walls are lined with interpretive photos and text. The pantry is stocked with ladles and scales as though Anne's foster mother Marilla were about to come in and start cooking. The kitchen is also outfitted with the same cast-iron stove, a new Waterloo No. 2, as in the novel. Climb the stairs to Anne's room to see her dress with puffed sleeves hanging on the closet door, her carpetbag set on a chair in the corner. There's also a

Visitors stroll Anne's storied Green Gable paths.

PRINCE EDWARD ISLAND

broken slate, representative of the time one of her classmates called her "carrots" (a dig at her red hair) and she broke a slate over his head.

One of the most popular artefacts in the house is a bottle of raspberry cordial. Fans of the books will remember that, in the first instalment of the series, Anne mistakes currant wine for cordial and serves her friend Diana a surplus of the alcoholic drink.

From July to September, Green Gables offers daily programming to help introduce visitors to the site. From a 20-minute guided tour of the grounds to a more extensive interpretive program about Cavendish as a community, there's usually something on each morning and afternoon to give visitors an overview of Montgomery's life and how her experiences in Cavendish were integral to *Anne of Green Gables*.

Period-costumed staff conduct heritage demonstrations on rug hooking, butter making, harness care, candle making, knitting, soap making, whittling, and more. The demos are included in the price of admission, and most range from 20 to 60 minutes each. There are also games and races and picnics.

Additional activities include sipping raspberry cordial while taking in an interpretive program, or making old-fashioned ice cream.

There are two trails at Green Gables. The Balsam Hollow Trail is an easy walk measuring 0.8 km (0.5 mi) round-trip. It begins with Lover's Lane, a former cow path, and wanders through woodlands and along a brook. The Haunted Wood Trail is longer, 0.9 km (0.6 mi) one way, but it's an easy 45-minute stroll along a forested path that passes Cavendish Cemetery, where L. M. Montgomery was buried upon her death in 1942,

and leads to the site of Montgomery's Cavendish home.

SITE OF MONTGOMERY'S CAVENDISH HOME

The site of the Cavendish home where Montgomery grew up is located a quarter mile east of Green Gables. None of the original buildings remain, but there are plenty of recognizable natural features, including the fields that surrounded the home, the lanes and gardens Montgomery would have strolled, and the trees she used to sit under to read and write.

Placards and interpretive signage dot the landscape, pointing out significant areas and stories about the former homestead, which belongs to John Macneill, Montgomery's great-grandson. A bookstore and museum offer additional information.

How to Get There

If driving from New Brunswick, Cavendish is a 50-km (31 mi) drive along the Trans-Canada Highway to the opposite side of the island from the Confederation Bridge and Borden-Carleton. From Nova Scotia, Northumberland Ferries regularly cross the Northumberland Strait May through mid-December to Wood Islands; from there, Cavendish is a 90-km (56 mi) drive northwest. From Charlottetown, Cavendish is a 34-km (21 mi) drive along Rte. 2.

When to Go

The full slate of programming is offered at Green Gables July through Labour Day. Summer also provides the best opportunity to take advantage of the wide, sandy shoreline at Cavendish and to enjoy the attractions of nearby Prince Edward Island National Park.

L. M. MONTGOMERY'S CAVENDISH NATIONAL HISTORIC SITE
(Lieu historique national du Cavendish-de-L.-M.-Montgomery)

INFORMATION & ACTIVITIES

HOW TO REACH US
Green Gables Heritage Place, 8619 Rte. 6, Cavendish, PE. Phone (902) 963-7874. pc.gc.ca/greengables.

SEASONS & ACCESSIBILITY
The site is open daily May 1 to October 31. Special appointments may be made from April 15 to 30 and November 1 to 30.

ENTRANCE FEES
$7.80 per adult, $19.60 per family/group.

PETS
Leashed animals are allowed on-site, though not in buildings.

ACCESSIBLE SERVICES
All buildings at Green Gables, including the first floor of the house, are accessible to visitors with disabilities. Closed-captioning is available in all of the theatres.

THINGS TO DO
Summer activities include demonstrations, interpretive talks, and guided and self-guided hikes. See the website for details.

SPECIAL ADVISORIES
Certain trails and sections of the site may be closed for maintenance or forest restoration. Check the website for updates.

CAMPGROUNDS
Cavendish Campground (in Prince Edward Island National Park) 357 Graham's Ln., Cavendish, PE C0A 1N0. (902) 672-6350. pc.gc.ca/eng/pn-np/pe/pei-ipe/activ/activ-menu/camping/cavendish.aspx. Sites $27–$36; oTENTiks $120.

HOTELS, MOTELS, & INNS
(Rates are for a 2-person double, high season, in Canadian dollars, unless otherwise noted.)

Anne Shirley Motel and Cottages 7542 Rte. 13, Cavendish, PE C0A 1N0. (800) 561-4266. anneshirley.ca. 36 rooms, $109–$165.
Bay Vista Motel and Cottages 9517 Cavendish Rd. W, Bayview, PE C0A 1E0. (902) 963-2225. bayvista.ca. 31 rooms, $69–$135.
Green Gables Cottages 8663 Cavendish Rd., Rte. 6, Cavendish, PE C0A 1N0. (902) 963-2722. greengablescottages.com. 40 rooms, $120–$164.

PRINCE EDWARD ISLAND SITES

PORT-LA-JOYE–FORT AMHERST
ROCKY POINT, PE

Ruins and interpretive plaques testify to the role the French-built Port-la-Joye–Fort Amherst played in the struggle for control of North America. At the entrance to Charlottetown Harbour, the fort was a point of entry for many settlers, and home to early Acadian farms. In the 18th century, it was also one of two locations where the alliance between the Mi'kmaq and the French was renewed annually through ceremony and gift giving. Designated NHS: 1958. 191 Hache Gallant Dr. (902) 566-7050.

PRINCE EDWARD ISLAND SITES

DALVAY-BY-THE-SEA
YORK, PE

Located inside the boundaries of Prince Edward Island National Park, Dalvay-by-the-Sea is a sprawling homestead originally built in 1896–99 for Alexander McDonald, then president of Standard Oil of Kentucky. The home was the site of many lavish parties and celebrations before it became a summer hotel in 1932. Today, the many dormers, bay windows, and gables mark Dalvay as a fine example of Queen Anne Revival architecture in Canada. Designated NHS: 1990. 16 Cottage Crescent. (902) 672-6350.

PROVINCE HOUSE
CHARLOTTETOWN, PE

Province House is the dominant landmark in Charlottetown's Great George Street Historic District. Before this structure was built in the 1840s, the legislature of Prince Edward Island met in local taverns and houses. With the construction of this beautiful neoclassical building, the legislature was able to host such events as the Charlottetown Conference of 1864, the first of a series of discussions that ultimately led to the Confederation of Canada. Designated NHS: 1966. 165 Richmond St. (902) 566-7050.

CONFEDERATION CENTRE OF THE ARTS
CHARLOTTETOWN, PE

Adjacent to Province House, where conversations about a united Canada first began, sits the Confederation Centre of the Arts. Built in the brutalist style during the 1960s, the centre was meant to inspire Canadians by referencing both the development of the country and a national dedication to arts and culture. Inside, distinct pavilions offer a theatre, art gallery, and public library. Designated NHS: 2003. 145 Richmond St. (902) 628-1864.

ARDGOWAN
CHARLOTTETOWN, PE

Ardgowan is the former home of William Henry Pope, a lawyer, newspaper editor, politician, and a father of Confederation. This Gothic Revival–style house, flanked by a small carriage house and beautiful garden, lies on the outskirts of Charlottetown. In September 1864, Pope hosted a lunch for delegates attending the first of three conferences about the possible union of the British North American colonies, which led to the Confederation of Canada in 1867. Designated NHS: 1966. 2 Palmers Ln. (902) 566-7050.

GOVERNMENT HOUSE
CHARLOTTETOWN, PE

Located just west of Charlottetown's Great George Street Historic District, this 1830s neoclassical residence is an architectural jewel fronted by an expanse of well-manicured lawn. A two-storey gabled portico, verandas, and wood-shingle cladding lend a simple elegance to the building, now the official residence of the lieutenant governor of Prince Edward Island. When first built, it was the seat of colonial executive power in the province. Designated NHS: 1971. 1 Terry Fox Dr. (902) 368-5480.

ST. DUNSTAN'S ROMAN CATHOLIC BASILICA
CHARLOTTETOWN, PE

A fine example of high Victorian Gothic Revival architecture, St. Dunstan's was designed and built by Québec architect François-Xavier Berlinguet. It took about ten years (from 1896 to 1907) to build. The stone facade, with its towers and pinnacles, remains dark and imposing, but the interior is more English-inspired. This design discrepancy is the result of a 1913 fire that substantially damaged the structure, calling for a redesign. Designated NHS: 1990. 65 Great George St. (902) 894-3486.

PRINCE EDWARD ISLAND

Canoers at sunset in Kejimkujik National Park and Historic Site

MAINLAND NOVA SCOTIA

Along with New Brunswick, Ontario, and Québec, Nova Scotia is one of the four original provinces of the Dominion of Canada. It comprises the mainland peninsula as well as the large island of Cape Breton and a number of other smaller islands. The Mi'kmaq and other Indigenous Peoples had been in this region for hundreds of years by the time Europeans arrived in the late 15th century or possibly earlier. Home to Port-Royal (see pp. 31–32), one of the earliest European settlements in North America, mainland Nova Scotia also boasts

Canada's oldest national historic site, Fort Anne (see pp. 30–31), as well as Grand-Pré (see pp. 26–29), where visitors can explore the landscape and remains of one of the nation's largest Acadian settlements. After the Seven Years' War (1756–1763), Nova Scotia prospered, attracting more immigrants from Europe and expanding its fishing and shipbuilding industries. The other historic sites in this region weave a vibrant tapestry of culture, commerce, and conflict, much of it centred on the provincial capital of Halifax.

Grand-Pré Memorial Church and statue of Evangeline

▶ GRAND-PRÉ

GRAND-PRÉ, NS
Designated 1982; Inscribed WH 2012

Grand-Pré National Historic Site and World Heritage site was once home to a prosperous Acadian agricultural community. The Acadians were descendants of French colonists who settled along the shores of the Bay of Fundy more than 300 years ago.

Their communities prospered despite the struggle between England and France for control of the region. Although the peninsula that is today Nova Scotia changed hands many times in the colonial era, the Acadians wished to stay on their farms and aspired to remain neutral. But in 1755 the British chose to deport the Acadians; their communities were destroyed and they were scattered among the English-speaking American colonies to the south.

In 1682, Pierre Melanson moved his family from the Acadian settlement of Port-Royal to the rolling uplands of Grand-Pré, overlooking extensive marshlands on the shores of the Bay of Fundy. Many other

Acadians followed his lead, eager to establish their own farms.

As they had done around Port-Royal, the Acadians used techniques from their homes in western France to dyke and drain the marshland, reclaiming arable lands where they might plant grain and raise cattle. It was a massive undertaking, but one that, after the soil was desalinated, yielded superior crops. By 1750, Grand-Pré had become one of the largest Acadian population centres.

The Acadian settlements at the eastern end of the Bay of Fundy were removed from the military presence at Port-Royal/Annapolis Royal, but in times of war the conflict touched their communities. During the War of the

Austrian Succession (1740–48), a French force en route to retake Annapolis Royal called on the Acadians to provision and support them. In 1747, French forces and their Indigenous allies attacked British troops from Annapolis Royal billeted for the winter at Grand-Pré. Between 1751 and 1755, the French again encouraged and pressured Acadians to move into French territory and to help to defend their fort at Beauséjour, at the eastern end of the Bay of Fundy.

In 1755, amid mounting tensions on the eve of the Seven Years' War, the lieutenant governor and the Council of Nova Scotia told a delegation of Acadians that all Acadians would have to swear an unconditional oath of allegiance to the British king. When the delegates refused, the council arrested them and began the process that would lead to the deportation of almost the entire Acadian population.

Roughly 2,200 Acadians were deported from the lands around Grand-Pré, constituting a third of the roughly 6,000 deported from the province of Nova Scotia that year.

By 1764, when the British allowed Acadians to return to Nova Scotia, their lands had been claimed by settlers from New England, forcing the Acadians to other parts of the east coast, including Cape Breton and the western shore of Nova Scotia, New Brunswick, Prince Edward Island, and Québec.

In 1907, John F. Herbin, who popularized Acadian history in a series of books about Grand-Pré, bought 5.5 ha (13.6 acres) of land on which the original Grand-Pré community had stood. Though the parish church, houses, farm buildings, storehouses, and windmills were long gone, the landscape drew the Acadian diaspora from across North America. Many were looking to connect with a home they never knew, through a history they had only heard. Many came via the Dominion Atlantic Railway, which had a main rail line running through Grand-Pré. Years later, Herbin sold his property to the railway, with two caveats—that the site be developed as a memorial park and that a parcel of land be deeded to the Acadian people on which a memorial would be built. The lands were transferred to the Canadian government in 1956–57.

In 2012, UNESCO inscribed the landscape of Grand-Pré on the World Heritage List. The national historic site, designated in 1982, lies at the heart of this landscape. Grand Pré means "great meadow," and a drive or a walk through the hamlet perfectly illustrates why the land ended up with this name.

EXPLORING GRAND-PRÉ

Visitors can explore the national historic site on their own, or join one of the many interpretive talks and guided tours (available July to August). Start in the visitor centre and then walk the grounds, being sure to see the view over "La Grande Pré," a large meadow created through dyking as well as the various works of art that depict the Acadian successes, struggles, and eventual deportation.

Designed by architect Terry Smith-Lamothe, the visitor centre tips its hat to the 1605 Habitation at Port-Royal (see pp. 31–32) as it appeared in an early sketch of the village. The centre's siding and the trim work surrounding the windows and doors imitate the log construction of the early Acadian settlers. The centre's colour scheme matches that of the Acadian flag. Images of maple and French willow trees are found throughout, and the trusses of the atrium are modelled after the branches of a family tree.

The "Réveil" mural by artist Wayne Boucher, meant to represent the past, present, and future of the Acadian people, complements the design. Boucher's representation of the Acadian flag puts the Deportation Cross—the cross at Hortonville (previously known as Pointe Noire), on the shores of the Minas Basin, site of the actual deportations—at the centre of the work.

A multimedia presentation relates Acadian life before the deportation, and the deportation itself. Acadians were put in the holds of ships when deported, and the theatre itself was designed as a ship's cargo hold. In another exhibit, Acadian agricultural practices are explained through audio-visual media, a maquette of the landscape, and a reconstructed dyke and *aboiteau* (sluice). Displays include original *aboiteaux* and other artefacts.

Outside, stroll through the Victorian gardens (see below) where the statue of Evangeline and other monuments and sculptures stand among duck ponds, flower gardens, a kitchen garden, and an orchard— a perfect place to enjoy a picnic.

Filled with art, the Memorial Church is a monument to the

Picnickers enjoy Grand-Pré's grounds and duck pond.

deportation. Must-see works include Smith-Lamothe's stained-glass window, an evocative picture of the deportation from Pointe Noire, and the paintings by Claude Picard, large-scale realist works depicting significant moments in Acadian history.

Located a short walk from the church is a stone cross erected by Herbin, built from what he believed to be the remnants of Acadian residences. The cross commemorates the site of the old Acadian cemetery.

The site's blacksmith shop is an original building from the post-deportation era that was transplanted to Grand-Pré from the Acadian community of Wedgeport.

EVANGELINE

Modelled on a 1917 design by sculptor Louis-Philippe Hébert, the life-size bronze statue of Evangeline was created by his son, Henri, who had been commissioned by the Dominion Atlantic Railway (owned by the Canadian Pacific Railway [CPR]). The statue was inspired by American poet Henry Wadsworth Longfellow's 1847 "Evangeline: A Tale of Acadie," which recounts the fictional trials of an Acadian girl named Evangeline as she searches for her fiancé, Gabriel, in the wake of the deportation.

By erecting the monument, the CPR hoped to increase visitation to Grand-Pré, and in turn, the sale of rail tickets. Interest in the poem brought many U.S. tourists to Nova Scotia, encouraging the province to develop its history for tourism.

From the time of Longfellow, Evangeline has represented the tragic struggles of the Acadians during and after the 1755 deportation. She has become the physical embodiment and symbol of perseverance and survival of a people. The statue depicts

GRAND-PRÉ NATIONAL HISTORIC SITE
(Lieu historique national de Grand-Pré)

INFORMATION & ACTIVITIES

HOW TO REACH US
2205 Grand-Pré Rd., Grand-Pré, NS.
Phone (902) 542-3631 or (866) 542-3631.
parkscanada.gc.ca/grandpre.

SEASONS & ACCESSIBILITY
The site is open daily from the Friday of the
Victoria Day weekend to the Monday of
the Thanksgiving weekend (in October).
The grounds are accessible year-round,
weather permitting.

SOCIÉTÉ PROMOTION GRAND-PRÉ
P.O. Box 150, Grand-Pré, NS B0P 1M0.

LES AMI(E)S DE GRAND-PRÉ
P.O. Box 246, Port Williams, NS B0P 1T0.
rootsweb.ancestry.com/~nsgrdpre.

ENTRANCE FEES
$7.80 per adult, $19.60 per family/group.

PETS
Leashed pets are allowed in outdoor areas.

ACCESSIBLE SERVICES
The site is fully accessible.

THINGS TO DO
Learn the Acadian story through exhibits
at the visitor centre. Join a guided tour.
Wander the grounds, being sure to see
the Memorial Church, Evangeline statue,
transplanted blacksmith shop, and gardens. The cultural festival Acadian Days
takes place in July (check website for
details and dates).

CAMPGROUNDS
**Land of Evangeline Family Camping
Resort** 84 Evangeline Beach Rd., Wolfville,
NS B4P 2R3. (902) 542-5309. evangeline
campground.wordpress.com. $33–$46.

HOTELS, MOTELS, & INNS
*(Rates are for a 2-person double, high season,
in Canadian dollars, unless otherwise noted.)*

Evangeline Inn & Motel 11668 Nova Scotia
Trunk 1, Grand Pré, NS B0P 1M0. (888)
542-2703. evangeline.ns.ca. 23 rooms,
$115–$145.
Slumber Inn 5534 Prospect Rd., New
Minas, NS B4N 3K8. (902) 681-5000.
slumberinn.ca. 76 rooms, $102–$126.
Olde Lantern Inn & Vineyard 11575 Hwy. 1,
Wolfville, NS B4P 2R3. (902) 542-1389.
oldlanterninn.com. 4 rooms, $119–$147.

a young girl in simple skirt and top,
looking over her shoulder, having one
last look at her homeland.

ACADIAN DAYS

Every year in July, Acadian Days,
organized by the Société Promotion
Grand-Pré and other partners, fills
Grand-Pré with the sound of music
and the smell of Acadian and sometimes Cajun dishes. During this two-
day festival, Grand-Pré hosts public
lectures on a variety of subjects from
history and archaeology to genealogy,
culture, and much more. A number
of activities take place on Sunday,
including art workshops, guided
tours, demonstrations, and more,
while music fills the air with the
strains of traditional Acadian tunes.

How to Get There
From Rte. 101, take exit 10 toward
Wolfville. Follow Rte. 1 in a westerly
direction for 1 km (0.6 mi), and then
turn right (north) on Grand-Pré Road
for another kilometre.

When to Go
The site is normally open daily from
mid-May to mid-October. July's Acadian Days offers a firsthand experience of Acadian culture.

Fort Anne is Canada's oldest historic site.

▶ FORT ANNE

ANNAPOLIS ROYAL, NS
Designated 1917

Located at the confluence of the Annapolis and Allain Rivers, Fort Anne is the oldest national historic site in Canada. Today, a 19th-century British barracks sits inside the 17th-century French fort that overlooks salt marshes, green hills, and endless waterfront.

In 1605, years before the Pilgrims landed at Plymouth Rock, French explorers settled the shores of the Annapolis River. The site of Fort Anne offered fields suitable for the growth of wheat and other crops. The French did not build at this location until after 1613, when an English expedition burned the first French settlement to the ground. This point of land was also the site of Charles Fort (see p. 33).

What to See & Do

It takes roughly two hours to see the interpretive exhibits and exterior features of Fort Anne, including the 1708 powder magazine and 1701 black hole (pick up a map from the Officers' Quarters). Earthen ramparts speak to the area's tumultuous military history. The 1702 earthworks are the earliest Canadian example of a Vauban-style fortification—and one of the best surviving examples in North America.

The museum offers further insight into the fort, including one of the only original copies of the 1621 Nova Scotia Charter, the document that gave the province its name. Other artefacts illustrate the early presence of Mi'kmaq, Scots, and Acadians. The heritage tapestry is both beautiful and functional: It depicts 400 years of life in the area. It took 100 volunteers and 3 million stitches to create the 5.5-m-by-8.5-m (18 by 28 ft) piece.

For a different perspective on Fort Anne, visit after dark on one of the Historical Association of Annapolis Royal's Candlelight Graveyard Tours (*tourannapolisroyal.com*). A 19th-century mourner, in period costume, guides guests through the cemetery by lantern light, pointing out significant headstones and talking about the lives and customs of those who shaped Fort Anne and the region of Annapolis Royal.

How to Get There

Fort Anne is 205 km (127 mi) west of Halifax. Take Hwy. 101 to exit 22 and go north on Rte. 8. Proceed through the traffic lights on St. George Street in Annapolis Royal, and then take the second left into Fort Anne.

When to Go

The grounds are open year-round, but building access and programming are only offered from June 1 to September 30.

INFORMATION

HOW TO REACH US
323 St. George St., Annapolis Royal, NS B0S 1K0. Phone (902) 532-2397. pc.gc.ca/fortanne.

ENTRANCE FEES
$3.90 per adult.

ACCESSIBLE SERVICES
Limited; contact the park for more details.

HOTELS, MOTELS, & INNS
Garrison House Inn 350 St. George St., Annapolis Royal. (902) 532-5750. garrisonhouse.ca. 7 rooms, $89–$149.

Port-Royal, founded by French colonists in 1605

▶ PORT-ROYAL

PORT ROYAL, NS
Designated 1923

Tucked inland from the Bay of Fundy, Port-Royal National Historic Site sits on the north shore of the Annapolis Basin. It is the site of one of the earliest European settlements in North America, begun as the dream of Pierre du Gua de Monts, a French nobleman.

Henry IV of France had granted de Monts a monopoly on the fur trade across a significant area along the northeastern part of the continent. De Monts financed the colony with money from private investors, and Samuel de Champlain helped establish it in 1605.

Fertile soil, ample fish and game, and support from the local Mi'kmaq people meant early success in the colony. However, the settlement was put on hold when Henry IV revoked its monopoly status. Some colonists returned to France. Others chose to follow Champlain along the St. Lawrence River to establish the Habitation of Québec.

The rustic Habitation at Port-Royal stood for just eight years, but the community was painstakingly re-created in 1939–1940. The design is typical of rural French architecture in the 17th century, with houses surrounding a courtyard inside a wooden stockade.

What to See & Do

Tours and activities at Port-Royal cater to adults and kids alike. Great attention has been paid to every detail of the Habitation: the layout of the grounds, the clothing worn by interpreters, the furnishings, and more. Interpreters are happy to answer questions about the community.

Interpreters patrol the grounds in military uniform.

INFORMATION

HOW TO REACH US
53 Historic Ln., Port Royal, NS B0S 1K0. Phone (902) 532-2898. pc.gc.ca/portroyal.

ENTRANCE FEES
$3.90 per adult.

ACCESSIBLE SERVICES
Limited; contact the park for details.

HOTELS, MOTELS, & INNS
Annapolis Royal Inn 3924 Hwy. 1, Annapolis Royal. (888) 857-8889. annapolisroyalinn.com. 30 rooms, $89–$150.
A Seafaring Maiden B&B 5287 Granville Rd., Granville Ferry. (888) 532-0379. aseafaringmaiden.com.

Daily demonstrations (May–Oct.) give visitors an idea of what life would have been like for the European settlers, as well as for the Mi'kmaq who lived in the area long before Port-Royal was built.

The gun platform and palisade offer incredible views of the Annapolis River, the Annapolis Basin, and Goat Island. Visit the wigwam to learn about Mi'kmaq culture. Check the website for scheduled programs.

How to Get There

Port-Royal is roughly 200 km (124 mi) from Halifax. From Hwy. 101, take exit 22 and continue north on Rte. 8 to Annapolis Royal. At the traffic lights, turn right on Rte. 1, and cross the causeway. Take the first left and follow signs for the site.

When to Go

The grounds are open year-round. The buildings are open May 20 through October 8, daily June 21 to September 3, and closed Sunday and Monday rest of time.

MAINLAND NOVA SCOTIA SITES

FORT EDWARD
WINDSOR, NS

On a hilltop near Windsor, all that remains of Fort Edward is its squat two-storey blockhouse, replete with a range of gun slits for both cannons and rifles. Built by the British in 1750, it was used during the expulsion of the Acadians and during both the Seven Years' War and the War of 1812. At that time, the larger site consisted of a palisaded square, complete with four bastions, ramparts, barracks, and a provisions storehouse. Designated NHS: 1920. 67 Fort Edward St. (902) 798-2639 (summer only).

CHARLES FORT
ANNAPOLIS ROYAL, NS

Like many of the fortifications in Nova Scotia, time has erased Charles Fort from the landscape. Built in 1629 by Scotsman Sir William Alexander to establish a Scottish colony, "Nova Scotia," it was only used for a few years. In the 1630s, the region was restored to France by way of a peace treaty. A plaque marks the location of the former fort and the settlement that gave the province its name. Designated NHS: 1951. Prince Albert Rd. (902) 532-2397 (summer) or (902) 532-2321 (winter).

MELANSON SETTLEMENT
PORT ROYAL, NS

Today, the former Melanson Settlement looks like an idyllic slice of unused farmland butting against the banks of the Annapolis River. In the 17th and 18th centuries, however, it was an active Acadian family farming settlement. Before the Acadian deportation of 1755, four generations of the Melanson family lived here. Visitors can see remnants of their unique methods of agriculture present in the dyke systems that desalinated seaside marshland. Designated NHS: 1987. 3870 Granville Rd. (902) 532-2321.

MAINLAND NOVA SCOTIA SITES

KEJIMKUJIK
MAITLAND BRIDGE, NS

The landscape of Kejimkujik tells a story—that of the Mi'kmaq, the Indigenous People who lived in the area well before the first Europeans began arriving during the 1600s. Their history can be read in the interconnected lakes and rivers the Mi'kmaq once travelled, as well as in the park's age-old petroglyphs and habitation sites. Hiking trails, paddling routes, guided tours, and more help visitors explore the park. Designated NHS: 1994. 3005 Main Pkwy. (902) 682-2772 (summer).

BEAUBASSIN
FORT LAWRENCE, NS

This bucolic landscape of hayfields, pastures, and marshland on the southeast edge of Fort Lawrence Ridge was once a major Acadian settlement, Beaubassin. Here, residents farmed, raised livestock, and traded with people in New England, the French, and Indigenous Peoples. Founded in 1671–72, the community was burned to the ground in 1750, falling victim to the ongoing battle between French and English. Only ghost impressions of former buildings remain. Designated NHS: 2005. Hwy. 4.

FORT LAWRENCE
FORT LAWRENCE, NS

Fort Lawrence was built on the ruins of the village of Beaubassin (see above), on the east side near the Missaguash River. At one time, there was a labyrinth here of embankments and trenches, barrack frames, and blockhouses for British defences. The fort was abandoned in 1755, after the British overtook nearby Fort Beauséjour (see pp. 64–65) and claimed it under the name Fort Cumberland. The footprint of the former fort's earthworks is visible. Designated NHS: 1923. Fort Lawrence Rd.

YORK REDOUBT
FERGUSON'S COVE, NS

The York Redoubt played a significant role in the Halifax Defence
Complex from the late 18th century
through the Second World War, and
it remains a largely preserved site
today. The redoubt's strategic positioning on a bluff overlooking Halifax
offered a clear view of the city's harbour, making it a key component of
British fortifications in the area. Visitors can walk among the redoubt's 27
buildings and related structures. Designated NHS: 1962. York Redoubt
Crescent. (902) 426-5080.

PRINCE OF WALES TOWER
HALIFAX, NS

The squat stone structure at Point
Pleasant Park is a beautiful example
of a British martello-style tower, a
small round fort generally with two
interior storeys and thicker walls facing the coast. The first of its type to
be built in North America, it was constructed by the British in 1793. Its
purpose was to defend the sea batteries at Point Pleasant from potential
French attack. Interpretive panels
explain the significance of the tower
and its strategic location. Designated
NHS: 1943. 5718 Point Pleasant Dr.
(902) 426-5080.

FORT MCNAB
HALIFAX, NS

Located on McNabs Island, near the
mouth of Halifax Harbour, the late
19th-century British Fort McNab
acted as a gatekeeper to the harbour,
guarding the outer channels of the
waterfront. The outermost battery
of the Halifax Defence Complex,
it was outfitted with long-range,
breech-loading guns. Additionally,
the fort included an examination station that checked incoming ships to
ensure they didn't pose a threat to
port security. Designated NHS: 1965.
McNabs Island. (902) 426-5080.

Dating from 1749, Halifax Citadel was a Canadian Army command centre during the First World War.

▶ HALIFAX CITADEL

HALIFAX, NS
Designated 1951

The Halifax Citadel commands a hilltop overlooking Halifax Harbour. Since its first incarnation in 1749, the star-shaped fort has been rebuilt four times. It was first built to counter the French base at Louisbourg, and served through the American Revolution, Napoleonic Wars, Victorian era, and the First and Second World Wars, but it was never attacked.

That's part of the reason why the site remains such a pristine example of early east coast fortifications. It is also one of five sites that form the Halifax Defence Complex—a collection of forts and batteries built by the British and Canadian militaries over the years to guard the entrance to Halifax Harbour, which served as the North Atlantic base for the British Royal Navy, and later the Royal Canadian Navy.

The first Citadel was built in 1749, to protect the new colony of 2,500 British settlers who had landed in Chebucto Harbour. The hilltop was immediately identified as the best place from which to watch for a possible attack. The early palisade walls were made of wood.

Efforts were made in the 1760s to repair the Citadel, but by 1776, with the American Revolution breaking out, the site was in ruins and had to be rebuilt. The second fortification expanded on the first (including a barracks tower for 100 soldiers), but it too was made of wood and thus suffered in the coastal climate.

In 1796, the hilltop was cut back for the third citadel, the first one sited directly at the top of the hill. The Citadel, built under the aegis of Prince Edward, Duke of Kent, was named Fort George, after the prince's father. Again built of wood, this iteration was in ruins by the 1820s. Because of renewed tensions with the United States, it was decided to build a permanent stone structure on the site. Flaws in the planning process slowed the build, however, and the new and improved Citadel wasn't finished until 1856. It would fall into disrepair over the years, but not like its predecessors had.

In 1906, the British transferred the Citadel to the Canadian Department of Militia and Defence, where it was used as soldier barracks, a prison camp, and a command centre during the First World War. As military technologies advanced in artillery and aviation, the features that had made the fort's positioning strategic became obsolete. In the 1930s, repairs were done on the Citadel's sagging walls through the National Works Program for depression relief. It was brought back into service during the Second World War, but by the late 1940s, after years of underuse, the fort was beginning to go to ruin. Its restoration was taken on by Parks Canada in the 1950s.

Historians, researchers, archaeologists, engineers, masons, and more all worked together, often using decades-old techniques and technology to ensure the fort was authentically reproduced, using wood, brick, and stone. Additionally, many of the rooms within the Citadel have been outfitted with original artefacts to give visitors an idea of what the fortifications would have looked like during their heyday. Of these, one of the most popular rooms is the Soldiers' Barracks, where members of the 78th Highland Regiment lived with their families. Original headgear and heavy backpacks are on display for visitors to touch and try on.

The Town Clock, which faces Brunswick Street, is perhaps the most recognizable symbol of the Citadel—and one of the most well-known landmarks in all of Nova Scotia. The three-tiered octagonal tower bears a clock face built by the House of Vulliamy, a famous London-based clockmaker. A gift from Prince Edward, Duke of Kent, the clock was installed in 1803, and the original gears and inner workings (including cable-suspended weights) are still intact. The clock is still wound manually twice weekly.

PROGRAMMING

A 60-minute tour (offered in both French and English) is included with admission and gives visitors the opportunity to explore the grounds of the Citadel. Costumed guides from the Halifax Citadel Regimental Association share stories of the Citadel in all its incarnations, and interpreters play the roles of a British soldier and his family. In character, they will talk about what life was like on the hill as well as the role the Citadel played in the protection of Halifax and as a gatekeeper to the country.

The immersive, three-hour Soldier for a Day program (fee) offers participants the opportunity to find out what it was like to be a 19th-century soldier. After a fitting for a complete

The star-shaped fortification overlooks Halifax Harbour.

uniform—including a kilt!—participants march to Parade Square to learn how to run drills and, for those over the age of 16, fire a rifle. (Those age 8 to 15 learn to play the field drum that the British Army used.) For an additional fee, adults (ages 16+) may pretend they're one of the 78th Highlanders and fire three rounds using an authentic 1869-era Snider-Enfield rifle.

Ghost tours (Friday and Saturday nights, July to October) paint the Citadel in a different light. These guided walks are held when Citadel Hill is bathed in darkness, and the passageways, cobblestone alleys, and ditches are shadowy and lit only by candlelight. See the stone-walled prison cells that held prisoners convicted of minor offences.

Additional activities cater to young visitors; check the website for details.

ARMY MUSEUM

Located on the second floor of the Citadel's Cavalier Building, the museum focuses on the Atlantic Canada's military efforts over the last 400 years, with emphasis on the contribution of Halifax to Canadian defence during the two World Wars.

The museum has a collection of medals—each telling the story of a Canadian soldier—that dates back to the earliest days of Canada's military history. There is also a German Iron Cross, reportedly found in the plane flown by Rudolph Hess (Hitler's second in command) when he went from Germany to Scotland in 1941, allegedly attempting to orchestrate peace talks.

Don't miss the exhibit of trench art, unique sculptural works created by soldiers using the materials they had on hand in the trenches. Everything from empty bullet cartridges and enemy helmets, to belt buckles and badges became fodder for soldiers looking for a creative outlet. A modern-day contrast to this art is that of artist and army reservist Jessica Wiebe. Drawings of the locals and her fellow soldiers depict her time serving in Afghanistan.

The exhibit "The Road to Vimy and Beyond" recounts the stories of Canadians who fought in the First World War, with a focus on Nova Scotian military.

Guided walks lead through barracks, alleys, and prison cells.

HALIFAX CITADEL NATIONAL HISTORIC SITE
(Lieu historique national de la Citadelle-d'Halifax)

INFORMATION & ACTIVITIES

HOW TO REACH US
5425 Sackville St., Halifax, NS B3K 5M7.
Phone (902) 426-5080. pc.gc.ca/eng/lhn
-nhs/ns/halifax/index.aspx.
Army Museum of the Halifax Citadel:
(902) 422-5979. armymuseumhalifax.ca.

SEASONS & ACCESSIBILITY
The site is open year-round, but hours and
services change with the seasons. Regular
activities and programming are scheduled
from early May to the end of October. The
rest of the year, programming is limited to
ghost walks and prearranged tours.

HALIFAX CITADEL REGIMENTAL ASSOCIATION
5425 Sackville St., Halifax, NS B3K 5M7.
(902) 426-1990. regimental.com.

ENTRANCE FEES
$11.70 per adult, $29.40 per family/
group (June 1-Sept. 15); $7.80 per adult,
$15.60 per family/group (May, Sept. 16–
Oct. 31).

PETS
Leashed pets are permitted on the
grounds, but not inside the buildings.

ACCESSIBLE SERVICES
Much of the site is wheelchair accessible,
including the ramparts, Army Museum,
majority of ground-level exhibits, and
washrooms. Films are closed-captioned.
Designated parking areas for those with
mobility challenges.

THINGS TO DO
Regular military demonstrations, including cannon firings, sentry charges, and
pipe and drum performances, bring the
Citadel alive. Programming includes walking tours, an on-site museum, and a daily
noon gun firing. The restored Soldiers'
Barracks and schoolroom are full of artefacts that provide a glimpse into the lives
of 19th-century soldiers and their families.

In addition, there are ghost walks and
special seasonal events, including Victorian Christmas celebrations in November.

SPECIAL ADVISORIES
The weather and temperatures change
often in Halifax. Bring a light jacket or
sweater and wear comfortable shoes.

CAMPGROUNDS
Woodhaven RV Park 1757 Hammonds
Plains Rd., Hammonds Plains, NS B4B 1P5.
(902) 835-2271. woodhavenrvpark.com.
$30–$48.

HOTELS, MOTELS, & INNS
*(Rates are for a 2-person double, high season,
in Canadian dollars, unless otherwise noted.)*

Lord Nelson Hotel 1515 S. Park St., Halifax,
NS B3J 2L2. (902) 423-6331. lordnelson
hotel.ca, 280 rooms, $139–$219.
Atlantic Corporate Suites 596 Bedford
Hwy., Halifax, NS B3M 2L8. (902) 880-
0889. atlanticcorporatesuites.com.
15 rooms, $60–$275.
Prince George Hotel 1725 Market St., Halifax, NS B3J 3N9. (902) 425-1986. prince
georgehotel.com. 201 rooms, $129–$279.

How to Get There
There are two vehicle entrances—one
on Sackville Street, the other on Rain-
nie Drive. By foot from the waterfront, the Citadel is easy to find. Start
walking uphill and look for the signal
flags that fly over the ramparts. The
steep stairs in front of the old town
clock lead to the Citadel entrance.

The sidewalk from the Sackville
Street entrance is a more gradual
climb. Metro Transit also has a stop
just a short walk from the Citadel.

When to Go
The site is open year-round,
but most programming is offered
between May and October.

Nearly a million immigrants passed through Pier 21 into Canada.

▶ PIER 21 AND THE CANADIAN MUSEUM OF IMMIGRATION

HALIFAX, NS
Designated 1997

Between 1928 and 1971, Halifax's Pier 21 was a gateway to Canada. Almost one million immigrants entered the country through its doors, entrenching the place in the lives and memories of Canadians. Originally built to be a cargo shed, the building is now celebrated as an iconic Canadian historic site.

IMMIGRATION GATEWAY

Although it was built as a cargo shed, Pier 21 was converted into a complete immigration facility, including spaces for processing immigrants and their baggage, facilities for overnight accommodation and detention, dining rooms, and a hospital. One of the most recognizable interior features of the building was its large assembly hall. Immigrants waited there for civil and medical examination. These exams were usually done quickly, as prospective immigrants were screened before coming to Canada. During Pier 21's years of operation, not many immigrants were refused entry, but factors for refusal included a person's health, occupation, financial resources, education, and perceived ideology or racial identity.

Once immigrants passed these inspections, they proceeded to an annex building through an overhead walkway. Along the way, customs officers checked their hand baggage.

Larger bags were checked on the ground floor of the annex building. Despite the amount of baggage moving through the buildings, the customs process generally only took a few minutes for each person.

After this process, an immigrant might wait for several hours before boarding a train. The train cars used at Pier 21 for immigrants were often older models with wooden seating and wood stoves for cooking. The museum features a reproduction of the interior of one of these cars, called a colonist car. Immigrants travelling across the country spent several days in these simple accommodations. Other travellers, such as tourists, generally joined modern trains at the nearby rail station.

The years after the opening of Pier 21 in 1928 were marked by a massive decline in immigration. The government put restrictive policies in place as part of a response to the Great Depression, so for approximately a decade the new facility was relatively quiet. In addition to a reduction of the overall numbers of immigrants per year, from more than 100,000 to fewer than 20,000, the policies also led to a higher proportion of immigration by land from the United States rather than via ocean ports.

With the outbreak of the Second World War, Pier 21 became the embarkation port for the hundreds of thousands of Canadians who served overseas. Some civilians still entered Canada in wartime via Halifax alongside the military traffic, but the traffic was very limited due to the wartime restrictions on passenger shipping and the tight immigration regulations that remained in force. During the war, valuable items ranging from gold bullion to cultural and historic treasures also arrived from overseas at Halifax's ocean terminals for safekeeping in Canada.

In the wake of the world war, immigrants from all over Europe, including Britons, Netherlanders, Poles, Germans, Italians, and Ukrainians, arrived in Halifax as displaced people or refugees, as war brides and their children, or as conventional immigrants. All told, about 500,000 newcomers landed here in the decade following the war. Amid these waves, Pier 21 was briefly the busiest ocean port of arrival in Canada. With the advent of air travel as the 1960s progressed, the waterfront immigration facility at Halifax was no longer needed and Pier 21 closed in 1971.

Today, the historic waterfront shed houses the Canadian Museum of Immigration at Pier 21.

MUSEUM HIGHLIGHTS

The Canadian Museum of Immigration at Pier 21 houses two permanent exhibitions on the history of the site and on the broader history of immigration to Canada. These exhibitions feature immersive and interactive displays; they are complemented by temporary exhibitions and public programs, with some touching on the contemporary Canadian immigrant experience.

The permanent exhibition on the history of Pier 21 in Rudolph P. Bratty Exhibition Hall interprets the era when the building served as an immigration gateway to Canada from 1928 to 1971, and as an embarkation and disembarkation point for military personnel serving overseas during the Second World War. Visitors are immersed in history through first-person stories—of newcomers and those who welcomed them— archival photos, film, and artefacts. Immersive environments such as a colonist railcar and a ship's cabin make it easy to imagine being tossed at sea in a tight ship's quarters or heading west aboard a train. An interactive customs challenge allows visitors to see if valued items from home will be allowed in or confiscated. Visitors can also dress in period costumes of immigration officials and Red Cross volunteers.

The new Canadian Immigration Hall tells the broader story of more than 400 years of immigration history in Canada. Supplemented by both historic and contemporary examples, exhibits include the stories of those groups that were encouraged to immigrate to Canada, and of those that were discouraged. Here visitors can learn about some of the collective and individual achievements of newcomers as well as explore objects symbolizing individual feelings of belonging as immigrants sought acceptance within Canadian society. Within this thematic exhibition, a timeline of events and decisions important to the history of immigration in Canada allows visitors to situate themselves in time.

In the Canadian Immigration Hall, a series of interactives allow visitors to discover how immigration has touched and influenced all aspects of Canadian life. Visitors can follow the changing immigration trends on the multimedia Immigration Waves map, browse the oral history collection in the BMO Oral History Gallery to view and hear firsthand accounts of the immigrant experience, try their hand at packing one lone suitcase for their entire immigration journey, or test their knowledge about Canada with a citizenship test.

The museum also has the Ralph and Rose Chiodo Gallery, a large temporary exhibition space featuring new exhibits every year. A recent example is "Canada: Day 1," the museum's own exhibition about the experiences of immigrants during their first days in Canada. Past exhibits include *Empress of Ireland: Canada's Titanic,* produced in partnership with the Canadian Museum of History, which explored the 1914 sinking of a Canadian ocean liner during Canada's immigration boom years. Another past exhibition is "Peace: The Exhibition," developed by the Canadian War Museum, which explored issues of war, peace, and immigration.

Smaller exhibitions and displays are featured in the museum's central lobby areas. Examples include "The Wheel of Conscience," a sculptural monument designed by architect Daniel Libeskind. This monument commemorates the Jewish refugee ship M.S. *St. Louis* and was produced in partnership between Immigration, Refugees, and Citizenship Canada and the Centre for Israel and Jewish Affairs. Other past exhibitions and displays have included "A Perilous Crossing," developed by the Canadian Science and Technology Museum, about the recent wave of migrants fleeing violence and instability through dangerous voyages across the Mediterranean. "Perfect Landings," developed in partnership

Pier 21 became a full immigration station in 1928.

Red Cross nurses helped care for newcomers.

Stoves warmed railcars called colonist cars.

Once cleared, newcomers took trains west.

with Skate Canada, featured figure skaters, coaches, and builders of the sport of figure skating who were immigrants to Canada.

SCOTIABANK FAMILY HISTORY CENTRE

The Scotiabank Family History Centre offers reference services and is located on the ground level of the museum. The centre reaches beyond the years of Pier 21—1928 to 1971—with information on topics covering

The Oral History Gallery

PIER 21 NATIONAL HISTORIC SITE AND THE CANADIAN MUSEUM OF IMMIGRATION

(Lieu national historique du Quai 21 et le Musée canadien de l'immigration du Quai 21)

INFORMATION & ACTIVITIES

HOW TO REACH US
1055 Marginal Rd., Halifax, NS B3H 4P7. Phone (902) 425-7770. pier21.ca.

SEASONS & ACCESSIBILITY
The museum is open year-round. Check the website for current hours.

ENTRANCE FEES
$10 per adult, $26 per family.

PETS
Only service pets are permitted inside the museum.

ACCESSIBLE SERVICES
All floors of the museum are wheelchair accessible. The elevator floor numbers are shown in Braille. Parking spaces are reserved for wheelchair users. A wheelchair is available for use on a first-come, first-served basis. There are reserved wheelchair spaces in the Charles and Andrea Bronfman Theatre.

THINGS TO DO
Tour the museum's two permanent exhibits, filled with interactive displays. For a different perspective, join a guided tour.

Discover your family roots by, among other things, exploring immigration records and ship photos at the Scotiabank Family History Centre.

Watch the short film *In Canada*.

Visit the museum gift shop for unique souvenirs. The gift shop carries many items made in Canada, signature products, apparel, and books; it also has a children's section.

CAMPGROUNDS
Woodhaven RV Park 1757 Hammonds Plains Rd., Hammonds Plains, NS B4B 1P5. (902) 835-2271. woodhavenrvpark.com. $30-$48.

HOTELS, MOTELS, & INNS
(Rates are for a 2-person double, high season, in Canadian dollars, unless otherwise noted.)

Lord Nelson Hotel 1515 S. Park St., Halifax, NS B3J 2L2. (902) 423-6331, lordnelsonhotel.ca. 280 rooms, $139-$219.
Atlantic Corporate Suites 596 Bedford Hwy., Halifax, NS B3M 2L8. (902) 880-0889, atlanticcorporatesuites.com. 15 rooms, $60-$275.
Prince George Hotel 1725 Market St., Halifax, NS B3J 3N9. (902) 425-1986. princegeorgehotel.com. 201 rooms, $129-$279.

migration, nautical history, waves of immigration to Canada, ethnic groups, and genealogy. It holds immigration records from 1925 to 1935 on microfilm, and staff have access to arrival sources going back to 1865. Staff may also assist with information on all ports of entry into Canada, as well as seaports in the United States.

How to Get There

The national historic site and museum is located at 1055 Marginal Road. VIA Rail trains come into the station right next door. The Greyhound bus terminal is a short walk of less than half a kilometre (0.25 mi). Take Terminal Road toward the waterfront, and then follow it right as it curves around. The museum will be on the left.

When to Go

The museum is open year-round, with a slate of programming activities offered throughout the year. Check the website for more details.

MAINLAND NOVA SCOTIA SITES

HMCS SACKVILLE
HALIFAX, NS

The Canadian-built HMCS *Sackville,* currently docked beside the Maritime Museum of the Atlantic in downtown Halifax, is a prime example of the small warships used by Canada and its allies as convoy escorts during the Second World War. Once there were more than 200 of these tough little ships; now the *Sackville* is the last of the Flower-class corvettes in existence. Designated NHS: 1988. 1655 Lower Water St. (902) 429-2132 (summer) or (902) 427-2837 (winter).

HALIFAX PUBLIC GARDENS
HALIFAX, NS

Established in 1874, these lovely gardens are one of the few surviving Victorian gardens in Canada. Their original carpet bedding patterns, gently curving gravel walking paths, fountains, and statues remain in good condition. A centrally located bandstand provides a beautiful focal point, complete with traditional gingerbread woodwork and a bright, primary-colour paint scheme. The park is a favourite relaxation spot for visitors and Haligonians alike. Open May to November, 8 a.m. to dusk. Designated NHS: 1983. Four entrances; main gate at 5769 Spring Garden Rd.

ST. GEORGE'S ANGLICAN CHURCH/ROUND CHURCH
HALIFAX, NS

St. George's is Canada's only known 19th-century example of a round church. Heralded as a masterpiece of Palladian architecture, the church was begun in 1800 and completed 12 years later. Though damaged by the Halifax explosion of 1917, and further by a 1994 fire, the building has been restored in a way that has managed to retain its classical lines and proportions. Designated NHS: 1983. 2222 Brunswick St. (902) 423-1059.

MAINLAND NOVA SCOTIA SITES

ST. PAUL'S ANGLICAN CHURCH
HALIFAX, NS

For 96 years, St. Paul's served as the official garrison church of the local British army and navy establishment. An early example of Palladian architecture in Canada, the church was completed in 1750. Its design was probably based on a pattern that took its proportions from St. Peter's in London, England. Later expansions saw the addition of side aisles, a chancel, and a copper-clad steeple. The church was meticulously restored between 1984 and 1990. Designated NHS: 1981. 1749 Argyle St. (902) 429-2240.

PROVINCE HOUSE
HALIFAX, NS

Completed in 1819, this downtown Halifax landmark still serves as the legislative seat for Nova Scotia, making it the longest serving legislative building in the country. However, that's not the building's only claim to fame: This three-storey structure, a fine example of Palladian architecture, was also the site of the debates that led to freedom of the press and responsible government in Canada. Designated NHS: 1993. 1741 Hollis St. (902) 424-4661.

ST. MARY'S BASILICA
HALIFAX, NS

When it was built, beginning in 1820, St. Mary's was one of the first Roman Catholic cathedrals in Canada. It stands today as an incredible example of Gothic Revival architecture. It's difficult to walk through downtown Halifax without noticing the church's impressive triple portal and its tall central spire, added in 1874. Inside, the features are even more elaborate, including decorative stonework, stained-glass windows, and opulent doors. Designated NHS: 1997. 1508 Barrington St.

OLD BURYING GROUND
HALIFAX, NS

More than 1,200 grave markers fill the Old Burying Ground, located on the former outer limits of the settlement of Halifax. Today encircled by a stone wall, the inter-denominational graveyard features a unique Canadian collection of gravestone art from the 18th and early 19th centuries. Distinct styles, images, and carving skills are on display across the stones, speaking to the cultural traditions of early British North America. Designated NHS: 1991. Barrington St., north of Bishop St.

GOVERNMENT HOUSE
HALIFAX, NS

Government House, in the heart of historic Halifax, has served as the official residence of the lieutenant governor of Nova Scotia for more than 175 years. It was completed in 1805 at the direction of Sir John Wentworth, then governor of Nova Scotia. The Palladian-style stone mansion gives the impression of an English country estate rather than a colonial outpost, complete with a landscaped lot, ornate interior detailing, and curving front drive. Designated NHS: 1982. 1451 Barrington St. (902) 424–7001.

OLD TOWN LUNENBURG HISTORIC DISTRICT
LUNENBURG, NS

Brightly painted houses above Lunenburg Harbour call attention to a town whose gridiron layout is one of the earliest and most intact British model plans in Canada. The town's historic district is a well-preserved example of 18th-century settlement patterns. Its waterfront location speaks to long-established economic ties to the fishing and shipbuilding industries, and its architecture spans more than 240 years. Designated NHS: 1991; Inscribed WH: 1995. Lunenburg Harbour.

MAINLAND NOVA SCOTIA

Nova Scotia's Fortress of Louisbourg, built in 1713, overlooks the Atlantic Ocean.

CAPE BRETON

About a fifth of the population of Nova Scotia lives on Cape Breton. This hilly island just off the mainland's northeast coast is 175 km (109 mi) long and 120 km (75 mi) wide at its broadest point. At its centre lies Bras d'Or Lake, the primary waterway that connected the centuries-old communities of Mi'kmaq and other Indigenous Peoples who inhabited the island. The stunning saltwater lake is overlooked by the summer home of inventor Alexander Graham Bell (see pp. 54–57). Claiming the island as part of Acadia, the French

called it Île Royale. Although most of Acadia was ceded to the British with the Treaty of Utrecht in 1713, the French retained the island and, soon after, began building the Fortress of Louisbourg (see pp. 50–53), a fortified town that was both a key commercial port and a strategic military site. The British took Louisbourg in 1758, and five years later France ceded the island in the Treaty of Paris, which ended the Seven Years' War. Today, a causeway spans the 3-km-wide (1.8 mi) Strait of Canso to link Cape Breton with mainland Nova Scotia.

Firing cannons at the Fortress of Louisbourg

▶ FORTRESS OF LOUISBOURG

LOUISBOURG, NS
Designated 1920

Sitting on a small peninsula overlooking a harbour off the North Atlantic Ocean, the Fortress of Louisbourg is the largest reconstructed 18th-century fortified French town in North America. Between 1713 and 1768, the fortress played a profound role in the struggle for empire between Britain and France.

The French had come to the area in 1713, having lost their territories in Acadia and Newfoundland by the terms of the Treaty of Utrecht, which ended the War of the Spanish Succession. Their only remaining possessions in the region were two islands: Île Royale (modern-day Cape Breton) and Île Saint-Jean (Prince Edward Island). Eager to preserve the integrity of their maritime empire, the French began building a fortified town in 1719. The city housed government offices and a military garrison as well as a civilian population. By 1745, the Fortress of

Louisbourg had become one of the busiest harbours on the continent, a key port for the movement of goods between Europe, the West Indies, and the French and British North American colonies. It was also a critical military asset, strategically located to guard the approaches to the Gulf of St. Lawrence, the main shipping route to Québec and interior North America.

The first attack on the fortress came in 1745 during the War of the Austrian Succession (1740–48), when Louisbourg became a battleground in the much larger dispute between Britain and France. Armed with the information that Louisbourg's fortress wasn't in prime shape, British forces invaded. Within 46 days, they had overtaken the site. It was a short-lived ownership, however. Three years later, Louisbourg was returned to the French under the Treaty of Aix-la-Chapelle. When hostilities renewed in 1756, the French and British both amassed naval and army power in the region. The final attack on the fortress began in 1758. The siege by a combined British army and navy force of 30,000 lasted for seven weeks. To guard against the fortress being restored to the French in the future, the British destroyed its walls. They launched an assault on Québec the following year.

In 1961, the Canadian government began a $25 million project to re-create roughly a quarter of the original town and its fortifications as they would have appeared in the 1740s, before the first attack—soldiers' barracks, stone bastions, an artillery, merchant houses and stores, a bakery, and more.

In the process, archaeologists discovered not only the ruins of buildings and fortifications but also more than 5.5 million artefacts that reveal much about daily life at Louisbourg—on land and at sea. Many of the artefacts can be viewed in the on-site open-drawer research collection.

The fortress spans 5 ha (12 acres). Enter through the Dauphin Gates and pass soldiers' barracks and stone bastions to reach the city proper. Here, dozens of buildings stand, some reserved for military use (the artillery storehouse, the armoury, and forge) and some for the general populace (residences, merchant businesses, a bakery, and more).

UNIQUE EXPERIENCES

One of the most popular experiences at Louisbourg is the cannoneer program, with two versions offered. The short program allows visitors to try on the traditional dress of a soldier assigned to firing the cannon. A lesson in firing is included, followed by participation in a parade march that concludes with the firing of a cannon. The daylong program begins with a private tour of the grounds that speaks to its history and military life. A complete costume fitting is followed by an artillery workshop, a full meal at one of the on-site restaurants, and the opportunity to fire the cannon later in the afternoon.

For another authentic experience, take the Healing Gardener Garden Tour. This focuses on a collection of five present-day gardens, each built on the site of one that was original to Louisbourg. The gardens, which range in style from formal to raised bed, are cultivated the way they would have been in the 1700s. They're planted with herbs, fruits, and vegetables—useful plants that could either feed a family or serve a medicinal function. These were identified when seeds were discovered in the site's excavation.

All guided tours and experiences come at an additional cost.

WALKING TRAILS

Louisbourg has roughly 8 km (5 mi) of walking trails. The trails show off not only the area's man-made heritage but also its natural heritage. Marigolds, wild strawberries, tansy, sweetgrass, starflowers, spruce trees, and the official flowers of the province, mayflowers, are some of the typical east coast flora seen along the

CAPE BRETON

trails. Rabbit, deer, coyote, weasels, fox, and all kinds of birds number among the fauna.

The 2-km (1.2 mi) Lighthouse Trail is a looping path that follows the curve of the coast. It leads to incredible vistas and is dotted with interpretive panels that explain the significance of the flora and fauna in the area. It also offers a close-up view of Louisbourg Lighthouse. This isn't the original lighthouse, but it is standing in the same location as the original, which was, when it was erected in 1734, the first lighthouse in Canada. The Lighthouse Trail connects with a more rugged trail being developed by the Coastal Connections Trail Association.

The Old Town Trail runs 2.25 km (1.4 mi) along the shore of Louisbourg Harbour. Interpretive panels along the way tell the story of the

Costumed interpreters tell of life in the summer of 1744.

Reenactors store barrels of provisions.

place that was once known as Old Town, the history beginning 300 years ago and running to present day. This is an easy trail and one that's wheelchair accessible.

A handful of shorter interpretive trails take visitors to incredible views or to significant on-site structures. The 351-m (0.2 mi) Mi'kmaw Trail runs through the woods and up to a lookout that provides a panoramic view of Louisbourg Harbour. The Royal Battery Trail is a 678-m (0.4 mi) loop that follows the perimeter of the former battery on its way to a sweeping harbour view. Finally, the 178-m (0.1 mi) Wolfe's Redoubt Trail leads to an earthen-work redoubt.

Perhaps the most impressive trail is the Ruins Walk. This 2.3-km (1.4 mi) path snakes through the remains of the original 18th-century town, three-quarters of which lies in ruins. Start in the national historic site's reconstructed section of town and follow a series of interpretive panels that explain such features as the foundations of King's Hospital, the Island Battery, and a convent.

18TH-CENTURY DINING

In the 1740s, Louisbourg innkeepers ran waterfront cabarets where off-duty soldiers spent their time and money gambling, gossiping, and eating. Two restaurants at Louisbourg are designed to relate this experience to visitors, with servers costumed in period dress.

The Grandchamp Inn and Hôtel de la Marine are both reconstructions of the original 18th-century buildings that fulfilled this function when the fortress was operational. Both serve 18th-century-style fare, including pea, vegetable, or fish soup, mussels and bread, beef stew, cod filet, and more. Opt for the upper-class meal and dine

FORTRESS OF LOUISBOURG NATIONAL HISTORIC SITE
(Lieu historique national de la Forteresse-de-Louisbourg)

INFORMATION & ACTIVITIES

HOW TO REACH US
259 Park Service Rd., Louisbourg, NS B1C 2L2. Phone (902) 733-3552. pc.gc.ca /louisbourg.

SEASONS & ACCESSIBILITY
Closed weekends post-Thanksgiving Day to pre-Victoria Day; open daily Victoria Day to Thanksgiving Day. Hours vary by season; check with the site.

FORTRESS OF LOUISBOURG ASSOCIATION
265 Park Service Rd., Louisbourg, NS B1C 2L2. (902) 733-3548. fortressoflouis bourg.ca.

ENTRANCE FEES
$17.60 per adult, $44.10 per family/group in peak season; $7.30 per adult, $18.10 per family/group rest of year. Free admission on Canada Day.

PETS
Registered service dogs are allowed. Otherwise, pets are only allowed on the Louisbourg Lighthouse Trail, Old Town Trail, and at the recreational areas along Kennington Cove Road. They must be leashed.

ACCESSIBLE SERVICES
Period construction techniques mean limited accessibility. Not all buildings are accessible. When the visitor centre is open, a bus is available that accommodates manual wheelchairs. Parts of the Lighthouse Trail are accessible, though loose gravel and inclines pose mobility challenges. Staff will work with guests to find solutions for accessibility issues.

THINGS TO DO
During the summer, the site offers guided tours and other programming. Year-round, the site stages various special events and activities; call for dates, as these change annually. Hiking trails available year-round.

Two beaches are nearby, Kennington Cove and Anson's Cove, their wide, flat, sandy strands perfect for swimming and spending the day. Special events are often organized at the beaches.

CAMPGROUNDS
Lakeview Treasure Campground 5785 Louisbourg Hwy., Cape Breton, NS B1C 2G4. (902) 733-2058. louisbourgcamp ground.com. $20–$36.50.

HOTELS, MOTELS, & INNS
(Rates are for a 2-person double, high season, in Canadian dollars, unless otherwise noted.)

Cranberry Cove Inn 12 Wolfe St., Louisbourg, NS B1C 2H9. (902) 733-2171. cran berrycoveinn.com. 7 rooms, $105–$160.
Louisbourg Harbour Inn 9 Lower Warren St., Louisbourg, NS B1C 1G6. (902) 733-3222. louisbourgharbourinn.com. 7 rooms, $129–$155.
Point of View Suites at Louisbourg Gates 15 Commercial St. Extension, Louisbourg, NS B1C 2J4. (888) 374-8439. louisbourg pointofview.com. 19 rooms, $125–$299.

CAPE BRETON

as an 18th-century sea captain might have, in a private setting.

How to Get There
Take Trans-Canada 105. At Bras d'Or, follow Hwy. 125 to Sydney and turn off at exit 8. Turn right on Rte. 22 and stay on it to the village of Louisbourg. Then follow the signs to the national historic site.

When to Go
Summer affords the best opportunity for activities; it's also the best time to see the gardens. Visit in July also to participate in CultureFête, a celebration of the multiculturalism of Cape Breton. Off-season, visitors can walk among the buildings and along the site's trails, and take part in special activities such as Heritage Day.

The museum at Alexander Graham Bell National Historic Site has three main halls.

▶ ALEXANDER GRAHAM BELL

BADDECK, NS
Designated 1952

Alexander Graham Bell National Historic Site, on a hill overlooking Bras d'Or Lake's Baddeck Bay, commemorates Bell's life and work. The museum's collection includes Bell's own notes, his library of 1,500 books, and objects from various experiments. The Bell family, who still own Beinn Bhreagh, Bell's estate across the bay, donated many of the artefacts.

Alexander Graham Bell may be best known for inventing the telephone, but it's just one accomplishment in a career that spanned telecommunication, transportation, medicine, and more. He also was responsible for various aircraft and hydrofoil boats, a metal jacket that acted as an early iron lung, and an audiometer that was able to detect hearing issues. He also conducted extensive research into techniques for teaching speech to the deaf and sought alternative fuels.

Bell, who emigrated from Scotland to Canada at age 23, first visited Baddeck in 1885, when he was in his late 30s. Charmed by the social and intellectual life of the village, Bell and his wife Mabel established here their summer home, Beinn Bhreagh ("beautiful mountain" in Gaelic), which Bell visited annually until his death in 1922. In fact, the graves of both Bell and Mabel are located on the grounds. Though Beinn Bhreagh isn't accessible to visitors, it acts as an important visual touchstone for the national historic site—the estate's headlands are visible across the water from the museum's rooftop deck. There, Bell, who had already had success with the telephone, performed experiments in sound transmission, medicine, aeronautics, marine engineering, and more in a laboratory on the property.

And although many of Bell's accomplishments would go on to have far-reaching global impact, his presence in Baddeck had an unexpected positive local impact on the economic and social life of the small coastal village. Upkeep of Beinn Bhreagh provided many with jobs, as did Bell's continuous experimentation, which often required assistants.

MUSEUM EXHIBITS

The museum chronicles Bell's life and work in three main halls through various exhibits. Gain an overview of Bell's life in Beinn Bhreagh with the exhibit "Home," which also tells the story of his wife Mabel. An adjacent timeline gives global context to the events in Bell's life and how they related to what was going on in the world at the time.

Mabel was an influential person in Bell's life. Like her husband's mother, Mabel was deaf, her hearing destroyed by disease when she was a young girl. Bell began teaching the deaf in the early 1870s, and the couple met when Mabel was one of his private students. They married in 1877, when she was just 19.

Mabel was not only her husband's confidante but also, in the case of his aeronautical experiments, his financial backer. In the early 1900s, with a strong belief in flight, she sold some real estate and gave the $20,000 profits to Bell and four of his colleagues. This gift helped establish the Aerial Experiment Association, which led to the creation of the *Silver Dart* (see p. 56), Bell's most successful airplane.

A strong and independent woman, Mabel advocated for women's education, especially in the field of science. She encouraged women to work toward change in health and home industries, as well as women's suffrage, children's labour, and children's education. She founded the first chapter of the Canadian Home and School Parent-Teacher Federation, the first Canadian Montessori School, and the Baddeck Public Library.

The "Sound and Silence" gallery illustrates the work Bell did to teach those with hearing impairments. In the "Ideas" portion of the hall, a mix of artefacts and audiovisual presentations complement the physical items illustrative of Bell's many accomplishments. "Air" details Bell's work with kites and airplanes, and contains a full-size replica of the *Silver Dart*. Finally, "Water" gives information on his work with hydrofoil boats and displays the original hull and a full-size replica of the HD-4 (see p. 56), Bell's most successful hydrofoil.

CAPE BRETON

Kite making is a family activity.

SILVER DART & HD-4

The *Silver Dart* was an early aircraft built by Bell's Aerial Experiment Association, an aeronautical research group that included engineers John Alexander Douglas McCurdy and Frederick W. Baldwin. In 1909, the aircraft took off from the ice of Baddeck Bay, making the first controlled flight in Canada. A variety of materials were used in its construction: wood, wire, bamboo, friction tape, steel tubing, and repurposed motorcycle wheels, among others.

The replica, completed in 2009, flew to mark the 100th anniversary of the plane's first flight. The *Dart's* wingspan measures 15 m (49 ft); its length, 12 m (39 ft). It weighs only 390 kg (860 lb). Many people marvel today, as they did at the time Bell invented it, that something so seemingly delicate could fly.

The original hull of the HD-4, a hydrofoil craft built by Bell and Baldwin at Beinn Bhreagh, stands nearby, as does a full-scale reproduction of the craft built in 1978. In 1919, the HD-4 was the fastest boat in the world, setting a world marine speed record of 70.86 miles an hour (114.04 km/h). The 18.5-m-long (61 ft), 4.5-tonne HD-4 was Bell and Baldwin's greatest achievement with hydrofoil craft.

PROGRAMMING

Visitors may explore the museum on their own or via a guided tour (fee). Of particular interest are the two White Glove Tours ("The Parlour" and "The Workshop"). Sharing with visitors how a museum conserves and protects precious artefacts, the tours are held in the actual artefact storage areas and feature items that would have been found in Bell's parlour or workshop, such as one of his notebooks filled with ideas, grocery lists, jokes, and other material, all jotted down in Bell's distinctive tiny handwriting. Other items include a preliminary small-scale maquette of one of Bell's larger inventions and a vacuum jacket, an invention that acted as a precursor to the iron lung, which saved thousands of lives during the years of widespread polio.

The site also offers a variety of hands-on programs (fee) for both adults and children, primarily during the summer months. In the kite-making program, kids make and decorate their own sled kite while learning about the history of Bell's work with aviation and how he made the leap from kites to airplanes. An all-ages workshop in building a tetrahedral kite teaches participants why and how Bell came up with this triangular kite design in his quest to build a craft appropriate for manned flight. Visitors can run other experiments too; call to find out which activities are offered on which days.

How to Get There

From Sydney, the closest airport, head west for about 20 minutes on Hwy. 125, and then take Trans-Canada 105 and continue west for about 45 minutes to Baddeck (exit 9). It's then 2 km (1.2 mi) to the site.

When to Go

The site is open daily from May 20 to October 30, but certain events and experiences are only offered in the summer months, such as *The Bells of Baddeck*, a musical drama that tells the story of how Bell and his wife Mabel came to Cape Breton, and daily kite-making sessions, in which kids and adults can create their own kites and fly them on the grounds.

ALEXANDER GRAHAM BELL NATIONAL HISTORIC SITE
(Lieu historique national Alexander-Graham-Bell)

INFORMATION & ACTIVITIES

HOW TO REACH US
559 Chebucto St. (Rte. 205), Baddeck, NS. Phone (902) 295-2069. pc.gc.ca/eng/lhn-nhs/ns/grahambell/index.aspx.

SEASONS & ACCESSIBILITY
Open May 20 to October 30, daily.

ENTRANCE FEES
$7.80 per adult, $19.60 per family/group.

PETS
Only service animals are permitted.

ACCESSIBLE SERVICES
The site is fully accessible for those with mobility issues. Film presentations are closed-captioned; a presentation is available for those with visual impairments.

THINGS TO DO
Tour the museum exhibits. Partake in regular interpretive programs, and hands-on experiences for kids and adults, such as making and flying kites, participating in experiments, and much more. For kids, there are toys, books, and interactive activities.

Two special activities of note: Aviation Day (usually the third Sunday of August) celebrates Bell's aviation achievements with workshops and activities. Harvest Home (the third Saturday in September) commemorates the relationship Bell and his wife had with the people of Baddeck, complete with activities for adults and children.

Elsewhere in the area, outdoor opportunities include hiking, kayaking, golfing, and whale-watching.

CAMPGROUNDS
Baddeck Cabot Trail Campground 9584 Trans-Canada Hwy., Baddeck, NS B0E 1B0. (902) 295-2288. baddeckcabottrailcamp ground.com. $28–$49.

HOTELS, MOTELS, & INNS
(Rates are for a 2-person double, high season, in Canadian dollars, unless otherwise noted.)

Auberge Gisele's Inn 387 Shore Rd., Baddeck, NS B0E 1B0. (902) 295-2849. giseles.com. 78 rooms, $115–$300.
Dunlop Inn 552 Chebucto St., Baddeck, NS B0E 1B0. (902) 295-3355. dunlopinn.com. 5 rooms, $105–$170.
Broadwater Inn and Cottages 975 NS-205, Baddeck, NS B0E 1B0. (902) 295-1101. broadwaterinn.com. 5 rooms and 9 cottage units, $80–$300.

CAPE BRETON

CAPE BRETON SITES

MARCONI
GLACE BAY, NS

Here in 1902, on this isolated point of land overlooking the ocean, inventor and electrical engineer Guglielmo Marconi exchanged some of the earliest transatlantic telegraph messages. At the time, there were four square towers, an operating room, and a powerhouse. Today, only footprints of the towers and the ruins of foundation walls remain. Designated NHS: 1939. 15 Timmerman St., Table Head. (902) 842-2530 (summer) or (902) 295-2069 (winter).

CAPE BRETON SITES

ROYAL BATTERY
LOUISBOURG, NS

The Royal Battery is located within the larger Fortress of Louisbourg National Historic Site (see pp. 50–53). As part of the French defence system, the battery's position on the harbour's north shore gave cannons a clear shot at approaching enemy ships. Despite this, the battery was surrendered to the British twice—in 1745 and again in 1758. The British disabled it in 1760. Now, only mounds and depressions reveal the outline of the former facility. Designated NHS: 1952. 265 Park Service Rd. (902) 733-3548.

WOLFE'S LANDING
KENNINGTON COVE, NS

From this site, between a rocky beach to the south and rolling grasses and forest to the north, British forces began the attack that would lead to the capture of Louisbourg (see pp. 50–53) in 1758. Under the leadership of Brig. Gen. James Wolfe, the initial landing eventually led French forces to evacuate. It was a definitive battle in the Seven Years' War, which ended French rule in Cape Breton. Designated NHS: 1929. Kennington Cove Rd., a few miles west of the Fortress of Louisbourg.

CANSO ISLANDS
CANSO, NS

Economically, the east coast is known for its strong ties to the fishing industry. The French first developed a fishing base on the Canso Islands—which had been inhabited by the Mi'kmaq for centuries beforehand—in the 16th century. British territory after 1713, Canso's three main islands (Grassy, George, and Piscatiqui) also served as staging areas for various battles in the French-British struggle for control of Canada. Designated NHS: 1925. School St.

GRASSY ISLAND FORT
CANSO, NS

The isles (including Grassy) that make up the Canso Islands have long been rich fishing grounds. As such, the islands were contested locations in the long war between the British and French. Twice, the British built fortifications to protect Grassy. One fell to ruin in the 1730s, and its successor was burned down during a French attack in 1744. Today, only depressions and rampart outlines are visible to give visitors an idea of the former fort's design. Designated NHS: 1962. Grassy Island.

ST. PETERS CANAL
ST. PETERS, NS

This man-made, 800-m (2,625 ft) channel connects the Bras d'Or Lake with St. Peters Bay on the Atlantic Ocean. In continuous operation since it was completed in 1869, the canal has undergone two enlargements and now accommodates transportation for commercial and industrial goods as well as pleasure craft. From the water, one can see the waterfront development that was fostered by the activity the canal promoted. Designated NHS: 1929. Hwy. 4. (902) 535-2118 (summer) or (902) 295-2069 (winter).

ST. PETERS
ST. PETERS, NS

Located on the southeast shore of Cape Breton, between St. Peters Bay on the Atlantic coastline and Bras d'Or Lake, the village of St. Peters bears evidence of Mi'kmaq settlements and of a French trading post and Acadian communities. Part of the site's significance is in the early role it played bringing together these two cultures. Here, the French used the Fort Saint-Pierre trading post to deal with the local Mi'kmaq. Designated NHS: 1929. (902) 733-2280.

New Brunswick's Carleton Martello Tower, a British military post on the Bay of Fundy

NEW BRUNSWICK

One of the four original provinces of the Confederation of Canada, forest-covered New Brunswick is the only province that is officially bilingual—English and French. The first people to settle here were the Mi'kmaq, who crossed from Nova Scotia and Prince Edward Island via the Chignecto Isthmus and Northumberland Strait. By the early 17th century, the French had claimed the area as part of Acadia. English speakers, including a flood of Loyalists fleeing the American Revolution, began arriving in the 1760s. By then, the imperial struggle

between France and Britain was well under way. Visitors can explore French-built forts, including Fort Beauséjour–Fort Cumberland (see pp. 64–65), as well as Carleton Martello Tower (see pp. 62–63), built by the British to defend the city of St. John against American attack during the War of 1812. Founded by Loyalist refugees and now one of the largest cities in New Brunswick, St. John owes much of its growth to the success of the timber industry, which has dominated the province's economy since the early 19th century.

Nineteenth-century uniforms hang in the barracks room.

▶ CARLETON MARTELLO TOWER

ST. JOHN, NB

Designated 1930

Located 70 m (230 ft) above the town of St. John, this squat stone tower built by the British in the early 1800s offers clear views not only of downtown St. John but also of the Bay of Fundy. Carleton Martello Tower is one of fewer than a dozen martello-style towers built by the British military forces in what was once British North America.

This hilltop position was the perfect vantage point from which to defend St. John against potential American land attacks during the War of 1812—at the time, New Brunswick was seen as offering a direct overland route to interior Canada. The tower didn't see action during the War of 1812 (in fact, it wasn't completed until 1815), but it did play a role in both the First and Second World Wars. In the first, the tower served as a detention centre for military deserters; in the second, it was used as an observation and fire command post, with a two-storey addition constructed for this purpose.

Carleton Martello has all the distinctive characteristics of martello construction: a circular shape and flat roof, a ground-floor storage space, and thick stone walls designed to absorb heavy artillery fire.

What to See & Do

Military history is certainly a reason why people visit Carleton Martello, but peaceful opportunities factor in as well. It's is a great place to picnic and to snap beautiful panoramas of downtown St. John, the Bay of Fundy, and, on a clear day, Nova Scotia.

Guide yourself through the tower and grounds, including the barracks room and powder magazine. In the summer months, demonstrations and reenactments entertain visitors. Costumed interpreters demonstrate military drills, mock attacks, and weapons handling, and then guests may try on uniforms and join in the action. Check with the site about special events, including ghost walks.

How to Get There

From Hwy. 1, take exit 120 (Digby Ferry) and follow the Parks Canada signs to Market Place, and then to Whipple Street. VIA Rail train service runs regularly to Moncton, roughly 150 km (93 mi) away.

When to Go

The site is open daily mid-June to September, and Monday through Friday in September and October. Closed rest of year. Note: The tower is closed for renovation in 2016–17.

INFORMATION

HOW TO REACH US
454 Whipple St., St. John, NB E2M 2R3. Phone (506) 636-4011. pc.gc .ca/eng/lhn-nhs/nb/carleton/index .aspx.

ENTRANCE FEES
$3.90 per adult.

ACCESSIBLE SERVICES
Limited; contact the park for more details.

HOTELS, MOTELS, & INNS
Chipman Hill Suites 76 Union St., St. John, NB E2L 1A1. (506) 693-1171. chipmanhill.com. 85 rooms, $95–$255.

NEW BRUNSWICK

Costumed interpreters share tales of the 1812 war era.

A reenactor demonstrates handling weapons.

The circular tower is a martello design.

Fort Beauséjour–Fort Cumberland, built in 1751 on the windy isthmus between Nova Scotia and New Brunswick

▶ FORT BEAUSÉJOUR–FORT CUMBERLAND

AULAC, NB

Designated 1920

The French built this star-shaped fortification on the Chignecto Isthmus to defend their claim to the territory that is today New Brunswick from British forces in Nova Scotia. Taken by the British in 1755, it would play an important role in the expulsion of the Acadians and stop an incursion during the American Revolution.

The Chignecto Isthmus is a land bridge between New Brunswick and Nova Scotia. For years, the spit was a major overland travel route for Indigenous Peoples and the Europeans who came later.

The French built Fort Beauséjour in 1751 to defend the Acadia colony against the British, who had built nearby Fort Lawrence the previous year. They held the site until June 1755, when a two-week siege ended in the British takeover of Beauséjour. In a cruel coincidence, the fort (now renamed Cumberland) later served as a stopover for Acadians being deported by the British.

The fort next saw battle in 1776, during the American Revolution.

Many of the recent settlers to Nova Scotia had New England roots and were drawn to the revolutionary cause. Jonathan Eddy organized a small militia, raising modest support in Massachusetts and among Indigenous Peoples, to launch an attack on the fort. The fort's small garrison was able to hold it until reinforcements came from Halifax, ending the Eddy Rebellion. The fort was reinforced during the War of 1812.

The fort is a good example of a Vauban-style fort, named for the French military engineer Sébastien le Prestre de Vauban. The star-shaped design includes low wall profiles with sloping earthworks, which provide defence from cannon fire as they cannot be penetrated and force the cannoneers to aim higher, missing the defence works. The stone ruins and underground casemates (where provisions would have been stored) have been stabilized and restored.

What to See & Do

At the visitor centre, artefact-filled exhibits give an overview of the fort and its history. Outside, a loop trail provides a self-guided tour of the fort via a series of interpretive panels. Learn what daily life was like for soldiers at the garrison and get a close-up look at the fort—and even enter the casemates.

The fort also commemorates hometown heroes whose efforts helped during the two World Wars. Albert Desbrisay Carter, for example, enlisted in St. John in 1914.

INFORMATION

HOW TO REACH US
111 Fort Beauséjour Rd., Aulac, NB E4L 2W5. Phone (506) 364-5080. pc.gc.ca/beausejour.

ENTRANCE FEES
$3.90 per adult.

ACCESSIBLE SERVICES
The visitor centre, museum, restroom, and a special trail are wheelchair accessible. An all-terrain wheelchair is available for loan. Audiovisual presentations are close-captioned and equipped with an FM loop.

HOTELS, MOTELS, & INNS
Marshlands Inn 55 Bridge St., Sackville, NB E4L 3N8. (506) 536-0170. marshlands.nb.ca. 18 rooms, $119–$124.

NEW BRUNSWICK

Earthworks helped protect the fort from cannon fire.

Provisions were stored in underground casemates.

He joined the Royal Flying Corps and became one of the top 15 Canadian aces, earning several distinguished medals.

Military history isn't the fort's only draw. Birders flock here for the variety of marsh birds that frequent the area—bald eagles and more—and, in mid- to late summer, for the wealth of shorebirds that gather in and around the Bay of Fundy.

On Canada Day, New Brunswick Day, and Acadian Day, the site stages special events and activities, which may include demonstrations of blacksmithing, spinning, and weaving. Check the website for more details.

How to Get There

Aulac is 58 km (36 mi) from Moncton. Take exit 513A off Trans-Canada 2 and follow the Parks Canada signs.

When to Go

The fort is open daily June 5 through Labour Day; closed rest of year.

NEW BRUNSWICK SITES

BOISHÉBERT
MIRAMICHI, NB

In 1756, a small group of Acadians fleeing the deportation by the British took refuge on an island (today's Beaubears Island) in the Miramichi River, naming their settlement for the French officer who led them, Charles des Champs de Boishébert. Defeated in 1760 and the refugees expelled, the settlement fell to ruin. All that can be seen today are cemetery remnants and a former church site, as well as cleared areas and paths along the point. Designated NHS: 1930. Hwy. 8, Northwest Bridge. (506) 876-2443.

BEAUBEARS ISLAND SHIPBUILDING
MIRAMICHI, NB

New Brunswick's history of shipbuilding goes back centuries, and Beaubears Island is an excellent example of why. Located in the Miramichi River, the second largest shipbuilding centre in New Brunswick, Beaubears boasted dense woods, perfect for providing raw materials, as well as the sloping terrain necessary for launching and repairing ships and vessels. Remnants of the 19th-century facilities that once serviced the industry include houses and barns. Designated NHS: 2001. Hwy. 8, Northwest Bridge. (506) 876-2443.

MONUMENT-LEFEBVRE
MEMRAMCOOK, NB

This sandstone building was erected in memory of Father Camille Lefebvre, founder of St. Joseph's College. As the first French language institution to grant university degrees in the Atlantic region, it had a major role in the renaissance of Acadian culture in the latter half of the 19th century. Today, the building serves as a cultural interpretive centre. Designated NHS: 1994. 480 rue Centrale. (506) 758-9808.

ST. ANDREWS BLOCKHOUSE
ST. ANDREWS, NB

The St. Andrews Blockhouse bears the distinction of being the only privately funded fortification from the War of 1812, having been funded and built by local citizens and militia. It may also be the only remaining blockhouse in the country from the war; however, it never saw active service. The two-storey square timber structure, whose second floor overhangs the first, is open to visitors during the summer months. Designated NHS: 1962. 23 Joes Point Rd. (506) 529-4270.

FORT GASPAREAUX
PORT ELGIN, NB

The French built Fort Gaspareaux in 1751 to prevent the British from accessing the north shore of the Chignecto Isthmus, a land bridge that connects present-day Nova Scotia with New Brunswick. The fort fell to the British shortly after Fort Beauséjour, at the other end of the isthmus, was taken in 1756. Once the British controlled the region, they burned the fort down as it lacked strategic value. Today, only traces remain of the fort as do nine graves of provincial soldiers killed in 1756. Designated NHS: 1920. Fort St.

OLD GOVERNMENT HOUSE
FREDERICTON, NB

Old Government House has served many purposes since its completion in 1828. Initially it was the residence for the governor of New Brunswick. Later the sandstone Palladian-style mansion housed a veterans' hospital and was used by the Royal Canadian Mounted Police, among other uses. Today, it has reverted back to its original role, serving as an official residence, but this time for the lieutenant governor of New Brunswick. Designated NHS: 1958. 20 Woodstock Rd. (506) 453-2505.

World-Class Heritage

Have you ever been to a place so inspiring you felt it should be safeguarded and shared with the world? That is exactly the sensation that the natural and cultural properties on the World Heritage List, administered by UNESCO's World Heritage Committee, are meant to convey. There are presently more than 1,000 sites on the list, which continues to grow, year after year.

United Nations
Educational, Scientific and
Cultural Organization

Organisation
des Nations Unies
pour l'éducation,
la science et la culture

World Heritage
in Canada

Patrimoine mondial
au Canada

Picturesque Old Town Lunenburg, Nova Scotia, established in the mid-1700s as a planned British colonial settlement

To be included, sites must satisfy criteria defined in the Convention Concerning the Protection of the World Cultural and Natural Heritage. Adopted in 1972, it supports the identification, protection, and preservation of heritage properties around the world. These sites must be of "outstanding universal value": That is to say, they must be of "cultural and/or natural significance which is so exceptional as to transcend national boundaries and to be of common importance for present and future generations of all humanity."

The selection process is long and rigorous. Countries that are signatories to the convention prepare a tentative list, which provides an inventory of their own places with strong potential. Then an extensive nomination is put together to demonstrate a site's outstanding universal value. Afterward, the nomination is submitted to a thorough evaluation by international advisory organizations, before being recommended to the World Heritage Committee for a final decision. The entire process can take several years. Once on the list, World Heritage sites are monitored to ensure that they are appropriately protected and managed, in order to keep their status.

The Great Wall of China and the Galápagos Islands are examples of the treasured places to receive this privileged status. There are equally remarkable World Heritage sites to explore in Canada, which include cultural landscapes, archaeological remains, buildings, and entire urban districts, as well as natural habitats, processes, and phenomena. These places, encompassing many national historic sites, are listed below with their dates of inscription:

CULTURAL SITES

L'Anse aux Meadows *(Newfoundland and Labrador, 1978)*
Head-Smashed-In Buffalo Jump *(Alberta, 1981)*
SGang Gwaay *(British Columbia, 1981)*
Historic District of Old Québec *(Québec, 1985)*
Old Town Lunenburg *(Nova Scotia, 1995)*
Rideau Canal *(Ontario, 2007)*
Landscape of Grand Pré *(Nova Scotia, 2012)*
Red Bay Basque Whaling Station *(Newfoundland and Labrador, 2013)*

NATURAL SITES

Nahanni National Park *(Northwest Territories, 1978)*
Dinosaur Provincial Park *(Alberta, 1979)*
Kluane/Wrangell-St. Elias/Glacier Bay/Tatshenshini-Alsek
(British Columbia, Yukon, and Alaska, U.S.A.; 1979)
Wood Buffalo National Park *(Alberta and Northwest Territories, 1983)*
Canadian Rocky Mountain Parks *(Alberta and British Columbia, 1984)*
Gros Morne National Park *(Newfoundland and Labrador, 1987)*
Waterton Glacier International Peace Park *(Alberta and Montana, U.S.A.; 1995)*
Miguasha National Park *(Québec, 1999)*
Joggins Fossil Cliffs *(Nova Scotia, 2008)*

NEW BRUNSWICK

Site of one of the world's best preserved buffalo jumps

Jones Falls Lock Station, Rideau Canal

Norse explorers likely founded L'Anse aux Meadows around A.D. 1000.

NEWFOUNDLAND & LABRADOR

The province of Newfoundland and Labrador is composed of the island of Newfoundland and the Labrador mainland. People have inhabited this region for 5,000 to 10,000 years, with the Inuit, Innu, Mi'kmaq, and other Indigenous Peoples probably arriving around 2000 B.C. Archaeological evidence at L'Anse aux Meadows (see pp. 72–75) indicates that the Norse reached the northern tip of Newfoundland around A.D. 1000 but soon left; Europeans didn't return until the late 15th century. A hundred years later the island's

coast hummed with European fisheries, while a thriving Basque whaling industry had developed in southern Labrador (see pp. 83–84). Settlement was slow and seasonal, and fishing predominated. By the 1600s, England and France controlled manufacturing and trade here. One of the last battles in their struggle for supremacy took place at Signal Hill (see pp. 76–79), near the modern-day provincial capital, St. John's. At nearby Cape Spear stands one of Canada's oldest surviving lighthouses (see pp. 80–83).

Sod-and-timber buildings blend into the landscape.

▶ L'ANSE AUX MEADOWS

ST. LUNAIRE-GRIQUET, NL
Designated 1975; Inscribed WH 1978

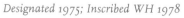

Tucked in a bay on the Atlantic Ocean, amid rolling green hills and rugged coastal rock, sits L'Anse aux Meadows. This is the spot where, about 1,000 years ago, a Norse expedition, en route from Greenland, stopped. The landscape is still marked with their sod-and-timber buildings that blend into the cliffs and coastlines of the landscape.

Here, at the tip of Newfoundland's Great Northern Peninsula, the remains of an early Norse encampment are of such significance that the site was inscribed on the UNESCO World Heritage List in 1978.

Over the years, many peoples have called L'Anse aux Meadows home, including the Dorset Eskimo. Though the remains of the Norse presence have been there for hundreds of years, they weren't discovered until the 1960s.

The first recorded voyages of the Norse to North America began in the 11th century. They touched the continent centuries before Columbus did, when a vessel from Greenland carried 30 men to this area. A low rolling coast and lush meadows captivated the Norse—as did the nearby streams alive with salmon, the sheltering forests that offer ample timber for construction, and the agreeable climate.

These forests were a significant find for the Norse, who had a dearth of suitable construction timber in Greenland. The following summer, they travelled home, with wood to show for their efforts. This bounty influenced more Norse to make the journey, eventually bringing livestock with them. L'Anse aux Meadows served as a base from which to explore the island and discover its richness of resources, especially timber, which they transported back to Greenland.

Eventually, tensions arose between the Norse and the Indigenous People native to the area—whom the Norse referred to as skrælings. There is no evidence to indicate that the Norse were driven back to Greenland; however, the settlement was eventually abandoned. When they departed, the houses, workshops, and small blacksmith's forge decayed and were reclaimed by the land.

Maybe that's why it was centuries before anyone realized what the remains of the site meant. In 1960, archaeologist Anne Stine Ingstad and her husband Helge Ingstad (a Norwegian writer and explorer) discovered Norse landing places along the east coast of the continent. They were led to the actual site of L'Anse aux Meadows by a local, George Decker, who thought the lumpy site might be of interest. What followed was an eight-year excavation involving archaeologists from Norway, Iceland, Sweden, and the United States. Together, they discovered the oldest European settlement in the New World.

EXPLORING THE SITE

When the Norse left Newfoundland hundreds of years ago, their sod-and-timber houses decayed though the ruins of the original buildings were clearly visible on the landscape. What you see today was reconstructed based on the extensive research done by an international team of archaeologists in the 1960s.

The reconstruction paints a clear picture of how the buildings would

have looked centuries ago. The site consisted of three major complexes. Each one had a residence and a workshop space for craftsmen, such as those who completed repairs on ships and boats, as well as blacksmiths who roasted bog ore in one workshop and then moved it to another for the smithing process.

The buildings were made of sod walls and roofs, overlaid with supporting timber frames. Each building was outfitted with a fireplace, typically simple, round pits used for heating, cooking, and lighting the house.

Costumed interpreters wander around the site, and they are happy to speak with visitors about any aspect of the area. Hands-on demonstrations encourage visitors to help spin fleece into yarn, learn to thread a bone needle, or pump the bellows in a working forge, where a blacksmith makes nails.

Inside the visitor centre, scale models based on archaeological research give the lay of the land, maps and old Norse literature further tell the story of the Norse, and exhibits of original artefacts found on-site reveal the past. These small, seemingly insignificant scraps of tools and other objects informed researchers about the day-to-day life and demographics of life in the settlement. For example, a bronze pin was found inside one of the site's fireplaces; worn to fasten a cloak, it's a uniquely Norse item and strong proof that the inhabitants here were Norse. Elsewhere, outside one of the buildings, archaeologists found a spindle whorl and a bone needle used for knitting. From these relics, considered domestic tools at the time, researchers deduced that not all the Norse in the area were men.

But perhaps the best evidence that L'Anse aux Meadows was a Norse site

Costumed interpreters are based on real village inhabitants.

Hands-on demonstrations cater to all ages.

is the slag (runoff from smelting and working iron) and rivets. Iron nails, square cut for ease of biting through wood, are a clear indication of European presence, not to mention that Canada's own Indigenous Peoples didn't forge using hot iron at the time.

For more insight, take a guided tour that highlights the cultural tapestry here, including additional stories and ancient Norse music.

SAGAS AND SHADOWS

The popular night-time Sagas and Shadows program (fee), offered Tuesdays and Saturdays in July and August, mixes Norse history and mythology. Costumed interpreters take on the role of the Norse who lived here for a few short years.

As visitors huddle together in the *skáli* (kitchen) of one of the sod buildings, they are treated to true tales from the Viking sagas, most of which date back to Iceland in the 13th and 14th centuries. Learn about Erik the Red and his exploits in Greenland, or listen to the myth of Norse gods Thor and Loki. Laugh along at the story of Gilitrutt—a tale that shares similarities with the more modern-day telling of Rumpelstiltskin. There's something for everyone—from conflict and battle, to the exploration of the seas and discovery of new lands.

HIKING

Sprawling across 80 sq km (31 sq mi), L'Anse aux Meadows is a beautiful place to simply wander. There's an incredibly diverse landscape including marshlands, icebergs, and wildflowers. The views of Islands Bay and the Atlantic beyond are incredible. Smell the juniper, crowberry, and salty ocean breeze. Enjoy the solitude of a meadow, or the novelty of visiting one of the black sand beaches in the area. Bring a picnic lunch and visit Muddy Cove, hugged on all sides by the harsh, rocky coastline.

L'ANSE AUX MEADOWS NATIONAL HISTORIC SITE
(Lieu historique national de L'Anse aux Meadows)

INFORMATION & ACTIVITIES

HOW TO REACH US
11 km (6.8 mi) N of St. Lunaire-Griquet, St. Anthony, NL. Phone (709) 623-2608 or (709) 458-2417. pc.gc.ca /lanseauxmeadows.

SEASONS & ACCESSIBILITY
May 30 to October 7, daily; shorter hours first and last couple of weeks. Closed rest of year.

ENTRANCE FEES
$11.70 per adult, $29.40 per family/group.

PETS
Leashed pets are permitted on the grounds, but not inside any buildings.

ACCESSIBLE SERVICES
The visitor centre (including the washroom), sod huts, and ruins are wheelchair accessible. From designated parking spots for those with mobility issues, an accessible boardwalk leads to the site.

THINGS TO DO
Meet costumed interpreters based on real Norse inhabitants of the former village. Listen to stories in the main hall and sit in on demonstrations of textile weaving and iron forging, with a chance to participate. The visitor centre provides context for the significance of this centuries-old site, exhibiting original artefacts found on-site. There's even a replica of a Norse *faering*, a small tender used to transport from the *knarr* (a merchant ship) to the shore or travel short distances along the coast. Absorb the natural beauty of the landscape by hiking the site's coastal and bog trails, which lead to incredible vistas.

CAMPGROUNDS
Pistolet Bay Provincial Park Rte. 437, Raleigh, NL A0K 4J0. (877) 214-2267. www.nlcamping.ca/PistoletBay. $18.

HOTELS, MOTELS, & INNS
(Rates are for a 2-person double, high season, in Canadian dollars, unless otherwise noted.)

Grenfell Heritage Hotel and Suites 1 McChada Dr., St. Anthony, NL A0K 4S0. (709) 454-8395. grenfellheritagehotel.ca. 20 rooms, $130–$170.
St. Brendan's Motel 132 Main St., St. Lunaire-Griquet, NL A0K 4X0. (709) 623-2520. stbrendansmotel.ca. 11 rooms, $100–$120.
Viking Village B&B Box 127, Hay Cove, L'Anse aux Meadows, NL A0K 2X0. (709) 623-2238. vikingvillage.ca. 5 rooms, $75–$92.

The easy 2-km (1.2 mi) Birchy Nuddick Trail travels inland to higher elevations that offer incredible views of the Atlantic. Interpretive panels explain the significance of the views and provide information on flora. One of the most exciting examples of northern plant life is the *Sarracenia purpurea*, commonly known as the purple pitcher plant, northern pitcher plant, or side-saddle flower, known to grow near the boardwalk. Moose are sometimes seen along the trail, as are various seabirds. Access the trail from the visitor centre parking lot.

How to Get There
L'Anse aux Meadows is at the tip of the Great Northern Peninsula, 433 km (270 mi) north of the town of Deer Lake, located on Trans-Canada 1, via the Viking Trail (Rte. 430) and Rte. 436.

When to Go
L'Anse aux Meadows is only open from spring to early fall, with its best hours at the height of summer. Visit in July for maximum enjoyment of the site, with full programming and warm, beautiful sunsets.

Cabot Tower, built in 1900 on rocky Signal Hill

▶ SIGNAL HILL

ST. JOHN'S, NL
Designated 1951

Standing atop Signal Hill feels like standing in another century. Here, a severe, rocky landscape rises to its highest point, topped by the imposing Cabot Tower that looks out over St. John's Harbour. This hill has been a military site since the 18th century—and in 1901, inventor Guglielmo Marconi achieved a telecommunications first here.

Because of its position high above St. John's, Signal Hill has been used for observation and communication purposes since 1704. That's where it gets its name. Before there was such a thing as ship-to-shore radio, signalmen kept watch on the hill, scanning the ocean for ships that might be headed into St. John's Harbour. The series of flags flown from signal masts were originally used for military purposes and then, years later, to signal merchant vessels.

This strategic location led to the hill becoming a site of harbour defences from the 18th century through the Second World War. Significant territorial battles, including the last battle in North America of the Seven Years' War, played out over this rough landscape.

In addition to being a major geographic landmark, Signal Hill also stands as a monument to the history of ongoing conflict between France and Britain. For centuries, beginning in 1696, the two cultures fought for dominion over St. John's, with the French gaining control in 1762.

In addition to various military fortifications, Signal Hill was home to three different hospitals between 1870 and 1920. Though none remain standing, it is important to note them because electrical engineer Marconi received the world's first transatlantic wireless signal on December 12, 1901, in one of them.

The Signal Hill Visitor Centre shares the history of the hill through tours, interactive displays, exhibits, and film. Visitors will learn about Signal Hill's role in military and communications history, discovering details on everything from the French attacks on St. John's in the 1700s through to the Second World War, when the hill was home to an American base manned by both American and Canadian soldiers.

But Signal Hill has more to offer than just history: Its spectacular view of the ocean makes Signal Hill one of the best places for whale-watching in St. John's. Visitors will most commonly see humpback whales, but fin, orca, and minke whales may be sighted too, as well as dolphins and porpoises. In May and June, icebergs commonly broken off from glaciers in Greenland may be spotted, too.

CABOT TOWER

Perhaps the most obvious landmark at the hill is a relatively recent addition. Though Cabot Tower looks like a relic from medieval times courtesy of its sandstone walls, buttressing, and crenellation, it was only completed in 1900. The tower was meant to simultaneously honour the 60-year reign of Queen Victoria (her Diamond Jubilee) as well as the 400th anniversary of the 1497 voyage (led by John Cabot) that led to the discovery of Newfoundland. In that year, Cabot landed at Cape Bonavista, roughly 300 km (186 mi) north.

Used for signalling functions for a number of years, Cabot Tower now features on its second floor the exhibit "Waves Over Waves," which highlights and interprets Marconi's discovery. You can also visit with

representatives of the Society of Newfoundland Radio Amateurs (SONRA), who operate a ham radio station from the tower throughout the summer season. There's also a small gift shop run by the Historic Sites Association of Newfoundland and Labrador.

MILITARY REENACTMENTS

In the summer months, the smell of gunpowder hangs in the air. From the beginning of July to the beginning of August, the award-winning Signal Hill Tattoo performs twice daily on Wednesday, Thursday, Saturday, and Sunday. Part of Parks Canada's commemoration of the First World War, the Tattoo program illustrates the history of the iconic Newfoundland Regiment, beginning in 1795, following it through the War of 1812, and concluding with the regiment's deployment overseas in 1914. The performance includes a show-stopping sequence of military manoeuvres, including musket, mortar, and cannon fire. The experience costs extra admission, but it's well worth the price to watch the precise movements of the performers, all dressed in period uniform.

Signal Hill was a military communications centre through the Second World War.

Another summer-only activity is the tradition of firing the noonday gun, a First World War–era cannon near Cabot Tower. For a fee, visitors may participate in the ceremony.

Additionally, when cruise ships leave St. John's Harbour, military interpreters (representing one of several regiments from 1861 to the First World War) will often mark their departure with three volleys of rifle fire, bidding farewell as the ships pass under the Queen's Battery at the edge of The Narrows.

HIKING TRAILS

Visiting Signal Hill is very much an outdoors experience. Roughly 8 km

Visitors participate in the noonday cannon firing.

(5 mi) of hiking trails wind around Signal Hill's rough topography. At various points along each trail, hikers are treated to views of everything from the endless expanse of the Atlantic Ocean to the closer, quieter waters of The Narrows—the channel that leads into St. John's Harbour— to the rugged coastline.

The easy 1.2-km (0.74 mi) Burma Road Trail leads to Cuckold's Cove Lookout. From there, visitors can turn back to their starting point near the Signal Hill visitor centre or continue on to Quidi Vidi, a historic fishing village. It boasts its own brewery and restaurant, a boon hikers looking for a mid-hike refreshment or bite to eat.

For something more challenging, tackle the 3.7-km (2.2 mi) North Head Trail, the longest, most difficult, and most popular trail at Signal Hill. From the parking lot at the top of Signal Hill, a series of boardwalks and stairs descend to a footpath that leads to the entrance to St. John's Harbour. Travelling along The Narrows, toward the city, the path connects with Lower Battery Road, a separate path that drops nearly 152 m (499 ft) in elevation over its

A cannon overlooks St. John's Harbour.

SIGNAL HILL NATIONAL HISTORIC SITE
(Lieu historique national de Signal Hill)

INFORMATION & ACTIVITIES

HOW TO REACH US
Signal Hill Rd., St. John's, NL. Phone (709) 772-5367. pc.gc.ca/signalhill.

SEASONS & ACCESSIBILITY
Visitor Interpretation Centre: Open Wednesday to Sunday mid-May to June; daily June to mid-September; and Saturday to Wednesday mid-September to mid-October. Closed rest of year.

Cabot Tower: Open Wednesday to Sunday mid-May to June; daily June to September 7; and Saturday to Wednesday September 8 to mid-October. Closed rest of year.

ENTRANCE FEES
$3.90 per adult, $9.80 per family/group.

PETS
Pets must be kept leashed and supervised.

ACCESSIBLE SERVICES
Bilingual service is available year-round. The Visitor Centre, its washrooms, and Lookout Trail are wheelchair accessible. The historic architecture of Cabot Tower makes it inaccessible to wheelchairs.

THINGS TO DO
Wander the site's trails, where interpretive signs help navigate the history of the place. Guided tours and exhibits give greater insight into the significance of Signal Hill. Check the website or call ahead to find out about timing for military reenactments and special events.

SPECIAL ADVISORIES
Because of Signal Hill's rugged, varied terrain—and often high winds—stay on the paths and refrain from walking too close to cliff edges, or climbing rock faces and wall ledges.

CAMPGROUNDS
Pippy Park Campground and R.V. Park 70 Nagles Pl., St. John's, NL A1B 2Z2. (709) 737-3669. pippypark.com. $23–$45.

HOTELS, MOTELS, & INNS
(Rates are for a 2-person double, high season, in Canadian dollars, unless otherwise noted.)

Hometel on Signal Hill 2 St. Joseph's Ln., St. John's, NL A1A 5V1. (709) 739-7799. hometels.ca. 23 rooms, $139–$179.
Ryan Mansion 21 Rennies Mill Rd., St. John's, NL A1C 3P8. (709) 753-7926. ryanmansion.com. 3 rooms, $355–$565.
Franklin Hotel 193 Water St., St. John's, NL A1C 1B4. (709) 754-9005. thefranklinhotel.net. 10 rooms, $179.

1.7-km (1 mi) length. This is the most difficult part of the hike. The trail is maintained, but in places it has no rails or handholds and runs close to the coastline over rough terrain. Because of this, visitors are encouraged to stay on the path. In the event of wet weather, intense fog, or strong winds, it's best to postpone this hike.

How to Get There
Most major airlines fly to St. John's. Alternatively, Marine Atlantic *(marineatlantic.ca)* operates a daily car and passenger ferry service from Nova Scotia to Port aux Basques. From there, take Trans-Canada 1 some 900 km (559 mi) across the island to St. John's. In town, travel east on Empire Avenue, Duckworth Street, or Water Street until you hit Signal Hill Road. The site is at the top of the road.

When to Go
Signal Hill and Cabot Tower are closed during the winter months. August is the best month for capitalizing on the various special events that take place.

Cape Spear boasts Newfoundland's oldest surviving lighthouse.

▶ CAPE SPEAR LIGHTHOUSE

ST. JOHN'S, NL
Designated 1962

A rocky peninsula on Newfoundland's east coast, Cape Spear is the easternmost point in North America. Atop the cliff sits a square, white lighthouse, its tower dome striped red and white. This is the oldest surviving lighthouse in Newfoundland. Inside, artefacts and furnishings evoke the lifestyle of the light-keeping family that lived here in the 1830s.

The Cape Spear Lighthouse has been operational since the mid-1800s. It was the first purpose-built lighthouse on the east coast of Newfoundland and served as the first signal for entering St. John's Harbour. Its construction was one of the first orders of business under Newfoundland's newly created legislative assembly.

Work on the building, which consists of a stone tower surrounded by a square wooden residence, began in 1834 and lasted two years. The two-storey lighthouse was operational by the fall of 1836. Over the years, there have been ten different light keepers, eight of whom were members of the Cantwell family. All of them, along with their wives and children, lived on-site, with the exception of Gerry Cantwell, keeper in the 1980s and '90s. He drove out daily from his home in St. John's.

Cape Spear's original light (the lens and light system) was first used at the lighthouse at Inchkeith, Scotland, where it had been installed in 1815. It had curved reflectors that concentrated the light rays from a collection of what were known as Argand burners. Lamps and additional reflectors were arranged on a rotating metal frame, to produce a 17-second flash of white light every 43 seconds.

As lighting technology progressed, the light changed with the times. In 1912, a glass dioptric system was installed, initially powered by oil, then acetylene in 1916, and finally electricity in 1930.

With the advent of the Second World War, and the threat of enemy submarines and raiders offshore, a coastal defence battery was established here in 1941, and artillery mounted to protect the entrance to St. John's Harbour. The landscape surrounding the lighthouse changed significantly during this period. Guns were connected to a system of magazines and ready rooms via underground tunnels. Barracks, mess halls, and canteens were built to serve the troops who were stationed here.

Today, little evidence remains of the cape's military history. When the war ended in 1945, most of Fort Cape Spear was demolished, leaving only the artillery emplacements. Visitors still come to see the wartime relics, though the cape is better known for its reputation as a great location for whale-watching, observing ships going into and out of St. John's Harbour, and taking in the natural beauty of the ocean and surrounding trails.

LIGHTHOUSE & GROUNDS

The lighthouse is open for self-guided tours. It has been restored to its original state, and furnished throughout to replicate the experience of visiting a light keeper's residence in 1839. Wander through the rooms, with their papered walls and antique, period-specific furniture, and see some original artefacts dating to the 1830s, and the year the lighthouse first became operational.

Visitors also learn the story of Fort Cape Spear, and how the cape was the ideal vantage point from which to watch for naval threats.

The site offers two daily interpretive tours (11 a.m. and 2 p.m.) that take visitors through the light-keeping and military history of Cape Spear.

The visitor interpretation centre has exhibits on lighthouse technology, including how different kinds of lights operated over the years.

In another building, a second former keeper's residence, is an art gallery that displays more than 60 paintings of Newfoundland lighthouses, all done by local artist Leslie Noseworthy.

A WHALE OF A FESTIVAL

Cape Spear has capitalized on its reputation as the best place in Newfoundland for whale-watching. Each summer, in mid-June, the site hosts the one-day Whale Festival, a whale-watching festival.

More than 22 species of whales migrate to the Newfoundland and Labrador coast from May to September, to eat capelin, krill, and squid.

Humpbacks are the most oft seen whales at the cape, putting on an incredible show as they breach and spout spray. Visitors regularly spot

Defence artillery, added during the Second World War

CAPE SPEAR LIGHTHOUSE NATIONAL HISTORIC SITE
(Lieu historique national du Phare-de-Cap-Spear)

INFORMATION & ACTIVITIES

HOW TO REACH US
P.O. Box 1268, St. John's, NL A1C 6M1. Phone (709) 772-5367. pc.gc.ca/capespear.

SEASONS & ACCESSIBILITY
Open Wednesday to Sunday mid-May to June; daily June to mid-September; and Saturday to Wednesday mid-September to October.

ENTRANCE FEES
$3.90 per adult, $9.80 per family/group.

PETS
Pets must be leased.

ACCESSIBLE SERVICES
The visitor centre, washrooms, and Second World War gun battery are wheelchair accessible. Bilingual guide service is available during the summer months.

THINGS TO DO
Guided tours and/or self-guided tours of the lighthouse and grounds, hiking, whale-watching. Sunday night lighthouse dinners, featuring fresh local food, take place from late June to late August.

SPECIAL ADVISORIES
The terrain is rocky and uneven (wear sturdy shoes), and there are high winds and irregular tides. Stay on designated trails and don't edge too close to the cliffs.

CAMPGROUNDS
Pippy Park Campground and R.V. Park 70 Nagles Pl., St. John's, NL A1B 2Z2. (709) 737-3669. pippypark.com. $24–$45.

HOTELS, MOTELS, & INNS
(Rates are for a 2-person double, high season, in Canadian dollars, unless otherwise noted.)

Hometel on Signal Hill 2 St. Joseph's Ln., St. John's, NL A1A 5V1. (709) 739-7799. hometels.ca. 23 rooms, $139–$179.
Ryan Mansion 21 Rennies Mill Rd., St. John's, NL A1C 3P8. (709) 753-7926. ryanmansion.com. 3 rooms, $355–$565.
Franklin Hotel 193 Water St., St. John's, NL A1C 1B4. (709) 754-9005. thefranklinhotel.net. 10 rooms, $179.

minke, sperm, and fin whales as well. Less common are orcas (the most easily recognizable), though visitors do still see them at times. Many different kinds of dolphins, porpoises, and seals appear too.

The festival includes special events, animal touch tanks, kids' activities, and, of course, ample opportunity for whale-watching. Staged predominantly in Cape Spear's main parking lot, it extends along a short hiking trail to the most easterly point of the site.

Local partners set up information booths to share facts and stories with visitors. Whale skeletons are often on display, and volunteers lead guided whale-watching at the coastline.

HIKING

Cape Spear boasts a couple of hiking trails, each showcasing spectacular scenery and the chance to see wildlife. In addition to the whales in the ocean, look to the sky for the many bird species that frequent Cape Spear: northern gannet, bald eagle, Atlantic puffin, Leach's storm-petrel, and murres, to name a few.

The 3.7-km (2.3 mi) Blackhead Path is considered a moderately difficult hike because of minor elevation changes and rough terrain. From it, gorgeous views can be had of the cliffs of Southside Hills, as well as of Cabot Tower (see p. 77). The path is somewhat exposed, which means the coastal wind, fog, and rain conditions can affect the state of the path, so watch your step. Along the way, you'll see all the sites on the Cape Spear property.

The more difficult Maddox Cove Trail measures 9.3 km (5.8 mi); it begins at the lighthouse and ends at Maddox Cove, a small town in Petty Harbour–Maddox Cove. The trail includes hills, a boardwalk, bogs, shoreline, and two river crossings. Weather along this path can be windier and wetter than what is experienced in nearby St. John's.

Both trails feature vegetation typical of this landscape, including stunted evergreens, blue flag iris, and Newfoundland's provincial flower, the pitcher plant.

These trails form part of the larger East Coast Trail System, which traverses 265 km (165 mi) of coastline. More information is available on the East Coast Trail Association website.

How to Get There

From St. John's, head west on Water Street to Leslie Street. Turn left at the light and go over the bridge. At the stop sign, go straight and continue for 15 km (9.3 mi) until you are on Rte. 11/Cape Spear Drive. The site is at the end of the road.

When to Go

The site is closed from October to mid-May. The most exciting time to go is mid-June, when the Whale Festival takes place.

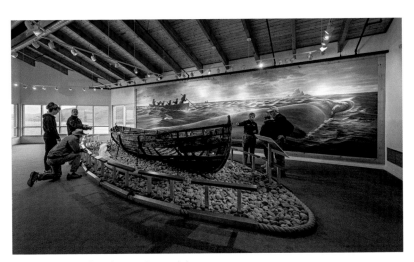

Restored chalupa, used by 16th-century Basque whalers

▶ RED BAY

RED BAY, NL

Designated 1979; Inscribed WH 2013

Labrador's Red Bay was once, in the mid-1500s, the centre of a booming business in whale oil production. Basque whalers from France and Spain came to these waters then to hunt bowhead and right whales for their blubber, which was rendered onshore into oil used for many purposes.

Red Bay, known as Butus to the Basques who used the site for several decades, is the largest—and the best preserved and most comprehensive—of several seasonal Basque whaling stations found along the northeastern coast of today's Canada. Underwater shipwrecks, a Basque cemetery, and the remains of rendering ovens, cooperages, and wharves tell the story of North America's first oil boom.

In 2013, the national historic site was also inscribed on the UNESCO World Heritage List, the world's highest recognition for a heritage place.

What to See & Do

At the Orientation Centre, don't miss the restored chalupa, the world's oldest known whaling boat. Then move on to the Interpretive Centre and its host of whaling artefacts, including a complete binnacle—the stand in which navigational instruments are placed so ship captains have easy access. Costumed interpreters relate stories of adventures, wrecks, and survival in 16th-century Labrador.

Outside, take the self-guided tour of the archaeological sites on Saddle Island, the heart of the Red Bay Basque whaling station, or hike the Boney Shore Trail and see whale bones discarded 400 years ago and spot icebergs from a lookout on the Tracy Hill Trail.

How to Get There

From Newfoundland, take Rte. 430 to St. Barbe. Take the Strait of Belle Isle ferry (drive-on/drive-off service; operates May–early Jan.) from Newfoundland to Blanc-Sablon, near the border of Québec and Labrador. From there, take Rte. 510 west/north to Red Bay.

From Labrador City in western Labrador, follow Rte. 500 east to Happy Valley–Goose Bay and then take Rte. 510 south to Red Bay.

INFORMATION

HOW TO REACH US
P.O. Box 103, Red Bay, NL A0K 4K0. Phone (709) 920-2142. pc.gc.ca/redbay.
Visitor centre: (709) 920-2051 or (709) 458-2417.

ENTRANCE FEES
$7.80 per adult, $19.60 per family/group.

ACCESSIBLE SERVICES
Accessible.

HOTELS, MOTELS, & INNS
Northern Light Inn Box 92, Main St., L'Anse au Clair, NL A0K 3K0. (709) 931-2332. northernlightinn.com. 70 rooms, $115–$159.
Whaler's Station 72-76 West Harbour Dr., Red Bay, NL A0K 2P0. (709) 920-2156. redbaywhalers.ca. 5 rooms, $95–$135.

When to Go

Open daily June 8 to September 28. Hours are shorter first and last couple of weeks; check the website for details.

Archaeological and natural treasures abound.

Since 1662, Castle Hill fortifications have overlooked Placentia Bay.

▶ CASTLE HILL

PLACENTIA, NL
Designated 1968

High on a hill on the east side of Placentia Bay stand the remains of military fortifications that date back to 1662. Below Castle Hill lies Placentia. This small town on Newfoundland's Avalon Peninsula played a pivotal role in the French and British struggle to control fishing rights around Newfoundland.

The waters around Newfoundland were historically rich with codfish. This is what drew Basque fishermen as early as the 16th century. The natural harbour of present-day Placentia quickly led the French government to found the colony of "Plaisance" here and to build the fortification on Castle Hill. This site, like many on the east coast, ended up being a battleground between French and British forces in the 17th and 18th centuries.

Though the French had excellent fortifications at Castle Hill (much of which remain), in 1708 British ships began a blockade of Placentia Bay to limit French access to supplies. The blockade continued until the 1713 Treaty of Utrecht gave the British rights to much of Newfoundland, and shifted the French to nearby Nova Scotia, where they built the Fortress of Louisbourg (see pp. 50–53).

What to See & Do

Castle Hill is a relatively small site, but visitors will find much of interest. Low, irregularly shaped rock walls—the breastworks—trace the forest line just below the summit, enclosing the fort. A few cannons aim out to the water. Wander through the ruins or along on-site hiking trails. Download Parks Canada's Explora app to serve as your own personal tour guide. Exhibits inside the visitor centre include a scale model of the fortifications and speak to what life was like for residents of the area in the 1600s.

During the summer, the site offers camping opportunities that are perfect for first-timers. Visitors need only pack a sleeping bag and pillow—Parks Canada staff take care of the rest, guiding campers through tent setup, meal preparation, fire building, and more. Conversations about Castle Hill's cultural value are part of the experience as the sun goes down and the sky opens up for stargazing.

How to Get There

From St. John's, head west for 90 km (56 mi) on Trans-Canada 1. Turn left onto Rte. 100 and travel 50 km (31 mi) south to the Freshwater–Argentia junction. Take a left to Placentia and Castle Hill.

When to Go

Castle Hill is open daily June through early September.

INFORMATION

HOW TO REACH US
24 Castle Hill Rd., Placentia, NL A0B 2Y0. Phone (709) 227-2401. pc.gc .ca/castlehill.

ENTRANCE FEES
$3.90 per adult, $9.80 per family/group.

ACCESSIBLE SERVICES
Accessible.

HOTELS, MOTELS, & INNS
Bridgeway Hotel 19 Prince William Dr., Placentia, NL A0B 2Y0. (709) 227-1700. bridgewayhotel.net. 12 rooms, $99–$115.

Interpreter at Ryan Premises, home of Newfoundland's most productive fishery

▶ RYAN PREMISES

BONAVISTA, NL
Designated 1987

The Ryan Premises buildings sprawl the shores of Bonavista's picturesque harbour. The white clapboard storehouses, the salty scent of sea air, and the waterfront views speak to Newfoundland's long history of commercial fishing.

Ryan Premises was the headquarters of James Ryan Ltd. Founded in 1869, the firm was involved in the inshore and Labrador fisheries, exporting salt fish to Europe and the West Indies. It grew to be one of Newfoundland's most successful fishery enterprises, integral to the regional economy and to the lives of local residents. At the time, the premises included store-houses for both fish and salt, a retail shop, various outbuildings (cooper-age, telegraph office, and so on), and the owner's residence. James Ryan Ltd. withdrew from the fishery industry in 1952 and operated as a general goods retailer until 1978, when the firm finally closed its doors. Although all of the retail inventory was sold off, a significant amount of furnishings, fixtures, and equipment now form part of the site's artefact collection, which includes thousands of objects.

What to See & Do

Knowledgeable interpreters greet visitors with stories and information about the site. The traditional wooden buildings house a multi-media exhibit about Canada's east coast fisheries. Called "Cod, Seals, and Survivors," it has been named North America's best indoor interpre-tive exhibit by the National Associa-tion for Interpretation. After learning about the past, walk into Bonavista and talk to locals about the town's present. On Canada Day and Parks Day, special events and activities take place on-site.

How to Get There

From St. John's, follow Trans-Canada 1 west to Clarenville. Take Rte. 230 (the Discovery Trail) to Bonavista, and then follow the signs. Alterna-tively, continue on Rte. 230 from Clarenville, turn onto Rte. 235 at

INFORMATION

HOW TO REACH US

P.O. Box 1451, Bonavista, NL A0C 1B0. Phone (709) 468-1600. pc.gc.ca/eng/lhn-nhs/nl/ryan/index.aspx.

ENTRANCE FEES

$3.90 per adult, $9.80 per family/group.

ACCESSIBLE SERVICES

Friendly.

HOTELS, MOTELS, & INNS

Captain Blackmore's Heritage Manor 7 Blackmore Rd., Port Union, NL A0C 2J0. (709) 469-2920. captainblackmores.com. 3 rooms, $95–$175.
Harbour Quarters Inn 42 Campbell St., Bonavista, NL A0C 1B0. (866) 468-7982. harbourquarters.com. 11 rooms, $149–$239.

Southern Bay, and follow route 235 straight to Ryan Premises.

When to Go

The site is open daily June through early September.

Traditional wooden buildings house modern exhibits.

NEWFOUNDLAND & LABRADOR SITES

HOPEDALE MISSION
HOPEDALE, NL

Established in 1782, the Moravian Mission at Hopedale provides a window into the early days of the Moravians in Labrador. Against the backdrop of this vast, barren coastal landscape, German, Czech, and British Protestants built a mission and trade post among the Inuit. Seven buildings remain, including mission houses, a church, a storehouse, and the dead house that served as a morgue. An interpretation centre provides context. Designated NHS: 1970. (709) 933-3864.

HAWTHORNE COTTAGE
BRIGUS, NL

Set among trees, ornamental flower beds, and vegetable gardens, this green-and-white cottage with a wraparound veranda, built in the picturesque style, dates to 1830. Initially sited 10 km (6.2 mi) away, the house was later moved to Brigus, where it became the home of Captain Robert A. Bartlett, who commanded many significant Arctic expeditions in the early 20th century, including Admiral Peary's 1905 Arctic expedition. Designated NHS: 1978. Corner of South St. and Irishtown Rd. (709) 753-9262.

GOVERNMENT HOUSE
ST. JOHN'S, NL

The Palladian-style Government House was built in 1827 with red sandstone quarried nearby and topped with a slate roof. Its establishment marked the transition of Newfoundland, then a British colony, from naval oversight to civilian government. It has been the official residence for the governors (1829–1949) and lieutenant governors of the province (1949–) since 1829. Designated NHS: 1982. 50 Military Rd. (709) 729-4494.

ST. JOHN THE BAPTIST ANGLICAN CATHEDRAL
ST. JOHN'S, NL

This cathedral located on a hillside site overlooking the harbour of St. John's marks the oldest Anglican parish in Canada. Construction began on the beautiful Gothic-style building in 1847. Designed by the English church architect George Gilbert Scott, and made of Irish limestone and local sandstone, it stands as a prime example of his work. Visitors can take tea in the church's crypt (which was never used as a crypt) and go on a guided tour. Designated NHS: 1979. 18 Church Hill. (709) 726-5677.

BASILICA OF ST. JOHN THE BAPTIST
ST. JOHN'S, NL

This Romanesque Revival basilica, which includes a church, school, and two convents, stands as the principal symbol of the Roman Catholic Church in the province of Newfoundland and Labrador. Many Catholics immigrated here from Ireland in the 18th and early 19th centuries. Despite their numbers, their rights were restricted with respect to worship, education, property, and political participation. These restrictions were finally lifted in 1832, when representative government was granted to the province. Designated NHS: 1983. 172 Military Rd. (709) 754-2170.

ST. THOMAS RECTORY/COMMISSARIAT HOUSE AND GARDEN
ST. JOHN'S, NL

This Georgian clapboard-sided structure was built in 1818–1820 as a residence for the assistant commissary general of Newfoundland's British garrison. After the garrison's withdrawal in 1871, the building became a rectory for the St. Thomas Anglican Church. During the First World War, it temporarily served as a hospital and convalescence home for recovering soldiers. Designated NHS: 1968. 5 Kings Bridge Rd. (709) 729-6730.

QUÉBEC

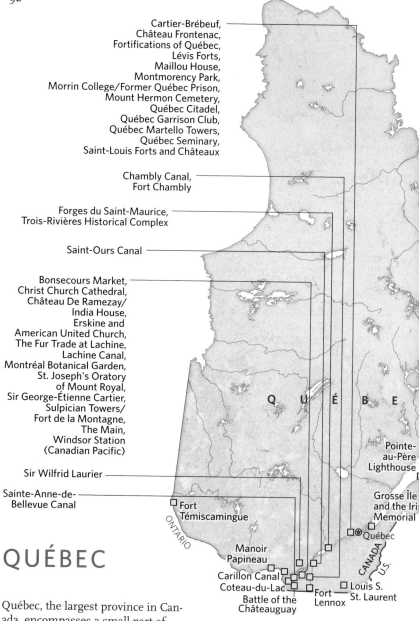

Cartier-Brébeuf,
Château Frontenac,
Fortifications of Québec,
Lévis Forts,
Maillou House,
Montmorency Park,
Morrin College/Former Québec Prison,
Mount Hermon Cemetery,
Québec Citadel,
Québec Garrison Club,
Québec Martello Towers,
Québec Seminary,
Saint-Louis Forts and Châteaux

Chambly Canal,
Fort Chambly

Forges du Saint-Maurice,
Trois-Rivières Historical Complex

Saint-Ours Canal

Bonsecours Market,
Christ Church Cathedral,
Château De Ramezay/
India House,
Erskine and
American United Church,
The Fur Trade at Lachine,
Lachine Canal,
Montréal Botanical Garden,
St. Joseph's Oratory
of Mount Royal,
Sir George-Étienne Cartier,
Sulpician Towers/
Fort de la Montagne,
The Main,
Windsor Station
(Canadian Pacific)

Sir Wilfrid Laurier

Sainte-Anne-de-
Bellevue Canal

Pointe-
au-Père
Lighthouse

Grosse Île
and the Iri
Memorial

Fort
Témiscamingue

ONTARIO

Manoir
Papineau

Québec

CANADA
U.S.

QUÉBEC

Carillon Canal
Coteau-du-Lac
Battle of the
Châteauguay

Fort
Lennox

Louis S.
St. Laurent

Québec, the largest province in Canada, encompasses a small part of what was once New France, French colonial territory in North America. At its height in the early 18th century, New France extended from the island of Newfoundland to the Rocky Mountains and from Hudson Bay south to the Gulf of Mexico. It began more

than a century earlier, with the founding of Québec City in 1608. British dominance followed the Seven Years' War (1756–1763), when the French ceded the cities of Québec and Montréal, and other parts of New France.

Costumed interpreter paints a scene at Saint-Louis Forts and Châteaux.
Page 90: Coteau-du-Lac blockhouse (top); the manor of Louis-Joseph Papineau (middle); Forges du Saint-Maurice (bottom) *Page 91:* Lachine Canal

NEWFOUNDLAND AND LABRADOR

Battle of the Restigouche

☐ National Historic Site (NHS)
⊛ Province capital city

0 mi — 200
0 km — 200

From 1791 to 1840, Britain administered the southern and eastern portions of present-day Québec as the colony of Lower Canada. The northern and western half was part of Rupert's Land, a vast swathe covering about a third of present-day Canada that was controlled by the Hudson's Bay Company. In 1841, in the wake of rebellions against the Crown in 1837–38, Britain united Lower Canada and Upper Canada (present-day southern Ontario) as the Province of Canada. With Confederation in 1867, the Province of Canada was split into the provinces of Québec and Ontario, which together with Nova Scotia and New Brunswick formed the Dominion of Canada. Québec's borders were solidified in 1912.

Today, most of Québec's population lives in the fertile St. Lawrence River Valley, between bustling Montréal and Québec City, the provincial capital, and more than three-quarters declare French as their first language—and in fact, it is the province's official language. The historic sites included in this chapter trace the history of French exploration and settlement, as well as relations with the Indigenous Peoples who inhabited the region. They also help illuminate the lucrative fur trade, which dominated commerce here for some 200 years, and highlight the contentious struggle between France and Britain for control of North America.

Scenic view from the Battle of the Restigouche interpretive centre

GASPÉSIE

The rugged Gaspé Peninsula, or Gaspésie in French, extends 240 km (149 mi) into the Gulf of St. Lawrence in southeastern Québec Province. Its name probably comes from a Mi'kmaq word meaning "land's end." For centuries Indigenous Peoples occupied the coasts, whose broad, stony beaches were well suited for drying the rich catches of cod and other fish found just offshore. And fishing continued to dominate the peninsula's economy for centuries. In 1534, Jacques Cartier claimed this region for France, and in his wake

several hundred French fishermen settled on the Gaspésie. British forces arrived in 1758, during the Seven Years' War (1756–1763), and destroyed the homes of the French settlers. Despite successfully sinking two British warships at the 1760 Battle of the Restigouche (see pp. 96–97), France lost the war and ceded the Gaspésie to Britain in the Treaty of Paris (1763). In the decades that followed, refugee Acadians and Loyalists fleeing the American Revolution added to the peninsula's population. The railway arrived in the 1890s.

Scale model of the French warship *Machault* at the interpretive centre

▶ BATTLE OF THE RESTIGOUCHE

POINTE-À-LA-CROIX, QC
Designated 1924

Nestled in an estuary at the mouth of the Restigouche River on the border between Québec and New Brunswick, two sunken ships lie undisturbed, telling remains of the last French-British naval battle over the lands of New France (the French colony that stretched along the St. Lawrence River).

During the Seven Years' War, the maritime power Britain had such a commanding control of the seas that it was able to hit the French in North America where it hurt time and time again—along the Atlantic seaboard, in the Ohio River Valley, and in the Lake Champlain region.

By 1760, the situation was not looking good for New France. The British had taken over Québec City, and their blockade of France's coastline was preventing much needed reinforcement French warships from coming to the colony's aid. However, in May three French frigates made it past the blockade and reached the Gulf of St. Lawrence. Learning of the presence of British ships in Québec,

Commander François Chénard de la Giraudais decided the three ships should take refuge in Chaleur Bay. As the British advanced, the French retreated into the estuary at the mouth of the Restigouche River.

The Battle of the Restigouche occurred in July 1760. The colonial powers warred for days in all-out gunfight in the river's shallow waters. Eventually the French had to abandon their ships, but before withdrawing to the shore they scuttled—or sunk—the 350-ton *Bienfaisant* and the powerhouse 550-ton *Machault* to prevent the British from taking their provisions. (The third ship, the *Marquis de Malauze*, was spared because it had captives aboard, but the British sank the ship after they captured it.) By September, the fate of New France was sealed.

Around 200 years later, in the 1960s, subaquatic archaeologists began excavating the site. Today, visitors can imagine the drama and the hardships of the 18th century through the warship remains now on display.

What to See & Do

Visit the interpretive centre to relive this dramatic chapter of Canadian history through recovered artefacts, reconstructions, and films. Explore the tween deck and Commander La Giraudais' council room. Admire the remarkable details of Fred Werthman's 1:32 scale model of the *Machault*—from its 26 cannons to its spiderweb of thin ropes. Between activities, take a break outside at a picnic table, enjoying views of the river and New Brunswick beyond.

How to Get There

The old battleground is just off Rte. 132, about 3 km (1.9 mi) west of the little town of Pointe-à-la-Croix.

INFORMATION

HOW TO REACH US
Rte. 132, Pointe-à-la-Croix, QC G0C 1L0. Phone (418) 788-5676. pc.gc.ca /restigouche.

ENTRANCE FEES
$3.90 per adult, $9.80 per family/ group.

ACCESSIBLE SERVICES
The museum is fully accessible; the outdoor area and the trail are limited.

HOTELS, MOTELS, & INNS
Quality Hotel & Conference Centre 157 Water St., Campbellton, NB E3N 3H2. (506) 753-4133. choicehotels .ca. 61 rooms, $109.
Comfort Inn 111 Val d'Amour Rd., Campbellton, NB E3N 5B9. (506) 753-4121. campbelltoncomfortinn .com. 59 rooms, $114–$129.

GASPÉSIE

When to Go

The Battle of the Restigouche site is open daily from late June until early September.

GASPÉSIE SITES

POINTE-AU-PÈRE LIGHTHOUSE
RIMOUSKI, QC

The mix of colours here are spectacular: the blue of the distant gulf waters, the crisp white buildings with cherry red roofs, the earthy tones of the rocky shore. This 1909 lighthouse—one of the tallest in Canada—is the third beacon built on this St. Lawrence–facing headland; the first was erected in 1859. Light and sound helped ship captains find their way to the river pilots waiting to guide them down the river. A visitor centre holds exhibits on river piloting and sound signal technology. Designated NHS: 1974. 1034 rue du Phare, Pointe-au-Père. (418) 368-5505.

Château Frontenac towers above the walled city of Old Québec.

QUÉBEC CITY REGION

Founded in 1608, Québec was built atop Cap-Diamant, a ridge overlooking the narrowing, island-dotted St. Lawrence River. When explorer Jacques Cartier arrived here in 1535, he discovered an Iroquoian village. By 1608, Samuel de Champlain had established a fur trading post and nomadic Algonquins had replaced the Iroquoian people. The city's name probably comes from an Algonquin word for "narrowing of the river." The location afforded the best access to inland fur traders, which made Québec a natural battleground in the imperial struggle

between Britain and France. In 1759, the British took control of the city. After the American Revolution, refugee Loyalists added to the English-speaking population, as did immigrants from Britain and Ireland in the 19th century. These days, the cobblestoned city has regained its French character, with an estimated 96 percent French speakers. The Historic District of Old Québec, comprising the Upper Town within the city walls and the Lower Town around Place Royale and the harbour, was inscribed on the World Heritage List in 1985.

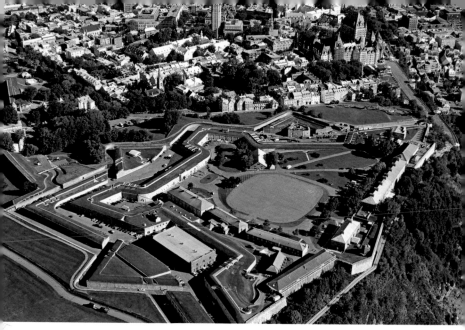

Québec Citadel, the largest British fortress in North America

▶ QUÉBEC CITADEL

Designated 1946

The Québec Citadel (or Citadelle) is an active garrison and the secondary residence of the governor general of Canada. Its star-shaped stone walls have formed a key part of the Fortifications of Québec (see pp. 104–107) for more than 200 years.

The Citadel sits on 37 acres in the heart of Old Québec. To get to the front gate, visitors must weave through a labyrinth of imposing stone walls. At Dalhousie Gate (the only original gate in the city), two guards dressed in crimson stand sentry in front of a large wooden door flanked by Greek columns. There's an air of grandeur to this place—the largest British fortress in North America—that humbles.

The French first drew up plans for a citadel on Cap-Diamant in 1716, but by 1759, when the British advanced on Québec City during the Seven Years' War, they still hadn't realized it. The British defeated the French on the nearby Plains of Abraham and

took Québec City, and they built the first fortress on this vantage point. They then built up the fort between 1820 and 1831, as part of Britain's effort to ramp up defences following a near American takeover during the War of 1812. Lt. Col. Elias Walker Durnford of the Royal Engineers designed this fortress as a complement to the existing Fortifications of Québec. The real selling point was the coverage afforded by the star-shaped layout and complementary bastions (that is, the projections at the points). With this design all angles could be covered by musket and cannon fire.

When the British troops left Québec City in 1871, B Battery of the

Regiment of Canadian Artillery took up residency. Notably, since 1920 the Citadel has housed the Canadian Armed Forces' only French-language regular force infantry regiment: the Royal 22e Régiment. One hundred fifty soldiers—both regular force and reservists—live and work here, including members of the acclaimed regimental band. Music has long been a part of this regiment, and the Royal 22e Régiment Band is very active on Québec's arts scene, giving concerts and participating in cultural events. Museum director Dany Hamel says there's a real pride in the long history of French-Canadian military service at the Citadel.

The Historic District of Vieux-Québec (Old Québec), which includes the Québec Citadel, was designated a UNESCO World Heritage site in 1985.

CITADEL HIGHLIGHTS

The Citadel is open year-round, but it offers summer visitors a real treat: the Changing of the Guard, a Citadel ceremony that dates to 1928. Visitors wishing to see it should plan to arrive by 9:30 a.m.; the ceremony starts at 10 a.m. and lasts about 45 minutes. Scarlet-clad sentries in bearskin hats march through the Citadel parade grounds while their commander bellows crisp orders for them to follow in perfect symmetry. The ceremony is offered daily June 24 to Labour Day (the first Monday of September).

After the ceremony, spend an hour following a guide around the grounds, soaking up stories, military activity, and stunning views of the city and landscape in equal measure (the grounds can only be toured with a guide because the Citadel is an active garrison). The tour ends at the Musée Royal 22e Régiment, Canada's second largest military museum, which is housed in a former barracks. Here, visitors are left to their own devices, freed to explore the interactive elements—interviews, video archives, and battle maps—inside the museum's permanent and temporary exhibits.

Notice the curator's efforts to place human stories centre stage: Read about the first woman to become a captain in the Royal 22e Régiment. Listen to testimonials from veterans and their family members. And admire the gun cum war diary that was used by a soldier in the Royal 22e Régiment during the First World War. He engraved this Lee-Enfield bolt-action rifle with the names of the places he fought during the war. He even gave the gun a name: Rosalie.

Of all the museum's features, Director Hamel says he's most proud of the Honour and Memory Medals Gallery. For each medal, visitors have access to the biography of the soldier who wore it, including comprehensive data about their service. The collection numbers about 300, and the museum invites anyone with a medal from the Royal 22e Régiment to submit to this growing gallery.

After exploring the museum, consider venturing over to the governor general's secondary residence, filled with Canadian-made antique furniture and artworks. Guided tours offer access to the staterooms, where the governor general welcomes dignitaries and honours Canadians. (Note: Unlike the Citadel museum, the governor general's residence is not open year-round. Call 418-648-4322 or 866-936-4422 for details.)

Throughout summer and fall, the Citadel offers guided night tours, in which visitors can spend about 90 minutes exploring "A Shrouded Fortress" by lantern light.

Je Me Souviens ("I Remember"): the Royal 22e Régiment motto—and Québec's

Royal guard with Batisse, the regiment's mascot

BUILDING 7: THE MEMORIAL

This small stone one-storey is not a building for the public; rather, it's a sacred space known by soldiers and museum staffers as the heart and soul of the regiment. Within it is the mausoleum of Gen. Georges-Philéas Vanier and his wife, Pauline.

Vanier, a founding officer of the Royal 22e Régiment, and thoroughly decorated for his bravery during the First World War, took command of the Royal 22e Régiment at the Citadel in 1925. And after some diplomatic postings in the 1940s, he was appointed the first French Canadian appointed governor general of Canada, in 1959.

The memorial also holds the Book of Remembrance. Every morning the Sergeant of the Guard comes to the memorial and carries out an honorific duty. He removes the glass covering over the Book of Remembrance and reads aloud the names of every soldier of the Royal 22e Régiment who died in combat. Then, he says, "*Je souviens*—I remember." The sergeant carries out this special tradition alone, without an audience.

BATISSE XI

Standing proud at each Changing of the Guard is Batisse the Goat, the Royal 22e Régiment's mascot. Her Majesty Queen Elizabeth II gifted Batisse I to the regiment in 1955. There have since been many successive Batisses—in fact, there's

QUÉBEC CITADEL NATIONAL HISTORIC SITE
(Lieu historique national du Citadelle-de-Québec)

INFORMATION & ACTIVITIES

HOW TO REACH US
1 Côte de la Citadelle, Québec, QC G1R 4V7. Phone (418) 694-2815. lacitadelle .qc.ca.

SEASONS & ACCESSIBILITY
The Citadel is open daily year-round, except for December 25 and January 1; check the website for specific hours, which vary by season. The last guided tour for the day leaves at closing time.

ENTRANCE FEES
$16 per adult, $32 per family (max. 2 adults and 3 children).

PETS
Only service dogs are permitted at the Citadel.

ACCESSIBLE SERVICES
A wheelchair is available on-site for guests with impaired mobility. Please contact the Citadel in advance of visit, or for more information.

THINGS TO DO
Enjoy the rare opportunity to tour an active military site. Learn how and why the fortress was built the way it was and why it matters that the commanding officer of the fort gives orders in French. Take a selfie with an esteemed goat. Check out the governor general's ceremonial home away from home. Enjoy the panoramic view of the St. Lawrence River.

SPECIAL ADVISORIES
• For security reasons, visitors are not allowed to wander freely throughout the site or in the Citadel. The Citadel is an active military base as well as the governor general's residence. Tours may be shortened or cancelled due to official ceremonies.
• Reservations are required for tours of groups of 15 or more people (418-694-2815).

HOTELS, MOTELS, & INNS
(Rates are for a 2-person double, high season, in Canadian dollars, unless otherwise noted.)

Hôtel Champlain Vieux Québec 115 rue Sainte-Anne, Vieux-Québec, QC G1R 3X6. (418) 694-0106 or (800) 567-2106. hotelsduvieuxquebec.com/en/hotel -champlain. 53 rooms, $149.
Manoir d'Auteuil 49 rue d'Auteuil, Vieux-Québec, QC G1R 4C2. (866) 662-6647. manoirdauteuil.com. 27 rooms and suites, $209–$379.

QUÉBEC CITY REGION

currently a small herd of goats all named Batisse. They take turns playing the mascot when the "main" Batisse needs a break, but each receives the "royal treatment" when it's his time in the spotlight. Every morning Batisse is brushed and his horns are painted gold. He's fitted with a silver head plate and a blue silk blanket (complete with regimental crest). When he's not working at the Changing of the Guard ceremony, Batisse enjoys parading about town and travelling across the country, stopping only to pose for photos.

How to Get There
Located in the heart of Old Québec, the Citadel sits atop Cap-Diamant next to the Plains of Abraham on the edge of the St. Lawrence River. There is free parking available on-site (max. two hours) and bike racks for cyclists.

When to Go
The Citadel is open year-round; however, summer is best for visitors wishing to see the Changing of the Guard. Autumn visitors may get the chance to meet Canada's governor general during the Fall Festival.

Fortifications have sheltered Old Québec since the 1700s.

▶ FORTIFICATIONS OF QUÉBEC

QUÉBEC, QC
Designated 1948

High above the St. Lawrence River, the Fortifications of Québec are a seamless reminder of the city's past life as a military stronghold. Its old stone walls snake around the centre of the city for nearly 5 km (3.1 mi). Today, Québec City is the only fortified city north of Mexico. It was recognized as a UNESCO World Heritage site in 1985.

Indigenous Peoples occupied this site for thousands of years before French explorer Samuel de Champlain established a "Habitation" at Québec in 1608. It resembled a small medieval castle, complete with a residence, a merchandise and supply store, and a redoubt (fort) for defence—with the whole lot ringed by a moat 4.5 m (14.7 ft) wide. In subsequent decades, modest and rudimentary structures were added to this basic foundation, but the city wasn't fully fortified until long after Champlain.

In 1690, an ambitious project was launched after the fall of Port-Royal

in Acadia: An enceinte—or defensive enclosure—was built. It consisted of 11 small stone redoubts joined by palisades. The improvised enceinte soon saw action. On October 16, 1690, a 2,300-man British army sailed up the St. Lawrence under the leadership of Sir William Phips, with the intention of taking Québec. But inside the enceinte, the governor of New France, Louis de Buade, Comte de Frontenac, stood ready with 3,000 militiamen and regulars. When Phips sent a messenger to demand Frontenac's surrender, the governor responded that he had no answer to give "save from the mouths of my cannon and from my musketry." The French successfully repelled this British invasion.

As Québec came to feature more prominently in a broader defensive strategy, France started investing more into defensive infrastructure. However, Québec remained a poorly connected patchwork of defensive projects, hindered by messy politics, until the fall of Louisbourg, in what is now Cape Breton Island, Nova Scotia, in 1745. After this French loss, Charles de la Boische, Marquis de Beauharnois, the governor of New France, ordered new, more comprehensive fortifications built.

But even these fortifications couldn't save the French from defeat. On September 13, 1759, French and British troops fought a fateful battle just outside the fortifications on the Plains of Abraham. After the British won, the French forfeited their prize military stronghold: Québec City.

Under new British leadership and the threat of an American invasion, Québec City's walls were intensified. A succession of architects—William Twiss, Gother Mann, and Elias Walker Durnford—strengthened fortifications along the heights of Cap-Diamant and introduced a squat, thick-walled martello tower into the defensive mix. In 1819, and for the next 10 years, Walker oversaw the building of the bastioned and irregular pentagonal, cliff-hugging Citadel (see pp. 100–103)—designed to be a final refuge for the British in the event of a civil uprising.

By the mid-19th century, many residents resented the limitations the massive infrastructure placed on the city's growth. Maintaining and restoring the walls was also a costly proposition. Thank goodness, Canada's then governor general, Lord Dufferin—a pioneer in Canada's 19th-century heritage conservation movement—saw the fortifications' heritage value. He lobbied for their preservation and eventually convinced municipal officials intent on tearing them down to hold their hammers.

In honour of Dufferin, the vast terrace that sits next to the Château Frontenac and overlooks the St. Lawrence River was named after him. During the summer, the terrace is filled with musicians, mimes, painters, and tourists—a scene that no doubt would have pleased its energetic and social namesake.

EXPLORING THE FORTIFICATIONS

Above all else, make time for one of the guided 90-minute walking tours, which begin at Dufferin Terrace. Wonderful views of Québec City unfold as the guide leads the tour group along the fortification walls. Throughout the tour, the guide points out architectural nuances and explains defensive strategies, fully detailing the history of this fortress—from Champlain's arrival to Old Québec's UNESCO World Heritage designation. Summer tours finish at the Artillery Park in time for a firing demonstration, where interpretive

Dauphine Redoubt, a barracks and storage facility

QUÉBEC CITY REGION

FORTIFICATIONS OF QUÉBEC NATIONAL HISTORIC SITE
(Lieu historique national du Fortifications-de-Québec)

INFORMATION & ACTIVITIES

HOW TO REACH US
2 rue d'Auteuil, Québec, QC G1R 5C2.
Phone (418) 648-4168. pc.gc.ca
/fortifications.
There are two visitor centres, phone
418-648-7016:
Frontenac Kiosk, Dufferin Terrace.
Interpretative Centre, Artillery Park (2 rue
d'Auteuil).

SEASONS & ACCESSIBILITY
This site is open year-round. Guided tours
(available May through September) begin
at the Frontenac Kiosk on Dufferin Terrace;
call the visitor centre for more information.

ENTRANCE FEES
$3.90 per adult, $9.80 for family/group.

PETS
Pets must be leashed at all times; they are
not permitted inside any of the buildings.

ACCESSIBLE SERVICES
Sites are partially wheelchair accessible.
All buildings at the Artillery Park are
wheelchair accessible. Contact the visitor
centre for more information.

THINGS TO DO
Walk along the fortifications' 4.6-km
(2.9 mi) wall. Thrill at the sound of a
black powder musket and the sight of the
18th-century French soldier firing it. Try
out one of the site's newest digital-based
activities: Imagine being a soldier under
siege during a role play, or use a tablet to
find clues among the fortifications' "talking
walls."

Run a hand along the original stones of
the fortifications' romantic gates. Spend
some time watching artists and tourists
mingle on the Dufferin Terrace and breathe
in the fresh air wafting off the St. Lawrence
River.

HOTELS, MOTELS, & INNS
*(Rates are for a 2-person double, high season,
in Canadian dollars, unless otherwise noted.)*

Hôtel Champlain Vieux Québec 115 rue
Sainte-Anne, Vieux-Québec, QC G1R 3X6.
(418) 694-0106 or (800) 567-2106.
hotelsduvieuxquebec.com/en/hotel
-champlain. 53 rooms, $174.
Manoir d'Auteuil 49 rue d'Auteuil,
Vieux-Québec, QC G1R 4C2. (866) 662-
6647. manoirdauteuil.com. 27 rooms and
suites, $209–$379.

guides dressed as French soldiers fire
black powder muskets, as they would
have done back in 1755.

Next, head over to the Dauphine
Redoubt, an imposing white building
in the heart of Artillery Park. Construction on the redoubt began in
1712, was paused in 1713, and resumed
in 1748 under the leadership of engineer Chaussegros de Léry. He also
built the long "New Barracks" next
door to the redoubt and a parade
ground, which would have been an
especially noisy place back in the
1750s with all the musket firing. Over
the course of 250 years, the building
was used first by the French and the

British for military purposes and
then by the Canadian government as
a cartridge factory.

Inside the redoubt a storage room
filled with oil, water, wine, beer, and
other supplies can be found on the
first floor. The second floor is set up
like a barracks. This one-window
room would have housed 12 to 20
French soldiers, and no doubt would
have been crowded and stuffy. Contrast this room with the British officers' quarters laid out on the third
floor, boasting opulent chandeliers
and fancy china.

Beyond the fortification sights, the
national historic site offers several

interactive activities at the Interpretation Centre in Artillery Park. Young children will enjoy the "Legend of the Talking Walls," in which they don a cape, grab a tablet and their choice of a magical sword or an enchanted bracelet, and search to find out who their chosen object belongs to by collecting clues from the "talking walls" of the fortifications. Older kids and adults might like to try out "The Fort's Mission," a role-playing game where participants have to make defensive decisions under pressure of an American siege.

How to Get There

The fortifications are in the central borough of Québec City—La Cité–Limoilou—embracing the historical district surrounding the upper town. Located in Artillery Park, the Interpretation Centre sits on Rue d'Auteuil, between Rue McMahon and Rue Saint-Jean.

When to Go

For an immersive, interactive experience, visit in July or August, when there might be 21 guides on shift—some in period costume—and a musket-firing demonstration at Artillery Park. For thinner crowds and smaller tour groups, consider visiting in the fall; Québec is also at its most colourful in autumn, with views from the fortifications taking in an explosion of fall foliage. During the winter, the site is only partially accessible, and may have snow on the ground.

QUÉBEC CITY REGION

French explorer Jacques Cartier landed here in the 1500s, and missionary Jean de Brébeuf a century later.

▶ CARTIER-BRÉBEUF

QUÉBEC, QC
Designated 1958

If this riverbank along the St. Lawrence could speak, it would tell tales of rowdy French explorers, deadly winters, enterprising Iroquoians, and of a missionary whose soul-saving journey in New France started on this riverbank and ended in martyrdom.

Between 1534 and 1542, Jacques Cartier led three expeditions to the New World in the name of François I of France, looking for a shortcut though North America to Asia. During his first voyage, Cartier chanced upon the nephews of Donnacona, the Iroquoian leader of the village of Stadacona (near present-day Québec City). Cartier took the young men to France to be trained as interpreters.

A year later the two young men, Domagaya and Taignoagny, helped Cartier navigate the St. Lawrence River and broker relations with local Iroquoians. After exploring Hochelega (present-day Montréal), Cartier and his 110-man crew wintered at the junction of the Lairet and Saint-Charles Rivers. A scurvy outbreak weakened the men, killing 25. If not for the cedar bark or balsam fir remedy Domagaya showed the French how to make, more may have died. When spring came, Cartier returned to France with some Iroquoian hostages, including Donnacona and his nephews; all but one died quickly upon arrival in their "new world."

In 1541, Cartier made one more expedition, under the leadership of Sieur de Roberval. They aimed to establish the first French colony in the New World—and failed. Cartier sailed home in 1542.

Several decades later, Jesuit missionary Jean de Brébeuf travelled to New France in 1625 with the hope of bringing the region's Indigenous Peoples to Catholicism. He built a residence on the north bank of the Saint-Charles, near Cartier's former wintering spot. There, he spent time with the Innu and the Chonnonton, but mostly he lived with the Wendat Confederacy—documenting his experiences. In the 1630s, smallpox and other diseases brought by Europeans devastated the Wendat. Once

INFORMATION

HOW TO REACH US

175 rue De L'Espinay, Québec, QC G1L 3W6. Phone (418) 648-7016. pc.gc.ca/cartierbrebeuf.

ENTRANCE FEES

Free for self-guided tour.

ACCESSIBLE SERVICES

Limited; contact the site for details.

HOTELS, MOTELS, & INNS

Best Western Plus Downtown Québec 330 rue de la Couronne, Québec, QC G1K 6E6. (418) 649-1919 or (888) 702-0876. hotelquebec .com/en. 177 rooms, prices vary. **Hôtel du Nord** 640 Saint-Vallier Ouest, Québec, QC G1N 1C5. (877) 474-4464. hoteldunord.qc.ca. 50 rooms, $104–$149.

welcoming (or at least tolerant) communities became reluctant or hostile. In 1649, Brébeuf was captured, tortured, and killed by the Iroquois during the Huron-Iroquois war. Pope Pius XI canonized him in 1930.

What to See & Do

This site is mostly an urban green space. Visitors may cycle, stroll, or find a patch of green to sit and contemplate how early exchanges between Indigenous and non-Indigenous people in Canada shaped the country. The park also hosts some family-friendly special events.

How to Get There

From Old Québec, take Rte. 175N. Exit at boulevard Hamel and continue straight to the site, which is on the right side of the road.

When to Go

The site is open June 24 through Labour Day, 1 p.m. to 5 p.m. only.

From 1865 to 1872, a three-fort complex was built in Lévis against potential U.S. invasion.

▶ LÉVIS FORTS

LÉVIS, QC
Designated 1920

Sometimes the greatest innovations never reach their full potential. Although the Lévis Forts proved useful as munitions warehouses during the two World Wars, they were built on the south shore of the St. Lawrence River to protect Québec from a possible American invasion.

In the 1860s, during the American Civil War, Britain ramped up defences in Canada, fearing that the northern states would try for new possessions should the Confederate Army prevail. A new railway line between Lévis and Maine made the British stronghold at Québec City especially vulnerable to a potential attack. So the British brought in defence experts. An army of royal engineers, soldiers, artisans, and labourers spent seven years (1865–1872) building three south-facing forts on the St. Lawrence, each unique in its construction. Meanwhile the American threat subsided. In the end, no wartime shots were ever fired from the Lévis Forts.

Fort No. 1 was the masterpiece of the three forts. To realize the asymmetrical pentagon, the British used sophisticated surveying technology to produce highly detailed maps that would set a new standard for Canada. They also experimented with new ways to prepare and pour concrete that would withstand Québec's cold winters. To complement the forts, they built a system of tunnels—some of which may be explored today.

In the 1960s, a group of volunteers dubbed "Friends of the Old Fort," led by Paul Théberge, helped save the fort from crumbling into oblivion. Parks Canada did all the major restoration work, which led to the opening of the site to the public in 1982.

What to See & Do

Peer 5 m (16.4 ft) down into the dry moat surrounding Fort No. 1. Explore the fort's underground passageways, vaulted tunnels, brick-vaulted caponiers, and the underground casemates. Learn who built the fort, what materials they used, and why. At the visitor centre, try on period costumes and sip gunpowder tea, a drink soldiers often indulged in.

How to Get There

From Hwy. 20, take the 327 northbound exit (Mgr. Ignace-Bourget). Drive 2.5 km (1.6 mi) and turn left onto Guillaume-Couture Blvd. Drive 700 m (0.4 mi), turn right, and then to the site.

When to Go

The site is open daily from the end of June to Labour Day, and on weekends from Labour Day to Canada's Thanksgiving Day.

INFORMATION

HOW TO REACH US
41 rue du Gouvernement, Québec, QC G6V 7E1. Phone (418) 835-5182. pc.gc.ca/levis.

ENTRANCE FEES
$3.90 per adult, $9.80 per family/group.

ACCESSIBLE SERVICES
Friendly; contact the site for details.

HOTELS, MOTELS, & INNS
Hôtel l'Oiselière de Lévis 165 rue President Kennedy, Lévis, QC G6V 6E2. (418) 830-0878 or (866) 830-0878. levis.oiseliere.com/eng. 84 rooms and suites, $119.

An interpreter shares stories of the Grande Maison—the ironmaster's house.

▶ FORGES DU SAINT-MAURICE

TROIS-RIVIÈRES, QC
Designated 1919

This spot just north of Trois-Rivières is rich with answers to potential Canadian trivia questions. Canada's first industrial community? Forges du Saint-Maurice. What did they specialize in? Iron and cast iron. For how many years? More than 150.

In 1730, the seigneur of Saint-Maurice, François Poulin de Francheville, received permission from the king of France to found the first industrial enterprise in New France. He set up a small forge on the king's land on the banks of a stream that flows into the Saint-Maurice River. Poulin was soon joined by a young French ironmaster named Pierre-François Olivier de Vézin. Vézin helped Poulin build a full-scale ironworks, a complex of workshops that became a major supplier of goods necessary for the development and defence of the colony.

Founders and moulders used the imposing blast furnace (some 8 m/26.2 ft wide and 7.5 m/24.6 ft tall) to produce iron bars for navy ships. Then, after the British conquered New France in 1760, the ironworks focused on producing castings for devices used in heating, cooking, and farming. In 1846, the French Crown sold the forges; the new owners started cranking out wagon wheels, and then later, pig iron for big industry, but business was increasingly competitive and the forges had to close down. This closure lasted five years. Then Trois-Rivières merchant John McDougall breathed new life into the complex for a couple of decades—before blowing the blast furnace out for good in 1883.

In the 1970s, the site underwent a huge archaeological excavation and Parks Canada has since restored and enhanced the forges—including the blast furnace and the Grande Maison (the ironmaster's house)—for historical interpretation.

What to See & Do

Enjoy an interpretive circuit that winds indoors and outdoors through archaeological vestiges and imaginative re-creations of what once was.

INFORMATION

HOW TO REACH US
10000 blvd. des Forges, Trois-Rivières, QC G9C 1B1. Phone (819) 378-5116. pc.gc.ca/eng/lhn-nhs/qc/saintmaurice/index.aspx.

ENTRANCE FEES
$3.90 per adult, $9.80 per family/group per day; $9.80 for adult, $24.50 per family/group per year.

ACCESSIBLE SERVICES
Friendly; contact the site for details.

HOTELS, MOTELS, & INNS
Hôtel-Motel Coconut 7531 rue Notre Dame Ouest, Trois-Rivières, QC G9B 1L7. (819) 377-3221 or (800) 838-3221. coconuthotelmotel.com. 38 rooms, $90–$202.
Super 8 3185 blvd. Saint-Jean, Trois-Rivières, QC G9B 2M4. (819) 377-5881 or (800) 454-3213. super8.com. 77 rooms, $107–$129.

At the Grande Maison, learn about the individuals who played key roles in the forges' history, dip down into the original cellars to browse historical iron goods, and revisit the old forges through a multimedia show. At the blast furnace, learn how cast iron was made. Save time to enjoy the scenic panorama down by the Saint-Maurice River, where remains of the lower forge and some lovely nature trails can be found.

How to Get There

The site is located on the west side of the Saint-Maurice River, about 15 km (9.3 mi) north of Trois-Rivières. From Trois-Rivières, simply head north on the Boulevard des Forges.

When to Go

The site is open from the Saturday before Saint-Jean-Baptiste Day (June 24) to Labour Day.

The Irish Memorial honours all who perished on Grosse Île.

▶ GROSSE ÎLE AND THE IRISH MEMORIAL

GROSSE-ÎLE, QC
Designated 1974

Steeped in stories both sad and inspiring, this picturesque island in the middle of the St. Lawrence River was the first stop in Canada for many hopeful European immigrants between the early 19th century and the 1930s. It was also a place of rampant disease, mass death, and brilliant innovation.

During the early 19th century, emigration and epidemics often went hand in hand. This was acutely felt in (what was then called) Lower Canada. In 1832, European immigrants sailing up the St. Lawrence to Québec City brought the cholera epidemic that was ravaging Europe along with them. In an effort to control the spread of disease, British authorities established a quarantine station on Grosse Île. The new station's efficiency was quickly tested. In 1834, the island was hit with another cholera outbreak. Cholera would strike again in 1849 and 1854, but not before an even deadlier typhus epidemic ravaged the island in 1847.

Although the quarantine station was active on Grosse Île from 1832 until 1937, 1847 is the year that jumps out of the history books. Nearly 100,000 immigrants reached Québec that year. More than half of them had left Ireland, then in the grips of the Great Famine.

The inexperienced staff on Grosse Île wasn't prepared to deal with the typhus these starved, sick, and exhausted people carried with them. Understaffed and severely under-resourced, they couldn't accommodate the hordes of sick men, women, and children. Dr. George M. Douglas, the station's medical superintendent, had 200 beds for the sick and 800 for the healthy, but 12,000 people were being held on the island, the sick and the healthy kept together in army tents. Others died on the anchored ships. As the sailing season came to an (ironic) close while services on the island were being upgraded, the chaos finally tapered.

All told, more than 5,000 people died while crossing the ocean on the so-called coffin ships, and more than another 5,000 were buried on Grosse Île. If there's a silver lining to this story, it's in the humanity of the doctors, priests, and carpenters who volunteered to come to the island crisis zone and help the victims. It's also in the French-Canadian families who took in about 700 Irish orphans.

THE GREAT FAMINE

There is a Gaelic inscription on the large Celtic cross on Grosse Île, which was erected in the early 1900s. According to Marianna O'Gallagher, the granddaughter of the cross's architect, it begins "Children of the Gael died in the thousands on this island having fled from the laws of the foreign tyrants and an artificial famine in the years 1847–48." Philippe Gauthier, supervisor of the national historic site, says the Gaelic message is far less politically neutral than the English and French translations.

The "foreign tyrants" alluded to in the inscription were the governing British of the day. The "artificial famine" was the Great Famine in Ireland brought on by the failure of a staple crop, potatoes, and then exacerbated by failures of government. In less than a decade, more than a million

Irish—about an eighth of the population—died of starvation, disease, and malnutrition. The country was riddled with political conflict, and a revolution was rumbling in its belly. More than a million people chose to emigrate; some headed for Canada. Between 1845 and 1848, an estimated 5,000 of these Irish died on Grosse Île.

Today, the Irish have a close connection to this island—and the island to them. On May 25, 1998, Grosse Île and the Irish Memorial National Historic Site was twinned with the National Famine Museum of Strokestown Park in County Roscommon, Ireland. Between 1841 and 1851, the population of Roscommon decreased by 80,000 people (31 percent), the highest population loss of any county in the country.

DR. MONTIZAMBERT

In 1869, at the age of 26, Dr. Frederick Montizambert became Grosse Île's new chief medical officer. The bacteriologist was tasked with replacing the dilapidated wooden huts and the flawed quarantine system with a better way of receiving immigrants and treating contagious diseases. A true public health devotee, Montizambert innovated toward this end for the next 30 years.

One of the first things he did to reduce sickness was to redesign the island's layout, so that the sick and the healthy were completely separated, work begun by Douglas in 1848. As immigration processes became more sophisticated, so did his inspection, disinfection, vaccination, and diagnosis procedures. In 1878, after some buildings on the island burned down, Montizambert lobbied the government for funding to build a modern, spacious hospital on the island that would specialize in infectious diseases.

In 1894, Montizambert's impact became widespread when the federal government made him superintendent of all Canadian quarantine stations; his ideas were soon adopted by stations in Halifax (Nova Scotia), New Brunswick, and British Columbia. Montizambert's devotion to the relatively new science of preventative medicine is believed to have saved Canadians from many more epidemic-induced deaths.

Montizambert devoted more than 50 years to the field of public health before he died at 86.

EXPLORING THE GROUNDS

As the ferry closes in on Grosse Île, a Celtic cross rises above the trees on a rocky cliff. And on the pier, a doctor and nurse—costumed staff—wait to whisk visitors to the disinfection building for an inspection and cleansing shower (don't worry—everyone stays dry).

During the high summer season, visitors may choose to follow a guide around the island or take a self-guided tour. Either choice will allow visitors to get a sense for what it must have been like for so many thousands of immigrants from Ireland and elsewhere who came to Canada with hopes of a better life. Buildings to explore include the first-, second-, and third-class hotels, a bakery, and the vaccination

A Celtic cross honours some 5,000 Irish emigrants.

Cholera and typhus patients filled hospital beds.

Visitors arriving by ferry land at a pier near the western end of the St. Lawrence River island.

and medical examination office.

Quiet reigns in the Irish cemetery, where thousands of Irish were buried. It's a short walk from the cemetery to the 14-m (45.9 ft) Celtic cross that overlooks the St. Lawrence. Designed by Jeremiah Gallagher and erected in 1909, the cross commemorates the thousands of Irish who died here. A chunk of granite knocked loose long ago from the cross during a thunderstorm soon will be incorporated into the Ireland Canada Monument in Vancouver (still in development as of June 2016).

The island's eastern sector, accessed via trolley or on foot, is the hospital sector. One of the original 12 lazarettos—or quarantine stations— still stands. Built in 1847, it's one of the oldest buildings on the island. Inside, an 1840s quarantine scene is re-created. Exhibits showcase artefacts left behind by Irish immigrants and detail the conditions they experienced on the coffin ships.

Be sure to save time to enjoy Grosse Île's wild lands, perhaps by hiking on the 2.5-km (1.6 mi) Mirador Trail, and watch the tide's dramatic pull in the aptly—if not so creatively—named Hospital Bay. The island is a wonderful place to appreciate the unique flora and fauna of the St. Lawrence Estuary. Almost 70 percent of the island is covered in forest—balsam fir, Canadian hemlock, and red maples—and about 11 percent is marshland, with vibrant skunk cabbage hiding among speckled alder. There's also plenty of wildlife to appreciate, including the harmless and rare (for Québec) ringneck snake, foxes, little brown bats, white-tailed deer (which are ubiquitous), great horned owls, and migratory snow geese.

A snack bar in the third-class hotel (near the ferry dock) has drinks and chips, but no sandwiches. Visitors are advised to bring their own food.

How to Get There

Grosse Île and the Irish Memorial National Historic Site is located 48 km (29.8 mi) downstream from Québec City. The island is reached via Croisières Lachance ferry (100 rue de la Marina, 418-692-1159 or 800-563-4643, *croisiereslachance.com*) from Berthier-sur-Mer. To get to Berthier-sur-Mer from Québec City, head south over Pierre-Laporte Bridge, take Hwy. 20E (toward Rivière-du-Loup), get off at exit 364, drive into Berthier-sur-Mer, and follow signs to the marina.

Alternatively, Air Montmagny (418-248-3545, *airmontmagny.com*) flies to the island from Montmagny Airport, but you must reserve a seat in the small plane at least 24 hours before the flight.

For information about departure times and tour lengths, contact the transportation companies directly.

When to Go

Site supervisor Gauthier recommends visiting the island in September. At this time of year, the weather is still warm and the crowds are thinner. At the end of September, the trees become gold and red kaleidoscopes as their leaves begin to turn.

Hospitals were built on the island's eastern half.

GROSSE ÎLE AND THE IRISH MEMORIAL NATIONAL HISTORIC SITE

(Lieu historique national de Grosse-Île-et-le-mémorial-des-Irlandais)

INFORMATION & ACTIVITIES

HOW TO REACH US
Grosse Île, QC. Phone (418) 234-8841. pc.gc.ca/grosseile.

SEASONS & ACCESSIBILITY
Open early May to mid-October (open daily June 23–Sept. 4; open Wednesday to Sunday May 4–June 22 and Sept. 5–Oct. 9).

ENTRANCE FEES
The Croisières Lachance ferry crossing and Air Montmagny air service to the island are both $65 per adult, and include entry to the site and guided visits. For child and/ or group rates, contact the companies (see "How to Get There," p. 115).

PETS
Guide dogs are welcome.

ACCESSIBLE SERVICES
This site is mostly wheelchair accessible. Contact the site for more information.

THINGS TO DO
Relive history. Explore the hills, forest, and marshes. Pick a quiet patch of green with views of the St. Lawrence to reflect.

SPECIAL ADVISORIES
• Check local weather forecasts and the level of difficulty of island activities before leaving. The site may have to close, especially in May and October, due to bad weather.
• Bring a lunch; there is no real food service on the island.

CAMPGROUNDS
Camping Orléans 3547 chemin Royal Saint-François-de-l'Île-d'Orléans, Île-d'Orléans, QC G0A 3S0. (418) 829-2953 or (888) 829-2953. campingorleans .com. $36–$55 per site per night. On the northern tip of Île d'Orléans, west of Grosse Île.

HOTELS, MOTELS, & INNS
(Rates are for a 2-person double, high season, in Canadian dollars, unless otherwise noted.)

La Camarine Hotel 10947 blvd. Sainte-Anne, Beaupré, QC G0A 1E0. (418) 827-5703 or (800) 567-3939. camarine.com. 31 rooms, $109–$149.
Château Mont-Sainte-Anne 500 blvd. du Beau-Pré, Beaupré, QC G0A 1E0. (866) 900-5211. chateaumontsainteanne.com. 214 rooms, $179–$639.

QUÉBEC CITY REGION SITES

MAILLOU HOUSE
QUÉBEC, QC

Lovers of 18th-century French architecture will appreciate this stone house in Quebec City's historic district. Architect Jean-Baptiste Maillou built it circa 1736 and lived there until he died in 1753. Later, military personnel, business leaders, and politicians used the building. The Chambre de commerce et d'industrie de Québec now uses it as an office, but visitors may enter the courtyard and admire the outbuildings. Designated NHS: 1958. 17 rue Saint-Louis.

MONTMORENCY PARK
QUÉBEC, QC

One of few parks in the walled city—and boasting a gorgeous view of the St. Lawrence—Montmorency Park had its share of uses as a cemetery, a worshipping place, and a political hot spot. This spot is where the Canadian parliamentary system began in 1792, and in 1864 politicians hammered out the Québec Resolutions here, establishing the framework for Canada's constitution. Designated NHS: 1966. Rue Port-Dauphin and Côte de la Montagne. (418) 648-7016.

QUÉBEC GARRISON CLUB
QUÉBEC, QC

Since the late 19th century, men of military, political, and economic distinction have been smoking cigars and contemplating dominoes moves in this clubhouse. (Only in the early 1980s did full membership become available to women.) It is the oldest military club in Canada perpetuating the British colonial tradition of social gatherings between military officers and influential members of civilian society still in existence. Visitors may only admire the château-style building, adorned with a steep mansard roof and pyramidal towers of cannonballs, from the outside. Designated NHS: 1999. 97 rue Saint-Louis.

SAINT-LOUIS FORTS AND CHÂTEAUX
QUÉBEC, QC

Explore the musty ruins of where colonial governors—first French and then British (from 1763)—once lived and ruled from Québec, the capital. During the 17th century, the French built four military forts and two châteaux here; in later years, gardens and sweeping terraces were added. Tour the archaeological crypt (May–Oct.) to see latrine pits and other historical gems dug up during excavations. Designated NHS: 2001. Rue Saint-Louis and rue du Fort. (418) 648-7016.

QUÉBEC CITY REGION SITES

CHÂTEAU FRONTENAC
QUÉBEC, QC

This cliff-top resort has perched on the edge of Québec's walled city since the 1890s. William Van Horne, then general manager of Canadian Pacific Railway, built it for train travellers, and it became the model for château-style railway hotels to follow. Many high-profile guests have since slept in one of the 600-plus rooms. Visit at night when the lights dazzle; guided (855-977-8977) or self-guided (with the hotel's app) tours are available. Designated NHS: 1981. 1 rue des Carrières. (866) 540-4460.

MORRIN COLLEGE/FORMER QUÉBEC PRISON
QUÉBEC, QC

Since the 1700s, people have done all kinds of things at 44 Chaussée des Écossais. They've been hanged; they've crammed for exams; they've published rare manuscripts. The site's also been home to a prison influenced by British reformer John Howard. Visit the library of the Literary and Historical Society of Québec (founded 1824) or take a guided tour about convict life or historical science experiments. Designated NHS: 1981. 44 Chaussée des Écossais. (418) 694-9147.

MOUNT HERMON CEMETERY
QUÉBEC, QC

Established in 1848 by the Protestant community in what was then a suburb of Québec City, this modest rural cemetery is renowned for its beauty. Among the curving hillsides and plentiful trees, take in artful grave monuments in a range of historic styles and a grand panoramic view of the St. Lawrence River. Guided tours of the cemetery are offered during the summer, and visitors can self-guide with the Québec City podcast tour throughout the year. Designated NHS: 2007. 1801 chemin Saint-Louis. (418) 527-3513.

QUÉBEC MARTELLO TOWERS
QUÉBEC, QC

In the early 19th century, the British built 200 or so martello towers—squat, cylindrical defensive forts—throughout their empire. Three such towers still stand along the Fortifications of Québec (see pp. 104–107), with views of the St. Lawrence and Charles Rivers. These towers were effective for their time, boasting thick cannon-resistant walls, strong interior arches, and flat roofs to support heavy guns. Seasonal exhibitions are staged. Designated NHS: 1990. 835 ave. Wilfrid-Laurier. (418) 649-6157 or (855) 649-6157.

QUÉBEC SEMINARY
QUÉBEC, QC

This French-Canadian landmark is rooted in religion and renowned for its contributions to education, shaping would-be priests since 1663. In 1852, priests here founded North America's first French-language university: Université Laval. Three letters on the Vieux-Séminaire's arched gateway speak both to the history and the modern mission of this place: SME, Séminaire des Missions-Étrangères (Seminary for Foreign Missions). Designated NHS: 1929. 1 rue de Remparts. (418) 692-3981.

TROIS-RIVIÈRES HISTORICAL COMPLEX
TROIS-RIVIÈRES, QC

Forming part of the downtown core, the five buildings in this complex were once two convents, a church, and two houses. A great fire destroyed many historic buildings in 1908, but this complex survived with its stone facades, gable roofs, and dormer windows intact. Today, the complex is a well-integrated representation of 18th-century French Canada. Designated NHS: 1962. 700, 732, 787, 802, and 834 rue des Ursulines. Trois-Rivières Tourism: (819) 375-1122.

The floating dock at Lachine Canal offers visitors canoes and paddleboats.

MONTRÉAL & WESTERN QUÉBEC

The largest French-speaking city in North America, the greater Montréal metropolitan area is home to almost half the population of Québec Province. Montréal is located on an island—the Island of Montréal—at the confluence of the St. Lawrence and Ottawa Rivers, an ideal settlement spot with a rich supply of natural resources. Although Iroquoian people once inhabited the island, they had disappeared by the end of the 1500s. The French founded Montréal in 1642, and over the next century it became the region's fur

trading centre. The fur trade continued to flourish in the decades following Britain's success in the Seven Years' War (1756–1763) but, with the advent of industrialization a century later, was gradually overshadowed by the lucrative lumber industry. By the end of the 19th century, the canal system around Montréal had been expanded (see pp. 133–138) and the city had become the main port in the region, as well as the heart of the nation's railway system. Today, Montréal is second only to Toronto in size and economic activity.

Manoir Papineau, home of French-Canadian advocate Louis-Joseph Papineau

▶ MANOIR PAPINEAU   MONTEBELLO, QC

Designated 1986

A winding, tree-lined driveway leads to the grand four-storey home that Canadian politician Louis-Joseph Papineau (1786–1871) wished to enjoy with his family, after spending decades staunchly defending political and cultural French Canada.

During the early 19th century, Papineau was elected several times to Lower Canada's House of Assembly and, later, to the Legislative Assembly of the Province of Canada. As the leader of the Parti Patriote, he fought for the political and cultural rights of French Canadians—and against the unification of Upper Canada and Lower Canada. In the 1830s, he used his law skills to help draft 92 resolutions outlining his party's grievances and demands, which the British government rejected.

He continued to argue for the rights and affirmation of French-speaking Canadians until the Rebellions of 1837–38, when he fled to the United States. Papineau stayed away—he went to France to research and document the history of New France—until granted amnesty in 1845.

He returned to his homeland—dubbed United Canada as of 1840—and began building this grand manor on the Petite-Nation seigneury, a 635-sq km (245 sq mi) stretch of forested land acquired from his father in 1817. The seigneury, named after an Algonquin tribe that used to live in the area, was home to more than 3,000 people by 1850. Papineau defended the feudal-esque seigneurial system as a safeguard against assimilation.

Today, his house looms large over the Ottawa River, a reminder of an agricultural tradition, the identity politics of a young nation—and a man who tried to navigate them.

What to See & Do

Enjoy authentic period decor on a guided tour (included with admission), or drop in for tea and a brief

19th-century etiquette primer. Flip through scrapbooks filled with old photos of the Papineau clan, or wander amid the woods and gardens. VIP tours (extra fee) offer a glimpse of Papineau's office and the frescoes in the attic granary, painted by Papineau's son-in-law, Napoléon Bourassa.

How to Get There

Manoir Papineau is about 55 minutes west of Ottawa by car. Take Hwy. 50E to exit 210, turn left on Rte. 323S, and then left again on Rue Notre-Dame.

When to Go

The site is open mid-May to mid-October (daily June 4–Sept. 5; Friday, weekends, and holidays during the shoulder seasons).

INFORMATION

HOW TO REACH US
500 rue Notre-Dame, Montebello, QC J0V 1L0. Phone (819) 423-6910. pc.gc.ca/manoirpapineau.

ENTRANCE FEES
$7.80 per adult, $19.60 per family/group.

ACCESSIBLE SERVICES
Limited; contact the site for details.

HOTELS, MOTELS, & INNS
Fairmont Le Château Montebello
392 rue Notre-Dame, Montebello, QC J0V 1L0. (819) 423-6341 or (866) 540-4462. fairmont.com /montebello. 211 rooms and suites, prices vary.

MONTRÉAL & WESTERN QUÉBEC

An interpreter explains artillery at Coteau-du-Lac military post.

▶ COTEAU-DU-LAC

COTEAU-DU-LAC, QC
Designated 1923

Nestled about 40 km (24.8 mi) southwest of Montréal, Coteau-du-Lac is home to the oldest lock canals in North America. You could easily lose hours admiring the 18th-century archaeological remains scattered about this gorgeous green countryside.

As far back as 6,000 years ago, nomadic groups were following spawning fish to this region; men caught their dinners using harpoons, fishgigs, and trotlines; women and children smoked the catch outside cone-shaped tents. And long before Europeans came to the region, Indigenous Peoples used Coteau-du-Lac to bypass the St. Lawrence River's most turbulent stretch—the Coteau Rapids. Later the French and Canadians managed to erect a rough stone breakwater. By doing so, they obtained a corridor of relatively calm water where they could haul their *bateaux*. This *canal rigolet* was put in place in 1749.

So, perhaps not surprisingly, the British picked this peninsula on which to build (1779–1781) a 100-m (328 ft) canal to provide a faster way to ship troops and merchandise. Shortly after the War of 1812 began, they also built fortifications here: an octagonal blockhouse, a powder magazine, a guardhouse, and other structures. Coteau-du-Lac never saw any fighting during the war—the American threat was neutralized farther up

the river—but the town was an important military post throughout the conflict, linking British strongholds at Montréal and Kingston.

What to See & Do
Take in some sunshine and some trivia on the outdoor circuit, exploring archaeological remains dating back thousands of years. For more outdoor recreation, search for herons and martins along the creek-adjacent nature trail. Inside the blockhouse, enjoy a popular multimedia presentation.

How to Get There
Take exit 17 off Rte. 20 and follow the signs to the site.

When to Go
The site is open daily June 18 through September 5.

The canal once carried British troops and supplies.

Built in 1803, this warehouse stored pelts for the North West Company.

▶ THE FUR TRADE AT LACHINE

LACHINE, QC
Designated 1970

It's easy to imagine voyageurs hauling heavy beaver, muskrat, and fox pelts through the doors of this old stone warehouse on the banks of the Lachine Canal. The North West Company (NWC), founded in 1779 by a group of mostly Montréal-based Scottish Canadians, built this warehouse in 1803.

Every spring, voyageurs set off from Lachine bound for Grand Portage (in Minnesota) and later Fort William (today's Thunder Bay), their canoes full of trading goods. These men were dubbed the "porkeaters" by their counterparts in the Northwest, the "winterers." The winterers paddled down to Grand Portage to meet the voyageurs, their birchbark canoes full of pelts to trade for the porkeaters' goods.

The NWC moved quickly from simply threatening the Hudson's Bay Company's long-held monopoly to dominating the fur trade by the early 19th century. In 1821, with competition having reached a costly boiling point, the two companies decided to merge under the name Hudson's Bay Company.

Forty years later, the fur trade was dwindling. In 1861, the warehouse found new purpose under the Sisters of Sainte-Anne, who used it until 1977. In 1984, Parks Canada converted it into an interpretive museum.

Today, Québec remains central to the Canadian fur trade, hosting 125 of 150 Canadian manufacturers. Among other people, the industry continues to employ trappers—about half of whom are Indigenous Peoples.

What to See & Do

Don a traditional sash and red toque and retrace—through an interactive exhibit—the routes trappers and voyageurs took. Admire the birchbark master canoe made by César Newashish, an Attikamek from the Manawan Reserve. Step into a room full of pelts and take a sniff. Finally, note the grand manor across the street from the warehouse, built in 1833 by Sir George Simpson, an HBC president.

How to Get There

From Hwy. 20, take exit 60 (32nd Ave.). Turn left on rue Victoria, right on avenue 25, and then left on boulevard Saint-Joseph. Parking is on the right side of the street.

When to Go

This site is open every day from June 18 through September 5.

INFORMATION

HOW TO REACH US
1255 blvd. Saint-Joseph, Lachine Borough, Montréal, QC H8S 2M2. Phone (514) 637-7433. pc.gc.ca/eng/lhn-nhs/qc/lachine/index.aspx.

ENTRANCE FEES
$3.90 per adult, $9.80 per family/group.

ACCESSIBLE SERVICES
Friendly.

HOTELS, MOTELS, & INNS
Fairfield Inn & Suites Montreal Airport 700 ave. Michel Jasmin, Montréal, QC H9P 1C5. (514) 631-2424. marriott.com. 160 rooms, prices vary.

Sir George-Étienne Cartier's home showcases upper-middle-class opulence.

▶ SIR GEORGE-ÉTIENNE CARTIER

MONTRÉAL, QC

Designated 1964

During the mid-19th century, lawyer, politician, and businessman Sir George-Étienne Cartier (1814-1873)—one of the Fathers of Confederation—lived in the east half of this neoclassical building from 1848 to 1855, and installed his family in the west half from 1862 to 1872.

Rural born, Cartier passed the bar in 1835, but his involvement with the Patriote cause and a consequent period of exile in the United States meant his law career got off to a slow start. Cartier made up for lost time by making clients out of some of Montréal's biggest players. In 1846, he married Hortense Fabre, the daughter of a former mayor and prominent bookstore owner.

Cartier channelled his legal expertise, networking skills, and passion for "responsible government" into a run for office in 1848. He represented Verchères (now a suburb of Montréal) from 1848 to 1858, and then Montréal-Est from 1861 to 1872, in the Legislative Assembly of the Province of Canada and in the federal parliament after Confederation. Meanwhile, he joined the Great Coalition in 1864 and is best remembered for the work he did to help bring about Confederation in 1867. No doubt, ideas about Confederation were sometimes debated in this house over elegant place settings.

In 1868, Queen Victoria honoured Cartier by making him a baronet. A few years later, in 1873, Cartier died from Bright's disease.

What to See & Do

Start in the "East House" to learn about Cartier's work, and then visit the "West House" to see how he relaxed. Here, the opulence of an upper-middle-class 1860s Montréal home is on display, much as it might have looked when the Cartier family lived here. Excerpts from the diaries of two of Cartier's daughters, Hortense and Joséphine, reveal glimpses of their bourgeois lives. Consider visiting in late December to enjoy Victorian-era Christmas activities: Sip old-fashioned drinks, hear Christmas stories at the foot of a

INFORMATION

HOW TO REACH US
456-462 rue Notre-Dame E, Montréal, QC H2Y 1C8. Phone (514) 283-2282. pc.gc.ca/eng/lhn-nhs/qc/etiennecartier/index.aspx.

ENTRANCE FEES
$3.90 per adult, $9.80 per family/group.

ACCESSIBLE SERVICES
Friendly.

HOTELS, MOTELS, & INNS
Hôtel Champ-de-Mars 756 rue Berri, Montréal, QC H2Y 3E6. (514) 844-0767 or (888) 997-0767. hotelchampdemars.com. 26 rooms, prices vary.
Hotel Pierre du Calvet 405 rue Bonsecours, Montréal, QC H2Y 3C3. (514) 282-1725 or (866) 544-1725. pierreducalvet.ca. 9 rooms, $350.

Christmas tree, or sneak a kiss under the mistletoe.

How to Get There

The house sits at the corner of Notre Dame and Berri in the eastern end of the historic district of Old Montréal. There is no parking on-site.

When to Go

The site is open Wednesday to Sunday and holidays from June 18 until September 5, and Friday to Sunday from September 9 to December 18.

Cartier championed "responsible government."

Women in Canadian History

In the 1970s, feminists pointed out that history was often written from a male perspective. Since then, historians have begun to study the important roles women have played in the past—in work, politics, religion, education, and the family.

In the early 1900s, women from across Europe immigrated to Canada.

Indigenous Peoples & Early Settlers

Indigenous Peoples interacted with the earliest European explorers and traders in the territories that now make up Canada. Newcomers sometimes married local women. Some, like Charlotte Small who assisted her explorer husband, David Thompson, taught skills the newcomers would need to survive. Thanadelthur, a young Dene woman, guided Hudson's Bay Company traders into her territory and also negotiated peace between her people and their traditional enemies, the Cree. Both women have been commemorated by the government of Canada as a national historic person (NHP).

In New France, European women who came as missionaries tried to convert Indigenous Peoples to Christianity. Arriving in 1639, the Augustines helped found the colony and built a hospital, the Hôtel-Dieu de Québec (today, a national historic site). Marie de l'Incarnation and fellow Ursulines played a similar role in education. After 1760, when the British took control of most of North America, English-speaking women helped build Canada as household members, whether as mothers, wives, daughters, or domestic servants. They assisted the men in clearing and farming the land, tended gardens, and kept dairies, all while maintaining homes, raising children, and supporting the founding of churches and schools.

Urbanization & the Women's Movement

During the 19th century, Canada became increasingly urban. Women began to work in factories, schools, and hospitals. As their independence grew, women formed their own organizations, yet they encountered barriers. It was widely believed that it was "natural" for men to govern the affairs of business, politics, and government. Thus women were not allowed to attend university or to enter most professions. Married women had few legal rights, and those who worked outside the home received lower wages than men.

Symbolic of these disadvantages, women were not even allowed to vote. In 1876, Dr. Emily Stowe (NHP) formed the first women's suffrage organization in Toronto to campaign for the vote. In the 1890s, the Woman's Christian Temperance Union endorsed women's suffrage, seeking the vote to influence government referenda on prohibition. Working-class women, such as Helena Gutteridge (NHP) of Vancouver, wanted the vote to gain a greater voice in trade unions and to advocate for better wages and working conditions. The suffragists achieved their first provincial victory in 1916, when Manitoba women gained the vote. It came two years after prominent author Nellie McClung (NHP) starred in a political satire at the Walker Theatre (a national historic site in Winnipeg), in which men had to beg women for the right to vote. Other provinces soon followed and, with some exceptions, most women could vote by 1940. They could also sit in the Senate, thanks to a successful legal challenge in 1929 that confirmed that Canadian women were "persons." This has been recognized as a national historic event.

After winning the right to vote and achieving fuller participation in Canadian society, women quietly contributed toward the making of a better Canada. When feminist activism re-emerged in the 1960s and '70s, however, women successfully fought for a Royal Commission on the Status of Women, which provided a blueprint for future directions. Since the 1970s, the women's movement has shifted its focus, fighting for the rights of Indigenous women, ethnic minorities, victims of violence, and LGBT communities, as well as ensuring that women were represented in the Charter of Rights and Freedoms.

The Famous Five fought for women to be "persons."

Uniformed interpreters and visitors relive the British-American battle.

▶ BATTLE OF THE CHÂTEAUGUAY

ALLAN'S CORNER, QC
Designated 1920

On October 26, 1813, on the banks of the Châteauguay River, 300 professional soldiers, volunteer militiamen, and Indigenous fighters banded together to rout 3,000 American soldiers—who were marching on Montréal in bid to gain Britain's North American colony during the War of 1812.

The Americans envisioned a two-pronged attack: General Hampton's troops would follow the Châteauguay River while General Wilkinson's men would travel through the upper St. Lawrence Valley. Lieutenant Colonel de Salaberry met the Americans coming up the Châteauguay, attacking them at Four Corners in New York State. Then his troops withdrew to Canada, setting up obstacles in their wake to slow the American advance. Near Allan's Corner, de Salaberry set his troops to digging trenches and prepared to defend the route.

The Battle of the Châteauguay broke out around 10 a.m. on October 26, 1813. Hampton's 3,000 soldiers and de Salaberry's 300-strong mix of militiamen, Indigenous fighters, and regular soldiers flexed their positions along the riverbank, trying to outsmart each other. By mid-afternoon, the Canadians had convinced the Americans to retreat, and by October 29 they had retreated across the border.

What to See & Do

Visit the Introductory Hall to learn about the architects and heroes of the battle. Then head over to the indoor lookout, where interpreters use an interactive scale model to explain how the battle played out; the lookout provides a lovely panoramic view of the grounds. The site's commemorative monument—a striking obelisk—was erected by the government in 1895. A 15-km (9.3 mi) riverside trail—suitable for bikes—runs between Ormstown and Howick and features 13 interpretive panels that map the hot spots of this historic battlefield.

How to Get There

Allan's Corner (a hamlet of the town of Howick) is a 45-minute drive (southwest) from Montréal. The easiest way is via Mercier Bridge. Take Rte. 138 to Howick. Turn right on Rang du Quarante, and then left on Rivière Châteauguay Road.

When to Go

The site is open daily June 18 through September 5.

INFORMATION

HOW TO REACH US
2371 Rivière Châteauguay Rd., Howick, QC J0S 1G0. Phone (450) 829-2003. pc.gc.ca/chateauguay.

ENTRANCE FEES
$3.90 per adult, $9.80 per family/group.

ACCESSIBLE SERVICES
Friendly, except for the belvedere.

HOTELS, MOTELS, & INNS
Hôtel Plaza Valleyfield 40 ave. Centenaire, Salaberry-de-Valleyfield, QC J6S 3L6. (450) 373-1990 or (877) 882-8818. plazavalleyfield.com/en/home. 123 rooms, $125.

Prime Minister Sir Wilfrid Laurier grew up in a modest mid-19th-century home much like this one.

▶ SIR WILFRID LAURIER

SAINT-LIN-LAURENTIDES, QC
Designated 1938

Before Prime Minister Justin Trudeau's "sunny days," Canada had Prime Minister Wilfrid Laurier's "sunny ways." Laurier led the country into the 20th century with characteristic optimism—an optimism that had its roots here in the Québec countryside.

While serving as Canada's seventh prime minister (1896–1911), Laurier made decisions that changed the face of western Canada—driving development during a time of mass industrialization and opening the gates wide to new immigrants. And he demonstrated a knack for resolving tense situations by brokering compromises that he deemed necessary in the name of national unity.

Laurier's grandfather bought this property—where Laurier was presumably born (in 1841)—at the turn of the 19th century. When the Canadian government decided to establish Laurier's birthplace as a national historic park in 1938, the quaint little brick residence on the property was assumed to have been Laurier's childhood home. This assumption has since been disproved: The house was actually built in 1870 by the subsequent property owners.

The "Robinette house" is therefore an interesting example of early 20th-century curatorship. It has a few ethnological objects relevant to Laurier's career and political life, but the emphasis is placed on immersing visitors—through period-era design, with more than 600 pieces of furniture and accessories—in a mid-19th-century family home. This is one of the first non-military sites that Parks Canada took efforts to preserve and re-create.

A house built in 1870 features effects from Laurier's era.

INFORMATION

HOW TO REACH US
945 12th Ave., Saint-Lin-Laurentides, QC J5M 2W4. Phone (450) 439-3702. pc.gc.ca/wilfridlaurier.

ENTRANCE FEES
$3.90 per adult, $9.80 per family/group. (Cash only.)

ACCESSIBLE SERVICES
Friendly, but the second floor of the house is not wheelchair accessible.

HOTELS, MOTELS, & INNS
Imperia Hotel 2935 blvd. De La Pinière, Terrebonne, QC J6X 0A3. (888) 472-3336. imperiahotel.com. 80 rooms, $149–$269.
Best Western Hôtel St-Jérôme 420 Mgr.-Dubois, Saint-Jérome, QC J7Y 3L8. (800) 718-7170. bwlaurentides .com. 50 rooms, $116.

What to See & Do
Start by getting a broad overview of Sir Wilfrid Laurier's life and career at the interpretation centre. Then dive into the historic house next door to gain insight into family life in the mid-19th century. Site interpreters tell visitors how the boy who became the first French-Canadian prime minister spent his early years. Green thumb enthusiasts will appreciate the vegetable garden outside.

How to Get There
The site is 50 km (31 mi) northeast of Montréal, in Saint-Lin-Laurentides. From Montréal, head north on Hwy. 25. Take exit 44, and then drive west on Rte. 339 to site.

When to Go
This site is open daily June 18 through September 5. The possibility of seeing guides dressed in period costume is greater on weekends.

Lachine Canal helped Montréal become a power centre.

▶ LACHINE CANAL

MONTRÉAL, QC
Designated 1929

The Lachine Canal runs from Montréal's Old Port to Lake Saint-Louis. As the head of the canal network linking the Great Lakes region and the Atlantic Ocean, it once helped establish Montréal as a power centre. Today, it offers a recreational escape for boaters, cyclers, and strollers.

In 1821, a group of Montréal merchants wanting to capitalize on trade booming in the Great Lakes region banded together to build a canal to bypass the difficult Lachine Rapids of the St. Lawrence River. Many Irish immigrants heeded their call for diggers and builders. And when the canal was widened in the 1840s to accommodate bigger boats, the Irish made up the bulk of the workforce again. Their work helped increase water flow, creating a new business opportunity: hydraulic power for sale. Water held back by the five locks was redirected into wheels or turbines, producing energy that was auctioned off to public buyers. Montréal's Sud-Ouest borough soon became a hub for industry, with businesses setting up along the banks of the canal (by 1945 more than 600 had sprung up).

In its heyday, just before the Great Depression, nearly 15,000 ships used the canal annually. But the canal was rendered obsolete—at least as far as shipping goes—when the St. Lawrence Seaway was built in 1959. Under the management of Parks Canada, the canal has since become a lively destination. The canal reopened to recreational navigation in 2002, and its popularity continues to grow.

What to See & Do

Take a walk or ride a bike (rentals available in the Atwater Market area) along the canal's pathway, where skyscrapers clash with centuries-old buildings and green spaces provide picnic places. The 14.5-km (9 mi) path stretches from the Bonaventure Expressway west of the Old Port to Chemin du Musée in Lachine.

134

Visitors with their own pleasure boat can take to the water, enjoying going through the locks. Kayaks and canoes are allowed too.

How to Get There

The Lachine Canal is an easily accessed urban park in Montréal. To learn about the metro stations, bus routes, and parking lots situated near the canal, visit the site's website.

When to Go

Open year-round. The path is maintained from April 15 to November 15, and the locks from mid-May to mid-October. The lockages schedule varies seasonally; call (514) 595-6594 for times.

INFORMATION

HOW TO REACH US
Phone (888) 773-8888. parks
canada.gc.ca/lachinecanal.

ENTRANCE FEES
None. Contact site for lockage fees.

ACCESSIBLE SERVICES
Friendly.

HOTELS, MOTELS, & INNS
Alt Hotel 120 rue Peel, Montréal, QC H3C 0L8. (514) 375-0220. althotels .com/en/montreal. 158 rooms, $154.
By boat: The five locks have wharves available for day and night mooring. Contact the lock operators through VHF-canal 68 during operating hours.

Sainte-Anne-de-Bellevue Canal was a key trade route around rapids in the Ottawa River.

▶ SAINTE-ANNE-DE-BELLEVUE CANAL
SAINTE-ANNE-DE-BELLEVUE, QC
Designated 1929

More than 150 years ago, Montréal and New York City were connected by a network of canals, used for bypassing unfriendly or inconvenient waters in the name of trade. The 58-m (190 ft) Sainte-Anne-de-Bellevue Canal formed a short yet important link in that network.

Constructed by the government of Lower Canada in the 1840s during Canada's canal-building heyday, this waterway skirts the southwestern tip of the Island of Montréal, bypassing the Ste. Anne's Rapids in the east channel of the Ottawa River, and thus connecting Montréal to the Ottawa River and the all-important Rideau Canal (see pp. 168–171). The St. Andrews Steamboat Company had been monopolizing upstream trade via their own nearby canal, and merchants in the Canadas (Upper and Lower) were keen to compete with this private company.

Until the period between the two World Wars, forest products made up the bulk of the goods shipped through this canal; later, it was sand and gravel. Standing on this quiet corner of the island today, it's hard to imagine a bustling industrial scene, but the canal played a key role in the North American timber trade.

In the early 1960s, the canal ceased to be used for commercial shipping, and in 1964 this waterway was reinvented as a recreational space (like many of Québec's heritage canals). Today, visitors might imagine steamships and lumber rafts flowing by as they stroll along the boardwalk, coffees or ice cream in hand.

What to See & Do

Learn more about the canal's history and operational nuances by reading the interpretive panels along the beautiful boardwalk. Watch the boats pass. Admire the remains of the first canal. Dine out at a restaurant terrace or find an inviting patch of grass on the canal's banks to sprawl out on and do some cloud counting.

Families with a penchant for old Mustangs might consider visiting in mid-June when Sainte-Anne-de-Bellevue hosts its annual vintage car

INFORMATION

HOW TO REACH US

170 rue Sainte-Anne, Sainte-Anne-de-Bellevue, QC H9X 1N1. Phone (514) 457-5546. pc.gc.ca/ste annecanal.

ENTRANCE FEES

None. Contact site for lockage fees.

ACCESSIBLE SERVICES

Friendly.

HOTELS, MOTELS, & INNS

Courtyard Marriott 20000 Trans-Canada Hwy., Baie D'Urfe, QC H9X 0B3. (514) 674-8000 or (888) 236 2427. marriott.com/hotels/travel /yulbd-courtyard-montreal-west -island-baie-d'urfe. 140 rooms, $149+. **By boat:** Overnight mooring services are available at a low cost both downstream and upstream of the canal. Contact the lock operators through VHF-canal 68 during operating hours.

show (cruisinattheboardwalk.com). During the one-day event, hundreds of custom-rebuilt muscle cars, hot rods, and classics are parked alongside the canal. Kids can play on inflatable games, and older folks can groove to the sounds of 1950s and '60s music.

How to Get There

The canal is located at the western end of the Island of Montréal. From Montréal, take Hwy. 20W, getting off at the Sainte-Anne-de-Bellevue exit. Alternatively, take Hwy. 40W and again look for the Sainte-Anne-de-Bellevue exit.

When to Go

Open year-round from sunrise until 11 p.m. The locks are maintained from mid-May to mid-October. The lockages schedule varies seasonally; call (514) 457-5546 for times.

The superintendent's house on scenic Saint-Ours Canal, once a timber trade hub

▶ SAINT-OURS CANAL   SAINT-OURS, QC

Designated 1987

The Saint-Ours Canal was the final link in the Richelieu canal system, an elaborate network that linked Montréal and New York via the Richelieu River. It played an essential role in the timber trade between Canada and the United States and the distribution of agricultural products.

The government of Lower Canada commissioned the Saint-Ours Canal's construction in 1829, but politics and financial setbacks kept the project on the shelf until 1844. When it finally opened in 1849, this one-lock canal helped boaters bypass the final obstacle on the Richelieu between Lake Champlain and the St. Lawrence River (the Chambly Canal—see pp. 160–161—farther south on the river, had been completed a few years earlier). Vessels on the St. Lawrence could now access Lake Champlain and then proceed to the Champlain Canal and the Hudson River.

The lock and mechanisms used to control the canal have seen several upgrades over the years. The current lock was completed in 1933 parallel and to the west of the original lock.

The original Saint-Ours Canal was complemented by a wooden dam that linked the west bank of the river to Darvard Island and helped regulate the Richelieu's water level. The old dam was replaced with a new, bigger model in 1969.

What to See & Do

Spoiled by scenic surroundings, the Saint-Ours Canal is wedged between the Richelieu River's east bank and the natural setting of Darvard Island. Visit the superintendent's house on the island to learn about the dams (old and new) and life on the island through original artefacts and interpretive panels. Exhibits explain how the 100-m (328 ft) canal was constructed and who toiled to build it. Outside, stroll the island's trail network, keeping an eye out for migrating birds.

Cross to the river's west bank to see the Vianney-Legendre Fishway, built in 2001. This ladderlike fishway allows species to bypass the Saint-Ours Dam so they can reach their breeding grounds.

How to Get There

The Saint-Ours Canal runs along Rte. 133N. From Montréal, head east on Hwy. 20, turn off at the Mont Saint-Hilaire exit, and follow the signs.

When to Go

Open year-round. The locks are maintained from mid-May to mid-October. The lockages schedule varies seasonally; call (450) 785-2212 for times.

INFORMATION

HOW TO REACH US
2930 chemin des Patriotes, Saint-Ours, QC J0G 1P0. Phone (888) 773-8888. pc.gc.ca/stourscanal.

ENTRANCE FEES
None. Parking $3.90. Contact the site for lockage fees.

ACCESSIBLE SERVICES
Friendly.

HOTELS, MOTELS, & INNS
By boat: Overnight mooring services are available at a low cost both downstream and upstream of the canal. Contact the lock operators through VHF-canal 68 during operating hours.

MONTRÉAL & WESTERN QUÉBEC

Carillon Canal visitors can picnic in the park and explore Carillon village.

▶ CARILLON CANAL

CARILLON, QC
Designated 1929

Situated on the left bank of the Ottawa River, the Carillon Canal harkens back to wartime tensions and wood-based economies. Explore the original canal remains, the Argenteuil Regional Museum, and the neighbouring hydroelectric power station.

Following the War of 1812, the British feared a potential American invasion. Wishing to establish a defence route linking Montréal, Ottawa, and Kingston that was free of impassable rapids, they built three canals on the Ottawa between 1819 and 1833: Carillon, Grenville, and Chute-à-Blondeau. The Carillon Canal opened in 1834, and it soon became a pipeline for the bustling timber trade. By 1873, the canal system was outdated; construction began on a second system with a complementary dam upstream. This new canal system moved a lot of pulpwood, lumber, and firewood in the last quarter of the 19th century. Later, Carillon was repurposed for tourism once it became more efficient to transport goods by rail.

Between 1959 and 1963, Hydro-Québec erected a major dam at Carillon. Around the same time, the canal system's original locks were replaced with a single, more effective lock, the biggest of its kind in Canada. This 200-tonne guillotine gate allows recreational boaters to drop 20 m (65.6 ft) in less than 40 minutes.

Close to the canal stand the stone barracks built by the British Army in the 1830s. This neoclassical building was probably designed to be a hotel, but the army used it as a barracks for a few years before it fulfilled its original mandate; in 1840, the building started accommodating people travelling by steamboat. A hundred years later the building was reinvented as the Argenteuil Regional Museum.

What to See & Do

Watch pleasure boats pass through the canal's massive gate. Enjoy a picnic in the charming park near the remains of the first Carillon Canal. Afterward, wander through Carillon village to admire heritage homes made of locally quarried stone. Stop

INFORMATION

HOW TO REACH US
230 Du Barrage St., Saint-André-d'Argenteuil, QC J0V 1X0. Phone (888) 773-8888. pc.gc.ca/carillon canal.

ENTRANCE FEES
None. Parking $3.90. Contact the site for lockage fees.

ACCESSIBLE SERVICES
Limited; contact the site for details.

CAMPGROUNDS
Voyageur Provincial Park 1313 Front Rd., Chute-à-Blondeau, ON K0B 1B0. (613) 674-2825. ontarioparks.com /park/voyageur. About 400 sites, $47 with electric outlet or $41 without.

HOTELS, MOTELS, & INNS
By boat: Overnight mooring services are available at a low cost both downstream and upstream of the canal. Contact the lock operators through VHF-canal 68 during operating hours.

at the Argenteuil Regional Museum (at the village's entrance) to view thousands of artefacts, a costumes room, a military kitchen, and a host of other permanent exhibits. For power enthusiasts, Hydro-Québec offers free 90-minute guided tours (May–Aug.) at the generating station.

How to Get There

The Carillon Canal runs along Rte. 344W. From Montréal, head west on Hwy. 40 and take the Pointe-Fortune exit. Then take the ferry to Carillon and follow Rte. 344W to the lock.

When to Go

Open year-round. The locks are maintained from mid-May to mid-October. The lockages schedule varies seasonally; call (450) 785-2212 for times.

MONTRÉAL & WESTERN QUÉBEC SITES

BONSECOURS MARKET
MONTRÉAL, QC

Browse boutiques for locally made jewellery, find a unique piece of art, or unwind with a hoppy brew here in Montréal's Old Port. From 1847 until 1963, this domed neoclassical building was a space for art, politics, and commerce. Dig underneath the market's stone walls and you might find ruins of mansions, remnants from a demolished theatre where Dickens played, and notes scribbled during City Hall meetings. Designated NHS: 1984. 300 rue Saint-Paul Est. (514) 872-7730.

CHÂTEAU DE RAMEZAY/ INDIA HOUSE
MONTRÉAL, QC

Flash back 200 years to a winter day in Montréal's Old Port and imagine smoke billowing from the high chimneys of this tidy-looking stone mansion. Originally built in 1705 by governor of Montréal Claude de Ramezay, this building (which was rebuilt after a fire in 1756) was used by men in suits, men toting beaver pelts, and men sporting "governor in chief" nametags. There's an on-site museum and flowers in the garden. Designated NHS: 1949. 280–290 rue Notre-Dame Est. (514) 861-3708.

CHRIST CHURCH CATHEDRAL
MONTRÉAL, QC

Beginning in the 1860s, if someone were looking for an influential Anglican in downtown Montréal on any given Sunday, they might have stopped by this church, which today is the seat of the Anglican Diocese of Montréal. Lean back to marvel at the Gothic Revival design, the steep gabled roof, the sculpted stonework, and the elegant spire before sliding through one of three arched entryways. Designated NHS: 1999. 635 rue Sainte-Catherine Ouest. (514) 843-6577.

MONTRÉAL & WESTERN QUÉBEC SITES

ERSKINE AND AMERICAN UNITED CHURCH
MONTRÉAL, QC

This Romanesque Revival church, built in the 1890s, boasts what is probably Canada's biggest collection of religious stained-glass windows by American artist Louis Comfort Tiffany. In 2008, the Montréal Museum of Fine Arts bought the church and poured 5,000 hours into restoring the 20 Tiffany windows, converting the nave into a 444-seat concert hall, and building a new six-storey pavilion for Québec and Canadian art next door. Designated NHS: 1998. 1339 rue Sherbrooke Ouest. (514) 285-2000.

MONTRÉAL BOTANICAL GARDEN
MONTRÉAL, QC

This 75-ha (185 acres) patch of nature started as the dream of a young botanist and a landscape architect in 1931. It became one of the world's most ambitious botanical gardens. Enjoy 22,000 plant species and cultivars, wander through the Garden of Weedlessness (one of 10 greenhouses), meditate in the Japanese Garden (one of more than 20 thematic gardens), and learn about the interesting experiments resident botanists are doing. Designated NHS: 2007. 4101 rue Sherbrooke Est. (514) 872-1400.

ST. JOSEPH'S ORATORY OF MOUNT ROYAL
MONTRÉAL, QC

In 1904, Montréal's Brother André initiated construction on a small wooden chapel on Mount Royal (aka Mont Royal), dedicated to St. Joseph. Over the next half century, this project evolved into a stunning complex featuring a large domed basilica, a limestone-faced crypt, and an elaborate garden with winding paths—making it the largest shrine in the world devoted to "the saint of everyday life." Designated NHS: 2004. 3800 chemin Queen-Mary. (514) 733-8211 or (877) 672-8647.

SULPICIAN TOWERS/
FORT DE LA MONTAGNE
MONTRÉAL, QC

In the 1680s and 1690s, the Sulpicians of Montréal—a Catholic society engaged in missionary work—erected a fort with four stone towers on the slopes of Mont Royal. Today, two remain: the west tower, which once housed the Indian school of Marguerite Bourgeoys, and the east tower, which housed the nuns. On-site illustrated panels detail the towers' history. Behind the towers is the Grand Séminaire de Montréal, a training ground for priests, established in 1857. Designated NHS: 1970. 2065 rue Sherbrooke Ouest. (514) 935-1169.

THE MAIN
MONTRÉAL, QC

Otherwise known as boulevard Saint-Laurent, the Main slices through the near middle of Montréal, separating east from west. Historically, English Montrealers clumped together in the west, whereas French Montrealers settled in the east. As new immigrants arrived, they congregated along the boulevard, creating a vibrant—and distinctly Canadian—cultural blend. Designated NHS: 1996. Boulevard Saint-Laurent, from Rue de la Commune in the north to Rue Jean-Talon in the south.

WINDSOR STATION
(CANADIAN PACIFIC)
MONTRÉAL, QC

Once the transportation heart of Canada, this heritage railway station pumped immigrants, westbound explorers, soldiers, and commercial goods across the country. It was built in 1888–89 to designs by American architect Bruce Price. Today, it stands (in all its limestone Romanesque Revival glory) at the corner of Canada Place in downtown Montréal as a reminder of the Canadian Pacific Railway's role in Canada's development. Designated NHS: 1975. 910 rue Peel. (514) 395-5164.

From the 1600s to the mid-1800s, fur trappers and traders plied the rivers and forests of northern Québec.

NORTHERN QUÉBEC

Encompassing most of the province of Québec, this large, heavily forested region extends from north of the St. Lawrence Valley and the cities of Montréal and Québec City to the Ungava Peninsula in the north, and westward from the Gulf of St. Lawrence to the shore of Hudson Bay. From the end of the 17th century until industrialization in the mid-19th century, fur trading dominated economic activity here. Essential to Canada's history, the fur trade spurred on exploration of the continent and encouraged relations with the First

Nations, whose centuries-old trading
routes and inland connections proved
vital to the trade's success. It also
helped shape the landscape of northern Québec, bringing with it not only
a network of trading posts but also an
intense, sometimes violent rivalry
between British fur traders, their
French-Canadian competitors, and
the First Nations. Although eclipsed
by manufacturing and other industries before the turn of the 20th century, the fur trade continues to play
an important economic role among
the Inuit of the Ungava Peninsula.

Home of the Timiskaming of the Algonquin Nation, the land became a European trading hub.

▶ FORT TÉMISCAMINGUE

DUHAMEL-OUEST, QC
Designated 1931

There's a place on Lake Timiskaming (Lac Témiscamingue) where the eastern shoreline protrudes like a fat fang, bringing it within 250 m (273 yd) of the western shore. Here, where the lake narrows dramatically, evidence of the early fur trade lies next to archaeological clues about how Indigenous Peoples lived here 5,000 years ago.

The Timiskaming, a band of the Algonquin Nation, called this place on Québec's western edge Obabjewong—which means "narrowed current." It turned out to be a natural site for a trading hub because it sat about halfway along the canoe route between Hudson Bay and the St. Lawrence River.

French settlers—keen to compete with English traders in Hudson Bay—first built a fort on this lake in 1679; however, the fort was destroyed just a few years later by the Iroquois, in 1688. In 1720, the French merchants picked up their hammers again and built Fort Témiscamingue on the shoreline's scenic tip. Eventually the fort was taken over by the

North West Company, which passed control to the Hudson's Bay Company (HBC) in 1821, when the two companies merged. Until it shut down the post in 1902, the HBC monopolized trade in this competitive, fur-rich region.

Marriages between French voyageurs (or their unlicensed brethren—the coureurs des bois) and Indigenous women in this region were common. According to the Timiskaming Métis Community Council, Métis families living around Timiskaming were deeply engaged in the fur trade: "The men in these families worked as voyageurs, guides, boat-builders, and carpenters. The women fished, hunted small game, cultivated, and produced beaded moccasins, mittens, and other items for the fur trade."

Indigenous and non-Indigenous relations were tested when Parks Canada accidentally uncovered a burial ground while working at Fort Témiscamingue in 1998. Algonquin (or Anishinabeg) occupied the site, development ceased, and the site closed for two years while Parks Canada and Algonquin communities negotiated a co-ownership plan. The park (fully) reopened in 2001, but as of February 2016 negotiations remain ongoing.

By 2007, Parks Canada had registered 125,500 artefacts from Euro-Canadian communities and 6,820 from Indigenous communities. Some of these artefacts are on display at the site's interpretive centre.

What to See & Do

Not much of the original fort remains standing, but follow a self-guiding visitor circuit to discover original artefacts and learn more about the fort's functions through interpretive panels and re-creations of trading post areas. The interpretive trail begins at the entrance gate.

After checking out the lakefront, head to the fortlike visitor centre. Inside, an impressionist mural sets the tone alongside shelves full of trading goods. Enter the exhibit room to retrace the history of the fur trade, or watch a screening of the 1964 documentary *The Voyageurs*.

Afterward, head to the woods. More than 80 percent of this several-hectares site is covered in trees. Admire the cedars and red pines scattered throughout the so-called "enchanted forest." Until June 2018, the forest will host 15 artworks by Christian Paquette made from wood materials and driftwood harvested from Lake Timiskaming.

INFORMATION

HOW TO REACH US
834 chemin du Vieux-Fort, Duhamel-Ouest, QC J9V 1N7. Phone (819) 629-3222. pc.gc.ca/temiscamingue.

ENTRANCE FEES
$3.90 per adult, $9.80 per family/group.

ACCESSIBLE SERVICES
Limited; contact the site for more details.

HOTELS, MOTELS, & INNS
Domaine TémiKami 128 rue Geneviève, Duhamel-Ouest Ville-Marie, QC J9V 1R2. (819) 629-3618. temikami.com/en/home. 15 rooms, $105. **Holiday Inn Express & Suites New Liskeard** 998029 Hwy. 11, New Liskeard, ON P0J 1P0. (705) 647-8282. 69 rooms, $156.

NORTHERN QUÉBEC

How to Get There

Fort Témiscamingue is about two hours north of the city of North Bay, Ontario. From North Bay, follow Ontario Rte. 63 and Québec Rte. 101 north to Chemin du Vieux-Fort in Duhamel-Ouest.

When to Go

This site is open from mid-June until early September

A fur trade exhibit along Lake Timiskaming

Interpreters in early 18th-century French uniforms patrol Fort Chambly's central courtyard.

SOUTHERN & EASTERN QUÉBEC

Modest mountains, plateaus, and beautiful plains characterize the fertile, mostly French-speaking region south of Montréal. Yet the idyllic setting—birthplace of Louis S. St. Laurent, Canada's 12th prime minister (see pp. 159–160)—belies the often violent history of this heavily contested area. The French began settling here in the early 17th century and, beginning with Samuel de Champlain, erected a series of forts to restrict the movement of the Iroquois and later to defend against British attack. During the American

Revolution (1775–1783) and the War
of 1812 (1812–1815), U.S. military forces
aimed to capture Montréal, and this
region witnessed several battles for
control of the city. Visitors can relive
the turbulent, complicated period at
Fort Chambly (see pp. 154–158), first
built by the French in 1665 and
exchanged several times by British
and American forces, and at Fort
Lennox (see pp. 148–151), erected on
an island in the Richelieu River. By
the mid-19th century, industry and
the labourious work of canal building
had taken the place of war.

British red coats line barracks walls at Fort Lennox.

▶ FORT LENNOX

SAINT-PAUL-DE-L'ÎLE-AUX-NOIX, QC

Designated 1920

Fort Lennox sits on Île aux Noix, a stunning patch of green in the middle of the Richelieu River, not far from the American border. The island was a seasonal hunting spot for Indigenous People, an important military theatre during the Seven Years' War and the War of 1812, and the location of a Second World War internment camp.

The French established the first fort on this tiny island in 1759. They'd been battling the British for five years and were still stinging from a significant loss at Québec City. By building fortifications on Île aux Noix, they hoped to fight off British advances on Montréal. The island's geography—with its narrow channels and elevated southern point—was ideal for a defensive stronghold.

When the British moved up the Richelieu River in August 1760, it was as part of a major three-pronged attack on Montréal. Brig. Gen. William Haviland led 3,400 British

troops up Lake Champlain. When they closed in on Île aux Noix, they found the French in a pretty bad state: outnumbered and lacking supplies, their fortifications incomplete. The British took the fort after a 12-day siege; the French had abandoned it, retreating for Montréal. Just over a week later, on September 8, 1760, the French surrendered Montréal to the British.

All was fairly quiet on Île aux Noix until 1775, when American forces occupied the island and used it as a base for an attack on Canada. A few months later, the Americans retreated to the island under the heat of a British counterattack, before withdrawing from the island altogether. In 1778, the British began fortifying the island in anticipation of further invasions.

During the War of 1812, the British were again moved to strengthen their position on the Richelieu. They established a shipyard on Île aux Noix and built a few warships. But when put to the test on Lake Champlain in the fall of 1814, their fleet proved no match for a stronger American fleet.

After this latest war, the Americans started building a large fort 15 km (9.3 mi) south of Île aux Noix. In response, the British built the stone fortifications seen today on the island between 1819 and 1829. They named the fort after Charles Lennox, a colonial administrator who, in 1818, recommended the fortifications on Île aux Noix be strengthened.

In subsequent decades, British forces used the fort as a base during the Rebellions of 1837–38 before eventually leaving the island in 1870.

The Canadian Militia used the site as a training ground until 1921. After that, Île aux Noix became a place for farming and summer getaways. And then, between 1940 and 1943, the island was converted to an internment camp (see below).

In the 1970s, the government began conserving and restoring the island's history in earnest.

ORIGINAL PEOPLE

The earliest evidence of Indigenous Peoples spending time on Île aux Noix dates back nearly 5,000 years ago. Clues turned up during archaeological digs suggest the island was more of a seasonal fishing and hunting spot than a permanent settlement. Experts hypothesize there was also a lot of trading activity here in the summer because found objects have their roots in different regions. These ancient artefacts—arrowheads, small stone knives, bits of pottery, and more—are not on permanent display, but some may be seen on certain summer tours.

"CAMP BOYS"

In 1940, Canada took in several thousand enemy aliens and prisoners of war at the request of Britain. What the two countries didn't realize at first was that 2,284 refugees from Nazism, most of them Jews, were included in the deportation. These men, many of them between the ages of 16 and 20, were sent to camps scattered throughout New Brunswick, Ontario, and Québec; 300 or so were sent to Camp "I" on Île aux Noix. When the British realized, shortly after sending these men, that they had made some crucial classification errors, they notified the Canadian government. But the government was slow to act and continued to intern some of these victims of the Holocaust behind barbed wire for as many as three years.

A reenactor shares drumming tips.

An exhibit in the officers' quarters relates the story of these refugees, dubbed "camp boys." In addition, there are video testimonials from some of the internees, describing their journeys from the frontlines of Europe to the interment camp on Île aux Noix.

EXPLORING THE FORT

It's easy to spend four or five hours at Fort Lennox. Try to arrive early, as the island is less busy in the morning. The five-minute ferry ride across the Richelieu River is just long enough to disconnect from the present world and prepare for a wonderfully immersive experience.

From the ferry dock, it's a two-minute walk to the fort, which sits on the southern part of the island. Consider starting with a guided tour, as the bulk of the activities are in the afternoon. That said, there are usually about five tours offered per day. The tours take in the powder magazine, the guardhouse, two warehouses, the officers' quarters, and the soldiers' barrack. All the buildings are preserved in their original state.

The soldiers' barrack in particular is worth seeing, and it is not hard to find: It is the longest and tallest building in the fort. The huge communal dorm room on the second floor is where British soldiers used to live along with their families. This room can only be seen on guided tours. It has been refurbished to look like it would have in 1833–35, when something like 60 British soldiers, 30 women, and 50 children lived here. The rows of bunk beds, neatly hung uniforms, muskets, ovens, and playing cards laid out on the long tables give a sense of the life of a 19th-century military family.

After the tour, spend time checking out the permanent exhibits about the interned refugees, the British officers, and the British engineers. Then consider having a picnic on the northern part of the island, under the shade of old deciduous trees. (Some food is available on-site, but it's advisable to bring a lunch.)

After lunch, consider joining one of the immersive tours, where visitors take on a new identity to role-play around the fort and are challenged to complete such fort tasks as loading one of the two historical cannon reproductions or reciting the steps required to fire a flintlock musket, and participate in the dreaded garrison inspection. Visitors who

Fort Lennox sits on Île aux Noix, in the Richelieu River.

FORT LENNOX NATIONAL HISTORIC SITE
(Lieu historique national du Fort-Lennox)

INFORMATION & ACTIVITIES

HOW TO REACH US
11 61e Ave., Saint-Paul-de-l'Île-aux-Noix, QC J0J 1G0. Phone (450) 291-5700. pc.gc.ca/fortlennox.

SEASONS & ACCESSIBILITY
Open late May to early October (open Mon.–Fri. May 23–June 21; daily June 22–Sept. 5; weekends and holidays Sept. 6–Oct. 10). The last crossing to the island leaves 75 minutes before closing time.

FRIENDS OF FORT LENNOX
1 61e Ave., Saint-Paul-de-l'Île-aux-Noix, QC J0J 1G0. (450) 291-3293.

ENTRANCE FEES
$7.80 per adult, $19.50 per family/group (includes ferry crossing). For visitors arriving in their own boat: $3.90 per adult, $9.80 per family/group.

PETS
Dogs on leashes are allowed in the park. Only guide dogs are allowed inside the fortifications (inside the museum).

ACCESSIBLE SERVICES
The ferry can only accommodate one wheelchair per crossing. On the island, the path is wheelchair accessible, and wheelchair-accessible washrooms are available at the fort and visitor centre. The barracks are not accessible. For more information, contact the visitor centre.

THINGS TO DO
Learn about the "real life of a soldier" from an interpreter dressed in a legendary Redcoat. Take part in a black powder musket-firing demonstration or try your hand at loading a cannon.

Learn about the women and children who lived alongside the soldiers of the British garrison. Discover heroic people who lived on Île aux Noix but had nothing to do with the military.

And enjoy the many quiet places around the island where you can disconnect from the digital world and reconnect with the natural one.

SPECIAL ADVISORIES
- Fishing on the banks of Île aux Noix is forbidden.
- Wood fires on the grounds of the national historic site are forbidden.

CAMPGROUNDS
Camping Grégoire 347 Rd. 221, Lacolle, QC J0J 1J0. (450) 246-3385. campinggregoire.com. $35–$45 per site. Wi-Fi available.

HOTELS, MOTELS, & INNS
(Rates are for a 2-person double, high season, in Canadian dollars, unless otherwise noted.)

Auberge Relay 4 Seasons Inn 579 Waterfront South, Noyan, QC J0J 1B0. (450) 294-2677 or (877) 294-2677. au4saisons.com. 18 rooms, $110–$120.

SOUTHERN & EASTERN QUÉBEC

---

complete their challenges get a reproduction of an 1831 British shilling to take home.

How to Get There

Fort Lennox is located at Saint-Paul-de-l'Île-aux-Noix, 60 km (37.3 mi) from Montréal and 12 km (7.5 mi) from the U.S. border. The parking area and information centre are in the village on the west shore of the Richelieu River. The ferry to Fort Lennox on Île aux Noix takes five minutes. Visitors may also take their own boat to the island, paying admission on arrival.

When to Go

July and August offer the most activities and programming. In fall, the crowds are thinner, the weather crisp, and the autumn colours vibrant.

Roots of Contemporary Canada

Many people think the story of Canada begins in 1867 with Canada's Confederation. Others point to 1759, when the British defeated the French in a decisive battle outside Québec City during the Seven Years' War. The resulting British-governed community of French descendants, called Canadiens, along with the long-established population of Indigenous Peoples, became the cornerstone of Canadian society.

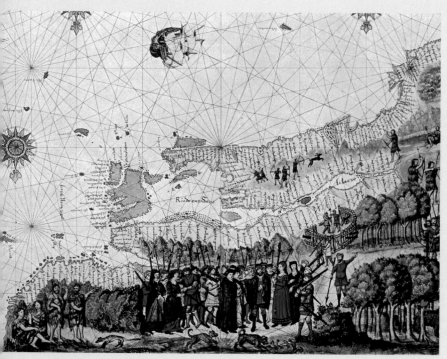

Lithograph of French explorer Jacques Cartier and colonists landing in Canada, 1547

But the story starts at least 13,000 years ago with the earliest Indigenous settlers. Not until the 1500s did Europeans begin arriving, starting with the French, who sent large numbers of colonists to North America. By the early 1700s, the territory of New France extended from Newfoundland to the Rocky Mountains and from Hudson Bay to the Gulf of Mexico. In 1763, when the Treaty of Paris ended the Seven Years' War, Great Britain gained control of most of this land.

In 1774, British governor Guy Carleton signed the Quebec Act, which guaranteed the Canadiens the right to practice Roman Catholicism and to use French civil law. However, the revolutionary Continental Congress in the American colonies denounced the Quebec Act as undemocratic. In 1776 Benjamin Franklin visited Montréal to help organize a revolutionary government, but he received a chilly welcome. With few exceptions, the Canadiens had no desire to renounce their religion, legal system, or culture.

The American colonies proceeded with their own revolution, and in 1778 Franklin secured the tide-turning support of the French Navy in Paris. When the British government decided in 1783 to recognize American independence, Carleton was furious. He tendered his resignation, but then agreed to oversee the evacuation of British Loyalists from the new United States to Canada, including thousands of former slaves.

Since 1775, when the British governor of Virginia proclaimed that slaves who fought the rebels would be freed, African Americans had been flocking to the Loyalist cause. Carleton had been helping them escape, mostly to Nova Scotia. These Black Loyalists had their names recorded in the *Book of Negroes*.

Between May 1782 and November 1783, battling pressure from the American patriots, Carleton evacuated some 30,000 troops and 27,000 Loyalist refugees to Canadian borders, including 3,500 African Americans. In 1783, George Washington demanded the return of all remaining escaped slaves. Carleton refused. Over the next few years, the northward exodus from the new United States continued as Loyalists experienced continued persecution. Many were people committed to maintaining their links with England and Scotland.

After 1783

The 1783 Peace of Paris ignored the contribution by Indigenous Peoples to the British cause. But Molly Johnson, the Iroquois widow of a British Indian agent for North America, persuaded four of the six Iroquois Nations to remain loyal to Britain. Her younger brother, Joseph Brant, who had been celebrated in London, followed her lead, and eventually secured a land grant for his people—now Brantford, Ontario.

The First Nations had long inhabited the lands that would become Canada, and would continue to play a key role, as would the first European settlers: the French. But after 1783, for the first time, a visible minority, the ex-African Americans, established a beachhead for multiculturalism. And down through the decades, Scottish refugees trickled into the east, and the new communities west of Québec would attract hundreds of thousands of English-speaking immigrants. Contemporary Canada was ready to be born.

— KEN MCGOOGAN

A uniformed guard on duty at Québec Citadel

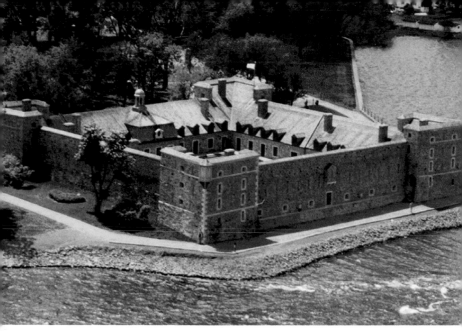

For three centuries Fort Chambly, on the Richelieu River, was central to defence in Canada.

▶ FORT CHAMBLY

CHAMBLY, QC
Designated 1920

Located on the banks of the scenic Richelieu River, Fort Chambly played defence often during the 17th, 18th, and 19th centuries. It had a role in the Iroquoian Wars, Anglo-French wars, American Revolution, and War of 1812.

Fort Chambly is well loved, and it bears the marks to prove it. The stonework in the fort's main entryway is inscribed with around 30 names of consequence to the fort's history: commanders, French officers who distinguished themselves in battle, and early explorers like Samuel de Champlain. Bougainville, Bourlamaque, Lévis, and Montcalm: These names and others were inscribed in 1883 by a local craftsman at the request of Joseph-Octave Dion, a Chambly resident who played a key role in preserving the fort.

With these inscriptions, Dion paid tribute to a site that saw its first fort go up in 1665. Visitors are often surprised to learn this first fort was actually made of wood. It was built by the Carignan-Salières Regiment, under the leadership of Capt. Jacques de Chambly. King Louis XIV of France sent this French contingent of soldiers to the colony at the request of New France residents. They wanted some help quashing the Iroquois League (Haudenosaunee Confederacy) in New France, as they found themselves repeatedly at war with the Iroquois during the last half of the 17th century.

Successful raids by the regiment's soldiers on Iroquois villages led to a peace agreement in 1667. After establishing this fragile peace with the league, hundreds of these French soldiers and officers settled in New

France (in fact, many place names in Québec reveal the influence of the regiment), with a few settling in Chambly. When relations between the Iroquois and the French soured again and hostilities renewed in the 1680s, Louis XIV sent Troupes de la Marine from France. These soldiers would form part of the permanent military force of Canada from 1683 until 1760. Like their predecessors in the Carignan-Salières Regiment, many of these men stayed in New France, helping to characterize the young and growing colony.

After many years, a new peace agreement—the Great Peace of Montréal—was signed in 1701 between the governor of New France, the Iroquois, and other First Nations. Afterward, the French soldiers began building a stone fort here in response to the threat of a British invasion. The huge square-shaped fortress they completed in 1711 was built to withstand rifle and cannon fire while ensuring no blind spots. Its prominent corner bastions and high curtain walls still stand today.

From 1760 to 1776, control of the fort bounced back and forth between nations: The British took it over during the Seven Years' War (in which France lost New France—also known as the Colony of Canada—to Britain), then the Americans during their war for independence from the British, and then the British again. During the War of 1812, the small community of Chambly was shaken up when the British strengthened the fort and stacked it with thousands of soldiers— ready for deployment in the war against the Americans. The fort itself was never attacked during the war.

In later years, Fort Chambly lost its strategic importance; it was left unoccupied in 1869.

A PASSIONATE MAN

If it were not for the passionate advocacy of Chambly resident and journalist Joseph-Octave Dion, Fort Chambly could be nothing but ashes and dust today. In 1854, an inspector had ruled against investing time or money into saving the disintegrating fort, and in 1869 the last troops pulled out, leaving the fort to crumble. Born in 1838, Dion grew up close to the fort; when he returned home to Chambly after spending several years in Montréal, he was reportedly alarmed to see the fort in such a sorry state.

Dion took it upon himself to mount a preservation campaign. In the 1870s, he laboured creatively to save the fort—fundraising, giving tours, lobbying politicians, and even publishing the first history of the fortification. In 1882, he succeeded in garnering some funding from the Department of Public Works to overhaul the fort. Then in 1886, Dion—who was living on the grounds of the fort—was made the fort's official guardian. He remained at the fort until his death in 1916.

BURIED TREASURES

In the mid-1970s, a lot of work went into restoring and enhancing Fort Chambly to its current appearance. At the same time, three seasons of intensive archaeological digs were carried out. These excavations turned up clues about everyday life—fragments of weapons, buttons, shoes, and so on—and about the way soldiers lived during the French era. Subtle differences in quality hint at class distinctions: No doubt the fine china belonged to the officers, whereas the soldiers ate their salted pork out of earthenware.

Interpreters in military uniform demonstrate soldiers' life in different eras.

A tent city grew outside the fort during the War of 1812.

A costumed interpreter greets guests.

Today, visitors can check out many of these artefacts in the fort's small museum, a series of rooms on the ground floor of a building that used to serve as barracks for the soldiers.

In the fort's courtyard, look for inlays of wood and concrete, outlining the original wood fort's stockade.

There's also evidence of two bakeries (bread was an important staple for soldiers). Finally, there's the mill: In 2011, maintenance workers accidentally discovered the foundations of a late 17th-century seigneurial mill. This was a place where farmers went to grind their wheat. Located at the heart of the seigneur's property, the fortified mill helped integrate the fort with the surrounding community.

EXPLORING THE GROUNDS

Begin any visit to Fort Chambly at the interpretation centre in the fort entrance. Here, visitors receive invaluable orientation to the site. In addition, a guide in period costume—and playing a character at the fort—will explain what it was like to live at the fort during the height of its military activity.

Next, proceed to the barracks, where visitors may hold examples of soldier weaponry. Another hands-on activity visitors may do in the barracks is attempt to master the antique scale to measure the daily rations of a French soldier (for example, 1½ French pounds of bread, ¼ French pound of salted pork, and ¼ French pound dried peas). After learning about what the soldiers ate, focus on what they wore: A guide takes visitors through the uniform—piece by piece—of a Troupe de la Marine.

In the soldiers' gallery, on the second floor of the barracks, the "Taste of Nouvelle-France" exhibit tantalizes the taste buds, offering tastings of the favourite dishes of French soldiers—like bread and chocolate. Stop at the machine that looks like a giant bubblegum dispenser to try a piece of dark chocolate, crafted from an 18th-century recipe. Note how it's bitter and a little spicy. On the way out, grab a leaflet full of historical recipes to try at home or add a family recipe to the international collection on the wall.

On a Discovery Tour visitors can learn about what it was like for the Carignan-Salières Regiment to build the first wooden fort at this site. What would they have eaten for breakfast? What tools did they use? Why build on this specific location? The guides can answer any question visitors may have.

After exploring the fort's grounds and buildings, take a walk in the wooded area around the site; enjoy the gorgeous scenery alongside the Richelieu River. Imagine the improvised tent city that sprang up here during the War of 1812, when British troops attacked Plattsburgh. Think about how this place might have looked when Champlain first sailed past, before the first fort was built. Interpretive panels throughout the park provide information that makes sense of the sights.

Reenactors give tours and perform military exercises.

SOUTHERN & EASTERN QUÉBEC

FORT CHAMBLY NATIONAL HISTORIC SITE
(Lieu historique national du Fort-Chambly)

INFORMATION & ACTIVITIES

HOW TO REACH US
2 rue De Richelieu, Chambly, QC J3L 2B9. Phone (450) 658-1585. pc.gc.ca/fort chambly.

SEASONS & ACCESSIBILITY
Open May 21 to October 10 (open daily June 22–Sept. 5; open Wed.–Sun. May 21–June 21 and Sept. 6–Oct. 10). The park closes at 11 p.m.

ENTRANCE FEES
$5.65 per adult, $14.20 per family/group per day; $67.70 per adult, $136.40 per family/group per year.

PETS
Pets must be leashed in the park and are not allowed inside the fort.

ACCESSIBLE SERVICES
This fort is fully accessible.

THINGS TO DO
Learn about the unique features of the fort by taking a tour. Watch reenactors perform military exercises in uniform and demonstrate how to fire a musket. Sign up for a culinary workshop. Explore the collection of centuries-old artefacts. Wander through the park.

SPECIAL ADVISORIES
• Fishing is forbidden close to the fort.
• Wood fires and barbecues are forbidden in the fort area.
• Swimming is forbidden.

CAMPGROUNDS
Domaine de Rouville 1925 chemin Rouville, Saint-Jean Baptiste, QC J0L 2B0. (450) 467-6867 or (866) 467-6867. domainederouville.com/en/. Has 1,800 sites for tent trailers, 150 sites for RVs, and 108 campsites (with water and electricity). Located at the foot of Mont Saint-Hilaire.

HOTELS, MOTELS, & INNS
(Rates are for a 2-person double, high season, in Canadian dollars, unless otherwise noted.)

Manoir Ramezay 492 rue Claude de Ramezay (Rte. 227), Marieville, QC J3M 1J6. (450) 460-3251 or (866) 460-3251. manoirramezay.com. 12 rooms and suites, $110–$140 for rooms.
Hôtel Objectif Santé 8665 chemin de Chambly, Saint-Hubert, QC J3Y 5K2. (450) 486-4816. hotelobjectifsante.com. $120–$140.

With more time on hand, consider biking or strolling alongside the Chambly Canal (see pp. 160–161). A bike trail—the canal's former towpath—runs from Fort Chambly all the way to Saint-Jean-sur-Richelieu.

How to Get There
Fort Chambly is about 30 km (18.6 mi) east of Montréal, via Hwy. 10E. Take exit 22 to Chambly and then follow the signs for Chambly. In Chambly, take Fréchette Boulevard to Bourgogne Street and turn right. The fort will be on the left (not too far after the bridge).

When to Go
In July and August, Fort Chambly brims with costumed guides: women wearing wide-brimmed sun hats and modest, long-sleeved blouses, and men dressed as 17th-century soldiers of the Carignan-Salières Regiment, among many other period interpreters. On summer weekends, reenactors at the national historic site perform a swivel-gun firing demonstration.

The site is popular in the summer; to avoid crowds of people, consider visiting in the spring and fall shoulder seasons.

The general store owned by the family of Canada's 12th prime minister, Louis S. St. Laurent

▶ LOUIS S. ST. LAURENT COMPTON, QC

Designated 1973

Louis S. St. Laurent, Canada's 12th prime minister, had what seems like an idyllic childhood. The oldest of seven children, he grew up speaking English with his mother and French with his father in a valley rich with rivers, south of Sherbrooke.

St. Laurent was born in 1882 in Compton; his family's home and adjacent general store were at the centre of the village's social world. At that time, a growing number of French speakers from other parts of Québec were settling in the eastern townships and changing their cultural character.

St. Laurent earned an impressive education despite his family's modest means. He passed a tough admission exam for Sherbrooke seminary and then went on to study at Laval University, where he mastered both the French Civil Code and British Common Law.

He found success in both commercial and constitutional law, eventually catching the eye of Prime Minister William Lyon Mackenzie King—who lured him into politics. St. Laurent worked as the justice minister during the Second World War and then as secretary of state for external affairs. He then succeeded King as prime minister and head of the Liberal Party, serving from 1948 to 1957.

After a decade spent developing social policies, joining defensive international alliances (NATO), and welcoming Newfoundlanders into the fold, St. Laurent retired. He died in 1973 at the age of 91. Today, the Compton home and store his parents bought in 1881 still stand, along with a small shed and a number of archaeological remnants.

What to See & Do

Authentic originals and reproductions abound on the St. Laurent property. Browse the neatly stacked vintage goods at the general store St. Laurent's father kept in Compton, including whalebone corsets and chamber pots. Afterward, visit the store's warehouse for a 20-minute multimedia show about Louis S. St. Laurent and take a tour of his childhood home, where more than 2,500 of the family's objects are on display.

How to Get There

Travelling from Montréal, take Hwy. 10E toward Sherbrooke. Take exit 121 and head south on Hwy. 55; then take exit 21 and go south on Rte. 141. At Ayer's Cliff, take Rte. 208 east to Compton.

When to Go

The site is open late June through late September, Wednesday to Sunday (and holidays).

INFORMATION

HOW TO REACH US
6790 Louis S. St. Laurent Rte., Compton, QC J0B 1L0. Phone (819) 835-5448. pc.gc.ca/stlaurent.

ENTRANCE FEES
$3.90 per adult, $9.80 per family/group.

ACCESSIBLE SERVICES
Limited accessibility.

HOTELS, MOTELS, & INNS
Auberge Le Bocage 200 chemin Moe's River (Rte. 208E), Compton, QC J0B 1L0. (819) 835-5653. lebocage.qc.ca. 4 rooms, $125-$250. Closed Mondays.

The only operating historic canal, Chambly has eight retractable bridges.

▶ CHAMBLY CANAL

CHAMBLY, QC

Designated 1929

The Richelieu River was an important transportation route into and out of the interior, and men tired of the labourious portaging required to bypass rapids dreamed of a canal on the river's left bank, southeast of Montréal. In the 19th century, this vision was slowly realized.

Work on the canal began in 1831 but was interrupted in 1834 by a lack of funds. Construction resumed in 1841, and the 20-km (12.4 mi) canal from Chambly to Saint-Jean-sur-Richelieu was completed by 1843. The project had important economic implications because the Richelieu was a major thoroughfare for timber traffic, carrying wood from the shores of Lake Champlain to Québec City, a centre of shipbuilding.

Living conditions for the canal workers were harsh. An estimated 500 to 1,000 diggers, masons, blacksmiths, and carpenters would get up at 5 a.m. to haul wheelbarrows full of earth and blow up rocks using gunpowder. They would get an hour for lunch and one for dinner. After getting off work at 7 p.m., these mostly immigrant workers would retire to 3.5-by-3.5-m (11.5 by 11.5 ft) huts, each crammed with a dozen men.

Today, the Chambly Canal is the only working component of Québec's historic canals network that has retained its original route, buildings, and turn-of-the-20th-century operating mechanisms, including 8 of the canal's 10 retractable bridges.

What to See & Do

The 20-km (12.4 mi) path that parallels the canal—the former towpath for horses pulling barges loaded with merchandise—is perfect for biking. Along the way, explore the locks, bridges, and quaint lockmasters' houses.

Summer visitors can also cruise the length of the canal via pleasure boat or kayak. During winter, enjoy a skate on the 400-m (0.25 mi) stretch of ice between Bridge No. 1, located on Bourgogne Avenue, and Lock No. 4, or don snowshoes for a trek along the canal pathway.

Kiosks at either end of the canal, run by the Friends of the Chambly

INFORMATION

HOW TO REACH US
Phone (888) 773-8888. pc.gc.ca/chamblycanal.
Locks Nos. 1-3 (Chambly area) 1751 Bourgogne Ave., Chambly, QC.
Lock No. 9 (Saint-Jean-sur-Richelieu area) 327 rue Champlain, Saint-Jean-sur-Richelieu, QC.

ENTRANCE FEES
None. $3.90 for parking. Contact the site for lockage fees.

ACCESSIBLE SERVICES
Limited; contact the site for more details.

HOTELS, MOTELS, & INNS
Auberge Harris 576 rue Champlain, Saint-Jean-sur-Richelieu, QC J3B 6X1. (450) 348-3821 or (800) 668-3821. aubergeharris.com. 48 rooms and 29 suites, $109–$194.
By boat: Take advantage of the overnight mooring service offered at several locations along the canal. Contact the lock operators through VHF-canal 68 during operating hours.

Canal, provide information about the canal and bike and kayak rentals.

How to Get There

The canal runs the length of Rte. 223. To get to Locks Nos. 1, 2, and 3, take exit 22 off Hwy. 10 and follow the signs for Chambly. To reach Lock No. 9 in Saint-Jean-sur-Richelieu, take exit 43 off Hwy. 35; then take Macdonald Street to Champlain Street and turn right. Lock No. 9 will be on the left.

When to Go

The canal is open year-round. The path is maintained from April 15 to November 15. The lockages schedule varies seasonally; call (450) 658-4381 for times.

ONTARIO

An interpreter leads a lantern-lit stroll at Fort Malden. *Page 162:* Retiring colours at Fort George (top); taps at Fort Henry Hill (middle); John MacDonald's Bellevue House (bottom) *Page 163:* Rideau Canal and Parliament

ONTARIO

Ontario has the largest population of any Canadian province, with more than half its residents living around one of several large urban centres, including Toronto, the provincial capital (and Canada's largest urban area), and Ottawa, the national capital. Its name comes from a Huron word for "beautiful water." Once covered by glaciers, Ontario is now laced with more than 250,000 lakes and accounts for about a third of the world's fresh water supply.

When the French arrived in the 17th century, the Indigenous Peoples in the region included nomadic Algonquian in the north and more settled Iroquois in the south. The British followed in the late 1750s and, in 1764, defeated the French and their allies to secure their position in the region. During the American Revolution (1775–1783), Britain used the Great Lakes area as a base of operations and, after the war,

established the first large, permanent settlement here as a home for the 6,000 to 10,000 Loyalists who fled to the area from the United States. Over the next century, large numbers of immigrants from the United States and Britain followed.

In 1791, the British Parliament passed the Constitutional Act, which created the provinces of Upper Canada (southern Ontario) and Lower Canada (southern and eastern Québec); the two provinces were united as the Province of Canada in 1841. At the time of Confederation in 1867, the Province of Canada was again divided, this time into the provinces of Ontario and Québec, which along with New Brunswick and Nova Scotia became the four original provinces of the Dominion of Canada. By then, Ontario had emerged as the nation's dominant manufacturer, a distinction the province continues to hold today.

National Historic Site (NHS)
Country capital city
Province capital city

Billings House,
Central Experimental Farm,
Château Laurier,
Laurier House,
Parliament Buildings,
Rideau Hall and Landscaped Grounds,
Royal Canadian Mint,
Victoria Memorial Museum

Diefenbunker/Central Emergency
Government Headquarters

Rideau Canal

Trent-Severn
Waterway

Peterborough
Lift Lock

Fort York,
George Brown House,
Gooderham and Worts Distillery,
Kensington Market,
Maple Leaf Gardens,
University College

O N T A R I O

Q U É B E C

Sault Ste.
Marie Canal

Fort St. Joseph

Ottawa

Bethune
Memorial House
Saint-Louis Mission
Mnjikaning Fish Weirs

Dundurn Castle,
?and Lee (Museum) Home,
HMCS Haida,
John Weir Foote Armoury,
Royal Botanical Gardens

Point Clark
Lighthouse

Toronto

Woodside

Butler's Barracks,
Fort George,
Fort Mississauga,
Hamilton and Scourge,
?ssissauga Point Lighthouse,
Navy Island,
Niagara Apothecary,
Niagara-on-the-Lake,
Queenston Heights,
Willowbank

Southwold
Earthworks

Bois Blanc Island
Lighthouse
and Blockhouse,
Fort Malden

Ann Baillie Building,
Bellevue House,
Fort Henry,
Kingston City Hall,
Kingston Fortifications,
Murney Tower

Merrickville Blockhouse

ONTARIO

0 mi   200

0 km   200

Battle of the Windmill,
Fort Wellington

Changing of the Guard, Parliament Buildings, Ottawa, Ontario

OTTAWA & KINGSTON

Canada's capital city, Ottawa sits on the Ottawa River in eastern Ontario. When the French first arrived here in the early 17th century, the Algonquian controlled the river, a key component of the fur trade and burgeoning timber industry. Less than 50 years later, they had lost their influence, overwhelmed by diseases like smallpox and further weakened by regular conflict with the Iroquois. Founded by the British in 1826, Ottawa served as a base for the construction of the Rideau Canal (see pp. 168–171), which connects Ottawa and the Lake Ontario

port town of Kingston, about 175 km (109 mi) southwest.

Loyalist refugees flocked to Kingston after the American Revolution, and the city's population and economy grew during the War of 1812. But Kingston's importance declined in the late 19th century after British military forces left and railroads began diverting commercial traffic away from the canal. Kingston boasts nearly 30 national historic sites, including Bellevue House (see pp. 172–175), a home of Canada's first prime minister, Sir John A. Macdonald.

The 202-km (126 mi) Rideau Canal runs past Ottawa's Parliament Hill (left).

▶ RIDEAU CANAL OTTAWA/KINGSTON, ON

Designated 1925; Inscribed WH 2007

An incredible feat of engineering, the Rideau Canal runs for 202 km (126 mi) through Ontario, winding from Kingston in the south to Ottawa in the north. A series of 45 locks at 24 lock stations allows boaters to easily navigate the lakes, rivers, and waters that are part of the canal.

In the early 1800s, tensions remained between Great Britain and the newly independent United States. The St. Lawrence River, which was necessary for shipping and transportation, lay exposed, a fact the British became acutely aware of during the War of 1812. The Americans already had an advantage: Much of the river's southern shore was on American soil.

After the war, the British government directed surveyors to map and plot potential safer routes from Montréal to the Great Lakes across the wilderness of eastern Ontario from the Ottawa River to Kingston on Lake Ontario. Plans were drawn up for a series of dams and locks that would open the corridor to much larger

boats. These lock sizes were, at a minimum, 41 m (134 ft) long and 10 m (33 ft) wide—the size of the steamboats that were starting to be used on the lakes. Plans were also made to establish fortified lockmaster houses and blockhouses at lock stations deemed especially vulnerable.

Work began in 1827. Many of the locks were built from stone quarried near the waterway (much of which passed through pure wilderness), with iron components forged by nearby blacksmiths. The entire process was contracted out to private firms and resulted in work for many individuals. Many of the labourers who had the most difficult jobs (hand-digging the pits for the locks and hauling quarried stone) were French Canadians or new arrivals from Ireland.

The canal officially opened in 1832. However, scandal marred the celebration. The canal ended up costing £800,000, well over the original estimate of £169,000. Despite the incredible feat of engineering, pushing a canal through the rocky terrain of eastern Upper Canada, the British government expressed shock at the final price and launched an investigation into expenditures. At the centre of the controversy was the man in charge of construction, Lt. Col. John By of the Corps of Royal Engineers. Though By was eventually found innocent of financial mismanagement, the controversy overshadowed his accomplishment.

Initially, the canal was a busier waterway than the St. Lawrence River. Its heyday ended in 1850, when new locks had subdued some of the more difficult rapids along the St. Lawrence, opening up the more direct route from Montréal to the Great Lakes.

Despite the downturn in shipping traffic, the canal remained a significant system for transportation through the First World War, after which the commercial traffic almost completely disappeared and the only thing that kept the canal from being dismantled was the cost of doing so.

But even as its commercial purpose was fading, the Rideau Canal was gaining new life as a recreational route. The canal passes through beautiful natural landscapes, with waterways that offer fishing, swimming, and the opportunity for recreational boating, something recreationists began taking notice of even before the end of the 19th century. Inscribed on the UNESCO World Heritage List in 2007, the canal now attracts thousands of visitors each year.

NATURAL LANDSCAPE

The gorgeous scenery through which the canal traverses is largely responsible for its 20th-century resurgence as a highly trafficked waterway, popular among cottagers, campers, and Sunday drivers. The landscape varies: limestone plains, with shallow soil and exposed limestone; rugged Canadian Shield; and the Napanee Plain—another broad expanse of exposed limestone surface.

Additionally, the draining and alterations carried out to create the canal resulted in perfect conditions for fish, including largemouth bass. The canal is home to one of Canada's most diverse fish communities as well as vast wetlands that are home to 42 rare plant and animal species.

Although the ecosystem is healthy, it has experienced ecological stress as a result of fishing, boating, and shore development. Parks Canada staff maintain an inventory of species considered to be at risk, endangered, and of special concern. Visitors are asked to aid in this data collection. They can do so by recording when and where they see animals such as the threatened Blanding's turtle, the southern flying squirrel, and the broad beech fern. Contact Parks Canada to find out which animals they're keeping an eye out for. Pick up official observation forms at visitor centres, or simply email the findings to the site.

LOCK STATIONS

Each of the 24 lock stations along the Rideau has its own draws and attractions, but the Ottawa locks are especially impressive. Here, eight locks step down the canal at the foot of

OTTAWA & KINGSTON

Parliament Hill, the seat of the federal government of Canada. In winter, the canal just to the south of the locks is full of people on ice skates, some recreationally and some, believe it or not, commuting to work! The nearby visitor centre offers canoe tours May through October (613-237-2309; fee). The 90-minute trips are taken in reproduction voyageur canoes (each measuring 8.3 m/27 ft in length) provided by the Canadian Canoe Museum. Each canoe accommodates up to 10 people. No experience is necessary: Trained guides are on hand to do all the paddling and navigation, as well as answer

The canal is a recreational haven.

Ice-skating near Parliament Hill is a winter tradition.

questions about the canal. Call the visitor centre to reserve a spot.

The Hogs Back Lock Station is another popular site because it's right next to Hog's Back Park—an urban park in Ottawa that offers access to waterfalls and green space in the city.

Burritts Rapids is notable for featuring the Tip to Tip Trail in addition to a lock station. Interpretive panels along this easy 2-km (1.2 mi) walking trail highlight features important to the construction of the canal. Merrickville, Jones Falls, and Kingston Mills also offer hiking opportunities.

At Jones Falls, the short but rugged Basin (Smithy) Trail crosses bedrock. It's an eye-opening experience, not only for the sights (towering white pine, red and white oak, and hemlock) but also for the thought that this was the kind of landscape workers had to blast through in the construction of the canal. Here, too, is the Redpath Trail, a roughly 1-km (0.6 mi) path that passes the lock, visitor centre, and wooded areas illustrative of the area's vegetation, such as the northernmost stand of pitch pine in North America near the dam.

The Smiths Falls lock features the canal's flagship interpretive centre. Many of the canal's lock stations have visitor centres, but Smiths Falls' is the largest. A former stone mill, the building is home to four floors of exhibits that highlight the life and legacy of the canal. Visitors can view such artefacts as replica Durham boats (the large wooden freighters used on the canal in the 1800s) and steamboats, and stand at a lookout where the Smiths Falls locks and impressive hydraulics system are in full view. There are also antique tools used in the construction of the canal, including an auger machine, compass, mason's mallets and chisels, stonecutting tools, and reproduction

RIDEAU CANAL NATIONAL HISTORIC SITE
(Lieu historique national du Canal-Rideau)

INFORMATION & ACTIVITIES

HOW TO REACH US
34 Beckwith St. S, Smiths Falls, ON K7A 2A8. Phone (613) 283-5170. pc.gc.ca /rideau.
   Many of the lock stations have a visitor centre, but the historic site's main visitor centre is in Smith Falls (address above).

SEASONS & ACCESSIBILITY
The lock stations are open daily May 20 to Labour Day, but with shorter hours Monday through Thursday compared to Friday, weekends, and holidays; open daily after Labour Day until Thanksgiving, with shorter hours Monday through Friday. Call for exact times.

FRIENDS OF THE RIDEAU
P.O. Box 1232, Stn. Main, Smiths Falls, ON K7A 5C7. rideaufriends.com/index.html.

ENTRANCE FEES
None.

PETS
Pets are permitted on-site, but they must be on a leash no longer than 3 m (9.8 ft) or kept in a cage or enclosure.

ACCESSIBLE SERVICES
Those in need of assistance with accessibility at any of the sites on the Rideau Canal can call Parks Canada operations staff to make accommodations at (613) 283-5170.

THINGS TO DO
Across the various lock stations on the canal, there are plenty of activities including camping, swimming, paddling, and hiking. Interpretive signage along hiking trails gives context to the surroundings. A number of visitor centres provide a comprehensive overview of the construction and significance of the canal system.

CAMPGROUNDS
Wesley Clover Parks Campground 411 Corkstown Rd., Ottawa, ON K2K 0J5. (613) 828-6632. wesleycloverparks.com. $30–$41.

HOTELS, MOTELS, & INNS
(Rates are for a 2-person double, high season, in Canadian dollars, unless otherwise noted.)

Best Western Colonel by Inn Smiths Falls 88 Lombard St., Smiths Falls, ON K7A 4G6. (613) 284-0001. smithsfallshotel .com. 40 rooms, $120–$150.
Rogers Motel 178 Lombard St., Smiths Falls, ON K7A 5B8. (613) 283-5200. rogers motel.ca. 16 rooms, $70–$90.
Tay Inn 125 Dufferin St., Perth, ON K7H 3A5. (613) 267-3300. tayinn.ca. 18 rooms, $99–$120.

OTTAWA & KINGSTON

surveying tools. One of the most interesting pieces is the journal of John Johnston, lockmaster at Merrickville from 1836 to 1869.
   Parks Canada–managed oTENTik accommodations—a hybrid cabin-tent—are available at Smith Falls, Upper Nicholsons, Upper Brewers, and Beveridges stations.

How to Get There
There are 24 lock stations along the canal, with some in cities, including Smiths Falls, Ottawa, Merrickville, and Jones Falls. Addresses for all locks can be found on the website.

When to Go
To see the gates and lifts in action, visit during the summer months (the locks are open mid-May through Thanksgiving in October). This is also peak camping season, and when most programming at various visitor centres takes place. Fall is beautiful for the changing leaves in this part of the province. Try for the end of September to get the best show of colour.

The designer of the early 1840s Bellevue House eschewed the Georgian style then popular in favour of the Italianate.

▶ BELLEVUE HOUSE

KINGSTON, ON
Designated 1995

Bellevue House sits on a lush, landscaped lot in Kingston's historic Western Liberties suburb. This green-and-white villa, a prime example of Italianate architecture, was briefly the home of Sir John A. Macdonald (1815–1891), Canada's first prime minister.

Though the house's architecture is notable, Macdonald's association with the house adds to its historic status. Macdonald lived here with his family for just over a year, from 1848 to 1849. Decades later, in 1867, Macdonald played a key role in bringing together Ontario, Québec, New Brunswick, and Nova Scotia as the Dominion of Canada.

Macdonald came to Canada from Scotland when he was five years old. His family settled in Kingston, living above the general store run by his father. As Macdonald grew up, so too did the city. In the 1820s, Kingston's population reached 3,000, making it a significant settlement in what was then Upper Canada.

When Macdonald turned 15, he began formal training to become a lawyer. Just five years later, he had a popular practice in the city. At the time, it was a natural progression for him to move from law into politics. In 1843, Macdonald ran for alderman in Kingston.

But Macdonald was already thinking beyond the city, and planning to become Kingston's representative to the Legislative Assembly of the Province of Canada. In the 1840s, Canada was a mere colony, encompassing parts of the countryside now known as Ontario and Québec. The province was run by a governor general, who was guided and informed by the Legislative Assembly.

The conservative Macdonald was elected to the assembly in 1844, with just a year's experience as alderman.

Macdonald was a new husband then, too, having married his wife, Isabella, in 1843.

Isabella is why the Macdonalds moved to Bellevue House. Afflicted with a never identified chronic illness, she had a terrible cough that wasn't helped by living in dirty downtown Kingston. So Macdonald began searching for cleaner, quieter accommodations for his bride and their new baby.

When he found Bellevue House, a mile from the city, it seemed the perfect respite. Surrounded by trees, with beautiful views and a constant breeze off Lake Ontario, the small family was happy there for a while. Tragically, Macdonald's one-year-old son died just a month into their stay. Still, he and Isabella remained, and Macdonald travelled into work every day while Isabella managed the household with the help of servants.

They were able to maintain this lifestyle for a year before expenses started piling up. A house that size, with a team of servants, became too much for Macdonald. It didn't help that Macdonald was also supporting his mother and additional family living in the city.

Eventually, the Macdonalds moved back to downtown Kingston, but tragedy followed them there as well. Isabella died in 1857, just as Macdonald's political star was rising even higher. Just 10 years later, he would realize his greatest achievement—helping advance confederation.

The concept of a united Canada wasn't one Macdonald was initially excited about, but as the colonies became more and more difficult to govern, he appreciated the idea of a cohesive country—a unified collection of colonies that operated on the same principles of peace, order, and good government.

Macdonald was one of a number of delegates who went to the Charlottetown Conference in 1864, where he spoke passionately and persuasively in favour of union. He did it again in Québec City later that year, arguing that a central government would give strength to all the British North American colonies. His pitch and personality played a big part in leading to the official Confederation of Canada on July 1, 1867. Macdonald was knighted by Queen Victoria for his efforts, and became the country's first prime minister.

THE HOUSE

Bellevue House was built in the Italianate architectural style by a Kingston merchant in the early 1840s. It was notable at the time for its departure in style from the more popular Georgian style, not only within Kingston but also within Canada as a whole. This fame wasn't necessarily positive, though, as Kingston's conservative populace felt that the house's design was pompous.

Nowadays Bellevue House is recognized in a more positive light—as an Italianate villa that serves as a rare

OTTAWA & KINGSTON

Bellevue is furnished in period decor.

example of this kind of architectural design in British North America. The unique colour combination of green-and-white siding, along with the elaborate exterior details (such as the scalloped fringe along the eaves, the columned veranda, and the balustrades), make the house stand out against its beautiful natural surroundings.

Just as much thought was put into the interior design. Bellevue House was built facing the south so that Lake Ontario would be visible from all the major rooms, including the drawing room, dining room, master bedroom, and the study, where Macdonald regularly retired to read and work in privacy. This orientation had the added bonus of filling each room with sunlight most of the day.

Guided tours (fee) of the house provide further insight into much of the house, which inside and out has been painstakingly re-created to the era when the Macdonalds lived here. The rooms are furnished with local period pieces (including four-poster beds, antique writing tables, and more) and a handful of artefacts that even belonged to the Macdonald family: a cradle, a travelling trunk, French and English dictionaries, and a set of the then popular Waverly

novels—a series of historical stories about Scotland.

HISTORIC GARDENS

The grounds at Bellevue House were as much a consideration for Macdonald as the house itself. Today, they look much the same way as they would have while the Macdonalds lived here, including the 0.2 ha (half acre) vegetable garden that yielded produce Isabella would have stored in the house's two root cellars.

The gardening practices are also true to the 1840s. The on-site gardeners refer almost exclusively to such decades-old guides as George Johnson's *Kitchen Garden* and J. J. Thomas's *Fruit Culturist*.

The grass at Bellevue is hand-cut using a scythe rather than a lawnmower, which accounts for its slightly ragged appearance. In the vegetable gardens, New Jersey tea, five-leaf akebia, devil's claw, and Moldavian balm are mixed in among the squash and other more recognizable species. These heritage varieties (or similar counterparts) add to the authenticity of the gardens.

The working gardeners wear period and task-specific work clothing, with broad-brimmed straw hats, heavy cotton work pants held up by leather suspenders for the men, and floor-length dresses for the women. The clothes may be for show, but the gardeners' efforts are not. These gardens produce several hundred pounds of vegetables each year, all of which goes to feed needy families by way of meal programs and community initiatives.

The vegetable garden is just one of three main components to the gardens at Bellevue House. The ornamental gardens cover the largest area. Walking through them, visitors

Bellevue's historically accurate vegetable garden

BELLEVUE HOUSE NATIONAL HISTORIC SITE
(Lieu historique national de la Villa-Bellevue)

INFORMATION & ACTIVITIES

HOW TO REACH US
35 Centre St., Kingston, ON K7L 4E5. Phone (613) 545-8666. pc.gc.ca/bellevue.

SEASONS & ACCESSIBILITY
Bellevue House is open daily July 1 (Canada Day) to Labour Day (first Monday in September), and Thursday through Monday Victoria Day weekend (last Monday before May 25) to July 1 and Labour Day to Thanksgiving (second Monday in October).

ENTRANCE FEES
$3.90 per adult, $9.80 per family/group.

PETS
Service dogs only.

ACCESSIBLE SERVICES
Bellevue House has wheelchair-accessible parking. The visitor centre is fully accessible and videos are captioned. A lift provides wheelchair access to the house's main floor. Paths through the gardens and grounds are also wheelchair accessible.

THINGS TO DO
Bellevue House is largely self-guided. Tour the grounds and take in the elaborate gardens. Visit the house and see artefacts from the year Sir John A. Macdonald spent living here with his wife, Isabella. Costumed interpreters are available to answer questions and help navigate the sprawling estate.

For kids ages 6 to 11, the site offers the Xplorers program; activities booklets, included with admission, make a bingo game out of spotting flora and fauna, and encourage kids to seek out various sights and demonstrations.

CAMPGROUNDS
Rideau Acres 1014 Cunningham Rd., Kingston, ON K7L 4V3. (613) 546-2711. rideauacres.com. $35–$52.

HOTELS, MOTELS, & INNS
(Rates are for a 2-person double, high season, in Canadian dollars, unless otherwise noted.)

Green Acres Inn 2480 Princess St., Kingston, ON K7M 3G4. (613) 546-1796. greenacresinn.com. 32 rooms, $129–$249.
Hotel Belvedere 141 King St. E., Kingston, ON K7L 2Z9. (613) 548-1565. hotelbelvedere.com. 19 rooms, $129–$199.
Residence Inn by Marriott Kingston Water's Edge, 7 Earl St., Kingston, ON K7L 0A5. (613) 544-4888. marriottresidenceinnkingston.com. 141 rooms, $200–$230.

OTTAWA & KINGSTON

will notice tall hardwoods planted in grassy lawns. A gazebo serves as a picturesque mount from which to admire planted beds.

The sweet-smelling orchard, the third component, is full of trees bearing heritage apple varieties, including Northern Spy, Russet, Tolman Sweet, and Baldwin.

How to Get There
Travelling via Hwy. 401, exit at Sir John A. Macdonald Blvd. (exit 615) and follow it south 5.5 km (3.4 mi) to Union Street. Turn left on Union and then right on Centre Street.

When to Go
Bellevue House closes for the winter months. Guided tours, themed historic dinners, and more are scheduled regularly between spring and fall. For the grounds, each season has its appeal: In spring, trees bloom in the apple orchards; during summer, the ornamental gardens spill over with a variety of flowers; and come fall, the trees and the harvest in the vegetable gardens make for a riotous show of colour. On Canada Day, admission is free, and visitors can expect games, tours, and refreshments.

Fort Wellington was a strategically important British garrison on the St. Lawrence River.

▶ FORT WELLINGTON

PRESCOTT, ON
Designated 1920

Built during the War of 1812, Prescott's Fort Wellington was to defend the St. Lawrence River, a significant shipping route, from attack by the United States. Today, the fort stands as one of the best preserved sites of its era.

Founded in 1810, Prescott was a significant port on the St. Lawrence River—one that linked Montréal and the Great Lakes. This made it a clear target for American forces, which, if successful in capturing the town, would have been able to cut off British shipping routes from the rest of Upper Canada. During the War of 1812, Fort Wellington served as home base for Prescott troops when they attacked and captured Ogdensburg, New York. Later, during the raids that followed the 1837 Rebellion in Upper Canada, this was the garrison for the soldiers who fought in the Battle of the Windmill in 1838 (see p. 179).

What to See & Do

Fort Wellington, with its imposing three-storey stone blockhouse looking down on the waterfront and 200-plus-year-old cannons on the ramparts that are still fired ceremonially today, can be self-guided. Visitors may interact with costumed interpreters, who bring the fort's history to life. Explore the fully furnished officers' quarters as well as the blockhouse (the largest of its kind in Canada), where soldiers lived with their families. Other buildings to peek into include the latrine, cookhouse, and guardhouse.

The fort hosts regular events and activities, such as rifle demonstrations. For an additional fee, Fort Wellington's cannon program will let visitors light the fuse on the fort's 19th-century muzzle-loading cannon. Kids' programming blends Canadian culture and heritage. Special events offered include Canada Day celebrations (complete with a traditional cannon firing) and the guided whiskey tastings that are a nod to the number of Scottish soldiers who were posted at the fort.

How to Get There

From Hwy. 401, take exit 716 to Edward Street. Turn left at off-ramp to head south on Edward Street. Turn left on King Street and left again on Vankoughnet Street.

When to Go

High season at the fort runs from Victoria Day weekend (the last Monday before May 25) to Thanksgiving (the second Monday in October). During this time, the site is open daily, offering a full slate of tours and activities.

INFORMATION

HOW TO REACH US
370 Vankoughnet St., Prescott, ON K0E 1T0. Phone (613) 925-2896. pc.gc.ca/wellington.

ENTRANCE FEES
$3.90 per adult, $9.80 per family/ group.

ACCESSIBLE SERVICES
The grounds and visitor centre are accessible; the blockhouse is not.

HOTELS, MOTELS, & INNS
Dewar's Inn on the River 1649 Cty. Rd. 2 RR#1, Prescott, ON K0E 1T0. (613) 925-3228. dewarsinnonthe river.com. 12 rooms and 5 cottages, $70–$95.

Two Canadian prime ministers called Laurier House home during their years of service, Laurier and King.

▶ LAURIER HOUSE

OTTAWA, ON
Designated 1956

Located in Sandy Hill, an upper-class neighbourhood in Canada's capital, Laurier House is a beautiful Second Empire–style yellow brick building with a wraparound veranda. It was the private residence of two prime ministers before there was an official prime ministerial address.

Wilfred Laurier, the country's first French prime minister, purchased the 1870s house in 1897, when his role as prime minister required him to live in Ottawa. He remained in the house until his death in 1919. When his wife died in 1921, she left the house to William Lyon Mackenzie King, who succeeded Laurier as head of the Liberal Party from 1919 to 1948. King would serve as prime minister for almost 22 of those years, the country's longest serving leader.

What to See & Do

Visitors may self-guide around the house and grounds, or join a White Glove Tour (fee) to see the private quarters of the Lauriers and explore off-limits areas. An interactive kitchen exhibit focuses on Canada's food rules, nutrition, and rationing during the Second World War.

How to Get There

From Hwy. 417 East, exit at Mann Avenue. Go to King Edward Avenue and head south to Rideau Street. Turn left on Rideau, and then make a right on Chapel Street; Laurier House sits at the corner of Chapel and Laurier East.

INFORMATION

HOW TO REACH US
335 Laurier Ave. E, Ottawa, ON K1N 6R4. Phone (613) 992-8142. pc.gc.ca/laurierhouse.

ENTRANCE FEES
$3.90 per adult, $9.80 per family/group.

ACCESSIBLE SERVICES
Only the visitor centre is accessible.

HOTELS, MOTELS, & INNS
Albert House Inn 478 Albert St., Ottawa, ON K1R 5B5. (613) 236-4479. albertinn.com. 17 rooms, $115–$195.
Lord Elgin Hotel 100 Elgin St., Ottawa, ON K1P 5K8. (613) 235-3333. lordelginhotel.ca. 355 rooms, $229–$259.

When to Go

Laurier House is open Thursday through Monday, Victoria Day weekend (last Monday before May 25) to Canada Day (July 1), and Labour Day (the first Monday of September) to Thanksgiving (second Monday in October); and daily, Canada Day to Labour Day.

OTTAWA & KINGSTON SITES

ANN BAILLIE BUILDING
KINGSTON, ON

The Ann Baillie Building was originally built in 1903–04 as a residence for student nurses who were completing apprenticeships at Kingston General Hospital. Named after a graduate and former superintendent of the school, it was designated a national historic site as a way to commemorate the training and professionalism of nurses in Canada. The building now operates as a museum of health care. Designated NHS: 1997. 32 George St. (613) 548-2419.

KINGSTON CITY HALL
KINGSTON, ON

Kingston City Hall occupies a full city block. Constructed in 1844, the neo-classical building was built to house the local government, customs house, a post office, a police station and jail, and a market. When Kingston, which had served as capital of the Province of Canada, was overlooked as Ontario's provincial capital, space was eventually rented out to a variety of businesses. Today, it functions again as two of its original uses—as town hall and the site of a summertime farmers market. Designated NHS: 1961. 216 Ontario St. (613) 546-0000.

MERRICKVILLE BLOCKHOUSE
MERRICKVILLE-WOLFORD, ON

Built over the course of a year, beginning in 1832, the Merrickville Blockhouse was meant to help defend Canada by securing the Rideau Canal (see pp. 168–171). The two-storey remains an excellent example of a defensive build. It gains strength from such features as a fire-resistant design, with thick, vented stone walls in the basement, and a lack of doors and windows. Designated NHS: 1939. 279 St. Lawrence St. (613) 283-5170.

BATTLE OF THE WINDMILL
PRESCOTT, ON

At the base of this white stone windmill lies the battlefield where, in 1838, British and Loyalist forces beat an invading force of Canadian rebels and American sympathizers. The rebel sneak attack on Prescott was foiled when their ships were detected so they landed instead at unguarded Windmill Point, but British and Loyalist militia quickly surrounded them. British gunboats cut off retreat across the St. Lawrence River. The fight lasted four days, with casualties on both sides. Interpretive panels and guided tours tell the tale today. Designated NHS: 1920. Cty. Rd. 2 E. (613) 925-2896.

OTTAWA & KINGSTON

A Beaux Arts masterpiece, the federal Parliament Buildings sit on a hill overlooking the Rideau Canal.

▸ PARLIAMENT BUILDINGS AND PUBLIC GROUNDS

OTTAWA, ON
Designated 1976

Sitting atop a hill in Ottawa overlooking the Rideau Canal, the Parliament of Canada comprises four buildings—the Centre Block, West Block, East Block, and Parliamentary Library. Tours of this national historic site must accommodate the business of running the country, making for an unpredictable but exciting experience.

Construction on the buildings began in 1859, two years after Queen Victoria chose Ottawa as the capital of the then Province of Canada. Almost immediately, the space proved insufficient for the government. In fact, quarters were so cramped during the 1800s that even the prime minister shared a desk with staff.

The government operated here until 1916, when a fire levelled most of the Centre Block. The Parliamentary Library survived the blaze for three reasons—the efforts of the firefighters, the direction of the wind, and the design of the library. Its first librarian, Alpheus Todd, had seen libraries burn before, all their holdings destroyed. He lobbied for the long hallway that separates the library from the Centre Block, and that inhibited the spread of the fire. The East and West Blocks, which are not physically attached to the Centre Block, also survived the fire.

To this day, no one knows the cause of the conflagration. Some say it was German military sabotage during the First World War. Others speculate that, as the building had recently been wired for electricity, faulty wiring was the culprit. A third theory blames smoking, which was allowed inside at the time.

Rebuilt between 1916 and 1922, the Centre Block today is a Beaux Arts masterpiece that makes use of Gothic design elements. When architects John Pearson and Jean Marchand decided to add a third floor to the new building, they realized that they could not use the remaining wall structures and stone foundation, and these were demolished. The new design incorporated a stone structure with a reinforced steel frame.

The East and West Blocks are High Victorian Gothic buildings characterized by polychromy as well as irregular massing and rooflines. Their limestone exterior is done in the Gothic Revival style.

Much of the Parliament Buildings is off-limits to visitors, with what can be seen accessible by guided tour only. The Peace Tower and the grounds of Parliament Hill (the latter designated a national historic site separate from the Parliament Buildings), however, are open to self-guided tours.

ARCHITECTURAL DETAILS

When architects Pearson and Marchand redesigned the Centre Block, they did so with an eye toward telling the story of the country up to that point, and leaving space to tell more in the future. For instance, the influence of the First World War is evident in the reconstruction of Victoria Tower, which once stood in the middle of Centre Block. When it was rebuilt, it was made much taller, and was renamed the Peace Tower.

Located inside the Peace Tower is the Memorial Chamber, dedicated to Canada's fallen soldiers. Staff are on hand to answer questions, but this is otherwise a space for quiet reflection. Inside are seven books of remembrance, each commemorating a different conflict and listing the names of those killed in action. Every day at 11 a.m., a ceremonial page-turning ceremony takes place. Visitors may call ahead to find out when the names of family members and loved ones will appear so they can make arrangements to be in the room at that time.

Elsewhere in the buildings, various decorative and architectural elements note events in the history of Canada. For example, there are depictions of provincial and territorial crests. In some spots, however, Newfoundland is missing—because the east coast island only joined the country in 1949. Similarly, Nunavut, one of Canada's three northern territories, joined the Confederation in 1999 and is therefore absent from a centenary stained glass in the House of Commons.

In fact, there are only two places on Parliament Hill where all 13 of Canada's provinces and territories are represented—in Confederation Hall and on the doors of the Senate.

TOURS

No two tours are the same. Trained guides hit on a number of key points about the buildings and their features, but each brings his or her own set of stories to the experience.

They might point out various aesthetic additions to the building over the years. When Pearson planned the Centre Block, he mapped out an elaborate decorative program, but he also left blank space where future sculptors might design and propose new features. Recent examples of this include a stained-glass window, installed in 2012, to commemorate the residential schools that First Nations children were placed in during the 19th and 20th centuries and the prime minister's historic apology to former students and their families. For decades, the schools removed children from native communities in an attempt to assimilate them into dominant Canadian culture. These panes, designed by Christi Belcourt, a Métis artist, are located above the west entrance to the Centre Block.

Elsewhere in the buildings, carved stone faces pay tribute to prime ministers and significant members of Parliament (such as Agnes Macphail, Canada's first female member of Parliament); journalists who have been part of the press gallery; Thomas Fuller, who designed the original Parliament Buildings; and Pearson, architect of the reconstructed Centre Block. As well, there are a number of unidentified faces, believed to be the likenesses of some of the stone carvers who did the work on the building.

Tours in July and August include the East Block, which is closed the rest of the year. Here, four heritage rooms are the main attraction: the former offices of Canada's first prime minister, Sir John A. Macdonald; Sir George-Étienne Cartier; the governor general; and the privy council. These offices have been restored to their original 19th-century appearance, based on photographs and renderings. The furniture pieces are not original, but they are either reproductions or original to the era. The East Block is where Canada was built in the years after Confederation, with MacDonald and co-premier Cartier sharing the decision making when it came to governing the country.

Finally, the Library of Parliament is a favourite among both staff and guests. The circular, spired building is beautiful inside and out. It holds more than 600,000 books. For the most part, these are books used as research materials by parliamentarians looking for information to help support legislation. However, there's also a historic collections vault. Books here include a $15 million copy of John James Audubon's *Birds of America*—a personal copy with notes scribbled in by the ornithologist; a book from 1558, based on interviews with early explorers of Canada; and a book signed by Queen Victoria.

DAILY EVENTS

Parliament Hill is one of several places in Canada you can hear a carillon, a musical instrument that consists of a collection of bronze bells. The Peace Tower Carillon has 53 bells.

Every weekday, the Dominion Carillonneur plays a recital. During the summer, concerts run an hour; the rest of the year, they are shorter. Each day's performance begins with "O Canada," the Canadian national anthem; after that, the playlist is up to the carillonneur. Visitors can find the daily time and scheduled program online.

The Dominion Carillonneur often creates his or her own arrangements. The current Dominion Carillonneur, Dr. Andrea McCrady, has been known

House of Commons, in the Centre Block

PARLIAMENT BUILDINGS & PUBLIC GROUNDS NATIONAL HISTORIC SITES

(Lieu historique national du Colline du Parlement)

INFORMATION & ACTIVITIES

HOW TO REACH US
111 Wellington St., Ottawa, ON K1A 0A4. Phone (613) 992-4793. parl.gc.ca.

SEASONS & ACCESSIBILITY
Guided tours of Centre Block are available year-round. Tours of East Block are available from July to early September. Hours depend on parliamentary business. Visit the website or call for information.

ENTRANCE FEES
None (tours also free).

PETS
Service dogs are allowed.

ACCESSIBLE SERVICES
The buildings are wheelchair accessible, with lifts throughout.

THINGS TO DO
Tours run regularly. Stroll the grounds. Go up the Peace Tower for a panoramic view of Ottawa.

SPECIAL ADVISORIES
The Parliament Buildings are undergoing extensive and long-term renovations. Centre Block is scheduled to be closed for 10 years, beginning in 2018.

CAMPGROUNDS
Ottawa's Poplar Grove Trailer Park Ltd. 6154 Bank St., Greely, ON K4P 1B4. (613) 821-2973. ottawaspoplargrovecamp.com. $30–$45.

HOTELS, MOTELS, & INNS
(Rates are for a 2-person double, high season, in Canadian dollars, unless otherwise noted.)

Fairmont Château Laurier 1 Rideau St., Ottawa, ON K1N 8S7. (613) 241-1414. fairmont.com/laurier-ottawa. 426 rooms, $389–$2,800.
Residence Inn Ottawa Downtown 161 Laurier Ave. W, Ottawa, ON K1P 5J2. (613) 231-2020. marriottresidenceinnottawa .com. 177 rooms, $160–$260.
Cartier Place Suite Hotel 180 Cooper St., Ottawa, ON K2P 2L5. (800) 236-8399. suitedreams.com. 72 rooms, $129–$169.

OTTAWA & KINGSTON

---

to arrange pop songs for performance on the bells. She once even played the *Star Wars* theme music.

The Changing of the Guard ceremony is a must-see event. From the end of June to the end of August, beginning at 10 a.m. daily, the Canadian Army's Ceremonial Guard marches on Parliament Hill, playing military drills and songs. There is always a big crowd for this, so it's best to find a spot around 9:30 a.m. The march begins at Cartier Square Drill Hall, a federal heritage building just south of Parliament Hill.

How to Get There

From Toronto, take Hwy. 401 E to exit 721A for Hwy. 416 N. Exit 75B merges onto Hwy. 417 E toward Ottawa. Take the right-hand exit 120 to Kent Street. From Kent, turn right onto Slater Street, and then left at the third cross street onto Metcalfe Street.

When to Go

Tours of Parliament run year-round, but they can be unpredictable depending on parliamentary business, press conferences, and more. Tours do not include the Senate or House of Commons chambers when Parliament is sitting; to increase chance of seeing these areas, visit during July or August, or on weekends. A weekend visit also allows visitors more time in the library. East Block is only accessible during July and August.

OTTAWA & KINGSTON SITES

BILLINGS HOUSE
OTTAWA, ON

One of the oldest homes in Ottawa, Billings House was built in 1828 by Braddish Billings, the first settler of Gloucester Township in 1812. The design is inspired by the Georgian architecture of New England, where Billings was born. Despite various renovations and additions over the years, the existing house stands more or less as it did in the mid-1800s. Billings House currently operates as a museum offering tours, guided interpretation, activities for children, and other events. Designated NHS: 1968. 2100 Cabot St. (613) 247-4830.

CENTRAL EXPERIMENTAL FARM
OTTAWA, ON

The federal government established this 426-ha (1,053 acres) farm in 1886. It reflects the era's philosophy of agriculture—where the aesthetic was picturesque and the approach was experimentation with regard to new farming technologies. At the time it was chosen, this parcel of land was 3 km (1.9 mi) from Parliament Hill. Its excellent soil type, as well as its access to land, water, and rail, made this an ideal location. Today, the farm lies well within city limits. Designated NHS: 1997. Arboretum, 960 Carling Ave.

CHÂTEAU LAURIER
OTTAWA, ON

It's impossible to walk through Confederation Square without being awed by Château Laurier. The hotel sits high on the banks of the Ottawa River, overlooking it and the Rideau Canal. Opened in 1912 by the Grand Trunk Pacific Railway, the hotel was initially an attempt to encourage guests to travel the railway's routes. The Château Laurier now operates under the Fairmont hotel chain. Designated NHS: 1981. 1 Rideau St. (800) 257-7544.

RIDEAU HALL AND LANDSCAPED GROUNDS
OTTAWA, ON

Since 1865, Rideau Hall has been the official home of the governor general of Canada. The large wooded estate, located near the Ottawa River, has a distinct British aesthetic. It features an elegant stone villa, idyllic open spaces, walking paths, and formal gardens. Originally owned by industrialist and lumberman Thomas McKay, it has seen many additions over the years, including a cricket pavilion. Free tours of the staterooms are offered. Designated NHS: 1977. 1 Sussex Dr. (866) 842-4422.

ROYAL CANADIAN MINT
OTTAWA, ON

In 1908, the Ottawa branch of the British Royal Mint opened with the production of a 50-cent coin. Prior to this, most Canadian currency was created in London, England. The Royal Canadian Mint, under the sole control of the Canadian government, was created in 1931. A refinery and a workshop flank the mint, a sandstone creation built in the late Gothic style, with towers and castle turrets to give it a fortified appearance. Designated NHS: 1979. 320 Sussex Dr. (613) 993-8990.

VICTORIA MEMORIAL MUSEUM
OTTAWA, ON

Victoria Memorial Museum was the first purpose-built federal museum in Canada. The Geological Survey of Canada (GSC) established it in 1843. This building, which the GSC shared with the National Gallery of Canada and Parliament, among others, opened to the public in 1912. Its castlelike appearance (a mix of Beaux Arts and Tudor Gothic styles) was indicative of the vision then Prime Minister Wilfred Laurier had for the capital city. Designated NHS: 1990. 240 McLeod St. (613) 566-4700.

OTTAWA & KINGSTON

The Diefenbunker's blast tunnel, in theory designed to divert the pressure wave of a blast away from the bunker

▶ DIEFENBUNKER/CENTRAL EMERGENCY GOVERNMENT HEADQUARTERS

CARP, ON
Designated 1994

Aboveground, an aluminum shed stands at the centre of a field, belying what lies below: a massive complex built during the Cold War to act as a shelter for Canadian government, military, and essential civilian institutions in the event of a nuclear war. Decommissioned in 1994, the bunker is now a museum, largely returned to the decor of the 1960s.

In 1959, with the Cold War mounting tensions in Canada, Prime Minister John Diefenbaker commissioned an underground bunker that, in the event of a nuclear attack, could serve as a protected hideaway for key members of the Canadian government and military. Officially named the Central Emergency Government Headquarters, the site was dubbed "Diefenbunker" by a newspaper.

A series of these bunkers were built from coast to coast, all connected by radio, and outfitted with enough rations and provisions to last 30 days. The thinking was that, from these bunkers, provincial and federal governments could work together to rebuild the country. Because Diefenbunker was located near the seat of the federal government, it was the largest bunker, built to accommodate up to 535 people.

The former farm site that was chosen for Diefenbunker was selected for its strategic location. Carp is 38 km

(23.6 mi) outside Ottawa, which put it within easy evacuation distance of the capital city. As well, its positioning in a natural valley west of Ottawa meant it was slightly safer in terms of experiencing potential fallout that might have been travelling with the area's easterly winds.

Construction of the four-storey, 9,290-sq-m (100,000 sq ft) complex began in 1959, under the code name Project Emergency Army Signals Establishment. It took less than 18 months to build and the labour of almost 1,000 men. Among other rooms, the bunker was outfitted with simple bedrooms and a kitchen for all personnel, a war cabinet, and a broadcast station for CBC radio.

Though never used for its intended purpose, Diefenbunker served as a functioning communications station for the Canadian Forces from 1961 until 1994. A staff of up to 150 people worked 24-hour shift rotations to take care of some of the country's most sensitive communications operations throughout the Cold War. During this time, the bunker was always stocked with enough fresh food for a week, and emergency rations for a full month.

Because of its significance, Diefenbunker was declared a national historic site at the time of its decommissioning in 1994. It was then sold to the township of West Carleton.

In 1995–96, to raise funds for a new library to be built in an exterior building on the Diefenbunker site, volunteers from Carp started offering tours of Diefenbunker. Some of the volunteers were former employees of the bunker. When these tours proved successful (they drew thousands in a number of days), the Diefenbunker Development Group formed to talk about the possibility of formalizing the tours. Canada's Cold War Museum

opened to the public in 1999, its mandate to increase interest in and understanding of the Cold War, both in Canada and the rest of the world.

Today, the museum attracts roughly 60,000 visitors annually.

THE BUNKER'S DESIGN

To construct something as blast-resistant and secure as Diefenbunker needed to be, there were many considerations. For instance, the heavy equipment required to keep the station operational (including generators and air-conditioning units) had to be located at the bottom of the building.

Because of the blast Diefenbunker would need to withstand in the event of war, it was overbuilt, with 385.6 kg of steel per cubic metre (650 lb/cubic yd) of concrete—this compared to the 68 kg (150 lb) of steel used for most construction. Overall, the bunker required 5,000 tons of steel and 24,470 cubic m (32,000 cubic yd) of concrete. It was built to withstand a nuclear blast of up to 5 megatons, from up to 1.8 km (1.1 mi) away.

Significant planning also went into decoration. Research was done on submarine psychology and how to reduce the chance of claustrophobia. Light, cheerful colours were chosen for rooms and hallways. Another tip taken from the navy is evident in

OTTAWA & KINGSTON

The Diefenbunker's unassuming entrance

the furnishings, some of which were anchored to the floor to guard against being displaced by shock waves.

Finally, a vault was installed on-site to house Canada's gold supply—800 tons of gold bars behind a 30-ton door that could only be opened by a group of four people, each with a different combination.

EXHIBITIONS

Diefenbunker has several permanent exhibitions, including "Canada and the Cold War" and "Cold War Berlin," and hosts roughly four travelling exhibitions each year. For the most part, however, the building itself is the most significant exhibition. To this end, it's full of re-created spaces that reflect what the bunker would have looked like during different periods in history.

The vault could hold 800 tonnes (882 tons) of gold.

The medical centre only had beds for a few patients.

The home fallout and community fallout rooms serve as examples of the kind of facilities Canadians were encouraged to build in the event of a nuclear war. To help citizens prepare for potential war, the government distributed pamphlets outlining 11 steps required to survive such a blast. These included tips such as keeping 14 days of emergency supplies on hand, knowing first aid, and knowing the municipal plan for war.

Other rooms not to be missed are the war cabinet, where the prime minister would have met with his cabinet during lockdown, and the decontamination showers near the bunker's entrance. In the event of an attack, personnel would have entered the bunker through the showers, fully clothed. Next, they would have put the wet clothing down a lead-lined chute and then entered a second shower. Afterward, Geiger counter measurements would determine whether or not there was any remaining radioactive residue. If so, up to six additional showers were required. Any additional concerns would have meant a visit to the medical centre and possible isolation.

SPECIAL ACTIVITIES

Each year, Diefenbunker hosts an artist-in-residence. This person is typically a visual artist, working anywhere from three to six months on a particular project. The goal is to highlight some aspect of the museum in a new and different way, through less traditional interpretive means. For example, in 2016, sculptor Anna Frlan, who works with steel, was the artist. Her work at the bunker focused on the connection between industrial steel and 20th-century weaponry production. The work created during these

DIEFENBUNKER/CENTRAL EMERGENCY GOVERNMENT HEADQUARTERS NATIONAL HISTORIC SITE
(Lieu Historique National Diefenbunker / Siège-Central-du-Gouvernement-d'Urgence)

INFORMATION & ACTIVITIES

HOW TO REACH US
3929 Carp Rd., Carp, ON K0A 1L0. Phone (613) 839-0007. diefenbunker.ca.

SEASONS & ACCESSIBILITY
The Diefenbunker is open daily (11 a.m. to 4 p.m.) year-round except in January and February, when it is closed on Mondays.

ENTRANCE FEES
$14 per adult, $40 per family/group.

PETS
Service dogs are allowed.

ACCESSIBLE SERVICES
Diefenbunker has wheelchair-accessible parking spaces. Some parts of the facility have limited accessibility, but the museum itself is largely accessible and has wheelchairs available for loan on a first-come, first-served basis.

THINGS TO DO
Wander through the museum's permanent and travelling exhibitions. Take a self-guided tour or join a guided tour of the bunker. Be sure to see the model of the bunker, which gives you a sense of its scale. Special events are offered regularly, including whiskey tastings for adults and summer spy camps for kids, which give them the opportunity to play espionage all summer long. Check the museum's website for current information.

CAMPGROUNDS
Breezy Hill Camping 3798 Graigner Park Rd., Kinburn, ON K0A 2H0. (613) 839-5202. breezyhillcamping.com. $45.

HOTELS, MOTELS, & INNS
(Rates are for a 2-person double, high season, in Canadian dollars, unless otherwise noted.)

Brookstreet Hotel 525 Legget Dr., Ottawa, ON K2K 2W2. (613) 271-1800. brookstreet.com. 276 rooms, $170–$210.
Comfort Inn Ottawa West Kanata 222 Hearst Way, Ottawa, ON K2L 3A2. (613) 592-2200. comfortinnkanata.com. 146 rooms, $109–$159.
Boston "T" Bed & Breakfast 106 Falcon Brook Rd., Kanata, ON K0A 1L0. (613) 836-8690. thebostontbandb.com. 3 rooms, $120.

OTTAWA & KINGSTON

residencies is featured in short-term exhibitions in various spaces throughout the museum.

"Escape the Diefenbunker" offers another way to experience the site. In this activity, groups of 12 or more are tasked with working through a number of the bunker's rooms, solving problems, and overcoming obstacles. The conceit of the event is this: The group discovers the museum is actually a cover for a secret spy organization—one that's planning an imminent attack. The group needs to find the bunker's communications room, stop the attack, and alert the outside world of potential disaster—with only a single hour to work together to save the world. Run by local Ottawa company Escape Manor *(escapemanor.com/ottawa)*, the experience is offered evenings from Thursday to Sunday.

How to Get There
From Ottawa, take Hwy. 417 west to exit 144 (Rte. 5 N/Carp Road N). Merge onto Carp Road/Rte. 5, on which Diefenbunker is located.

When to Go
Summertime provides the maximum slate of activities, although the winter months also offer plenty.

Urban Canada: Montréal, Vancouver, & Toronto

In 1867, only 19 percent of Canadians, roughly one in five, lived in an urban area. Today, four out of five people (81 percent) live in a "census metropolitan area" with a population of more than 100,000. Urbanization is Canada's great shared experience of the past 150 years.

Attractive to residents and businesses alike, Toronto has grown to become Canada's largest city and economic hub.

Throughout Canada's change and growth, its urbanization remains a constant, with economic development encouraging opportunity-seeking Canadians to leave farms for cities.

Eastern Canada vs. Western Canada

Demographically, Montréal in the east and Vancouver in the west tell different stories of urbanization. In 1867, with a population of just over 90,000, Montréal was the largest city in British North America. From then until about 1930, thanks mainly to Scottish and Irish immigrants, the city enjoyed a golden age as the economic centre of Canada.

Between 1883 and 1918, Montréal annexed nearby towns rich in French heritage, and became predominantly francophone. The Conscription Crises that came in 1917 (First World War) and 1944 (Second World War) pitted Montréal (and much of the province of Québec) against the rest of the country because the francophones opposed conscription, feeling no particular loyalty to Britain or

France. Later, the 1960s and '70s saw sociopolitical change and events (the Quiet Revolution and Trudeaumania in the 1960s, the 1970 October Crisis) and cultural highs (Expo 67, 1976 Summer Olympics) that transformed the city.

In 1980 and 1995, the political party Parti Québécois spearheaded two divisive referendums for Québec independence. Roughly 300,000 anglophones left Montréal and francophones from around the province moved in. In the end, Québec remained part of Canada, with French its primary language. With a population of 3.8 million, metropolitan Montréal is Canada's second largest city.

Demographically, Vancouver on the west coast is equally distinct. More ethnic Chinese live in Vancouver (over 17 percent) than anglophones in Montréal (13 percent). Chinese immigrants began arriving in British Columbia in 1858 to share in the Fraser Canyon gold rush, and later to work on the Canadian Pacific Railway, completed in 1885. The city was incorporated the next year, and then grew rapidly, from 5,000 in 1887 to 100,000 in 1900.

Vancouver became a major port (and Canada's third largest city) after the Panama Canal opened in 1914. The Great Depression of the 1930s hit the city hard. Vancouver expanded after the Second World War, building bridges, opening a second university (the first opened in 1905), establishing institutions, and, in 1967, creating the Greater Vancouver Regional District. The SkyTrain began running in 1985, part of an infrastructure expansion for Expo 86. Greater Vancouver is Canada's third largest metropolitan area, with 2.4 million people, and is its most densely populated city.

The Rise of Toronto

And what of Toronto, the capital of Ontario and Canada's largest city? Starting with 12,000 residents in 1837, the city boasted 56,000 by Canada's Confederation in 1867. The Great Toronto Fire of 1904 destroyed much of its downtown, but the city quickly recovered as immigrants arrived from Europe. Union Station opened in 1927 and the Royal York Hotel, a grand railway hotel, two years later. The population topped 1 million in 1951, and then doubled in the next two decades. In the late 1970s, Toronto became Canada's largest city and economic hub. The population of the Greater Toronto Area, 6.8 million in 2016, is projected to reach 9.4 million by 2041—and account for more than half of Ontario's population. One of the most multiethnic cities in the world, Toronto is an international beacon of pluralism.

— KEN MCGOOGAN

Montréal, the largest city in Québec

OTTAWA & KINGSTON

The Fort Henry Guard shows off its drum skills.

▶ FORT HENRY

KINGSTON, ON
Designated 1923

Fort Henry sits on a spit that juts into the St. Lawrence River between Navy Bay and Deadman Bay. The extensive stone fort never saw battle in the 1800s, but that does not explain its pristine condition. It actually underwent a substantial reconstruction during the Great Depression.

Fort Henry, in its first incarnation, was built during the War of 1812. Its strategic location on the St. Lawrence was key to British control of Upper Canada (present-day Ontario). Had the Americans taken Kingston, the British would have been completely cut off from their main source of supply downriver in Québec.

A completely new Fort Henry was built between 1832 and 1837 to protect the British shipyard, military depot, and the newly constructed Rideau Canal (see pp. 168–171), which linked Kingston with Ottawa, bypassing the vulnerable St. Lawrence. Fort Henry now sat at the juncture of three significant systems—the Rideau Canal, St. Lawrence River, and Lake Ontario.

By the late 1840s, Fort Henry was the hub of a series of defences and towers that were spread throughout Kingston. The British paid dearly to construct the fort (£70,000), which they could ill afford, illustrating how vital the project was.

Despite this investment, the British withdrew from the fort in 1870, handing it over to the newly created Dominion of Canada (united under Confederation in 1867). Canada was left to manage itself although British forces continued to reinforce the Canadian militia, train officers, and staff the position of general officer commanding. Canadian troops garrisoned the fort until 1891, at which point it was left to ruin.

The government of Ontario began initial discussions about the fort's restoration in 1935. Toronto architect William Somerville drew up the plans using the research of Kingston-born historian Ronald Way. The actual work, which was jointly funded by the Ontario and federal governments, took place between 1936 and 1938. Way ended up overseeing much of the initial research and day-to-day work that went into the restoration. Though it cost more than $800,000 (this during the Great Depression), the local community supported it, in part because it resulted in work for 100 to 200 labourers.

In a sense, Fort Henry is a legacy not only of military life and history in Canada but also of Canadian historic preservation. Way's approach went on to inform many of his fellow historians. An active member of the Kingston Historical Society, he had broad influence over historians and curators across the country. One of his most famous ideas was that of "the living museum"—having costumed interpreters reenact scenes that would have been commonplace while sites were operational. Way inaugurated this idea by having student volunteers from Queen's University dress as soldiers and reenact the Guard.

In 1958, the fort was transferred to the Ontario St. Lawrence Development Commission (later changed to St. Lawrence Parks Commission).

TOURING THE FORT

Visitors will discover a lot by simply wandering the site, which consists of an upper fort and lower fort, and chatting with costumed interpreters, who reenact the fort circa 1867.

The upper fort comprises the advanced battery, so named for a grouping of guns meant to guard against the possibility of attack from Lake Ontario. The battery is located not only at the highest point on the fort's premises, but in all of Kingston. The buildings flanking the battery would have served as commissariat stores during the 1840s.

In the lower fort, the wine cellar is a popular spot today, just as it was during the 1800s. The stone-walled room, with its curved ceiling and cool conditions, provided storage for beer, which the soldiers bought using the pence-a-day beer money that they received from the army. Alcohol consumption was a major cause of insubordination and desertion. For infractions like these, soldiers were sent to one of four sets of garrison cells. These too can be explored.

Soldiers looking to better themselves might have taken lessons in the schoolroom. The room was originally used to teach lessons to children of soldiers and, eventually, to soldiers themselves, as education was necessary for them to rise in rank, which could mean an improvement in their lives.

Oddly, one of the most interesting stories associated with the fort's various rooms starts in what's known as the privies. These rustic washrooms were flushed by way of a rudimentary

OTTAWA & KINGSTON

An aerial view reveals the fort's strategic positioning.

FORT HENRY NATIONAL HISTORIC SITE
(Lieu historique national du Fort Henry)

INFORMATION & ACTIVITIES

HOW TO REACH US
1 Fort Henry Dr., Kingston, ON K7K 5G8. Phone (613) 542-7388. forthenry.com.

SEASONS & ACCESSIBILITY
Lower fort, open May 16 to September 6; closed rest of year.

ENTRANCE FEES
$18 per person (lower fort). Upper fort free.

PETS
Service dogs are permitted.

ACCESSIBLE SERVICES
The main fort is mostly wheelchair accessible, with the exception of a few exhibits. The Discovery Centre is wheelchair accessible. Tours can be tailored to individual needs.

THINGS TO DO
Take a guided 50-minute tour (included with admission) or guide yourself around the fort. Stop by the Discovery Centre for additional context. Ask about after-hours ghost tours and other special events.

CAMPGROUNDS
Rideau Acres 1014 Cunningham Rd., Kingston, ON K7L 4V3. (613) 546-2711. rideauacres.com. $35–$52.
Ivy Lea Campground 649-1000 Islands Pkwy., Lansdowne, ON K0E 1L0. (800) 437-2233. stlawrenceparks.com. $37–$48.

HOTELS, MOTELS, & INNS
(Rates are for a 2-person double, high season, in Canadian dollars, unless otherwise noted.)

Green Acres Inn 2480 Princess St., Kingston, ON K7M 3G4. (613) 546-1796. greenacresinn.com. 32 rooms, $129–$249.
Hotel Belvedere 141 King St. E, Kingston, ON K7L 2Z9. (613) 548-1565. hotelbelvedere.com. 19 rooms, $129–$199.
Residence Inn by Marriott Kingston Water's Edge 7 Earl St., Kingston, ON K7L 0A5. (613) 544-4888. marriottresidenceinnkingston.com. 141 rooms, $200–$230.

system that collected water from the ramparts and parade square and then emptied into Navy Bay. In 1943, 19 German prisoners of war escaped by way of the drainage tunnels that carried the wastewater to the bay.

For a more focused exploration of the fort, take one of the hourly tours offered daily. And be sure to visit the Fort Henry Discovery Centre. The 900-sq m (10,000 sq ft) building has interactive exhibits that provide context and build on the experience of walking through the fort.

SPECIAL EVENTS

Fort Henry supplements its permanent programming with special exhibits and activities, including the annual Cannonball Crush, a challenging 5-km (3.1 mi) run that makes use of the fort's hills, ditches, and water traps; and Grape Escapes, a sampling from nearly 30 local wineries. In addition, for visitors interested in unique accommodations, the barracks are available for overnight rental for groups of 2 to 18 people. It includes access to a washroom as well as the staff lunchroom, where kitchen facilities are available.

One of the fort's most popular attractions is the Sunset Ceremony. Every Wednesday in July and August, at 8 p.m., the Fort Henry Guard (composed of university and college students) puts on a performance that's been recognized by Events and Festivals Ontario as one of the top 100 events in the province. Executed by one of the best precision drill units in the world, it is a period interpretation of 1860s military music and drills, complete with cannon firings.

How to Get There

From Toronto, take Hwy. 401 E to exit 623 for Hwy. 15/Rte. 15 toward Smiths Falls/Ottawa. Turn right on Rte. 15. Turn right on Rte. 2, and then left onto Constantine Drive/Fort Henry Drive. Take a slight right to stay on Fort Henry Drive.

When to Go

Fort Henry is only open during the summer months, with two fun-filled exceptions for the whole family: Fort Fright and Fort Frost. Running for a week at the end of October, Fort Fright turns Fort Henry into an epic haunted house, including indoor and outdoor scares that come complete with professional set design, animatronics, lighting, and more. Fort Frost, launched in 2016, blends modern and traditional winter activities and themed events in December and January.

OTTAWA & KINGSTON SITES

KINGSTON FORTIFICATIONS
KINGSTON, ON

The Kingston Fortifications National Historic Site encompasses five separate structures in and around Kingston Harbour: Fort Henry, Fort Frederick, Murney Tower, Shoal Tower, and Cathcart Martello Tower. Built as a defence system between 1832 and 1848, the fortifications were strategic for their location at the confluence of Lake Ontario and the St. Lawrence River, a major shipping route and gateway to the Great Lakes from the Atlantic Ocean. Designated NHS: 1989.

MURNEY TOWER
KINGSTON, ON

An important piece of the Kingston fortifications, Murney Tower is also exceptional for its example of a martello tower—a type of military structure renowned for the strength in its squat, stone construction. The thick limestone walls were considered fireproof and bombproof. Murney Tower was built in 1846 to keep watch over the western approaches to Kingston. The tower was used as a barracks almost right away, but it wasn't fully armed until 1862. Designated NHS: 1989. 18 King St. W. (613) 544-9925.

The scenic 386-km (240 mi) Trent-Severn Waterway in southern Ontario offers numerous recreational opportunities.

GEORGIAN BAY

Nearly the size of Lake Ontario, Georgian Bay—nicknamed "the sixth Great Lake"—forms the northeast arm of Lake Huron. Its eastern shore lies in the Canadian Shield, and the greyish pink granite rock formations that outline the shoreline make agriculture difficult. French explorer Samuel de Champlain began mapping the area in 1615, and in 1634 French Jesuits founded a mission here. The Algonquian and Huron First Nations used the bay as part of a major trade route that also included a series of rivers and lakes linking

Lake Huron with Lake Ontario.
Known as the Trent-Severn Waterway
(see pp. 202–203), this route played
an important role in the fur trade and
later incorporated the canals that
enabled permanent settlement and
the growth of the region's primary
industry: timber. By the turn of the
20th century, deforestation had felled
the timber industry. At the same
time, however, the region's rugged
beauty began to attract travellers.
Today, Georgian Bay, part of a
UNESCO biosphere reserve, is a
lively summer vacation destination.

The visitor centre for Bethune Memorial House, the birthplace of physician and humanitarian Norman Bethune

▶ BETHUNE MEMORIAL HOUSE

GRAVENHURST, ON

Designated 1997

Beautiful Bethune Memorial House, a moss green century home on tree-lined grounds, owes its historical significance to its association with Dr. Norman Bethune (1890–1939), who was born here. Bethune was a staunch early advocate of the accessible medical care system under which Canada operates.

Although Bethune only lived in the house until the age of three, it is remembered for him because of the large role he played in Canadian medical history. Originally, the house was the manse of the local Knox Presbyterian Church. Bethune was born there in 1890 while his father, Malcolm, a reverend, was preaching at the Gravenhurst church.

NORMAN BETHUNE

Bethune began studying medicine at the University of Toronto, but he took a break to spend time at Frontier College, where he arranged classes for immigrant workers in a northern Ontario bush camp. When the First World War was declared, he enlisted in the Canadian Army Medical Corps. Wounded while serving as a stretcher-bearer in Ypres, Belgium, Bethune returned to Canada and finished his medical degree, graduating in 1916. He re-enlisted, this time with the Royal Navy, in 1917, and went on to become the first chief medical officer of the newly formed Canadian Air Force in 1919. After completing his military service, he pursued postgraduate studies in England.

For a while, Bethune conducted a private practice in Detroit, Michigan. However, after contracting tuberculosis at the age of 36, he returned to Gravenhurst for treatment at the Calydor Sanatorium, and then additional treatment at the Trudeau Sanatorium in Saranac Lake, New York State. Frustrated by the rules at the treatment centres, he started looking into treatments on his own and demanded he receive artificial pneumothorax—a dangerous operation that pumps air into the chest. When he survived and recovered inside of a month, Bethune decided to focus on tuberculosis.

He worked with one of Canada's pioneering thoracic surgeons at Montréal's Royal Victoria Hospital. Later, he was put in charge of the Department of Thoracic Surgery at nearby Sacré Coeur Hospital in Cartierville. During this time, Bethune wrote journal articles on surgical techniques and improvements, many of which he designed himself.

Witnessing the impact of the Great Depression on the poor population of Montréal, who struggled to afford medical care, Bethune started to feel that the medical community needed to be concerned with the social as well as the medical causes of disease. In 1935, he set up a free clinic for jobless Montrealers. That same year, he joined the Communist Party and established an organization called the Montreal Group for the Security of the People's Health, in an effort to concentrate advocacy for public health care.

In 1936, Bethune, along with other Canadians who joined the fighting, went to Spain when the Spanish Civil War broke out, offering aid. There, he put together the world's first mobile, battlefront blood transfusion service—one that would collect blood from city donors, and transport it anywhere it was needed.

After Spain, Bethune travelled to China in early 1938 so he could be at the frontlines of the Second Sino-Japanese War (1937–1945). For nearly two years, he assisted medical personnel in the mountain ranges of the Shanxi-Hobei border region. When Bethune realized he was one of very few qualified doctors, he started teaching others the basics of first aid and sanitation. Eventually, he published manuals and booklets to further educate his colleagues, working toward a goal of educating and graduating doctors inside of a year, nurses in six months. Bethune even went so far as to establish a fully functioning medical centre, although sadly it was destroyed shortly after opening. Undaunted, Bethune conceived a mobile medical facility that could be carried on mules.

Bethune died in China in 1939 of blood poisoning contracted from treating a wounded soldier.

HOUSE & GROUNDS

When the house was built in 1880, it belonged to the Knox Presbyterian Church and served as its manse. It is representative of what a typical middle-class Victorian-style Gravenhurst home would have looked like in the 19th century, with a steeply pitched gable roof, brick chimneys, and clapboard siding. In the summer months, baskets of flowers line the veranda, where comfortable wicker chairs rock lazily.

At the time the house was constructed, the exterior of a home was viewed as an extension of the interior decor. Both were planned and designed to harmonize with each other. The grounds have been preserved and maintained to accurately

GEORGIAN BAY

reflect the Victorian landscape aesthetics of the 1890s.

Still, the house remains best remembered for its association with Bethune—and small details pay homage to him. For instance, bloodroot and lungwort have been planted in the flower gardens that line the front and sides of the house, intentionally chosen to symbolize the work Bethune did in the fields of blood transfusion and tuberculosis.

Visitors can tour the 1890s-era house on their own, but guided and private guided tours (fee) are also offered regularly during high season.

The two-hour guided tour (available in English, French, and Mandarin Chinese), which begins with a Chinese tea welcome, is comprehensive. As visitors are led

Bethune lived in this house until he was three years old.

Bethune's life is explained in the visitor centre.

through the house, exhibits and artefacts illustrate the stories told by interpreters. During the private tour, visitors are invited to look through a historic stereoscope at 3-D images of the 19th century and to play the Victorian pump organ in the parlour.

The house's extensive library contains most of the books that have been published on Bethune. Many of them are available in English as well as Chinese, with a few editions in other languages. Some of these books are contemporary, whereas others have been out of print for decades. The collection also includes interviews conducted with Bethune's family, friends, and colleagues, each of which was done specifically for Parks Canada.

A visitor centre interprets the site and offers guests the opportunity to handle historic objects, such as medical artefacts and personal diaries. Perhaps most interesting is the world's tiniest transcript of Mao Zedong's "In Memory of Norman Bethune"—an essay documenting the last months of the doctor's life in China. In the 1960s, this text was required reading in elementary schools in the country. Visitors may also watch a biographical video on Bethune, available in English, French, and Mandarin Chinese.

CHINESE GIFTS

Bethune Memorial House is full of family artefacts and period furniture from the doctor's time at the house, but more recent acquisitions also speak just as loudly to his legacy.

Because of the tireless work Bethune did in China during the Second Sino-Japanese War, he is still revered in China. Statues of Bethune can be found throughout the country,

BETHUNE MEMORIAL HOUSE
(Lieu historique national de la Maison-Commémorative-Bethune)

INFORMATION & ACTIVITIES

HOW TO REACH US
297 John St. N, Gravenhurst, ON P1P 1G4. Phone (705) 687-4261. pc.gc.ca/bethune.

SEASONS & ACCESSIBILITY
The site is open Wednesday through Sunday in June; daily July to mid-October; and Wednesday through Sunday mid-October to October 31. Open rest of year by appointment only.

ENTRANCE FEES
$3.90 per adult, $9.80 per family/group.

PETS
Service dogs are permitted.

ACCESSIBLE SERVICES
The visitor centre, including washrooms, and the first floor of the house are fully accessible for wheelchairs. The second floor of the house is not.

THINGS TO DO
Tour the house by self-guided or two-hour guided tour. Take a self-guided walk around the grounds. Check out the exhibits and artefacts in the visitor centre.

CAMPGROUNDS
Camp Hillbilly 1633 Hwy. 11S, Kilworthy, Muskoka, ON P0E 1G0. (705) 689-2366, hillbilly.on.ca, $40–$55.
Gravenhurst KOA 1083 Reay Rd. E, Gravenhurst, ON P1P 1R3. (705) 687-2333. koa.com/campgrounds/gravenhurst. Rates vary.

HOTELS, MOTELS, & INNS
(Rates are for a 2-person double, high season, in Canadian dollars, unless otherwise noted.)

Oakwood Motel 1060 Muskoka Rd. S, Gravenhurst, ON P1P 1K6. (705) 687-4224. oakwoodmotel.com, 10 rooms, $70–$120.
Residence Inn Gravenhurst Muskoka Wharf 285 Steamship Bay Rd., Gravenhurst, ON P1P 1Z9. (705) 687-6600. marriott.com. 106 rooms, $290–$600.
Taboo Muskoka Resort 1209 Muskoka Beach Rd., Gravenhurst, ON P1P 1R1. (800) 461-0236. taboomuskoka.com. 59 rooms, $122–$285.

GEORGIAN BAY

and the destroyed hospital that led to his mobile unit has been rebuilt.

A few times a year, delegations and representatives from the Chinese government will visit the Bethune Memorial House. They come bearing gifts, tokens of the warm feelings the country continues to have for Bethune. The collection of gifts at the house dates back 40 years and features commemorative plates, bronze statues, works of art, volumes of poetry, and books. Occasionally, visiting Chinese children will place flowers at the feet of one of the statues of Bethune.

How to Get There
From Toronto, take Hwy. 400N to Barrie. Keep to the left or centre lane to take Hwy. 11. Exit Hwy. 11 at Gravenhurst and follow the "Bethune Historic Site" signs north on Muskoka Road for 1.3 km (0.8 mi). Turn left on Brown Street, and then left on John Street North to reach the site's visitor centre.

When to Go
In spring and summer, the Bethune Memorial House gardens are glorious, full and lush with leafy trees and multicoloured blooms. But in the fall, the sight of Gravenhurst is spectacular, with foliage giving a vibrant, beautiful show, so plan to visit on a weekday or earlier in the season to avoid the crowds. Admission is free on Canada Day.

The Kirkfield Lift Lock, one of two such locks on the Trent-Severn Waterway

▶TRENT-SEVERN WATERWAY

BOBCAYGEON, ON
Designated 1929

The scenic Trent-Severn Waterway winds 386 km (240 mi) through southern Ontario's cottage country. Connecting Lake Ontario with Lake Huron, the waterway comprises lakes, rivers, and a dug canal between Trenton at the Bay of Quinte in the east and Port Severn at Georgian Bay in the west.

The Indigenous Peoples of Canada have used the Trent-Severn watershed since at least 9000 B.C., as evidenced by petroglyphs and burial mounds along its length. In the 17th century, it served as a major route for the fur trade. But it was the lumber industry in the 19th century that drove commerce and settlement, increasing the need for mills that would need dams, and the subsequent industry of moving people and goods to settlement.

The first lock, a small wooden one, was built at Bobcaygeon in 1833. Later locks were added over the years. Though originally intended for industry, the waterway was also used for recreation, with steamboats carrying tourists to the Kawarthas as early as the mid-1800s. The hydraulic Peterborough Lift Lock (see opposite), built in 1904, is the most famous of the locks.

What to See & Do

From July through October, Peterborough's Canadian Canoe Museum offers 90-minute tours (fee) of the canal in a voyageur canoe, guided by experienced interpreters. The lock at Peterborough is also home to one of Peterborough's many community gardens, with the vegetables grown here for local food security programs. Lock 24, near Lakefield on the Otonabee River, has oTENTik (a tent/cabin hybrid) camping available.

How to Get There

The waterway can be accessed at many points along its length. To reach the Peterborough Lift Lock Visitor Centre from Toronto, take Hwy. 401E and then Hwy. 115N. Exit toward Ashburnham Drive. Turn left on Neal Drive, left on Ashburnham Drive, and then left on Hunter Street East.

When to Go

The locks are open daily from May 20 to October 10. The hours are shorter May 20 to June 26, Monday through Thursday, and September 6 to October 10, Monday through Friday. Check the website for times.

INFORMATION

HOW TO REACH US
Peterborough Lift Lock Visitor Centre 353 Hunter St. E, Peterborough, ON K9H 7B5. (705) 750-4900. pc.gc.ca/trent.

ENTRANCE FEES
Boaters must purchase a pass.

ACCESSIBLE SERVICES
Limited.

HOTELS, MOTELS, & INNS
Comfort Inn Trenton 68 Monogram Pl., Trenton, ON K8V 6S3. (613) 965-6660. ramada.com. $130–$150.

GEORGIAN BAY SITES

PETERBOROUGH LIFT LOCK
PETERBOROUGH, ON

Completed in 1904 and able to lift boats nearly 20 m (65.6 ft), the impressive Peterborough Lift Lock on the Trent-Severn Waterway is still the world's highest hydraulic lift, and one of only two in North America (the other is also on the Trent-Severn Waterway). The lock operates on a balance system that moves water between two chambers, lifting and lowering vessels travelling the waterway. Designated NHS: 1979.
220 Hunter St. E. (705) 750-4953.

MNJIKANING FISH WEIRS
RAMARA, ON

More than 5,000 years old, the wooden stakes found in the Atherley Narrows are some of the earliest evidence of early fishery techniques in Canada. Here, late Archaic Indigenous Peoples guided fish toward the stakes, woven with vegetation, to be caught by nets or speared. The weirs were still in use by the Huron-Wendat up until the 1650s. Today, the Chippewas of Rama First Nation deeply value their role as stewards of the weirs. Designated NHS: 1982.

The sun sets over Fort George, a military garrison first established by the British in 1796.

TORONTO &
NIAGARA

Located on the northwest shore of Lake Ontario, energetic, modern Toronto, the capital of Ontario, is the most populous city in Canada. Three hundred years before French fur traders arrived in the mid-18th century, the Iroquois had established fortified villages throughout the region. The British conquered the area in 1759 and founded Toronto—originally named York—as a garrison to guard the border with the United States. Growth was slow, but the city boasted advantages, including a harbour and inland access. In 1834, the

city's name was changed to Toronto, from a Mohawk word meaning "where there are trees standing in the water."

Across Lake Ontario, and on the west bank of the Niagara River, lies the modest town of Niagara-on-the-Lake. Settled by refugee Loyalists in the decades following the American Revolution and briefly occupied— and burned—by American forces in 1813, the town is home to British-built Fort George (see pp. 206–209) and served as an important station on the Underground Railroad.

Fort George once served as the headquarters for the Centre Division of the British Army in Upper Canada.

▶ FORT GEORGE

NIAGARA-ON-THE-LAKE, ON
Designated 1921

Fort George sits on the banks of the Niagara River, just across the water from Fort Niagara in Youngstown, New York. It was established in 1796 by the British, who lost it during the War of 1812, retook it, and then abandoned it for the more strategically positioned Fort Mississauga.

All of the fort's buildings were reconstructed in the 20th century, except for the powder magazine—a brilliant example of 1700s-era construction, and one of the oldest buildings in southern Ontario.

The 1783 Treaty of Paris gave Fort Niagara to the Americans, but the British retained control of it until 1796. That year, they surrendered Fort Niagara and began building Fort George on the Canadian side of the river. Because the Niagara was an essential supply route, the British felt it necessary to construct a new post, not only to protect Newark (today's Niagara-on-the-Lake) from possible American attack, but also Navy Hall, a warehouse and wharf facility.

Numerous barracks, kitchens, and the powder magazine were built, as well as a Council House, residences, and storage facilities. Earthworks bastions and a wooden palisade surrounded the whole post. When the fort was finished in 1802, it was immediately named headquarters for the Centre Division of the British Army in Upper Canada.

In the War of 1812, the fort became home base for Maj. Gen. Sir Isaac Brock, the military commander of Upper Canada, who died nearby during the Battle of Queenston Heights in the fall of 1812. In May 1813, the fort was destroyed by cannon fire from Fort Niagara and captured during an American attack.

From May to December, the U.S. Army used Fort George as a base from which to invade Upper Canada. They were turned back twice, at the Battle of Stoney Creek (June 6) in Hamilton and at the Battle of Beaver Dams (June 24) in Thorold. In December, the British retook the fort and held it until the war's end. Though the British partially rebuilt Fort George after the war, they located barracks and other facilities on the far edge of the military lands, out of range of enemy gunfire. The fort was in ruins again by the 1820s.

Eventually, British forces abandoned Fort George in favour of Fort Mississauga (see p. 213), nearly 2 km (1.2 mi) downriver, and in a slightly more defensible area.

In the years that followed, the military lands were used for a variety of purposes, including farming, as part of a golf course, and as hospital grounds. Of course, they also continued to serve a military purpose, acting as a Canadian Militia summer training camp from the 1870s until the 1960s. During the First World War, 14,000 soldiers trained here and later fought in battles such as Vimy Ridge and Passchendaele. Soldiers trained here also fought in the South African War (1899–1902), the Second World War, and the Korean War, and acted as United Nations peacekeepers. This rich and diverse history is part of what led to Fort George being declared a national historic site.

EXPLORING THE FORT

Fort George is best experienced via a self-guided walking tour. Interpreters dressed in period clothing help guide visitors through the site, giving information and background on the day-to-day lives of the soldiers and families that lived here.

The lone original building at Fort George is the powder magazine, which dates to 1796. All of the other structures are reconstructions, but they—the blockhouses, officers' quarters, guardhouse, and more—serve as interpretive tools, accurately reflecting what life would have been like in the early 19th century. In them, visitors will find artefacts such as original muskets, pistols, carbines, rifles, and a four-pounder cannon, as well as an officer's uniform from a Swiss mercenary regiment that fought for the British during the War of 1812. There's also a uniform from General Brock's old regiment, and the coat of a New York State militia officer.

Pass through the soldiers' barracks, officers' room, and the on-site prison, and then finish by watching a musket demonstration.

A more recent Parks Canada addition to the site is the Agora. A round, modern pavilion made of concrete, glass, and cedar, it offers picnicking space to visitors. Large interior fireplaces warm it in the chilly fall, and roll-up walls allow for the breeze to pass through in the summer.

The Agora also has exhibits that showcase not only Fort George but the rest of the surrounding national historic sites, including Fort Mississauga, Butler's Barracks (see p. 213), the Battlefield of Fort George, and

TORONTO & NIAGARA

Soldiers' families also lived at the fort.

Queenston Heights (see p. 215), location of the iconic Brock's Monument. The histories of these sites are tied to one another.

Surrounded by what is now the grounds of the Niagara-on-the-Lake Golf Club, nearby Fort Mississauga is accessible by way of a pedestrian trail (funded by the Friends of Fort George) that begins at Simcoe and Front Streets.

To reach Butler's Barracks from Fort George, visitors can either drive 1.6 km (1 mi) or walk the Otter Trail. Named for Sir William Otter, who commanded Canadian troops in the 1885 Northwest Rebellion in Saskatchewan, the trail follows one of the old military trails that crisscrossed the former military reserve. It provides an easy link between Fort George and Butler's Barracks. It also connects with the Niagara River Recreation Trail (which runs all the way to Fort Erie) and the Waterfront Trail, if visitors wish to make a longer hike.

For something a little different, check in with the Friends of Fort George to find out about dates and times for ghost tours of Fort George.

FIFE AND DRUM CORPS

Drums and music have long been an integral part of the military. Drums were used to time marches, and music was a way of marking events. Horns and bagpipes were even used as systems of communication, to signal routines and events.

A drummer's duties at the fort were extensive. He called soldiers to events such as morning parade, inspection, and dinner. He announced the nightly closing of the gates, lights out, and lockup at the barracks. He also sounded marches and joined recruitment parties that moved through taverns and city streets. Least loved of all the drummer's duties was sounding out the lashes given to soldiers who had broken rules. This punishment often occurred in a public space, and a drum major counted out each lash in front of other soldiers and their families. This was done to make an example of the soldier, and to discourage others from similar behaviour. Finally, in active battle, a drummer sounded signal calls and served as a stretcher-bearer for the wounded.

At Fort George, the 41st Fife and Drum Corps has resurrected this tradition. The calibre of the Corps band means it's a celebrated troupe, not only at Fort George but also on the international stage. The Corps regularly travels throughout Canada and the United States to perform at other historic sites. The band is also frequently requested to participate in parades and festivals.

Since the 1980s, another band, this one composed of local student volunteers as well as of many

Musket demonstration by interpreters in period costume

FORT GEORGE NATIONAL HISTORIC SITE
(Lieu historique national du Fort-George)

INFORMATION & ACTIVITIES

HOW TO REACH US
51 Queens Parade, Niagara-on-the-Lake, ON L0S 1J0. Phone (905) 468-6614. pc.gc.ca/fortgeorge.

SEASONS & ACCESSIBILITY
The site is open daily May 1 through October 31; it's open weekend afternoons only November 1 to April 30.

FRIENDS OF FORT GEORGE
P.O. Box 1283, Niagara-on-the-Lake, ON L0S 1J0. (905) 468-6621. friendsoffortgeorge.ca.

ENTRANCE FEES
$11.70 per adult, $29.40 per family/group.

PETS
Pets must be leashed. Only service dogs are allowed inside buildings.

ACCESSIBLE SERVICES
All buildings are accessible except for the Octagonal Blockhouse, which has stairs.

THINGS TO DO
Tour the fort and interact with costumed interpreters. Try Hands-on History—for a fee, visitors may put on a red coat and fire a replica musket, just like soldiers would have done here 200 years ago. Relax with a picnic in the newly built Agora.

Check the website or call ahead to find out about special events and activities. Annual events include the celebrations on Canada Day (July 1) and the Fife and Drum Muster. There are also occasionally small concerts, lectures, commemorations, and more.

SPECIAL ADVISORIES
If visiting Fort Mississauga, allow golfers to play through before crossing the green. No bicycles, scooters, in-line skates, skateboards, or other vehicles are allowed.

HOTELS, MOTELS, & INNS
(Rates are for a 2-person double, high season, in Canadian dollars, unless otherwise noted.)

Harbour House Hotel 85 Melville St., Niagara-on-the-Lake, ON L0S 1J0. (905) 468-4683. niagarasfinest.com/properties/harbourhouse. 31 rooms, $325–$550.
Prince of Wales 6 Picton St., Niagara-on-the-Lake, ON L0S 1J0. (905) 468-3246. vintage-hotels.com/princeofwales. 110 rooms, $350–$500.
Riverbend Inn and Vineyard 16104 Niagara Pkwy., Niagara-on-the-Lake, ON L0S 1J0. (905) 468-8866. riverbendinn.ca. 21 rooms, $364–$424.

TORONTO & NIAGARA

members of the Fife and Drum Corps, has played period instruments (flutes, clarinets, bassoons, violins, French horns, and a serpent [a bass wind instrument]) and carried out marching drills that would have been used during the War of 1812. Some of their more popular marches include songs such as "The British Grenadiers," "The Girl I've Left Behind Me," and "The Downfall of Paris."

How to Get There
From the Queen Elizabeth Way, take Glendale Avenue/RR-89 (exit 38) to Niagara-on-the-Lake. Turn left on York Road, right on Airport Road, and then right again on Niagara Stone Road. Next, take a right on East and West Line, and then a left on Niagara Parkway, which becomes Queens Parade.

When to Go
The fort is open daily May through October. The fort is only open on weekends November through April. To see the Fife and Drum Corps perform, visit Wednesday through Sunday in July and August.

The HMCS *Haida* gained fame for her feats during the Second World War.

▶ HMCS HAIDA

HAMILTON, ON
Designated 1984

Sitting in a quiet corner of Hamilton Harbour is the HMCS *Haida*, the last surviving Tribal-class destroyer, with a reputation as "Canada's fightingest ship." The vessel is now moored at the edge of Lake Ontario's Waterfront Trail, in Bayfront Park.

In the distance, visitors can see the treed shores of the city of Burlington. This is home for the ship now, but in her heyday, the HMCS (Her Majesty's Canadian Ship) *Haida* served in the Second World War, the Korean War, and the Cold War.

In the 1930s, with war on the horizon, the British designed the new 114-m (374 ft) Tribal-class destroyer. Twenty-seven were built for use by Great Britain, Canada, and Australia. Of these, the *Haida* is the only one that remains.

The *Haida* began her stint in the Royal Canadian Navy in 1943, escorting supply convoys to Russia. The following year, the ship moved to the waters of the English Channel in preparation for D-Day, where she fought many successful battles against German warships. From

there, she went on to serve in the Korean War, where duties included blockading supply lines, protecting aircraft carriers, and shelling enemy supply trains. Throughout the 1950s, the ship operated training and goodwill missions before being decommissioned in 1963.

Over the course of 20 years of service, the *Haida* travelled 688,534.25 nautical miles, the equivalent of 27 times around the world.

What to See & Do

Explore the ship, seeing the living quarters, mess room, command centre, and guns up close. Get a glimpse of early computer technology in the transmission room, where a firing clock, used to fire the main guns, also monitors ship speed, wind, and wave measurements. Marvel at the

Haida's giant propellers, now sitting wharfside. Staff, students, and volunteers are available to direct and interpret the ship. Many volunteers have served with the Royal Canadian Navy and can give personal accounts of service. Show up early to witness the daily morning flag-raising ceremony, when traditional whistles are played.

How to Get There

From Toronto, take the Queen Elizabeth Way and exit at Hamilton's Burlington Street. Pass Wellington Street and turn right at John Street. Follow John until it ends at Guise Street. Turn right at Guise onto Catharine Street, and then left at Catharine and right at the entrance to Pier 9.

One of the *Haida*'s four radio rooms

INFORMATION

HOW TO REACH US
Pier 9, 658 Catharine St. N, Hamilton, ON L8L 8K4. Phone (905) 526-6742. pc.gc.ca/haida.

ENTRANCE FEES
$3.90 per adult, $9.80 per family/group.

ACCESSIBLE SERVICES
Inaccessible to wheelchairs.

HOTELS, MOTELS, & INNS
Staybridge Suites Hamilton 20 Caroline St. S, Hamilton, ON L8P 1C9. (905) 527-1001. staybridge.com. 129 rooms, $139–$379.
Sheraton Hamilton Hotel 116 King St. W, Hamilton, ON L8P 4V3. (905) 529-5515. sheratonhamilton.com. 300 rooms, $129–$299.

When to Go

The ship is open daily July 1 to August 31. From the Thursday before Victoria Day to June 30 and September 1 to Canadian Thanksgiving Sunday, the ship is open Thursday to Sunday. Closed rest of year.

TORONTO & NIAGARA SITES

DUNDURN CASTLE
HAMILTON, ON

Built in 1835 for Sir Allan Napier MacNab, a politician and businessman, Dundurn Castle sits atop Burlington Heights, between Hamilton Harbour and the serene Cootes Paradise. The 13-ha (32 acres) estate consists of a main residence built in the Italianate style, with surrounding buildings—a gardener's cottage, stable, former dovecote, cockfighting pavilion, and more—showcasing Gothic, classical, and Regency styles. Regular tours and events are offered on-site. Designated NHS: 1984. 610 York St. (905) 546-2872.

TORONTO & NIAGARA SITES

ERLAND LEE (MUSEUM) HOME
HAMILTON, ON

The birthplace of a movement that would eventually spread around the world, the Erland Lee Home stands as a symbol of Women's Institutes in Canada, which espoused the interests of rural and farm women. The organization's constitution was drafted here in 1897, at the home of Janet and Erland Lee, two co-founders of the Women's Institute. The institutes still promote women, families, and communities today. Designated NHS: 2002. 552 Ridge Rd. (905) 662-2691.

JOHN WEIR FOOTE ARMOURY
HAMILTON, ON

Located in the heart of downtown Hamilton's arts district, the armoury consists of the north drill hall, built in 1887–88, and the south drill hall, completed in 1908. Both red brick with stone trim, each hall speaks to a different era. The substantial brick of the north hall emphasized the significance of city militia units as the country's first line of defence; the modern facilities of the south hall reflected a subsequent phase of armoury construction and militia reforms. Designated NHS: 1989. 200 James St. N. (905) 528-2945.

HAMILTON AND SCOURGE
LAKE ONTARIO, ON

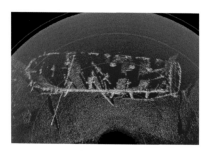

This national historic site is actually located at the bottom of Lake Ontario: The *Hamilton* and *Scourge* (both well preserved) went down 11 km (6.8 mi) north of Port Dalhousie. American merchant schooners, they were modified for military purposes at the beginning of the War of 1812 and capsized and sank during an August 1813 storm, killing all but a quarter of the more than 70 crewmembers on board. A commemorative plaque can be found in Hamilton's Confederation Park. Designated NHS: 1976.

ROYAL BOTANICAL GARDENS
BURLINGTON, ON

These gardens were established in the 1920s to beautify the road leading into Hamilton. The plan was radical at the time, departing from 19th-century ideals to focus on a series of gardens and conservation areas along a vehicular parkway. This included a rock garden built in an abandoned gravel pit. The gardens encompass 162 ha (400 acres) of display gardens and more than 930 ha (2,300 acres) of environmentally sensitive and diverse ecosystems. Designated NHS: 1993. 680 Plains Rd. W. (905) 527-1158.

BUTLER'S BARRACKS
NIAGARA-ON-THE-LAKE, ON

The British built Butler's Barracks after nearby Fort George (see pp. 206–209) was destroyed during the War of 1812. The barracks were named for John Butler and his Loyalist soldiers, who founded Niagara at the end of the American Revolution. Five of the 20 original buildings remain. The two-storey barrack building at Butler's Barracks would have once housed 100 soldiers. Today, it's home to the interpretive exhibits of the Lincoln and Welland Regiment Museum. Designated NHS: 1962. 51 Queens Parade. (905) 468-6614.

FORT MISSISSAUGA
NIAGARA-ON-THE-LAKE, ON

Originally built in 1814–16 and reconstructed in 1838–1840, Fort Mississauga is the only surviving example of its kind in Canada—a square central brick tower, buffered by a star-shaped earthwork of ramparts and ditches. Located at the mouth of the Niagara River, it acted as a counterpoint to the Americans' Fort Niagara on the river's other side. It is now surrounded by the greens of the Niagara-on-the-Lake Golf Club. Designated NHS: 1960. 223 Queen St.

TORONTO & NIAGARA

TORONTO & NIAGARA SITES

MISSISSAUGA POINT LIGHTHOUSE
NIAGARA-ON-THE-LAKE, ON

The lighthouse at Mississauga Point was the first one built on the Great Lakes. Constructed in 1804, the hexagonal stone tower and adjacent light keeper's house were both demolished when the British built Fort Mississauga (see p. 213) here in 1814, using the remains of the lighthouse to construct the fort's tower. No physical evidence of the lighthouse remains, but a plaque explains the site's significance. Designated NHS: 1937.

NIAGARA APOTHECARY
NIAGARA-ON-THE-LAKE, ON

A small, single-storey clapboard building in downtown Niagara-on-the-Lake, the apothecary is a fine example of a Confederation-era pharmacy. Operational from 1866 to 1964 (though the building dates to 1820), it's also one of the country's oldest continuously operating practices. The interior has been restored for use as a museum. Beautifully carved cupboards, black walnut cabinetry, plaster mouldings, and more give a glimpse into the past of commercial Canada. Designated NHS: 1968. 5 Queen St. (905) 468-3845.

NIAGARA-ON-THE-LAKE
NIAGARA-ON-THE-LAKE, ON

A visit to Niagara-on-the-Lake's historic district feels like a step back in time because much of it has been restored to its 19th-century appearance. The historic district stretches along the shore of Lake Ontario for 25 city blocks. Here, more than 90 buildings—including the district courthouse, also a national historic site—were built between 1815 and 1859, most designed in the British classical tradition. This gives a charming cohesion to the wide, tree-lined streets, the parks, and landscape. Designated NHS: 2004.

QUEENSTON HEIGHTS
NIAGARA-ON-THE-LAKE, ON

The Battle of Queenston Heights was a significant fight in the War of 1812, with British, Canadian, and Indigenous forces successfully defending the heights against an American invasion. The landscape tells the story—from the locations of the British batteries to military defence works, to the spot where Maj. Gen. Isaac Brock, a hero of the war, died. Brock is interred in the Brock's Monument, a commemorative column that towers over the battlefield. Designated NHS: 1968. 14184 Niagara Pkwy. (905) 262-4759.

WILLOWBANK
NIAGARA-ON-THE-LAKE, ON

Willowbank sits on the shores of the Niagara River, overlooking the border between Canada and the United States. The three-and-a-half-storey mansion was built in the early 19th century, a time when the upper-class members of Upper Canada established large country estates in what was considered wilderness. The house is currently home to the Willowbank School of Restoration Arts, which offers a diploma in heritage conservation. Designated NHS: 2004. 14487 Niagara Pkwy. (905) 262-1239.

NAVY ISLAND
NIAGARA FALLS, ON

During the 1760s, Navy Island was home to the shipyard that built the first British decked ships to sail the Great Lakes. The site also had an important role in the 1837–38 rebellions in Upper and Lower Canada. When the journalist and radical political reformist William Lyon Mackenzie failed to seize control of the government in 1837, he established a "government in exile" on Navy Island. Designated NHS: 1921. Niagara Pkwy.

TORONTO & NIAGARA

TORONTO & NIAGARA SITES

FORT YORK
TORONTO, ON

The wide green space of Fort York sits surrounded today by downtown Toronto's skyscrapers. Established in the early 19th century, the fort housed a garrison meant to entice settlers to the protected community that would become Toronto. Invading Americans burned down Fort York during the War of 1812, but the British rebuilt it. The fort boasts the largest collection of War of 1812 buildings in Canada, including seven buildings, a stone-lined earthwork, and a military cemetery at Strachan Avenue. Designated NHS: 1923. 100 Garrison Rd. (416) 392-6907.

GEORGE BROWN HOUSE
TORONTO, ON

This redbrick Beverly Street mansion was built for George Brown in 1875-77. One of the fathers of Confederation, Brown founded the *Globe* and used the Toronto-based newspaper to argue against the continuance of slavery in the United States during that country's Civil War. The house, where Brown lived until his death in 1880, now houses a museum, meeting space, and offices. Designated NHS: 1976. 186 Beverley St. (888) 773-8888.

GOODERHAM AND WORTS DISTILLERY
TORONTO, ON

Trinity Street is home to 30 brick-and-stone industrial buildings, all built between 1859 and 1927. The complex, which covers 5.25 ha (13 acres) on the eastern edge of downtown Toronto, was the site of operations for the Gooderham and Worts firm. Here, spirits were produced, packaged, stored, marketed, and developed. Taken together, the site's buildings speak to the history of the distilling industry and manufacturing process in 19th-century Canada. Designated NHS: 1988. Trinity St.

KENSINGTON MARKET
TORONTO, ON

Kensington is a busy, eclectic 27-ha (67 acres) neighbourhood in the heart of downtown Toronto, distinctive for its narrow streets and mixed-use buildings. Brightly painted houses have been converted into small storefronts selling fish, vegetables, clothing, and more. Apartments occupy upper floors. In rear alleys, short rows of 19th-century cottages are crammed onto miniature lots. Kensington can be viewed as a microcosm of Canada's ethnic mosaic. Designated NHS: 2006. Dundas West, Bellevue, Spadina, and College Sts.

MAPLE LEAF GARDENS
TORONTO, ON

Officially, the building is now known as the Mattamy Athletic Centre, but everyone still calls it Maple Leaf Gardens. Built in 1931, the Gardens was home to the Toronto Maple Leafs for 68 years, and it has maintained its iconic status despite the hockey team moving to newer facilities. Over the years, the Gardens has also hosted cultural, political, and religious events, and celebrities including Sir Winston Churchill, Muhammad Ali, and the Beatles. Designated NHS: 2007. 60 Carleton St. (416) 598-5961.

UNIVERSITY COLLEGE
TORONTO, ON

Completed in 1859, University College, the founding college at the University of Toronto, is one of the oldest collegiate buildings in Canada. The C-shaped Romanesque Revival building is positioned at the top of the central campus green. This location highlights the building's importance to the development of the University of Toronto as well as of a national system of government-supported, nondenominational postsecondary institutions. Designated NHS: 1968. 15 King's College Circle.

TORONTO & NIAGARA

The landscaped parkland of Fort Malden, on the banks of the Detroit River

SOUTHWESTERN ONTARIO

Fertile southwestern Ontario occupies a peninsula touched by three of the Great Lakes as well as Georgian Bay. Settled by the French in the early 18th century as part of New France, the area is home to the remains of a 16th-century First Nations village (see p. 223), a 17th-century French Jesuit mission (see p. 223), and several historic lighthouses. It fell under British control in 1763, and by 1812, as in the rest of southern Ontario, Loyalist refugees from the United States comprised the vast majority of the population. During

the War of 1812 (1812–15), local militias and Indigenous Peoples joined the British military in rebuffing invading U.S. forces, but not before they had destroyed Fort Malden (see pp. 220–221). Rebuilt by the British in the 1820s, the fort overlooks the U.S. border south of Windsor, one of the oldest continuous settlements in southwestern Ontario and the largest city here until the mid-20th century. In the decades following the end of the war, immigrants flocked to southern Ontario, with much of the region settled by the mid-19th century.

Period reenactments bring the 19th-century Fort Malden to life.

▶ FORT MALDEN

AMHERSTBURG, ON
Designated 1921

From the street, Fort Malden looks peaceful. It's hard to imagine a military past here, where beautiful brick buildings sit on landscaped parkland along the Detroit riverbanks. Step inside the fort, however, and soldiers' barracks, earthworks, and other evidence prove otherwise.

The remains of this once significant military stronghold did not form part of the original Fort Malden. Erected in 1796, the first fort was destroyed in the War of 1812. The British didn't begin rebuilding the garrison until the 1820s. At the time, with the British unsure about the future of the fort, the new construction numbered only a handful of buildings. It wasn't until the Upper Canadian Rebellions of 1837 that the fortifications were built up in earnest.

But by the mid-19th century, Fort Malden was no longer needed for defensive purposes, and the British turned its ownership over to the province of Ontario. In subsequent years, the fort served as a psychiatric hospital, and as a lumberyard and mill. Eventually, in 1937, the Canadian federal government acquired the lands and established the park that occupies the space today.

What to See & Do

The visitor centre features exhibits and a video that help tell the story of Fort Malden. The 45-minute guided tours (fee) give visitors a chance to listen to in-depth stories about the garrison during the War of 1812 and the Rebellions of 1837, as well as explanations for how the fort's ditches and defence systems worked. The fort's post-military uses are detailed too.

The fort has a unique on-site cafeteria: Visit the authentic soldiers' cookhouse for a meal of stew and teacakes, just like what would have been served in 1838 as part of supper— a meal introduced in an effort to improve the health and morale of the soldiers. (Food is not served in

September and October, but the cook-house can still be visited then.)

How to Get There

Travel south on Riverside Drive West and continue along Sandwich Street. Turn right on Ojibway Pkwy. North and continue onto Hwy. 18/Front Road. Turn right on Elm Avenue, and then left onto Laird Avenue.

When to Go

Open Wednesday to Sunday from Saturday of Victoria Day weekend (last Monday before May 25) to June 30; open daily July 1 to Labour Day (first Monday of September); open Wednesday to Sunday from Labour Day to the Sunday of Thanksgiving (second Monday of October).

INFORMATION

HOW TO REACH US
100 Laird Ave., Amherstburg, ON N9V 2Z2. Phone (519) 736-5416. pc.gc.ca/malden.

ENTRANCE FEES
$3.90 per adult, $9.80 per family.

ACCESSIBLE SERVICES
Limited.

HOTELS, MOTELS, & INNS
Guest House Getaway 8331 Middle Side Rd., Mcgregor, ON N0R 1J0. (519) 562-7711. 4 rooms, $135–$225. **Lexington Inn and Suites** 2130 Division Rd., Windsor, ON N8W 2A1. (519) 250-4657. lexingtonwindsor.com. 49 rooms, $89–$169.

SOUTHWESTERN ONTARIO

The extensive forested grounds and landscaped gardens at Woodside blaze with colour in the fall.

▶ WOODSIDE

KITCHENER, ON
Designated 1952

The yellow brick home that sits at the centre of Woodside was the boyhood home of Canada's longest serving prime minister, William Lyon Mackenzie King (1874–1950). Set amid 4.5 ha (11 acres) of forest, the house features original King family heirlooms and reproductions.

Originally built by a barrister in 1853, Woodside was home to various families. The Kings lived there for seven years (1886–93). King went on to act as the leader of the Liberal Party from 1919 to 1948, serving during that time as prime minister for a total of 22 years. Most significantly, he led the country through the Second World War. King was able to parlay the country's significant contribution to the war effort into a stronger international voice for Canada. Legislation introduced by his government was the first step in development of the modern Canadian welfare state.

What to See & Do

The interior of Woodside is furnished as it would have been in the 1890s, and the grounds are landscaped to re-create the feel of period gardens. There are guided and self-guided tours available.

How to Get There

In Kitchener, take Hwy. 85 and exit at Wellington Street, heading west. Turn right on Spring Valley Road; Woodside is on the left side.

INFORMATION

HOW TO REACH US
528 Wellington St. N, Kitchener ON N2H 5L5. Phone (519) 571-5684. pc.gc.ca/woodside.

ENTRANCE FEES
$3.90 per adult, $9.80 per family/group.

ACCESSIBLE SERVICES
The second floor is not wheelchair accessible.

HOTELS, MOTELS, & INNS
Crowne Plaza Kitchener-Waterloo 105 King St. E, Kitchener, ON N2G 2K8. (519) 744-4141. kitchener-hotel.com. 200 rooms, $119–$280.
Waterloo Hotel 2 King St. N, Waterloo, ON N2J 2W7. (519) 885-2626. thewaterloohotel.ca. 15 rooms, $165–$180.

When to Go

The site is open Monday through Friday, December 20 through September; the rest of the year, it is only open afternoons, Wednesday through Saturday.

SOUTHWESTERN ONTARIO SITES

POINT CLARK LIGHTHOUSE
POINT CLARK, ON

Automated since the mid-1960s, Point Clark Lighthouse still stands as a beacon, warning ships away from a dangerous shoal on Lake Huron. One of six imperial-style towers built on Lake Huron and Georgian Bay, Point Clark was completed in 1859 as part of an effort to make the lake safer for increased commercial and passenger traffic. The 27.5-m (90 ft) tower is made from local limestone. The former lighthouse keeper's residence now houses a museum. Designated NHS: 1966. 530 Lighthouse Rd., Huron-Kinloss. (705) 526-9804.

SAINT-LOUIS MISSION
TAY, ON

When Jesuit missionaries came to the area in the 1640s, they gave the name Saint-Louis to a village established by the Ataronchronon, who were part of the Wendat Confederacy. Located beside the Hogg River, the site is now just a field surrounded by freshly planted pine and a mixed hardwood forest. The only interpretation is offered by a stone cairn that explains the site's significance as the place where missionaries Jean de Brébeuf and Gabriel Lalement were captured when the Iroquois attacked the village in 1649. Designated NHS: 1920.

BOIS BLANC ISLAND LIGHTHOUSE AND BLOCKHOUSE
AMHERSTBURG, ON

In 1838, Canadian rebels, along with their American allies, drove British militia off Bois Blanc Island and set up camp. The next day, the rebels' botched attack on nearby Amherstburg led to their capture. In the wake of the attack, the British constructed further defensive positions on the island, including three blockhouses. The limestone lighthouse and one recently reconstructed blockhouse are all that is visible today. Designated NHS: 1955. Southern tip of Bois Blanc Island. (519) 736-5416.

SOUTHWOLD EARTHWORKS
IONA, ON

Archaeological evidence recalls the community of Iroquoian-speaking people, known as the Chonnonton, who built on this site in the 15th and 16th centuries. Twentieth-century excavations revealed closely spaced longhouses and well-preserved earthworks, consisting of a double ring of earthen mounds that would have supported the village palisades. Along with a commemorative plaque, these are the only visible evidence of the former village. Designated NHS: 1923. About 3 km (1.9 mi) south of Iona on Iona Rd. (Rte. 14). (519) 322-2365.

SOUTHWESTERN ONTARIO

The Attikamek Trail on South St. Marys Island, at Sault Ste. Marie Canal National Historic Site

NORTHERN ONTARIO

Most of the northern part of Ontario lies under the Canadian Shield— a vast area of exposed continental crust topped with a thin layer of soil. Although generally unsuitable for agriculture, this region rich with minerals (cobalt, copper, zinc, gold, and more) has played an important role in the nation's timber and mining industries, which both had their beginnings here in the late 19th and early 20th centuries. Most cities in northern Ontario owe their origins to Canada's railroads, which carried minerals and lumber to factories in

the south, eventually pushing Toronto ahead of Montréal in overall economic production. Because it could accommodate the large commercial ships of the day, the Sault Ste. Marie Canal (see pp. 228–229) on the St. Marys River, completed in 1895, also helped with the transportation of raw materials and labourers between northern and southern Ontario. Today, the number of trees in this region has been dramatically decreased due to logging, but northern mines remain a vital part of Ontario's economy.

Displays and interactive features in the Fort St. Joseph visitor centre make sense of the fort's archaeological remains.

▶ FORT ST. JOSEPH   ST. JOSEPH ISLAND, ON

Designated 1923

St. Joseph Island sits at the rugged northwestern end of Lake Huron. Remote and isolated on the lake, it was in the late 18th century and early 19th century home to the most westerly outpost of British North America—Fort St. Joseph.

The fortifications here symbolize the military and commercial alliance that existed between the British and the Indigenous Peoples of the region in the years between the American Revolution and the War of 1812.

In 1796, the British evacuated the post of Michilimackinac in Michigan Territory, which they had held since the end of the American Revolution in 1783, and built their own fort on Lake Huron. They chose St. Joseph Island for its proximity to Fort Mackinac and for its waterway transportation routes. During the War of 1812, they attacked Mackinac Island, capturing the fort there. The Americans later retaliated by burning Fort St. Joseph to the ground. After the war, Fort Mackinac was returned to the United States, and the British chose to establish a new post on nearby

Drummond Island, with Fort St. Joseph's remaining buildings relocated there.

Today, only limestone ruins are visible of the former fort.

What to See & Do

Exploration of Fort St. Joseph is self-guided. A total of 6 km (3.7 mi) of hiking trails wind past former settlements and burial grounds and through forests on their way to Huron's limestone beaches. Guides and interpreters are available to explain the significance of each of the ruins, which include the outlines of a blockhouse, guardhouse, powder magazine, and bakehouse, among other buildings.

For something special, participate in a ghost walk (fee), where costumed guides lead visitors by candlelight through the ruins of the old fort, telling tales of former residents of the island.

The visitor centre features a theatre, museum, and displays.

How to Get There

St. Joseph Island is 45 km (28 mi) east of Sault Ste. Marie, Ontario. Take the bridge from Trans-Canada 17 and follow the Parks Canada signs for the 37-km (23 mi) drive to Fort St. Joseph National Historic Site.

When to Go

The site is open daily from July 1 to Labour Day (first Monday of September), and Monday to Friday mid-May through June and after Labour Day to Thanksgiving in October.

INFORMATION

HOW TO REACH US
Box 220, Richards Landing, ON P0R 1J0. Phone (705) 246-2664. pc.gc .ca/eng/lhn-nhs/on/stjoseph/index .aspx.

ENTRANCE FEES
$3.90 per adult, $9.80 per family/ group.

ACCESSIBLE SERVICES
Limited.

HOTELS, MOTELS, & INNS
Clansmen Motel 1430 Richards St., Richards Landing, ON P0R 1J0. (705) 246-2581. clansmenmotel.ca. 6 rooms, $70–$80.

NORTHERN ONTARIO

Fort St. Joseph was built from limestone quarried on nearby Lime Island.

A chimney mysteriously stands apart at the fort.

The ruins of one of Fort St. Joseph's buildings

The Sault Ste. Marie Canal links Lake Huron and Lake Superior.

▶ SAULT STE. MARIE CANAL

SAULT STE. MARIE, ON
Designated 1987

The locks and waterways of Ontario crisscross the province, all the way from the St. Lawrence River in the southeast to Lake Superior in the northwest. When the Sault Ste. Marie Canal, which links Lake Huron and Lake Superior, was completed in 1895, it was the final piece of a navigational system still in use today.

The newly constructed Sault canal not only boasted the world's largest lock at the time, but also the first lock operation in the world to run off its own power station.

Measuring 274 m (899 ft) long and 18 m (59 ft) wide, the original lock chamber was built to hold the large freighters, steamers, schooners, and barges of the day. The chamber has since been reconstructed to hold smaller recreational boats.

Besides the canal itself, the site's significance extends to the surrounding buildings, including those on North St. Marys Island. The red sandstone Administration Building, Superintendent's Residence, Canalmen's Shelter, Powerhouse, Stores Building, and four motor houses (two at either end of the lock) contributed to the day-to-day operation of the canal, and give the site its current character.

A novel means of controlling water flow into the lock, the Emergency Swing Dam is the only one of its kind in Canada and one of few ever constructed in the world. It was successfully used in 1909 after an accident in the canal tore away several of the lock gates.

What to See & Do

Take in the cultural heritage by exploring the Powerhouse and other buildings. Site staff are always available to answer questions and conduct guided tours (fee). The natural heritage of the area is on display along the easy 2.2-km (1.4 mi) round-trip Attikamek Trail, which begins across the lock gates on South St. Marys Island. Hiking along here, visitors might see bald eagles, ducks, and geese.

The visitor centre has exhibits and a gift shop.

How to Get There

Follow Hwy. 17E into the city until the highway turns into Trunk Road. Follow it to the end where it becomes Wellington Street East, and then stay in the left lane to take Elgin Street. Turn left on Elgin and follow it to Queen Street East. Follow Queen and turn left on Huron Street. Take the right-hand lane to Canal Drive and turn left.

INFORMATION

HOW TO REACH US
1 Canal Dr., Sault Ste. Marie, ON P6A 6W4. Phone (705) 941-6262. pc.gc.saultstemariecanal.

ENTRANCE FEES
None.

ACCESSIBLE SERVICES
Accessible.

HOTELS, MOTELS, & INNS
Algoma's Water Tower Inn and Suites 360 Great Northern Rd., Sault Ste. Marie, ON P6B 4Z7. (705) 949-8111. watertowerinn.com. 176 rooms, $109–$189.
Fairfield Inn and Suites 633 Great Northern Rd., Sault Ste. Marie, ON P6B 5A1. (705) 253-7378. marriott.com. 82 rooms, $164–$184.

NORTHERN ONTARIO

Relaxing at the 1897 Superintendent's Residence

When to Go

The visitor centre is open from mid-May to the Friday before Thanksgiving (second Monday in October). The site is open daily from July 1 to Labour Day (first Monday of September), and Monday to Friday mid-May through June and after Labour Day to closing. The lock is open daily from mid-May to mid-October.

The Administration Building was built out of red sandstone excavated during the construction of the canal.

PRAIRIE
PROVINCES

South Saskatchewan River, Batoche *Page 230:* Fort Walsh, a North West Mounted Police post in Saskatchewan (top); a child tries on the uniform of the North West Mounted Police (middle); tepees at Head-Smashed-In Buffalo Jump, Alberta (bottom) *Page 231:* Bar U Ranch, Alberta

□　National Historic Site (NHS)
⊛　Province capital city

0 mi　　　　　　　　　　　200

0 km　　　　200

PRAIRIE PROVINCES

Bounded in the east by Lake Superior and in the west by the Rocky Mountains, the three prairie provinces—Manitoba, Saskatchewan, and Alberta—abound with natural resources, including fertile soil and oil and natural gas reserves. The prairie itself stretches across the southern portions of the provinces.

For thousands of years Indigenous Peoples inhabited this region, numbering some 20,000 to 50,000 by the mid-17th century. European and Canadian fur traders arrived in the 1640s, and the region soon became the centre of the competitive fur trade, with the Hudson's Bay Company (founded in 1670), French traders, and later the North West Company (founded in 1779) all vying for control of the lucrative industry. Nevertheless, the region remained sparsely settled until the second half of the 19th century, when many Canadians began migrating west. People from the United States, Great Britain, and Europe followed later in the immigration boom of the 1890s and early 1900s.

The expanding nonnative population threatened the First Nations, whose way of life was likewise jeopardized by the steep decline in the number of buffalo, upon which they

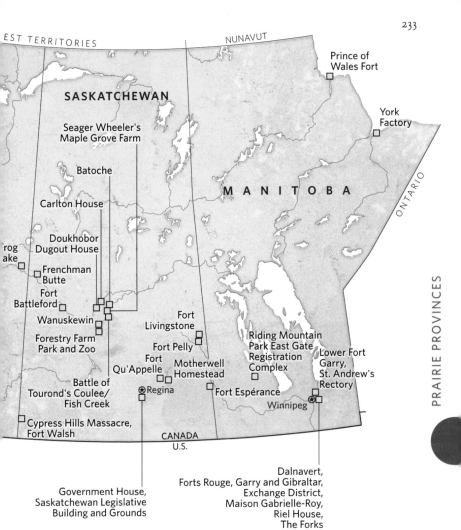

EST TERRITORIES

NUNAVUT

SASKATCHEWAN

Seager Wheeler's
Maple Grove Farm

Batoche

Carlton House

rog
ake

Doukhobor
Dugout House

Frenchman
Butte

Fort
Battleford

Wanuskewin

Forestry Farm
Park and Zoo

Battle of
Tourond's Coulee/
Fish Creek

Cypress Hills Massacre,
Fort Walsh

Fort
Livingstone

Fort Pelly

Fort
Qu'Appelle

Motherwell
Homestead

Regina

Fort Espérance

Prince of
Wales Fort

York
Factory

M A N I T O B A

ONTARIO

Riding Mountain
Park East Gate
Registration
Complex

Lower Fort
Garry,
St. Andrew's
Rectory

Winnipeg

CANADA
U.S.

PRAIRIE PROVINCES

Government House,
Saskatchewan Legislative
Building and Grounds

Dalnavert,
Forts Rouge, Garry and Gibraltar,
Exchange District,
Maison Gabrielle-Roy,
Riel House,
The Forks

depended for food and other resources. In a series of seven numbered treaties negotiated with the Canadian government in the 1870s, the Indigenous Peoples of the prairie exchanged their centuries-old sovereignty over the land for the promise of economic and educational compensation. Reserves on which the First Nations could live were also created. In 1885, some of the First Nations allied with the Métis, people of mixed European and Indigenous heritage, in their struggle to safeguard their way of life. Consuming Saskatchewan and parts of Alberta, the five-month-long Northwest Resistance ultimately failed; however, distinctive Métis cultural traditions remain strong. In 2003, the Canadian government officially recognized the Métis as an Indigenous group.

Winnipeg grew up around The Forks, site of the first permanent European settlement in the Canadian West.

MANITOBA

The province of Manitoba lies midway between Canada's Atlantic and Pacific coasts. Indigenous Peoples—the Assiniboine, Ojibwa, Cree, and other First Nations—have inhabited this land since about 4000 B.C. Some 100 years after the first European explorers arrived in the early 17th century, the Hudson's Bay Company (HBC) began to establish a series of trading posts throughout the region. Historic HBC sites like The Forks (see pp. 240–243), York Factory (see pp. 250–251), Prince of Wales Fort (see pp. 248–249), and Lower Fort

Garry (see pp. 236–239) help outline the history of the fur trade and relations with First Nations in the west. Following Manitoba's admission to the Confederation in 1870, the province experienced a population boom and, with the arrival of the Canadian Pacific Railway in the 1880s, was transformed into a national transportation hub. Capital city Winnipeg became the centre of Canada's grain industry and today hosts historic sites associated with the fur trade, the Métis, and urban life in the late 19th and early 20th centuries.

Costumed interpreters bring to life the Lower Fort Garry of the mid-1800s.

◗ LOWER FORT GARRY

ST. ANDREWS, MB
Designated 1950

Established by the Hudson's Bay Company (HBC) in 1830, and operated as a company post until 1911, Lower Fort Garry was also where First Nations and representatives of the British Crown gathered to make the first of the Numbered Treaties.

TREATY NO. 1

As a major business site for the Red River Settlement, Lower Fort Garry was the place where farmers and trappers came for supplies. It was also where the surrounding Indigenous communities (Anishinabe [Ojibwa] and Mushkegowuk [Swampy Cree] First Nations and Métis) came to trade their leather goods, farmed crops, and dried fish with the HBC. Many would also take part in the annual buffalo hunts or work on the farms. That made the fort a fitting location for the negotiation and signing of Treaty No. 1 between the

First Nations and the Crown in 1871.

Eleven in total, the Numbered Treaties promised Indigenous Peoples reserve lands, annuities, and the continued right to hunt and fish on unoccupied Crown land. They were signed between 1871 and 1921 as the Canadian government pursued settlement, farming, and resource development in the west and north.

Also known as the Stone Fort Treaty, Treaty No. 1 set the stage for negotiations with First Nations throughout western Canada. "Stone Fort" refers to the 1.5-ha (3.7 acres) HBC fort comprising several buildings within a stone wall on the site. The fort, along with a number of restored and reconstructed buildings beyond the wall, make up one of the most impressive collections of early stone architecture in western Canada. The HBC donated the complex and land to the federal government in 1951, and since then many of its structures have been restored to the 1850–1860 period.

A VITAL HUB

After the government of Canada acquired the HBC's lands in the west (in 1870), various government officials and functions occupied the fort's facilities together with fur trade officials; as a result, the fort has been both witness and symbol for much of western Canada's early history. As an HBC post for decades, Lower Fort Garry was a centre for industry and transport in the Red River Settlement as well as a supply and distribution centre for the fur trade. Its location near the junction of the Red and Assiniboine Rivers made it a major shipping port for a while. HBC's York boats would make the 1,100-km (684 mi) journey from Hudson Bay to the Red River Settlement, which included dozens of gruelling portages.

York boats were the transportation workhorse of the HBC in western Canada. They were made with heavy timber and had sterns angled upward at 45 degrees, making beaching and launching easier. They could be operated by oar or by sail, carried lots of cargo, and were yet still light enough to be dragged over log rollers by its crew when portaging was necessary. Lower Fort Garry has some of these legendary boats, including a historically accurate reproduction approximately 12.8 m (42 ft) long.

ARCHITECTURE & NOTABLE BUILDINGS

Lower Fort Garry encompasses several different architectural designs popular during the fur trade era, making it a significant collection of trade structures demonstrating early stone architecture. The fort itself is constructed with limestone, one of only three stone forts built by the HBC. Its ramparts still stand, making it the oldest intact stone fur trading post in North America.

With wood readily available just north of the site and a generous supply of limestone at the fort, several different methods of construction were used in the settlement. Designs often featured both stone and wood, and the current historic buildings are examples of construction techniques used 150 years ago.

Taking a tour around the fort offers ample opportunity to see the early stone building practices firsthand. The two main techniques used were colombage pierroté (half-timbered construction with the infill between the posts and studs made of stone rubble and lime plaster, or colombage) and Red River frame construction (timber-frame structure with horizontal log infill also known as post on sill). The former construction method was used to build the Men's House and the Annex to the Big House. The latter technique can be seen best in the Southwest Bastion, which was used for storage and now houses an exhibit showcasing fur trade architectural techniques.

After becoming familiar with the site in the visitor centre, explore the site's many buildings. Nine of the 13 buildings have been furnished to represent their appearance during the mid-1800s. A guided 90-minute tour (fee) offers a great introduction to the

MANITOBA

fort as well as behind-the-scenes information. The tours are available on weekends in May and June, and daily in July and August.

A gravel pathway from the visitor reception area links to the other buildings and to the main stone-walled fort. The fort encloses many of the main structures, such as the Big House, the oldest and largest of the buildings. It is an elegant example of the type of dwelling HBC posts had for the officers or business executives of the company.

Foundations still remain of many of the buildings of the Industrial Complex, in use from the mid-1840s through the mid-1870s. These include a malt house, distillery, limekiln, gristmill, and York boat–building shed. Other structures inside the fort include the Ross Cottage (currently

An interpreter in period dress plays a traditional tune.

Numerous women and children lived at the fort.

closed), which was used as a guest cottage for many years and even rented out, and the Farm Manager's House, one of the last Red River frame buildings left in Canada, which was moved to Lower Fort Garry in 1970 to represent what was used for this purpose in the 1850s. There is also an Indigenous encampment, blacksmith's shop, fur loft/sales shop, warehouse, and the 1850 Men's House, which served as a residence for the labourers and tradesmen who came from other communities.

Countless historic objects or artefacts on display throughout the site help tell the story of Lower Fort Garry. For instance, a wooden plough located in the warehouse was made by local stonemason Duncan McRae. Stonemasons were in high demand in the early days of the Red River Settlement. The plough was among the first to be made at the fort, and it is likely one of the oldest surviving ploughs in western Canada. Around the mid-19th century, this type of ox- or horse-drawn plough was widely used in the Red River Settlement. They were pulled through farmers' fields in long straight lines, creating ridges and furrows in the earth to turn up nutrient-rich soil in preparation for seeding crops.

Because much of the site is outdoors, be sure to dress in layers in the spring, and bring a hat and sunscreen for hot summer days. Dress warmly for a winter visit as historic buildings are closed. Also, wear comfortable walking shoes; the buildings are spread out across the site.

How to Get There

Lower Fort Garry is a half hour's drive (32 km/20 mi) north from downtown Winnipeg and a few minutes south of Selkirk on Hwy. 9 (Main Street). It is accessible by bus; scheduled runs

LOWER FORT GARRY NATIONAL HISTORIC SITE
(Lieu historique national de Lower Fort Garry)

INFORMATION & ACTIVITIES

HOW TO REACH US
5925 Hwy. 9, St. Andrews, MB R1A 4A8. Phone (204) 785-6050 or (888) 773-8888. pc.gc.ca/fortgarry.

SEASONS & ACCESSIBILITY
The fort's grounds are open year-round. The buildings are closed early September to mid-May.

FRIENDS OF LOWER FORT GARRY
(204) 785-8577. folfg.com.

ENTRANCE FEES
$7.80 per adult, $19.60 per family/group per day; $19.60 per adult, $49.00 per family/group per year.

PETS
Dogs are allowed in most of the historic buildings and the visitor centre, but they must be kept on a leash at all times. (In some buildings, dogs are allowed only if they can be carried.) Owners are responsible for cleaning up after their dogs and for their dog's behaviour.

ACCESSIBLE SERVICES
Motorized carts are available for transporting visitors with limited mobility to the historic grounds. Wheelchairs and strollers are available on loan. All pathways are gravel. The visitor centre is entirely accessible, but not all of the historic buildings are fully accessible.

THINGS TO DO
From May to September, costumed interpreters bring the site to life, portraying life in the Red River Settlement in the 1850s, be they company clerks, aboriginal trappers, York boatmen, blacksmiths, farmers, or gentry. Period demonstrations include wool spinning and dyeing, blacksmithing, as well as traditional Indigenous crafts.

At the Fun Historic Trades Workshops (fee), offered several times a week in July and August, visitors may bake a bannock (a traditional Indigenous biscuitlike bread), prepare tallow candles from scratch, and more. Check the website for times.

CAMPGROUNDS
There is no camping on-site. Nearby campgrounds include **Selkirk Municipal Park** (204-785-4953), **Willow Springs Campground** (204-485-1344), and **Birds Hill Provincial Park** (888-482-2267).

HOTELS, MOTELS, & INNS
(Rates are for a 2-person double, high season, in Canadian dollars, unless otherwise noted.)

Bridgeview Bed & Breakfast 1246 Breezy Point Rd., Selkirk, MB R1A 2A7. (204) 482-7892. bridgeviewretreat.com. $85.
Canalta Selkirk 1061 Manitoba Ave., Selkirk, MB R0C 0P0. (844) 484-7474. canaltahotels.com. 84 rooms, $139–$360.
Evergreen Gate Bed & Breakfast 1138 River Rd., Selkirk, MB R1A 4A7. (877) 901-0553. evergreengate.ca. 3 rooms, $115–$129.

MANITOBA

from Winnipeg and Selkirk take place Monday through Friday via Beaver Bus Lines *(beaverbus.com)*.

When to Go
Lower Fort Garry is open year-round, but hours and services change with the seasons. From mid-May to early September, most historic buildings are open and fees apply. Outside of this time frame, the grounds are open (entrance free), but the historic buildings are closed. Some programming may happen in the off-season; check the website for details.

For families, Wednesdays throughout the summer are Children's Day, when kids can carry out such chores at the fort as picking vegetables for dinner, taking part in a North West Mounted Police drill, packing a fur bale, and building a tepee.

Visitors flock to The Forks for its historical significance and its numerous recreational offerings.

▶ THE FORKS

WINNIPEG, MB
Designated 1974

Located at the junction of two major rivers—the Red and Assiniboine—and the heart of Turtle Island, The Forks was a focus for the site of the first permanent European settlement in the Canadian West that would later become the city of Winnipeg. It has witnessed many key historical events in western Canada.

Long before European explorers arrived, The Forks was a traditional Indigenous Peoples' stopping place for camping, gathering provisions, and trading with other First Nations. During the 1600s, Indigenous trading networks began circulating European goods as well, acquired from traders farther east. Europeans themselves established a presence in The Forks area during the 1730s.

In the 19th and 20th centuries, The Forks was a staging point for fur trade, exploration, and settlement. For a century, it served as the yards of major railways, including the Canadian Northern, the Grand Trunk Pacific, and the Canadian National Railway. The small settlement of Winnipeg grew into the principal metropolitan centre of western Canada, and became Canada's Gateway to the West. As both a railway and riverboat junction, The Forks served as an entry point for thousands of immigrants. In 1872, the Canadian government built two immigration sheds at The Forks, each of which could accommodate 500 people. The Canadian government designated The Forks a national historic site in 1974, and its historical legacy as a hub for people and significant activities continues to this day, serving as a vibrant public gathering place that is Winnipeg's top tourist destination.

INDIGENOUS MEETING PLACE

Archaeological remains of two camp-fires along the banks of the Assiniboine River channel, west of today's Forks Market, show that Indigenous Peoples used the confluence of the Red and Assiniboine Rivers as early as 4000 B.C. By 1000 B.C., they were camping in the area for extended periods of time, taking advantage of the area's rich food resources. Large runs of fish, including sturgeon, sauger, and walleye, travelled from the headwaters of the Red and Assiniboine Rivers to Lake Winnipeg. The river-bottom forests and prairies that surrounded and extended beyond the river junction were plentiful in deer, elk, bear, and, in winter, bison. Artefacts from this era originate from as far away as the Lake Superior region and northern Texas, demonstrating how The Forks played many important roles to these peoples. It was not only a provisioning site but also a traditional transition area between the prairies and the woodlands on seasonal migration routes, and part of a transcontinental trade route.

The Forks was occupied by the Nakoda (Assiniboine) First Nations people when French explorers first heard of the region. The Nakoda had moved north into this area during the 17th century when they split from the Dakota (Sioux) in Minnesota. The Nakoda soon assumed the role of fur trade middlemen between other First Nations groups and Europeans. They used the rivers to conduct commerce with trading posts located hundreds of miles away.

The Forks NHS has a collection of more than 190,000 recovered artefacts illustrating the early inhabitants' way of life. The recoveries were almost exclusively made from Fort Gibraltar I and II. Parts of these areas are now occupied by the Variety Heritage Adventure Park, and the north point interpretive node behind the Oodena Celebration Circle. Artefacts include projectile points, or arrowheads, used for hunting purposes by the First Nations groups living in this area from 200 B.C. to A.D. 1750. Hunting was an essential part of life on the prairies. Glass bead artefacts were also found. Beads were imported from Europe and were a popular fur trade item for the First Nations and Métis people. Beads were used to decorate items of clothing and were also made into earrings, necklaces, and hair adornments.

THE RAILWAY ERA: 1886-1923

The Forks was a key site of early railroad development on the prairies, with the railway arriving in 1885. The railway connected Manitoba with ice-free ports and world markets, helping to build the agriculture industry.

Rail yards of the three major railways took over The Forks, and many of the present-day buildings date from this time period. Union Station (1908–1911), designed and built by Warren and Wetmore Architects (the same architects who designed New York's Grand Central Station), is still used as a passenger railway terminal as well as an office building. The Boiler's and Brakes Structure (1889), the oldest building at The Forks, is now the Manitoba Children's Museum. The National Cartage Building is now the Johnston Terminal, and the Grand Trunk Pacific Railway Stable Building (1909–1912) and the Great Northern Railway Stable Building, also designed by Warren and Wetmore, are joined together to form The Forks Market.

MANITOBA

The Forks was long a seasonal trading centre and campsite for Indigenous Peoples before the Europeans came.

A skater takes to the ice in The Forks.

A large urban green space, The Forks has much to offer.

THE FORKS TODAY

Get a sense of the 3.6-ha (8.9 acres) site by taking to the various pathways lacing through this historic green space, which are perfect for strolling or cycling. The Red River walkway offers views of historic St. Boniface, downtown Winnipeg, and the dramatic L'Esplanade Riel pedestrian bridge that connects the centre of Winnipeg with the historic French Quarter. Interpretive panels throughout the site describe the site's cultural and historical import, detailing significant people and events.

Important public art pieces are located here as well. In the orientation circle at the site's main entrance, Manitoba artist Marcel Gosselin's "The Path of Time" sculpture uses sunlight to showcase people's

THE FORKS NATIONAL HISTORIC SITE
(Lieu historique national de La Fourche)

INFORMATION & ACTIVITIES

HOW TO REACH US
45 Forks Market Rd., Winnipeg, MB R3C 4S8. Phone (204) 983-6757 or (888) 773-8888. pc.gc.ca/forks.

ENTRANCE FEES
$3.90 per adult, $9.80 per family/group per day; $67.70 per adult, $136.40 per family/group per year.

ACCESSIBLE SERVICES
The Forks is fully accessible for those with mobility issues. Access to the river walk is by ramp and all paths are graded with accessibility in mind.

THINGS TO DO
Guided walking tours (fee) are available Friday to Monday from the end of May to the end of August, in both English and French. A free guided tour at the Variety Heritage Adventure Park takes place twice daily, Friday to Monday, in July and August. Call or check the website for times.

HOTELS, MOTELS, & INNS
(Rates are for a 2-person double, high season, in Canadian dollars, unless otherwise noted.)

Fort Garry Hotel 222 Broadway, Winnipeg, MB R3C 0R3. (204) 942-8251. fortgarry hotel.com. 240 rooms, $209–$319.
Humphry Inn & Suites 260 Main St., Winnipeg, MB R3C 1A9. (877) 486-7479. humphryinn.com. 128 rooms, $179–$229.
Inn at the Forks 75 Forks Market Rd., Winnipeg, MB R3C 0A2. (877) 377-4100. innforks.com. 117 rooms, $197–$369.

Additional visitor information:
The Forks (888) 942-6302. theforks.com.
Tourism Winnipeg (204) 943-1970 or (855) 734-2489. tourismwinnipeg.com.

influence on this land. As the sun tracks across the sky, different pictographs of tools cut into a bronze shell are reflected onto a centre block of Tyndall limestone. Also located along the Red River walkway are 21 bronze ceremonial gambling sticks. They are a tribute to the Indigenous history at The Forks and were created by internationally acclaimed Indigenous artist Robert Houle.

At the Variety Heritage Adventure Park, Parks Canada teamed up with Variety, the Children's Charity of Manitoba, to bring history to life. The award-winning one-of-a-kind park has seven play zones based upon key historical themes of The Forks, such as the First Peoples zone, where kids can discover the many uses for a single bison. Similarly, kids can take a trip in a Hudson's Bay Company York boat in the Fur Trade zone or ride the rails on the *Countess of Dufferin*, the first locomotive train on the prairies, in the Iron Horse zone. The park also features representations of the Red and Assiniboine Rivers, with a portion serving as a splash pad in the summer.

How to Get There
The Forks is in the centre of Winnipeg. By car, turn south from Pioneer Avenue or William Stephenson Way onto Waterfront Drive (Israel Asper Way). If travelling north along St. Mary's Road/Main Street, there's also a turn-in to The Forks just over the Main Street Bridge (on Queen Elizabeth Way).

The closest Winnipeg Transit (204-287-RIDE, *winnipegtransit.com*) bus stop is #10907.

When to Go
The Forks National Historic Site is open year-round, but most activities are offered in the summer months.

Associated with Louis Riel, the Riel House is emblematic of a Métis household in the mid-1880s.

▶ RIEL HOUSE

WINNIPEG, MB
Designated 1976

Designated a national historic site in 1976, Riel House was the Riel family home from its construction around 1880 until 1969. It thus holds a strong connection to Louis Riel (1844–1885), Métis leader and a founder of the province of Manitoba, and its architecture demonstrates the nature of Métis settlement in Manitoba.

The Métis developed as the descendants of unions between First Nations women and French-Canadian and European men. They have a unique cultural identity, and helped to shape Canada.

As a spokesman for Métis resistance to Canadian expansion in the Red River area, Louis Riel helped form a provisional government in 1869 after the Hudson's Bay Company's administration broke down. The ensuing negotiations led to the creation of the province of Manitoba in 1870. Forced into exile in the United States in part because of the execution of a captive by the provisional government, Riel returned to the Northwest in 1884 to represent a group, largely of Métis, in their struggle for land rights. The next year he led the ill-fated 1885 conflicts, often spoken of in our history books as the Northwest Rebellion, and was subsequently hanged for treason.

Though Louis Riel never lived in the house, he visited here briefly in 1883 and lay in state in the home after he was hanged. The house has been restored and furnished to how it appeared in 1886 to offer a glimpse into the family's life and that of the Métis community, shortly after Riel's death.

Riel House is a rare surviving example representing how the Métis settled in Canada. The house's size, shape, structure, and design are typical of 19th-century Red River–frame Métis houses; in fact, the frame is one of the only surviving elements of the original home.

What to See & Do

Take a self-guided tour through Riel House, where interpretive panels and 800-plus artefacts, items that represent a blending of Indigenous and European cultures, tell the story of what life was like for the Riel family in 1886, specifically during its time of mourning. Look for the reproduction of a broken white statuette of St. Joseph, the patron saint of the Métis people. It's said that when Riel was praying in his cell after he had been arrested, the statue fell off a shelf and broke. He took this to be an omen of bad things to come.

How to Get There

Riel House is located in the residential area of South St. Vital at 330 River Road in Winnipeg. By car, turn south from Bishop Grandin Boulevard onto River Road. Winnipeg Transit (877-311-4974, *winnipegtransit.com*) offers bus service from downtown.

When to Go

Riel House is only open July 1 to August 30; open daily, but closed Wednesday mornings.

INFORMATION

HOW TO REACH US
330 River Rd. (St. Vital), Winnipeg, MB. Phone (204) 983-6757. pc.gc.ca/riel.

ENTRANCE FEES
$3.90 per adult, $9.80 per family/group.

ACCESSIBLE SERVICES
Partially accessible for wheelchairs.

HOTELS, MOTELS, & INNS
Best Western PLUS Pembina Inn & Suites 1714 Pembina Hwy., Winnipeg, MB R3T 2G2. (877) 269-8811. bestwesternpembina.com. 104 rooms, $153–$197.
Canad Inns Destination Centre Fort Garry 1824 Pembina Hwy., Winnipeg, MB R3T 2G2. (204) 261-7450 or (888) 332-2623. canadinns.com. 106 rooms, $115–$160.
Capri Motel 1819 Pembina Hwy., Winnipeg, MB R3T 2G2. (204) 269-6990. 67 rooms, $75–$95.

Additional visitor information:
Tourism Winnipeg (204) 943-1970 or (855) 734-2489. tourismwinnipeg.com.

MANITOBA

The furnishings of Riel House reflect both Métis and European traditions.

MANITOBA SITES

ST. ANDREW'S RECTORY
ST. ANDREWS, MB

Built in 1851–54 as a residence for the parish Anglican priest, St. Andrew's Rectory was rebuilt by Parks Canada in the 1980s. The rectory occupies a prominent hilltop location overlooking the Red River. The building is a prime example of mid-19th-century Red River architecture, with clean lines, limestone construction, and a wooden veranda. The landscaping reflects the 1860s. House open July and August; grounds open year-round. Designated NHS: 1962. 374 River Rd. (204) 785-6050.

FORTS ROUGE, GARRY, & GIBRALTAR
WINNIPEG, MB

Three forts differently sited at the confluence of the Red and Assiniboine Rivers show the fur trade evolution in the west. Fort Rouge (circa 1738) was part of the trade's expansion on behalf of France. The North West Company's 1810–11 Fort Gibraltar was destroyed in 1816 in a conflict with the Hudson's Bay Company, rebuilt, and, when the two companies merged in 1821, renamed Fort Garry. Damage led to its replacement by nearby Upper Fort Garry, itself partially demolished in 1882. The northern gate of Garry is the only visible remnant of the three forts. Designated NHS: 1924. The Forks, 45 Market Rd. (204) 983-6757.

MAISON GABRIELLE-ROY
WINNIPEG, MB

Maison Gabrielle-Roy presents the achievements of the great Franco-Canadian author Gabrielle Roy, who found inspiration for her books in these environs. Roy lived here for close to 28 years. The residence is now a museum, dedicated to ensuring that her literary legacy lives on within the vibrant cultural scene in Manitoba. Designated NHS: 2009. 375 Deschambault St. (204) 231-3853.

DALNAVERT
WINNIPEG, MB

Dalnavert was built in 1895 as the family home of Sir Hugh John Macdonald, the son of Canada's first prime minister and one of Winnipeg's leading citizens when the city was the economic power-house of western Canada. The restored house exemplifies the Queen Anne Revival style. It is now a museum with a visitor centre and heritage garden. Designated NHS: 1990. 61 Carlton St. (204) 943-2835.

EXCHANGE DISTRICT
WINNIPEG, MB

More than 100 heritage buildings built between 1880 and 1913 make up the Exchange District in downtown Winnipeg. These 20 city blocks of architecturally significant structures illustrate the city's key role in the west as a centre of finance, manufac-turing, and grain and wholesale trade. This colourful neighbourhood is now home to shops, restaurants, and galleries, and it has an urban park right at its core. Designated NHS: 1997. North of Portage Ave. and Main St. (204) 942-6716.

MANITOBA

RIDING MOUNTAIN PARK EAST GATE REGISTRATION COMPLEX
WASAGAMING, MB

Built as part of the Canadian govern-ment's Depression relief program, Riding Mountain National Park's East Gate Registration Complex com-prises three buildings: a warden's sta-tion, a gatekeeper's cottage, and the gate. With the only original national park gate from the 1930s still stand-ing, the complex features the rustic design style, a hallmark of national park building construction at that time. The gate's truss bridge and twin cupolas remain the eastern gateway into the park. Designated NHS: 1992. 1 Wasagaming Dr. (204) 848-7275.

Gun emplacements look out over the mouth of the Churchill River.

▶ PRINCE OF WALES FORT

ESKIMO POINT, MB
Designated 1920

Built by the Hudson's Bay Company (HBC), the Prince of Wales Fort was one of the fur trading empire's subarctic outposts during Canada's early years. This national historic site on Hudson Bay at the mouth of the Churchill River also includes the fort's winter harbour at Sloop Cove and Cape Merry, a defensive battery across the river, opposite the fort.

In the late 17th and early 18th centuries, Hudson Bay was the scene of English/French imperial rivalry. On several occasions, French forces captured HBC trading posts and nearly drove the English company out of business. Anxious to avoid such defeats in the future, in 1730 the HBC began building a stone fort at the mouth of the Churchill River, which was considered reasonably defensible.

However, the massive size of the fort, a European star-shape design with four protruding bastions, combined with the small construction crew, short building season, and the many tasks needed to survive in the subarctic, made for slow progress: It took more than 40 years to complete.

Throughout the HBC's operations here, nearby Dene (Chipewyan) and Cree families provided the post with meat, fish, cold-weather clothing, and snowshoes. They served as guides and couriers, trappers, provisioners, and consumers—they were crucial to the success of the HBC's fur trade.

What to See & Do

Visits to the Prince of Wales Fort are by guided tour only because of the danger posed by polar bears (with a higher probability of encounters July to early December). Bear monitors accompany the tours to ensure visitor safety. Book them with Parks Canada or a local tour operator.

At the multilevel fortification, visitors get a sense of the challenges faced by those living here in the 18th century. The tours usually include time for visitors to do some exploration within the fort on their own, perhaps to revisit the powder magazine or climb up to the cannon-lined stone parapets, among other things.

The site offers a couple special guided hikes: the summertime Sloop Cove Hike (book through Sea North Tours, *seanorthtours.com*), an easy 4-km (2.5 mi) hike along the shore of Hudson Bay from Sloop Cove (reached via Zodiac boat) to the fort, watching seabirds, spotting beluga whales, and finding fossils hundreds of millions of years old; and the wintertime (at the end of March) annual Trek to the Fort, an 8-km (5 mi) round-trip, mostly over sea ice (contact the Parks Canada Churchill office for dates and details).

Cape Merry has little interpretive signage; therefore, a guided tour is recommended.

How to Get There

There is no road into Churchill. Train service departs Winnipeg three times a week (VIA Rail, *viarail.ca*). Churchill is connected by daily flights from Winnipeg and a weekly flight from Thompson.

The Prince of Wales Fort is across the river from Churchill; it is accessible by boat or helicopter, available through commercial companies. Cape Merry Battery is 1.5 km (1 mi) by road north of Churchill. Bus transport and vehicle rentals are available; walking is not recommended because of the polar bear risk.

When to Go

Prince of Wales Fort is only open via guided tour (fee) in July and August, weather permitting.

MANITOBA

Cape Merry Battery is open mid-June to August for both self-guided tours (though Parks Canada recommends a guide because of polar bear risk) and guided (fee) tours. Free guided tours are available in October and November.

Rugged, star-shaped Prince of Wales Fort

A circa 1800 painted panel found in the depot building, showing a scene of everyday life at the fur trade depot

▶ YORK FACTORY

GILLAM, MB

Designated 1936

York Factory was an isolated but vital fur trade hub for more than 250 years. It played a critical role in the French-English struggle on Hudson Bay for control of the fur trade, as an important Hudson's Bay Company (HBC) trading post and entrepôt, and in the expansion of the fur trade into the interior of western Canada.

York Factory's current location near the mouth of the Hayes River is actually the third incarnation of the factory. The French and English battled for control of the original York Factory (built 1684), and each captured it at different times until 1713, when the Treaty of Utrecht gave the HBC exclusive trading rights on Hudson Bay. Later, York served as the main HBC entrepôt, providing the vital trade and transshipment link between the vast fur resources of the interior of North America and the markets of Europe.

Over the next century, it changed to a warehousing and transshipment depot with considerable administrative responsibilities. At its peak in the mid-19th century, the factory boasted more than 50 buildings, including a church, hospital, and school, and a large staff of officers, clerks, tradesmen, and labourers, as well as a seasonal workforce of Indigenous traders and hunters. The establishment of new southern supply lines after 1860 diminished York Factory's role by the end of the century to a regional trading post. Only two buildings, two visible ruins, a cemetery, remnants of planned landscapes, and archaeological remains exist today on the 102-ha (252 acres) national historic site.

What to See & Do

Visitors may wander at will around the grounds. Make sure to visit the depot building, the centre of the York Factory. Its rooms are filled with cannons, a fur press, a church pulpit, and ornate iron stoves stashed amid tables crowded with trade items like copper kettles, blankets, knives, and guns. Stroll along the wooden boardwalks over boggy tundra to the ruins of a powder magazine and cemetery.

Self-guided tours are available using printed materials or the Parks Canada Explora interactive tour. Loaded with maps, pictures, quizzes, and information about the rich history of York Factory, the Explora app allows you to explore York Factory at your own pace. Devices with the app may be signed out on-site if you do not have a smartphone.

Be aware that weather conditions are unpredictable at York Factory and can force a stay longer than anticipated. Take warm clothing, rubber boots, bug repellent, and two or three days of extra supplies. The average temperature in summer is 13°C (55.5°F), and a severe temperature drop is common in June and July when the wind comes off the frozen Hudson Bay. There is a 40 percent chance of daily rain, and high winds and high tides (up to 4 m/13 ft) are frequently experienced.

Polar bears may be encountered at any time at York Factory, with the greatest risk of an encounter mid-July

INFORMATION

HOW TO REACH US
P.O. Box 127, Churchill, MB R0B 0E0. Phone (204) 675-8863 or (888) 773-8888. pc.gc.ca/yorkfactory.

ENTRANCE FEES
None.

ACCESSIBLE SERVICES
Limited; contact the site for more details.

CAMPING
Safe camping locations and washroom facilities are available in Parks Canada's fenced compound. No reservations required.

HOTELS, MOTELS, & INNS
Aurora Garden Motel & Suites 88 Mattonnabee Ave., Gillam, MB R0B 0L0. (204) 652-6554. 35 rooms, $135.

Additional visitor information:
Travel Manitoba (800) 665-0040. travelmanitoba.com.

MANITOBA

to mid-September. Parks Canada staff provide polar bear monitoring for tours of the site. Please observe all directions given by staff.

How to Get There
Charter air transportation to York Factory is available from various points in northern Manitoba. VIA Rail *(viarail.ca)* has limited train service to nearby Gillam. From Gillam, take a plane or charter boat to the site. Visitors can also paddle the Hayes River; paddlers should register with the Parks Canada Churchill office and the Royal Canadian Mounted Police at their departure point.

When to Go
York Factory is open July and August (weather permitting).

York Factory's depot building (in background)

Horseback riding, Fort Walsh National Historic Site

SASKATCHEWAN

Admitted to the Confederation in 1905, landlocked Saskatchewan is the only province in Canada with no natural boundaries. Its name comes from a Cree word for "swiftly flowing river," and evidence suggests that the Cree and other Indigenous Peoples have inhabited this territory since at least 10,000 B.C. As in neighbouring Manitoba, the first Europeans to make inroads here were 17th-century fur traders. Most settlers, however, arrived after the establishment of the North West Mounted Police (NWMP) in the 1870s.

Travellers can experience the life of an early settler and agricultural pioneer at Motherwell Homestead (see pp. 260–261) and also visit Fort Walsh (see pp. 258–259) and other NWMP posts erected to negotiate relations with First Nations and help maintain law and order. The Northwest Resistance ended in May 1885 with the defeat of the Métis at Batoche (see pp. 254–257). In subsequent decades, myriad immigrants settled in the territory, including Quakers as well as Doukhobors fleeing persecution in Russia (see p. 269).

Batoche focuses on the lifestyles of the Métis community between 1860 and 1900.

▶ BATOCHE

BATOCHE, SK

Designated 1923

This peaceful rolling parkland filled with prairie sage, songbirds, and rabbits was the final battlefield of the Northwest Resistance of 1885, a Métis uprising born from years of the Métis people feeling excluded from the growth and development of the Canadian West.

Batoche National Historic Site commemorates this armed conflict between the Canadian government and the Métis provisional government as well as the history of the community of Batoche, home of Métis culture and heritage. Located on the South Saskatchewan River north of Saskatoon, the 810-ha (2,002 acres) site encompasses the battlefield, surviving elements of the surrounding community such as the distinctive river lot layout, and the vestiges of the Métis village, including a church and rectory. The village was located where Carlton Trail—the primary overland trade route between Fort Edmonton (in present-day Alberta) and Fort Garry in Winnipeg (Manitoba) for much of the 19th century—crossed the South Saskatchewan River.

THE MÉTIS

The term "Métis" is now used to encompass all people of mixed descent who have family roots in the fur trade, and who identify themselves as distinct from Euro-Canadian and First Nations cultures in the area west of the Great Lakes. The Métis were known by the Nehiyawak (Cree) as "their own bosses" or "the people who own themselves," but they also worked for the Euro-Canadian trading companies as hunters, guides, interpreters, and freighters. Such opportunities were more limited after the two major companies merged in 1821, but rising demand for bison hides was good news for the hunting and trading economy. By 1850, the Métis had successfully challenged the HBC's fur trade monopoly and many were trading independently with the First Nations peoples in the West. They were prominent and prosperous members of many western communities.

The Métis of Red River had resisted Canadian annexation in 1869, and succeeded in winning provincial status for Manitoba the following year. However, the political and economic benefits developed slowly and unevenly, and both land and power increasingly fell into the hands of Euro-Canadian newcomers. Disenchanted Métis moved west into central Saskatchewan, where they turned their fathers' and grandfathers' winter hunting camps into permanent settlements. In 1873, François-Xavier Letendre dit Batoche built a ferry where the Carlton Trail crossed the South Saskatchewan River. By 1885, the riverbank community that bore his name numbered about 500 people.

Just as they did along the Red River in Manitoba, the Métis in Batoche laid their farms out in river-lot fashion—long but narrow lots (up to 3 km/1.9 mi long but only a couple hundred metres wide), so everyone had access to the river and neighbours were nearby—cultivating a small portion of them, but living principally by freighting, trading, and raising cattle.

NORTHWEST RESISTANCE OF 1885

In the 1870s, the Canadian West was going through a difficult transition:

Game was scarce, bison hunting economies were no longer sustainable, and agriculture was beset with problems and not yet profitable. First Nations negotiated treaties with the Crown, but the food, equipment, and retraining that had been promised was not always forthcoming or of good quality; the Métis lacked even such indifferent support. Petition after petition seemed to fall on deaf ears, and tension and frustration grew. Finally, after a particularly cold and hungry winter, the tension burst into violence in March 1885.

The Northwest Resistance, also known as the Northwest Rebellion, culminated in the Battle of Batoche. The Battle of Batoche was fought over four days from May 9 to May 12, 1885. Fewer than 300 Métis and First Nations people led by Louis Riel and Gabriel Dumont defended Batoche from a series of rifle pits, which they had dug along the edge of the bush surrounding the village. The North West Field Force, commanded by Maj. Gen. Frederick Middleton and numbering 800 men, attacked the defences directly and used feinting manoeuvres to draw the Métis and First Nations into vulnerable positions. The North West Field Force soon captured Riel and pursued their remaining opponents into the northern forests.

The settlement of Batoche carried on into the early 1900s, but after the Canadian Pacific Railway bypassed it, the population declined. By 1915, only one store remained in the village.

EXPLORING BATOCHE

Take a self-guided tour of the site or, in July and August, join one of the guided 90-minute Journey Through Time tours (fee). The tour is suitable for the whole family. Along the way,

SASKATCHEWAN

authentically costumed Métis settlers tell their stories of living by the South Saskatchewan River on the site of the last battle of the 1885 resistance. Stops on the tour include the original rifle pits, where fighters hid from cannon fire and bullets, and the rectory, which still bears bullet holes in the wall.

Batoche offers a system of walking trails, including the 1.5-km (0.9 mi) South Saskatchewan Meander, along the river, and the Carlton Trail, which follows a portion of an old trading route. Please note that because of riverbank erosion, portions of the trails have been altered or closed.

Young visitors try out traditional Métis toys.

For visitors with limited mobility or anyone who wishes a less physically demanding option for touring the site, the Batoche Shuttle is an open-sided vehicle that can transport up to 48 visitors. The shuttle takes visitors throughout the East Village where Riel's provisional government of Saskatchewan was headquartered. Along the way, take in the scenic views of the prairies dotted with wildflowers and the trembling aspen forest. Tours can be booked in advance, but they also run throughout the day Monday to Friday between May and June, and daily in July and August.

How to Get There

Batoche is an hour's drive north of Saskatoon (88 km/54.7 mi). Follow Hwy. 11 north to Rosthern, and then Hwy. 312 east to Rte. 225. Batoche is 11 km (6.8 mi) north of this junction, on Rte. 225.

When to Go

Off-peak times are quieter, but the full slate of programming activities is offered in July and August, and July's Back to Batoche Days are not to be missed.

Caught in the crossfire of the Northwest Resistance of 1885, the rectory (left) still bears bullet holes in its walls.

BATOCHE NATIONAL HISTORIC SITE
(Lieu national historique de Batoche)

INFORMATION & ACTIVITIES

HOW TO REACH US
RR#1 Box 1040, Wakaw, SK S0K 4P0.
Phone (306) 423-6227. pc.gc.ca/batoche.

SEASONS & ACCESSIBILITY
Open Monday to Friday in May and June
and September to Thanksgiving in October; open daily July and August; closed in
winter. Check the website for specific
dates.

FRIENDS OF BATOCHE HISTORIC SITE
(306) 423-5687. Gift shop located on-site.

ENTRANCE FEES
$7.80 per adult, $19.60 per family/group
per day; $19.60 per adult, $49.00 per
family/group per year.

ACCESSIBLE SERVICES
All buildings are wheelchair accessible.
Special needs equipment such as golf
carts are available upon request, as are
all-terrain baby joggers; most of these services are free of charge and are on a first-
come, first-served basis. The Batoche
Shuttle provides tours ideal for those with
limited mobility.

THINGS TO DO
In addition to the regular interpretive living
history, special activities offered on-site or
nearby include geocaching and the Back to
Batoche Days.

Geocache treasure hunt: Using a
smartphone or GPS from the visitor centre,
track down clues to discover hidden treasures throughout the site. During the hunt,
find out more about the role of women and
children in the Northwest Resistance;
uncover the story of Monsieur Batoche in
the East Village; and learn about the North
West Field Force rifle pits. Ideal for all ages
and abilities.

Back to Batoche Days: Every third week
of July, the nearby Back to Batoche
grounds play host to a lively celebration of
Métis culture. Visitors can watch jigging
competitions or try doing a Red River jig
for themselves. Various cultural
performers take to the stage throughout,
and traditional Métis art such as intricate
beading is also on display.

SPECIAL ADVISORIES
- The site covers an extremely large area
  that contains numerous depressions,
  brush-filled areas, and natural hazards
  such as gopher holes. Comfortable and
  supported footwear is suggested for the
  varied terrain.
- Ticks, mosquitoes, and other small
  insects are found here. In particular, ticks
  are found in tall grassy or wooded areas
  and drop from leaves or blades of grass.
  To avoid tick bites, wear long sleeve
  shirts and pants. Check for ticks periodi-
  cally and check your pets.
- Black bears occasionally come on the
  grounds. Please check with the visitor
  centre for the latest bear sightings.
- Visitors are also encouraged to view the
  South Saskatchewan River from the dock
  as the water is fast moving. Swimming is
  not advised. Visitors may go paddling on
  the river, but should always wear a floata-
  tion device.

CAMPGROUNDS
Valley Regional Park. Just north of Rosthern. (306) 232-5600. valleyregionalpark
.com.

HOTELS, MOTELS, & INNS
*(Rates are for a 2-person double, high season,
in Canadian dollars, unless otherwise noted.)*

Academy Bed and Breakfast 402 9th
Ave., Rosthern, SK S0K 3R0. (306) 232-
5633. academybandb.ca. 3 rooms,
$70–$95.
Rosthern Hotel 8016 Saskatchewan St.,
Rosthern, SK S0K 3R0. (306) 232-4841.
8 rooms, $62.

Additional visitor information:
Prince Albert Tourism (306) 953-4385.
princealberttourism.com.
Tourism Saskatoon (800) 567-2444.
tourismsaskatoon.com.

SASKATCHEWAN

New recruits swear allegiance to the North West Mounted Police at Fort Walsh.

▶ FORT WALSH

Designated 1924

Fort Walsh was the most important, largest, and most heavily armed fort of the North West Mounted Police (NWMP) during their early years in the West. It was constructed in 1875 to bring Canadian law and order to the area. The NWMP at this fort also patrolled the international border to assert Canadian sovereignty.

Fort Walsh only existed for eight years, but in that time it served as the watchdog and peacekeeper during a period of tremendous change. Although equipped and prepared for war, the NWMP used diplomacy and conciliation to avoid much of the violence that often characterized other frontiers.

A major reason Fort Walsh was established was to help with First Nations relations. The Northwest Mounted Police encouraged them to enter into treaty agreements with the federal government. As well, NWMP surgeons were the only doctors in the area and attended to the needs of Indigenous Peoples. In turn, the Indigenous Peoples actively assisted the NWMP in ending the illegal whiskey trade. Fort Walsh also

maintained diplomatic relations with the Lakota peoples when they arrived in Canada following historic battles in the United States.

The Mounties at Fort Walsh and elsewhere were not just peacekeepers, however. They also carried out customs responsibilities. They did the work of quarantine inspectors as herds of horses and cattle were brought into Canada. Their wagons distributed the mail. NWMP officers were magistrates and justices of the peace. They were law and order, and infrastructure. They were ambassadors of the new Dominion government, and advisers to that government. And when their terms of service expired, they were among the first settlers and businessmen in the Canadian West.

What to See & Do

Start at the visitor centre to get an overview of the site, and then proceed around the fort and the former town-site. As visitors wander through the buildings and grounds, costumed interpreters in period dress reveal what life was like at an 1870s working fort. Visitors may even test bartering skills with trade activities at Fort Walsh's trading post, learning such things as how much buffalo robes were worth in the 1870s.

For a taste of the natural environment, take to a couple of walking trails. A 550-m (601 yd) trail wanders through the Cypress Hills forest along the beautiful Battle Creek. For something longer, there's the new 5-km (3.1 mi) backcountry loop.

For something special, visit in August when Fort Walsh hosts Trades Day, a family-friendly, fun-filled day of firing cannons, wagon rides, Métis dances, historic trades, and cultural demonstrations as well as NWMP/RCMP drills! Call (403) 893-3833 for more information.

Because of the high altitude of the Cypress Hills, weather may vary drastically from the surrounding

INFORMATION

HOW TO REACH US
P.O. Box 278, Maple Creek, SK S0N 1N0. Phone (306) 662-2645 (administration office) or (306) 662-3590 (site; May–Oct.). pc.gc.ca/walsh.

ENTRANCE FEES
$9.80 per adult, $22.00 per family/group per day.

ACCESSIBLE SERVICES
Limited, and the terrain is variable; contact the site for more details.

SPECIAL ADVISORIES
Do not approach or feed the deer, moose, elk, and other wildlife.

CAMPGROUNDS
Camping facilities (no services) are located 10 km (6.2 mi) west along the Graburn Gap Road. The nearest full-service facilities are 40 km (24.9 mi) away in **Cypress Hills Interprovincial Park** (cypresshills.com).

HOTELS, MOTELS, & INNS
Commercial Hotel 26 Pacific Ave., Maple Creek, SK S0N 1N0. (306) 662-2988. maplecreekcommercialhotel.ca. 14 rooms, $75–$132.

SASKATCHEWAN

Raising the Union Jack

lower-elevation areas. Go prepared with a hat, rain gear, and all-terrain footwear. Bring bug spray, sunscreen, and drinking water.

How to Get There

Fort Walsh is 55 km (34.2 mi) southwest of the town of Maple Creek, off Trans-Canada 1.

When to Go

Fort Walsh is open May through September. It's open daily in July and August, and Tuesday through Saturday in May, June, and September. Check the Parks Canada website for specific dates.

The Motherwell Homestead illustrates the life of prairie homesteaders in the late 1800s.

▶ MOTHERWELL HOMESTEAD

ABERNETHY, SK
Designated 1966

The 3.6-ha (8.9 acres) Motherwell Homestead was designated a national historic site in 1966 because of its association with the career of William Richard Motherwell, and as an illustration of a prairie homestead of western Canada's settlement period planned around scientific farming principles.

An early Saskatchewan settler, Motherwell came west from Ontario to take advantage of Canada's homestead policy, which offered free quarter sections of land on the prairies to those willing to establish farms. He was among the first to homestead the area, in the spring of 1882, and became a community leader. He became Saskatchewan's first minister of agriculture and later served as a federal minister of agriculture. The two-storey stone house he built, known as Lanark Place, would become an Abernethy area landmark.

Motherwell was one of a number of individuals whose efforts revolutionized agriculture on the prairies. He embraced new farming methods,

and as a politician, he was a firm supporter of agricultural research and tireless in his efforts to publicize new findings. He was a great proponent of dryland-farming techniques that were essential to successful agriculture and settlement on the prairies.

What to See & Do

Start at the visitor centre and then take a self-guided tour (free Explora official tour app available) through the homestead. Travel down the path alongside the large vegetable garden to Lanark Place, the fully furnished stone house where the Motherwell family lived. Visit the barnyard, a large Ontario-style barn, complete with livestock.

The 1.5-km (0.9 mi) Stueck Nature Walk takes you through a farmer's field to a nearby wetland area with a variety of birds and an observation platform. Access the trail from the picnic area—an inviting place to sit and enjoy a peaceful prairie oasis—near the parking lot.

How to Get There

Motherwell Homestead is 3 km (1.9 mi) south of Abernethy on Hwy. 22. Abernethy is 100 km (62 mi) east of Regina on Hwy. 10.

When to Go

The site is open Monday through Friday in May and June, and daily July to September. Check the website for specific dates.

INFORMATION

HOW TO REACH US
P.O. Box 70, Abernethy, SK S0A 0A0. Phone (306) 333-2116. pc.gc.ca /motherwell.

ENTRANCE FEES
$3.90 per adult, $9.80 per family/ group per day; $9.80 per adult; $24.50 per family/group per year.

ACCESSIBLE SERVICES
Friendly.

HOTELS, MOTELS, & INNS
BraeBurn Inn 750 Bay Ave. S. Fort Qu'Appelle, SK S0G 1S0. (306) 332-5757. braeburn.sk.ca. 9 rooms, $99–$149.

SASKATCHEWAN

Fort Battleford was a North West Mounted Police post between 1876 and 1885.

▶ FORT BATTLEFORD

BATTLEFORD, SK
Designated 1923

An early North West Mounted Police (NWMP) post (established 1876), Fort Battleford presided over and assisted in some of the most pivotal events in the history of western Canada, including the negotiations between First Nations and the Canadian government for Treaty No. 6.

The NWMP established the rule of Canadian law and order while Battleford, the first capital and seat of government for the newly formed and then much vaster Northwest Territories, grew into a thriving community.

The fort extended the Canadian government's interests in the West through the role of the NWMP from 1876 to 1885. During the Northwest Resistance of 1885 (see p. 255), the fort was important as a refuge for settlers, as a military operations base for the battles of Cut Knife Hill and Fort Pitt, and in the search for Mistahimaskwa (Big Bear), a powerful Plains Cree chief who resisted signing Treaty No. 6 and tried to advocate peacefully for his people. Fort Battleford was also the site of the surrender of Pîhtokahânapiwiýin (Poundmaker), another Plains Cree chief, to General Middleton's forces on May 26, 1885.

What to See & Do

Fort Battleford offers a glimpse into life in the late 1800s with the newly formed NWMP. Visit authentically refurbished buildings, from the spartan guardhouse and prison to the more refined commanding officer's house.

Rent a pair of headsets at the visitor centre and take a self-guided audio tour (or use the free Explora

INFORMATION

HOW TO REACH US
P.O. Box 70, Battleford, SK S0M 0E0. Phone (306) 937-2621 (March 1–Oct. 31). pc.gc.ca/battleford.

ENTRANCE FEES
$3.90 per adult, $9.80 per family/group per day.

ACCESSIBLE SERVICES
Friendly. Electric scooters are also available.

CAMPGROUNDS
Eiling Kramer Campground Adjacent to Fort Battleford. (306) 937-6212.

HOTELS, MOTELS, & INNS
Gold Eagle Lodge 12004 Railway Ave. E, North Battleford, SK S9A 3W3. (306) 446-8877. goldeaglelodge.com. 112 rooms, $160–$270. **Tropical Inn** 1001 Hwy. 16 Bypass, North Battleford, SK S9A 3W2. (306) 446-4700. tropicalinns.com/north battleford. 119 rooms, $119–$159.

official tour app), discovering 15 fact-filled spots around the fort. Along the way, explore five original NWMP buildings and learn about the role that Fort Battleford played in the armed conflict of 1885.

To temper your history with a little recreation, Fort Battleford boasts a nine-hole disc golf course suitable for everyone from beginners to experts. Players see beautiful views along the North Saskatchewan River as they stroll the course. A round of disc golf is included in the entrance fee, and staff will help explain it to newcomers to the sport. It's as simple as throwing a Frisbee.

Various special activities and events are held too. Every July, Fort Fest combines historic activities and trades demonstration with modern entertainment, music, and games.

A NWMP firing demonstration at Fort Battleford

Visitors can see historic weapons demonstrations, NWMP on horseback, and telegraph demonstrations, among other things. And in August, the fort hosts a few lantern-lit Summer Ghost Walks, after-hours tours where you can hear stories of the ghosts who stalk the corridors and haunt the rooms of this historic site. Check the website for specific dates.

Bring sunscreen, sunglasses, a hat, and water bottles. The terrain is varied and can have hazards such as gopher holes so it's advisable to wear supportive footwear.

How to Get There

Fort Battleford is 153 km (95 mi) northwest of Saskatoon in the town of Battleford.

When to Go

The site is only open May through August; Monday through Friday in May and June, and daily in July and August. Check the website for specific dates.

SASKATCHEWAN SITES

BATTLE OF TOUROND'S COULEE/FISH CREEK
FISH CREEK, SK

This site commemorates where the Métis, led by Gabriel Dumont, and Cree and Dakota First Nations held back the advancing North West Field Force during the Northwest Resistance of 1885. It was the first time the Métis encountered the Canadian military. The 36-ha (89 acres) site comprises the main battleground as well as archaeological remains and landscape features associated with the battle. Designated NHS: 1923. 25 km (15.5 mi) south of Batoche. (306) 423-6227.

FORT ESPÉRANCE
SPY HILL, SK

Located in the Qu'Appelle Valley between Rocanville and Spy Hill, this archaeological site is believed to contain the remains of two late 18th- and early 19th-century fur trade forts, both known as Fort Espérance. Stone monuments mark the spot where the fort, which was the North West Company's primary pemmican depot, once stood. (Pemmican was dried meat, traditionally bison pounded into coarse powder and mixed with melted fat.) Designated NHS: 1959. 18 km (11 mi) southeast of Spy Hill off Hwy. 600. (306) 333-2116.

SASKATCHEWAN SITES

FORT LIVINGSTONE
PELLY, SK

Built in 1874–75, the inaugural head-quarters of the North West Mounted Police was also the first capital of the Northwest Territories (1876–78), serving as the temporary seat of government while new government buildings in Battleford were being constructed. A prairie fire destroyed the fort in 1884. The 48.5-ha (120 acres) national historic site is also home to a garter snake hibernaculum, which was present when the fort was established. Designated NHS: 1923. 16 km (10 mi) north of Pelly. (306) 333-2116.

FORT PELLY
PELLY, SK

For almost half a century, Fort Pelly was the headquarters of the Swan River District of the Hudson's Bay Company. It was built in 1824, the latest in a series of fur trade posts in this location dating back to 1793. A new and more substantial fort was built here in 1856, and housed fine herds of cattle and horses. Abandoned in 1912, the fort was sold in 1921, at which time all of its buildings were torn down or removed. Designated NHS: 1953. 5 km (3 mi) west and 10 km (6.2 mi) south of Pelly. (306) 333-2116.

FRENCHMAN BUTTE
PARADISE HILL, SK

Frenchman Butte marks the location of an armed battle between Plains Cree warriors under the lead of Wandering Spirit and the Canadian troops commanded by Gen. Thomas Strange, as part of the 1885 Northwest Resistance. Rifle pits are still visible along the contours of the rolling landscape at this 7.2-ha (17.8 acres) site, located along Little Red Deer Creek in western Saskatchewan. Designated NHS: 1929. 11 km (6.8 mi) west of Paradise Hill. (306) 937-2621.

CYPRESS HILLS MASSACRE
MAPLE CREEK, SK

Here, American traders attacked a Nakoda camp in a horse dispute, resulting in a loss of more than 20 Indigenous Peoples' lives. The June 1, 1873, massacre spurred Prime Minister Macdonald to complete the formation of a federal police force for the West, and in 1874 the North West Mounted Police marched westward. One of their first priorities was to investigate the massacre. The site has reconstructions of two former trading posts. Designated NHS: 1964. 2 km (1.2 mi) south of Fort Walsh NHS (see pp. 258–259). (306) 662-2645.

WANUSKEWIN
SASKATOON, SK

Located in the Tipperary Creek Conservation Area, the 20 archaeological sites contained within the 146-ha (361 acres) area represent nearly 6,000 years of cultural history relating to the Northern Plains First Nations. A medicine wheel, camps, tepee rings, and stone cairns give clues to daily life in earlier times. The heritage park has a visitor centre, gift shop, and restaurant, all featuring traditional First Nations culture. Designated NHS: 1986. Northeast of Saskatoon on RR #4 Penner Rd. (306) 931-6767.

FORESTRY FARM PARK AND ZOO
SASKATOON, SK

Currently owned and operated by the city of Saskatoon, the Forestry Farm Park and Zoo was originally a forest nursery station, established by the federal government in 1913. The farm helped address the challenges of settlement and agriculture on the prairies by developing new and scientific farming methods. Today, there are ornamental plantings, picnic grounds, and a zoo. Designated NHS: 1990. 1903 Forestry Farm Park Dr. (306) 975-3382.

SASKATCHEWAN

The First Peoples of Canada

For many years, the voices of Inuit, Métis, and First Nations peoples, who together make up the Indigenous Peoples of Canada, were not heard at national historic sites. This is slowly changing. Today, some of these important places convey the rich history and knowledge of Indigenous Peoples; others tell a story that demonstrates how people have connected to these spaces over thousands of years.

A First Nations woman, circa 1960s, wears a traditional basket and tumpline.

Many Voices, Many Stories to Tell

Some national historic sites are places to maintain and renew connections with the past. Situated next to the cold, clear waters of Great Bear Lake, in the Northwest Territories, Saoyú-Ɂehdacho National Historic Site is recognized for how its significant natural resources are fundamental for the continuation and transmission of the Sahtúgot'įnę (Bear Lake People) culture. The Sahtúgot'įnę believe that all the land is sacred, especially Saoyú-Ɂehdacho, as it is a place of "teaching and learning."

Through such places, with their associated stories, elders pass on the culture, history, cosmology, spiritual values, law, ethics, land use, and traditional lifestyles of the Sahtúgot'įnę. The intergenerational transmission of traditional knowledge and important cultural values are fundamental to understanding the meaning of this place. Every year, a camp is held at Saoyú-Ɂehdacho, in which youth and elders participate in cultural learning activities, including telling stories, drying caribou and fish, gathering and preparing traditional medicines, and conducting spiritual ceremonies and celebrations, such as the fire teaching and the first kill ceremony.

Other sites seek to connect visitors with Indigenous perspectives on the past. The Métis community leads and participates in the history presented at Batoche National Historic Site (see pp. 254–257) in Saskatchewan. An example of their involvement is a program developed to preserve Métis women's history of resistance and survival through a community storytelling circle that honours their untold stories. This innovative approach was a response to Métis Elders, who indicated their wish for more participation in the development and presentation of cultural programming at Batoche. The program recognizes the divergent and complementary viewpoints of history so that different perspectives can be honoured and shared with visitors. It also encourages visitors to see the Métis as a vibrant people, moving beyond conflicts of the 19th century to connect Indigenous history to the present day.

In the far north, one of Canada's most unusual sites, Inuksuk National Historic Site, is situated at Enukso Point, on the southwest corner of Baffin Island, on the shore of Foxe Basin, approximately 88 km (54.7 mi) west of Cape Dorset, Nunavut. *Inuksuk*, an Inuit word meaning "likenesses of men," are stone constructions found across the Canadian Arctic. Built by Inuit, they can function as landmarks, memorials, kayak stands, meat platforms, pillars supporting drying lines, or elements of caribou drive fences. Collectively known as *inuksuit*, the cairns consist of carefully piled stones that can be as large as 1.8 to 2.1 m (6 to 7 ft) in height, sometimes figurelike; smaller inuksuit may be composed of two balanced stones or single standing stones. At Enukso Point, these cairns, which vary in size and complexity, may be up to 2,000 years old. They are testament to the creativity and artistry at work in maximizing the naturally occurring resources in this harsh environment.

A Shared Future

The stories told at national historic sites continue to expand, evolve, and be enriched by the sharing—in partnership with Indigenous Peoples—of the rich and vibrant cultures, languages, traditions, and histories of First Nations, Inuit, and Métis peoples. Working together to broaden how we define, understand, and communicate the past to national historic site visitors gives hope for a promising, shared future.

— JOHN MCCORMICK, *Mohawk,*
Consultation Manager, Parks Canada

An 11,400-year-old projectile point from Gwaii Haanas

SASKATCHEWAN

SASKATCHEWAN SITES

GOVERNMENT HOUSE
REGINA, SK

The former residence of the lieutenant governor of the Northwest Territories from 1891 to 1905 and of Saskatchewan from 1905 to 1945, this two-storey brick mansion is now part of a large complex, with the offices of the lieutenant governor of Saskatchewan, a museum, an interpretive centre, and gardens. Government House is one of the few surviving territorial government buildings. Designated NHS: 1968. 4607 Dewdney Ave. (306) 787-5773.

SASKATCHEWAN LEGISLATIVE BUILDING AND GROUNDS
REGINA, SK

A three-storey structure with a soaring central copper-clad dome, the 1912 building is situated on 17 ha (42 acres) of landscaped grounds. Together, the Saskatchewan Legislative Building and Grounds are considered among the finest examples of Beaux Arts design and the City Beautiful movement in Canada. Inside, the rotunda is the focal point; it features marble Ionic columns and intricately carved symbols of royalty and public art. Designated NHS: 2005. 2405 Legislative Dr. (306) 787-5416.

CARLTON HOUSE
FORT CARLTON, SK

Consisting of the remains of forts constructed on the banks of the North Saskatchewan River between 1810 and 1885, the site was the location of a major Hudson's Bay Company trading post. Building foundations exist from the 1855 fort, as does a reconstruction of Carlton House, which includes the palisade, a fur and provisions store, clerk's quarters, tepee encampment, and a stockade. Designated NHS: 1976. Fort Carlton Provincial Park, 27 km (16.7 mi) west of Duck Lake on Hwy. 212. (306) 467-5205.

DOUKHOBOR DUGOUT HOUSE
BLAINE LAKE, SK

This site features the remains of a log timber and earthbound dwelling built into the slope of a ravine, near the North Saskatchewan River. The house illustrates the adaptive and resourceful strategies Doukhobor settlers used in 1899. Fleeing religious persecution in Russia, Doukhobors were offered sanctuary by the Canadian government. The house holds symbolic importance to descendants of those settlers. Designated NHS: 2008. 8 km (5 mi) southeast of the town of Blaine Lake on Petrofka Rd. (306) 497-3140.

SEAGER WHEELER'S MAPLE GROVE FARM
ROSTHERN, SK

This 17-ha (42 acres) farmstead recognizes the agricultural contributions of Seager Wheeler—farmer and pioneering seed breeder who developed varieties of wheat and fruit suited to western Canada during the period of the "wheat boom" (1898–1940). Learn about his innovations in direct seeding and visit the extensive English flower garden. Designated NHS: 1994. 6.5 km (4 mi) east of Rosthern. (306) 232-5959 or (306) 232-5596.

FORT QU'APPELLE
FORT QU'APPELLE, SK

Established in 1864 as a Hudson's Bay Company (HBC) trading post, the fort now only has one original building, which houses a museum with First Nations, HBC, and North West Mounted Police artefacts. Overlooking the Qu'Appelle River, the fort was designated a national historic site because of its role as a major provisioning post for the southern prairies and as the site of the negotiations for Treaty No. 4 in 1874. Designated NHS: 1953. 198 Bay Ave. N. (306) 332-5751.

SASKATCHEWAN

Alberta's Head-Smashed-In Buffalo Jump protects one of the world's oldest, largest, and best preserved buffalo jumps.

ALBERTA

Alberta today boasts the largest oil and gas reserves in the nation. Historically, however, agriculture dominated the region, as did the fur trade, in which the Hudson's Bay Company and the North West Company built competing trading posts until their merger in 1821. Rocky Mountain House (see pp. 276–277) preserves several posts constructed by the two rivals. Homesteaders began arriving in droves in the 1890s, just a decade after the Bar U Ranch (see pp. 272–275), one of Canada's largest and longest lasting cattle ranches, was

established south of Calgary. The influx further disrupted the lives of the Blackfoot and other Indigenous Peoples, who depended on the quickly diminishing buffalo for food and raw materials. Alberta has one of the world's best preserved buffalo jumps, a hunting practice that eventually ended with the buffalo's near extinction in the late 19th century (see pp. 278–282). Home to a North West Mounted Police fort since 1875, Edmonton became the province's capital city after admission to the Confederation in 1905.

The Bar U Ranch played a critical role in shaping the ranching industry across Canada's West.

▶ BAR U RANCH

LONGVIEW, AB
Designated 1991

For anyone who has ever wondered how ranching evolved in Canada, look no farther than the Bar U Ranch. Alberta has long been known for ranching, and the Bar U—in continuous operation as a cattle ranch from 1883 until 1991—epitomizes why. It is the only national historic site that commemorates the history and importance of ranching in Canada.

Set in the rolling foothills with spectacular views of the distant Rocky Mountains, the Bar U headquarters site is nestled in a creek bottom, sheltered from prevailing winds and shaded by cottonwood trees. Many of the ranch's buildings are strung out along a "main street" with sheds, barns, storage buildings, and residential structures roughly grouped by function.

Beyond these modest buildings, corrals, and fences lie the crucial grasslands. This land has been the home of Indigenous Peoples for many thousands of years. Bison, and then cattle, thrived in this environment where warm Chinook winds expose slopes of nutritious rough fescue for winter grazing. The native drought-resistant fescue grasses are essential to the story of life in the foothills.

BAR U HISTORY

The Bar U was one of the first and most enduring large corporate ranches of western Canada. It opened up the prairie to beef production, providing food for the local population and developing export markets in Britain and eastern North America. A workforce with diverse origins kept the Bar U running: Canadians, upper-class Englishmen, Indigenous

Peoples, Europeans, Americans, and Chinese were all employed.

Turning grass into beef and hence into money is key to a rancher's success. When the Bar U was established, its owners had access to very inexpensive leases of huge tracts of land. At one point these leases took in 63,940 ha (158,000 acres)—a block of land 29 by 29 km (18 by 18 mi). Beyond these leased lands were also vast stretches of "free grass" available to ranchers. As settlers began to take up land in western Canada in the 1890s, these huge leases were reduced: Eventually the Bar U lands included leased and deeded land amounting to 24,280 ha (60,000 acres) on which about 8,000 head of cattle grazed.

From 1881 to 1902, Fred Stimson and his partners in the North West Cattle Company (NWCC) operated the Bar U. They acquired the original leases, and Stimson brought 3,000 head of cattle from Idaho to stock the ranch. Stimson succeeded in pulling together the essential elements of a ranching business: capital, grass, cattle, labour, and above all else, markets. Originally from western Québec, Stimson lived with his family at the ranch for 20 years, directly managing the huge spread. The main street of the headquarters site evolved during this time.

Under George Lane—a former NWCC ranch foreman—and his partners (operating 1902 to 1925), the ranching operation diversified. More hay and grains were planted for feed, and the ranch achieved an international reputation for its purebred Percheron draft horses (a versatile workhorse breed originating from France). Taking advantage of the need for good heavy work horses on new farms and in heavy construction of western Canada, Lane built the Bar U

into the largest Percheron breeding operation in the world in the early 1900s, with a herd of more than 1,000 horses. It was the cornerstone of a business empire that included several other ranches and farms. New barns, corrals, and feed preparation facilities to accommodate the Percherons as well as residential buildings were built at this time to reflect the diversification and growth of the ranch. Lane is remembered in western Canada as one of the four ranchers—known as the Big Four—that established the Calgary Stampede.

During the Patrick Burns era (1927–1950), the Bar U became part of an integrated agricultural business that linked ranches, feedlots, meatpacking, and wholesale and retail operations. An experienced and resilient owner, Burns steered his ranches through the Depression, cutting back operating costs and investing in long-term improvements. He scaled down the Percheron operation, and several buildings were adapted to store grain. Following Burns's death in 1937, the ranch was run by a management group. Operations were modernized and grain was grown in huge quantities to feed cattle and hogs during the Second World War. The Bar U remained one of the largest ranches in the country until 1950, after which the executors of the Burns' estate sold land to other ranchers.

J. Allen Baker bought the headquarters site and part of the Bar U lands on which he ranched for 27 years. The Wambeke and Nelson families then owned the property before Parks Canada bought 148 ha (366 acres), including the headquarters site, in 1991.

Throughout its operation, the Bar U has seen its share of famous (and infamous) people pass through its gates. In 1919, Edward, Prince of

ALBERTA

Wales, wanted to experience a cowboy ranch and so was taken to the Bar U, then under Lane's ownership. He became so enthralled by the experience that he bought the neighbouring ranch. Bar U horse breaker Harry Longabaugh, a cowboy from Wyoming, gained notoriety later on as the Sundance Kid, an accomplice of the outlaw Butch Cassidy. American western artist Charlie Russell also stayed at the ranch to create a series of now famous oil paintings.

The Bar U has stood the test of time. Its long and close association with the ranching industry and the survival of many buildings from its early operations make it an ideal place to experience Canada's ranching heritage.

EXPLORING THE BAR U

The Bar U uses a living history approach to present the ranching industry of the past, and also links it to present-day ranching. Its buildings have been carefully restored to show ranch life in the first half of the 20th century. Costumed guides, horses, and livestock bring the past to life, revealing life on a working ranch from the 1880s to the 1940s.

Start at the visitor centre, which houses a reception area, rangeland exhibit, theatre, gift shop, and restaurant. From there, pick up an illustrated map guide and wander the site on foot, take a guided walking tour (fee), or hop aboard a horse-drawn wagon ride (fee).

The Bar U has the largest collection of historical ranch buildings in Canada, and many of them are operational. The original ranch headquarters situated along Pekisko Creek are still intact. One of the most popular structures is the cookhouse, where the smell of fresh baking fills the air. Watch live demonstrations as the blacksmith prepares horseshoes or the saddle maker repairs a rein. As you move from building to building, costumed interpreters bring the ranching history to life, sharing the stories of the men and women who made the Bar U famous.

On a wagon ride pulled by Percheron draft horses—the "gentle giants

Saddles, reins, and more hang in the stables.

Spurred boots complete a cowboy's outfit.

BAR U RANCH NATIONAL HISTORIC SITE
(Lieu historique national du Ranch-Bar U)

INFORMATION & ACTIVITIES

HOW TO REACH US
P.O. Box 168, Longview, AB T0L 1H0.
Phone (403) 395-2212. pc.gc.ca/baru.

SEASONS & ACCESSIBILITY
The ranch is open mid-May through September. See the website for specific dates.

FRIENDS OF THE BAR U HISTORIC RANCH ASSOCIATION
(403) 395-3993, friendsofthebaru.com.

ENTRANCE FEES
$7.80 per adult, $19.60 per family/group per day; $19.60 per adult, $49.00 per family/group per year.

PETS
None permitted.

ACCESSIBLE SERVICES
The visitor centre is wheelchair accessible.

THINGS TO DO
In addition to tours, historic demonstrations, and more, the Bar U hosts several popular annual events. In June, competitors aim to prepare the best beef stew and biscuits at the Chuckwagon Cook-Off, cooking everything over an open campfire.

On Canada Day, admission is free for an Old West celebration full of hands-on activities, from making rope to churning butter or ice cream. And on the second Sunday in August, the ranch stages its biggest event: the Old Time Ranch Rodeo. It showcases teams of working Alberta cowboys competing in events such as wild cow milking and broke horse racing.

CAMPGROUNDS
Chain Lakes Provincial Park On Hwy. 22, approximately 10 minutes south of the ranch. (403) 627-1165. albertaparks.ca /chain-lakes-pp.

HOTELS, MOTELS, & INNS
(Rates are for a 2-person double, high season, in Canadian dollars, unless otherwise noted.)

Twin Cities Hotel 105 Morrison Rd., Longview, AB T0L 1H0. (403) 558-3787. twincitieshotel.ca. 10 rooms, $75.
Blue Sky Motel 114 Morrison Rd., Longview, AB T0L 1H0. (403) 558-3655. 10 rooms, $99.

Additional visitor information:
Cowboy Trail Tourism Association thecowboytrail.com.
Travel Alberta (800) ALBERTA. travel alberta.com.

ALBERTA

of ranching"—visitors hear the stories of George Lane and his amazing herd of Percherons, as well as learn about seven decades of ranching history and discover why the Bar U location is ideal for ranching.

Several activities give visitors a fuller sense of ranch life. At Roundup Camp, relax under the shade of cottonwood trees while enjoying bannock (biscuitlike bread, traditional in the Indigenous community) and cowboy coffee made over a roaring fire. Hear cowboy poetry, songs, and legends around the campfire. And cowpokes of all ages can try their hand at roping a steer, mastering the skill of looping a rope over the head of a model steer.

How to Get There
The Bar U is approximately 95 km (59 mi) south of Calgary on Hwy. 22, 13 km (8 mi) south of Longview. From Calgary, go south on Hwy. 2, and then west on Hwy. 540. The ranch is just west of the junction of Hwys. 540 and 22 (aka the Cowboy Trail).

When to Go
The ranch is open mid-May through September, with a full slate of activities offered in the summer months.

Fur traders transported their goods up and down inland waterways in York boats, large, heavy wooden rowboats.

▶ ROCKY MOUNTAIN HOUSE

ROCKY MOUNTAIN HOUSE, AB

Designated 1926

The remains of several early 19th-century fur trade forts can be found at Rocky Mountain House. The first was established by the North West Company (NWC) in 1799, and a rival post was built nearby just days later by the Hudson's Bay Company (HBC). The two companies competed fiercely throughout the West until they joined forces in 1821.

The posts were small and remote, but they brought international trade goods like tea, firearms, gunpowder, axes, glass beads, copper pots, and more to Indigenous Peoples. During Rocky Mountain House's 76-year history, eight First Nations and the Métis brought furs and pemmican to trade. Its occupation was not continuous during the fur trade, and posts were rebuilt and replaced over the years using at least four different sites.

Explorer, fur trader, and mapmaker David Thompson used the NWC post as a base for finding a pass across the Rocky Mountains. First Nations guides helped Thompson create two fur trade routes through the Rockies: Howse Pass

(see p. 299) and Athabasca Pass (see p. 298). The Athabasca Pass route became necessary after the introduction of guns changed the balance of power between the Pikani and the Ktunaxa First Nations. The Pikani were angry with the NWC for trading guns to the Ktunaxa, and barricaded them from using Howse Pass.

What to See & Do

In the visitor centre, see original artefacts excavated from the fort sites, a reproduction trade room where guests can pose in period costume, and interactive displays about the fur trade era at Rocky Mountain House.

Outside, explore the two interpretive trails. The wheelchair-accessible

0.9-km (0.6 mi) round-trip Chimney Trail circles through the archaeological remains of the last two HBC forts. The last fur trade post (1868–1875) was actually the first Alberta archaeological site within the Parks Canada system. The 3-km (1.9 mi) round-trip David Thompson Trail follows in the footsteps of the mapmaker. The trail winds along the North Saskatchewan to the oldest fort sites.

Later, relax by the fire at the Trapper's Tent as interpreters narrate stories of their ancestors. Or try your hand at traditional Métis activities, including baking a bannock—traditional Indigenous biscuitlike bread—over an open fire, making dream catchers, and playing games that require survival skills such as observation, intuition, estimation, and hand-eye coordination.

How to Get There

Rocky Mountain House is 6 km (3.7 mi) west of the town of Rocky Mountain House on Hwy. 11A.

When to Go

Open daily mid-May through September 4; open Thursday through Sunday the rest of September.

INFORMATION

HOW TO REACH US
392077 Rge. Rd. 7-5, Rocky Mountain House, AB T4T 2A4. Phone (403) 845-2412. pc.gc.ca/eng/lhn-nhs/ab /rockymountain/index.aspx.

ENTRANCE FEES
$3.90 per adult, $9.80 per family/ group per day.

ACCESSIBLE SERVICES
Limited; contact the site for more details.

CAMPGROUNDS
The site offers traditional camping in one of three First Nations Tipis (each sleeps six) or several Métis Trappers Tents (each sleeps two in beds, four more on sleeping mats). Enhanced Heritage Camping Kits, complete with a buffalo hide to furnish your tent, a period cooking kit, and a fire-starting kit, are available. For reservations, call (403) 845-2412 or email rocky.info@pc.gc.ca.

Additional visitor information:
Town of Rocky Mountain House (403) 845-2866. rockymtnhouse .com.

ALBERTA

ALBERTA SITES

FROG LAKE
FROG LAKE, AB

Frog Lake is where Plains Cree led by Big Bear camped, resisting reserve life in hopes of negotiating better terms with the government. Rising tensions resulted in a deadly conflict led by Cree warrior Wandering Spirit on April 2, 1885. Frog Lake National Historic Site includes a cemetery marked by a cairn and plaque that recalls the nine lives lost that day. Designated NHS: 1923. Located on the First Nations Reserve of Frog Lake. Fish Lake Rd. (306) 937-2621.

Head-Smashed-In Buffalo Jump stages authentic First Nations drumming and dancing performances in the summer.

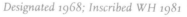

▶ HEAD-SMASHED-IN BUFFALO JUMP

FORT MACLEOD, AB

Designated 1968; Inscribed WH 1981

Scanning the sprawling landscape where the foothills meet the Great Plains in southwestern Alberta brings to life the history of Head-Smashed-In Buffalo Jump, one of the world's oldest, largest, and best preserved buffalo jumps. In fact, UNESCO inscribed this Plains peoples' archaeological site on the World Heritage List in 1981.

A buffalo jump refers to a method of communal hunting practiced by the Indigenous Peoples of the northern plains for more than 6,000 years. Buffalo were the foundation of life for the Plains peoples, providing an essential food source and raw materials for clothing and lodging. Because of their understanding of the regional topography and bison behaviour, the Plains peoples were able to hunt bison by stampeding them over a cliff. They then carved up the carcasses in a camp below the cliffs.

This archaeological site, known around the world, preserves the remarkable history of the Plains peoples, with artefacts dating back to 4400 B.C., such as the remains of tools, bone, arrowheads, darts, and butchering implements. The structural remains include a massive and deep—more than 10 m (33 ft)—deposit of bison bone at the base of the cliff, a nearby camping area where the hunters and their families lived and processed the carcasses, as well as long rows of cairns on top of the cliff, all leading toward the jump. These cultural remains are largely undisturbed—one of the only sites of this nature to remain virtually intact.

As a result, the site has provided archaeologists with a unique opportunity to trace the evolution of communal bison jumping from its earliest beginnings to its eventual abandonment in the 19th century.

Head-Smashed-In was one of the most heavily used jumps on the northern plains, with an estimated 100,000 or more buffalo killed at the site. It lies at the very southern end of the Porcupine Hills. The rolling nature of these hills is one of the key reasons why this is one of the premier bison kill sites in North America. Although most other buffalo jumps are simply steep drops at the edge of a broad prairie, the topography at Head-Smashed-In offered critical cover for the hunters to use in manipulating the herds.

ANATOMY OF A BUFFALO JUMP

The site is composed of four elements: First, a natural grazing area attracted herds of buffalo. Second, long lines of stone cairns helped the hunters direct the buffalo to the cliff. Thousands of these small piles of stones can still be seen marking the "drive lanes" that extend more than 14 km (8.7 mi) into the gathering basin. To start the hunt, "buffalo runners" enticed the herd to follow them by imitating the bleating of a lost calf. As the buffalo moved closer to the drive lanes, the hunters circled behind the herd and scared the animals by shouting and waving.

The third element is the cliff. As the buffalo stampeded over the edge of the 10-m (33 ft) cliff, they fell to their deaths. The sandstone cliff just north of the Head-Smashed-In Interpretive Centre is the actual jump site. This cliff is just one of several locations used as buffalo jumps

along the tail end of the Porcupine Hills. The Calderwood jump is visible just 1 km (0.6 mi) north of Head-Smashed-In.

Finally, the site had a flat area immediately below the cliff where the hunters camped while they butchered the buffalo. A few tepee rings and stones used to anchor tepees against the wind can still be seen. Much of the meat obtained from the buffalo carcasses was used to make pemmican. Pemmican is a nutritious staple food made by pounding grease, marrow, and sometimes berries with dried meat; it can be preserved for years.

THE NIITSITAPI

A culture formed around the buffalo for Indigenous Peoples of the northern plains. The buffalo supplied them with almost everything they needed to survive—clothing, tepees, bowstrings, cooking utensils—and, of course, food.

The Head-Smashed-In site is situated on the traditional domain of the Niitsitapi. The Niitsitapi were hunters and gatherers who moved with the buffalo, as well as because of the weather and the seasons. It was a structured movement known as the seasonal round. For almost half the year, the Niitsitapi bands lived in winter camps along a wooded river valley. In spring, the buffalo returned to the plains to forage. Soon after, the bands would leave their winter camps to follow and hunt the buffalo.

The use of buffalo jumps for killing buffalo represents an advanced collaboration in how the Plains peoples survived. To conduct a hunt and process the kill required small bands of people to unite and organize themselves in ways that would benefit the larger group.

ALBERTA

The buffalo assumed sacred status to early peoples and became a focal point for many religious and cultural activities. The abundant supply of buffalo afforded the Niitsitapi the time and opportunity to develop a rich spiritual and cultural life. In short, communal buffalo hunting was the catalyst for the development and growth of native Plains culture as we know it.

With the buffalo herds diminishing rapidly, Treaty No. 7 was signed in desperation in 1877. The Niitsitapi were settled on reserves in southern Alberta and forced to adapt to an entirely new way of life.

The Niitsitapi played a critical role in the development of the Head-Smashed-In Buffalo Jump National Historic Site, and continue to contribute, particularly as interpreters, to tell of their history and culture.

EXPLORING THE SITE

Taking in the landscape at Head-Smashed-In Buffalo Jump is a crucial part of understanding the story of what transpired here. It's worth noting the striking architecture of the interpretive centre. Only about 10 percent of the total surface area of the building is visible, with the remainder tucked into the cliff and covered with soil and vegetation. This placement of the building affirms the importance of not intruding on the landscape so that visitors can clearly picture the story of the buffalo jump.

Before exploring the jump area, learn that story first inside the interpretive centre, where five levels of exhibits explore buffalo hunting culture, the art of driving the great herds from the cliff, the eventual demise of the buffalo hunting culture, and the work of archaeologists at Head-Smashed-In. The theatre plays a reenactment of the hunt throughout the day.

Exit outside on the top level of the centre to access a paved trail that leads to spectacular views of Head-Smashed-In Buffalo Jump Cliff, Calderwood Buffalo Jump and Vision Quest Hill to the north, the prairies to the east, and the Rocky Mountains to the south.

A short interpretive hike beneath the cliff winds through the camp and processing areas. For more information, see the admissions desk and pick up a copy of the "Lower Trail Guide." This wilderness hike is not suitable for strollers or people with mobility issues.

For a more in-depth understanding of the jump, consider the guided four-hour round-trip, off-trail Hike to the Drive Lanes, which follows in the footsteps of the early Plains peoples. A Niitsitapi guide tells stories along the way of how the Plains peoples hunted the mighty buffalo. The hike (fee) is only offered May through October on the first Saturday of the month. Register in advance as space is limited. Dress appropriately for inclement weather, and bring lunch and water. (It is not recommended for small children.)

SPECIAL SUMMER EVENTS

In July and August, the site offers two unique activities. The first is the always popular Drumming and Dancing on the Plaza. Every Wednesday, twice daily (11 a.m. and 1:30 p.m.), Indigenous dancers perform to the beat of Niitsitapi drumming and singing. Hear stories of how drumming and dancing connect us with the ancient buffalo hunting culture. Sit with a Niitsitapi elder, interact with the performers, and take photos.

Plains Indians' tepees were easy to transport and able to be quickly put up and taken down.

A Blackfoot traditional dancer

Informative displays explain the buffalo hunting culture.

ALBERTA

The second activity, Run Amongst the Buffalo (fee), is staged Mondays and Fridays at 1 p.m. This three-hour experience immerses participants in the basics of how Plains peoples hunted buffalo. Take part in a traditional Niitsitapi blessing, taste dried buffalo meat, and reenact the buffalo jump. Try throwing an ancient spearthrower and take home your own arrowhead. Register in advance as space is limited.

How to Get There

Head-Smashed-In Buffalo Jump is 18 km (11.2 mi) north and west of Fort Macleod on secondary Hwy. 785. It is approximately 180 km (112 mi) south of Calgary on Hwy. 2.

When to Go

The centre is open year-round, but more special events and activities are scheduled in the summer months.

HEAD-SMASHED-IN BUFFALO JUMP NATIONAL HISTORIC SITE

(Lieu historique national Le précipice à bisons Head-Smashed-In)

INFORMATION & ACTIVITIES

HOW TO REACH US
Box 1977, Fort Macleod, AB TOL 0ZO. Phone (403) 553-2731. headsmashedin.org.

SEASONS & ACCESSIBILITY
The site is open daily year-round, except on Christmas Eve, Christmas Day, New Year's Day, and Easter Sunday.

ENTRANCE FEES
$12 per adult, $30 per family per day; $40 per adult, $100 per family per year.

PETS
Only service animals are allowed on-site and inside the museum.

ACCESSIBLE SERVICES
The centre as well as the trail to the lookout at the top of the building are wheelchair accessible. A limited number of wheelchairs are available to borrow for use in the centre. The Lower Trail is not recommended for those with mobility issues and is not wheelchair accessible. Exhibit text is available in Braille.

THINGS TO DO
Learn the story of the buffalo jump through five levels of exhibits in the interpretive centre. Explore the jump surroundings on a couple of walking paths. Participate and/or take in special activities such as drumming and dancing, a guided hike to the drive lanes, and more.

SPECIAL ADVISORIES
Severe weather may lead to temporary closures. Call (403) 553-2731 to check if the site is open.

CAMPGROUNDS
Daisy May Campground 249 Lyndon Rd., Fort Macleod. (403) 553-2455 or (888) 553-2455. daisymaycampground.com. More than 110 sites with full hook-up, power, and water; log camping cabins; and nonserviced sites.

Additional visitor information:
Town of Fort Macleod (403) 553-4425. fortmacleod.com.
Chinook Country Tourist Association (403) 320-1222 or (800) 661-1222. exploresouthwestalberta.ca.

ALBERTA SITES

FORT WHOOP-UP
LETHBRIDGE, AB

Established in 1869 by Montana traders, Fort Whoop-Up was the earliest and largest American whiskey trading post in southern Alberta. The fort traded liquor with Indigenous Peoples after such trade was banned in the United States. Its notorious nature was one factor that led to the formation of the North West Mounted Police to maintain law and order. The site now has a museum depicting life at the fort in the 1800s. Designated NHS: 1963. 200 Indian Battle Park Rd. (403) 329-0444.

BEAULIEU
CALGARY, AB

A late 19th-century residence situated on spacious landscaped grounds in central Calgary, Beaulieu, also known as Lougheed House, was home to the family of Sir James Alexander Lougheed (1854–1925), a prominent lawyer and senator. Beaulieu is a rare surviving example of the grand sandstone houses once known in Calgary, and also a fine example of the Victorian Eclectic architecture style. The house is open to the public (fee) Wednesday through Sunday. Designated NHS: 1992. 707 13th Ave. SW. (403) 244-6333.

FORT CALGARY
CALGARY, AB

The North West Mounted Police established Fort Calgary in 1875 at the junction of the Elbow and Bow Rivers, where it soon became the focal point of the settlement of Calgary (thus the reason for its national historic site designation). Sitting on a 12-ha (29.7 acres) park, the present fort, complete with barracks and other buildings, is a reconstruction of the original wooden one; it features interpretive exhibits of Calgary's past. Designated NHS: 1925. 750 9th Ave. SE. (403) 290-1875.

GOVERNMENT HOUSE
EDMONTON, AB

Government House, a three-storey sandstone mansion with a view of the Saskatchewan River, was purpose-built to serve as the official residence for the lieutenant governors of Alberta, and did so between 1913 and 1938. It is an excellent example of period architecture. Its imposing size and ornamental detail were designed to reflect Alberta's new provincial status. Free public tours are available on Sundays and holiday Mondays. Designated NHS: 2012. 12845 102 Ave. NW. (780) 427-2281.

ALBERTA

ROCKIES

The Banff Park Museum, which dates to 1895, moved to this building in 1903. *Page 284:* Main entrance of Cave and Basin National Historic Site (top), Banff; touring the Cave and Basin by lantern (middle); looking toward Athabasca Pass (bottom) *Page 285:* Abbot Pass Refuge Cabin, Banff National Park

Jasper House

Jasper Park Information Centre

Yellowhead Pass

Athabasca Pass

☐ National Historic Site (NHS)

0 mi   50

0 km   50

ROCKIES

Forming the boundary between British Columbia and Alberta, the Rocky Mountains are the birthplace of Canada's national parks system. Archaeological evidence indicates that the human presence in the Rockies goes back about 4,000 years. Before Europeans arrived, Indigenous Peoples traversed this rugged shale and limestone landscape, migrating over the range's southern passes in fall and winter to hunt buffalo on the Canadian prairie.

In 1793, Scottish explorer and fur trader Sir Alexander Mackenzie traced one of the northern routes to become the first European to cross the Rockies. Explorer Simon Fraser

followed soon after and, in 1805, established the first mountain trading post. In 1887, the natural hot springs at the base of Sulphur Mountain, which had a reputation for healing, became part of Canada's first national park, Banff. Today, visitors to Cave and Basin National Historic Site (see pp. 288–291) in Banff can tour the cave and explore the natural history of the surrounding wetlands.

Other national historic sites in the Rockies also trace the development of Canada's national parks, from fine examples of the rustic design tradition in park architecture to the grand, castlelike resort hotels of the early 20th century. The oldest surviving federal building in the park system, the Banff Park Museum (see pp. 293–294) features more than 5,000 natural specimens arrayed in habitat displays, a radical new approach in the early 20th century. By then, the Canadian Pacific Railway (CPR), whose own history helped determine the course of Canada's national parks, had established a land route that connected the prairie provinces with coastal British Columbia and helped open the nation's interior for settlement. Rogers Pass (see pp. 292–293) commemorates the CPR's last hurdle to a national railway.

Today, the Rockies boast two UNESCO World Heritage sites—Canadian Rocky Mountain Parks and Waterton-Glacier International Peace Park—each home to several national historic sites featured in this chapter.

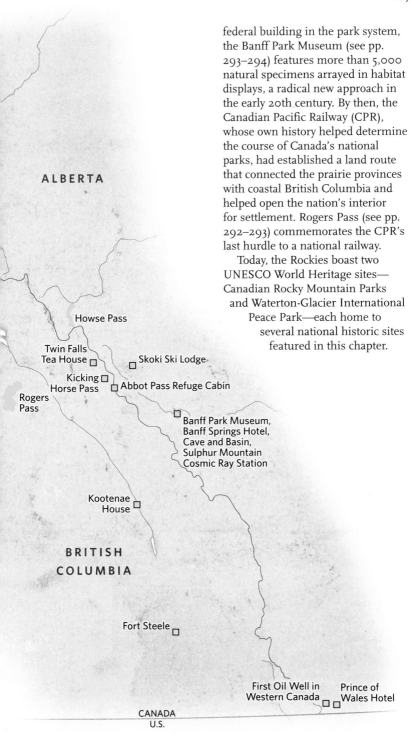

ALBERTA

Howse Pass

Twin Falls
Tea House

Skoki Ski Lodge

Kicking
Horse Pass
Abbot Pass Refuge Cabin

Rogers
Pass

Banff Park Museum,
Banff Springs Hotel,
Cave and Basin,
Sulphur Mountain
Cosmic Ray Station

Kootenae
House

BRITISH
COLUMBIA

Fort Steele

First Oil Well in
Western Canada

Prince of
Wales Hotel

CANADA
U.S.

ROCKIES

Indigenous Peoples long knew of the Banff hot springs waters before railroad workers discovered them in the 1880s.

▶ CAVE AND BASIN

BANFF, AB
Designated 1981

Hot springs have long been popular for their healing properties and relaxing nature, and those at Cave and Basin are no different. For more than 10,000 years, Indigenous Peoples travelled through Alberta's Bow Valley, and oral histories tell of the restorative healing powers of the Banff hot spring waters.

The Cave and Basin National Historic Site, at the bottom of Sulphur Mountain in Banff National Park, holds naturally occurring, emerald green warm mineral springs both inside the cave and outside in a basin. These thermal springs are where Canada's national park system was born.

In 1883, the Canadian Pacific Railway (CPR) arrived in the Bow Valley. Three railway workers, William and Tom McCardell and Frank McCabe, decided to stay in the area over the winter to try their hand at trapping and prospecting. But instead of finding furs and gold, the three men discovered the thermal springs, which they then tried to lay claim to with plans to commercialize them and strike it rich.

Indigenous Peoples in the area had long known about the hot springs, but these three CPR workers brought the Cave and Basin springs to wider public attention at a time when the Bow Valley was being transformed by the railway. Various private ownership claims led to a public inquiry, and in 1885 the federal government intervened and established the Hot Springs Reserve, a 26-sq-km (10 sq mi) public land reserve encompassing the hot springs on Sulphur Mountain, including the Cave and Basin site.

Two years later, the Hot Springs

Reserve became the centre of Canada's first national park, Rocky Mountains Park, now known as Banff National Park. Today, Parks Canada is responsible for more than 10 million sq km (3.9 million sq mi) of protected area, roughly 167 national historic sites, more than 44 national parks, and 4 marine conservation areas—and it all began with the Cave and Basin.

WHAT ARE THE HOT SPRINGS?

Hot springs are natural features of the Bow Valley. Most of the rain and snow that falls on the slopes of nearby mountains ends up in the Bow River. But some of it filters down through cracks and pores in the rock, pulled by gravity to a depth of 3 km (1.8 mi) below the surface.

As it descends, the water becomes hotter and hotter, heated by Earth's molten core. When the water boils and the pressure mounts, it must seek a route back up to the surface. The temperature of the springs depends on several factors, including the time of year (lower in spring because of mixing with meltwater) and altitude (lower altitude means more mixing with colder groundwater). The water is hot at the Upper Hot Springs, for instance, and warm at the Cave and Basin.

Once at the surface, the spring water flows down the lower slopes of Sulphur Mountain toward the Cave and Basin Marsh. Along the way, and in the marsh itself, this warm mineral water creates a rich oasis for a diversity of plant and animal life. Brilliant pink bacteria, white and blue-green algae, small fish, insects, and endangered snails thrive in the water. (The tiny endemic Banff Springs snail, only 5 mm [0.2 in]

long, about the same size as an apple seed, is a federally protected species.) Delicate orchids, harmless garter snakes, and 80 percent of Banff's bird species can also be found here at different times of the year.

Visitors often wonder about the sometimes pungent sulphurous odour at the site. Some bacteria in the thermal waters metabolize the sulphate (SO_4) it contains. In the process, the sulphate is converted to the aromatic hydrogen sulphide (H_2S) gas.

EXPLORING THE CENTRE & GROTTO

Reopened in 2013 after it underwent a nearly $14 million renovation, the Cave and Basin National Historic Site offers year-round interactive programming and exhibits that show how the discovery of the hot springs led to the system of national parks, national historic sites, and national marine conservation areas that Canadians have chosen to protect and enjoy today.

In the renovated historic stone bathing pavilion, explore the interactive exhibits of Story Hall and enjoy a giant four-screen, high-definition journey through Canada's stunning protected areas.

Included with the price of admission to the Cave and Basin centre, the 45-minute guided Discovery Tour allows visitors to experience firsthand how the thermal springs were discovered, and how the discovery started one of the world's greatest conservation movements. Dip a hand in the steamy waters at the touch fountain, meet colourful characters from the past, and hear the water bubble and drip on the walk through the narrow tunnel to reach the underground

ROCKIES

cave, a shimmering cavern of jewels. The Discovery Tour is only offered twice daily (11 a.m. and 2:30 p.m.) from May to September.

To experience a different side of the Cave and Basin, visit after dark with only a lantern for light! Join a small group of visitors on the 25-minute Lantern Tour (fee) to learn the tales of the discovery and days of old. Lights, sounds, and the help of a fog machine conjure up the past, including the tour's host, the ghost of David Galletly, an early caretaker of the Cave and Basin. While Galletly discusses the history of the site, carefully walk through the unlit tunnel to visit the shadowy cave. Entering the cavern in the dark means your other senses become heightened. The water drips louder, the minerals smell stronger, and even the air feels hotter. Listen to Galletly's stories and watch as the lanterns create dancing shadows on the walls. The tour is offered Saturday nights, June through August. Reservations are recommended (403-845-3524).

WALKING TRAILS

Two short interpretive boardwalk trails explain the history of the area and the array of plants and animals that flourish in this warm springs habitat. The

An emerald green mineral pool at Cave and Basin

Discovery Boardwalk Trail above the bathing pavilion takes visitors to the cave vent and the location of the former hotel. See the two smaller springs bubbling from the mountainside and the pools filled with pink bacteria, white and green algae, small fish, and insects. Explore the Marsh Boardwalk Trail below the building to find out more about the natural history of this area. Look for the fish and bird life that live in the wetlands. The area is a favourite for bird-watchers and wildflower enthusiasts alike.

Two longer trails—the 7.4-km (4.6 mi) round-trip Sundance Trail and the 2.5-km (1.6 mi) Marsh Loop—let visitors enjoy safe walks in the unique environment of the thermal springs with the potential to see wildlife such as deer, elk, coyotes, snakes, and birds.

FIRST WORLD WAR INTERNMENT EXHIBIT

Parks Canada has created an exhibit to increase awareness about Canada's First World War internment operations from 1914 to 1920. The exhibit, located adjacent to the Cave and Basin National Historic Site centre, includes interactive touch-screen, mixed media, and two-dimensional displays.

When the First World War began in 1914, there was widespread suspicion in Canada that immigrants from enemy countries—Germany, Austria-Hungary, and later Turkey and Bulgaria—might be disloyal. Under the War Measures Act, the federal government passed regulations that allowed it to monitor and even intern some of these immigrants. During and immediately after the World War, more than 8,500 people were interned as prisoners of war across the country.

CAVE AND BASIN NATIONAL HISTORIC SITE
(Lieu historique national Cave and Basin)

INFORMATION & ACTIVITIES

HOW TO REACH US
311 Cave Ave., Banff, AB T0L 0C0. Phone (403) 762-1566. pc.gc.ca/eng/lhn-nhs/ab/caveand basin/index.aspx.

SEASONS & ACCESSIBILITY
Hours vary seasonally. Open Wednesday to Sunday, from January to mid-May and October through December; open Tuesday to Sunday from mid-May through June and September; and open daily July and August. See website for specific dates and hours.

ENTRANCE FEES
$3.90 per adult, $9.80 per family/group per day.

PETS
None permitted.

ACCESSIBLE SERVICES
Fully accessible, with the exception of the lower marsh boardwalk.

THINGS TO DO
Take a guided tour of the cave, or two self-guided interpretive trails aboveground and two longer walking trails. Visit the museum in the restored bathhouse. Kids age 6 to 11 can discover hidden secrets at the birthplace of Canada's national parks with their own free Xplorers guide filled with fun activities and games. Booklets are available at the front desk.

SPECIAL ADVISORIES
- Refrain from touching the thermal waters or straying from the boardwalk trails as this may compromise the habitats of endangered wildlife.
- Do not approach any wildlife, such as deer or elk, that may be encountered on the trails.
- The site has a significant outdoor component; it's advised to wear comfortable shoes and to bring an extra layer for the outdoors.

HOTELS, MOTELS, & INNS
(Rates are for a 2-person double, high season, in Canadian dollars, unless otherwise noted.)

Rimrock Resort Hotel 300 Mountain Ave., Banff, AB T1L 1J2. (403) 762-3356. rimrockresort.com. 343 rooms, $438–$638.
Buffalo Mountain Lodge 700 Tunnel Mountain Rd., Banff, AB T1L 1B3. (403) 762-2400. crmr.com. 108 rooms, $309–$379.

Additional visitor information:
Banff & Lake Louise Tourism
(403) 762-8421. banfflakelouise.com.

ROCKIES

Four internment camps opened in Canada's western Rocky Mountain national parks: at Banff, Jasper, Mount Revelstoke, and Yoho. Internees did a variety of work, including constructing roads, improving facilities, and clearing land. Through their labour, the internees played an important part in building Canada's western national parks. The internment camp in Banff was established at Castle Mountain in July 1915, and then it was moved to the Cave and Basin that November. The Banff camp closed in July 1917.

How to Get There
The Cave and Basin is located in Banff, Alberta. Banff is 128 km (80 mi) west of Calgary on Trans-Canada 1. A number of commercial shuttles and buses offer transportation to Banff from downtown Calgary or the Calgary International Airport.

When to Go
The national historic site is open year-round, with both winter and summer programming; the trails may be in poor hiking condition in the wintertime.

Canada's first transcontinental rail line crossed over Rogers Pass.

▶ ROGERS PASS

GLACIER NATIONAL PARK, BC
Designated 1971

The discovery of Rogers Pass, a historic travel corridor through the Selkirk Mountains, helped overcome the last major obstacle of a national railway. The pass formed part of the Canadian Pacific Railway's main line from the mid-1880s to 1917.

The pass played a pivotal role in the development of Canada as a nation. Completion of the railway fulfilled Prime Minister John A. Macdonald's 1871 promise of a land connection to British Columbia. It also opened up the nation's interior to settlement.

The Canadian Pacific operated the Rogers Pass line for 30 years despite its steep grade and susceptibility to avalanches. But the Connaught Tunnel was built in 1916 to bypass it. When Trans-Canada 1 officially opened in 1962, Rogers Pass again became part of a national transportation route.

Rogers Pass, now at the centre of Glacier National Park, is an outdoor enthusiast's paradise, its setting the perfect place for numerous outdoor activities, including wildlife viewing, mountaineering, caving, fishing, cycling, and hiking.

What to See & Do

Visitors should check in at the Rogers Pass Discovery Centre, housed in a reproduction of a historic railway snow shed, for a site overview before exploring the surrounding area. Staff can also provide updates on facility, trail, and weather conditions.

Four short, easy interpretive trails in the pass area provide good insight into the cultural and natural history of the pass—the Abandoned Rails Trail, the Loop Brook Trail, the 1885 Rails Trail, and the Glacier House Trail. Several trails from the Illecillewaet Campground lead into the Illecillewaet and Asulkan Valleys. They range from a gentle loop through the woods to all-day grinds that wend up to spectacular alpine ridges and viewpoints.

In the summer, the park offers campfire talks most evenings in July and August, and guided strolls most summer afternoons.

How to Get There

On Trans-Canada 1, Rogers Pass is reachable by bus or car. The closest communities are Golden, 80 km (50 mi) east of the pass, and Revelstoke, 72 km (44.5 mi) to the west.

When to Go

Rogers Pass is accessible year-round, but many visitor facilities are closed in winter. The hours for Rogers Pass Discovery Centre vary by season. Check the website for specific dates.

Day-use areas open with the spring snowmelt, usually mid- to late June, and are closed after Canadian Thanksgiving in early October.

INFORMATION

HOW TO REACH US
P.O. Box 350, Revelstoke, BC V0E 2S0. Phone (250) 837-7500. pc.gc.ca/rogers.

ENTRANCE FEES
$3.90 per adult, $9.80 per family/group per day; $9.80 per adult, $24.50 per family/group per year.

ACCESSIBLE SERVICES
Friendly; contact the site for more details.

Additional visitor information:
Tourism Golden (250) 344-7125. tourismgolden.com.
Tourism Revelstoke (800) 487-1493. seerevelstoke.com.

ROCKIES

Banff Park Museum's animal dioramas were considered novel when they were first created in the 1910s.

▶ BANFF PARK MUSEUM

BANFF, AB
Designated 1985

The Banff Park Museum, with collections initially created by the Geological Survey of Canada, opened in 1895. At the time, it was one of only about 20 museums in Canada. The museum was moved to its current building in 1903.

Norman Bethune Sanson, the museum's curator from 1896 to 1932, actively collected in the field. He eventually assembled more than 5,000 specimens native to the Rockies. Early on, the museum explored both natural and human history, but its focus had narrowed to natural history by the late 1950s. The museum was refurbished in 1985, but its exhibits maintain interpretation styles from the 1914 era, commemorating its early approach to the interpretation of natural history.

The 1903 museum building is the largest and most elaborate example of the early phase of the rustic design tradition in the national parks, using decorative cross-log construction. The quality of materials and craftsmanship throughout makes the building a showpiece and landmark for Banff National Park.

The two-storey museum is somewhat reminiscent of a pagoda with its overhanging shingled roof eaves. The large windows and roof lantern allowed for natural lighting throughout the museum as it was built before electricity was available in Banff. The interior wood finishings, including trim, display cases, and other furnishings, are for the most part original to the building.

What to See & Do

Sanson's impressive collection—ranging from lifelike taxidermic bears and bison to minerals and plants, to birds, bugs, and butterflies—gives an up-close look at Banff's wildlife and a glimpse into how people studied and displayed nature more than a century ago. The exhibits also showcase the changing attitudes people had about wildlife and natural resource management.

Like in many modern natural history museums, the animals

are exhibited in habitat dioramas. But when Dr. Harlan Smith, an archaeologist with the National Museum in Ottawa who worked with Sanson, designed the Banff Park Museum's sheep and goat exhibit in 1914, such a presentation was considered novel.

Real antlers, furs, and even fossils can be handled and examined in the Interactive Discovery Room.

How to Get There

The museum is in downtown Banff, next to the Bow River Bridge and Central Park. Banff is 128 km (80 mi) west of Calgary on Trans-Canada 1.

When to Go

The museum is open daily in July and August, and Wednesday through Sunday mid-May through June and September to early October. Check the museum's website for specific dates and hours.

INFORMATION

HOW TO REACH US
91 Banff Ave., Banff, AB T1L 1K2. Phone (403) 762-1558. pc.gc.ca/eng/lhn-nhs/ab/banff/index.aspx.

ENTRANCE FEES
$3.90 per adult, $9.80 per family/group.

ACCESSIBLE SERVICES
The first floor of the museum is wheelchair accessible; contact the site for more details.

HOTELS, MOTELS, & INNS
Banff Caribou Lodge & Spa 521 Banff Ave., Banff, AB T1L 1H8. (403) 762-5887. bestofbanff.com. 184 rooms, $309–$399.

Additional visitor information:
Banff & Lake Louise Tourism (403) 762-8421. banfflakelouise.com.

ROCKIES SITES

SULPHUR MOUNTAIN COSMIC RAY STATION
BANFF NATIONAL PARK, AB

Located at the top of Sulphur Mountain in Banff National Park, this observation station was built by the National Research Council in 1956 as part of Canada's contribution to the 1957–58 International Geophysical Year (IGY), a scientific undertaking involving more than 60 countries. Ninety-nine cosmic ray stations were in operation worldwide during the IGY, nine in Canada. Because of its high elevation (2,383 m/7,818 ft), Sulphur Mountain was the most important Canadian station. It closed in 1978 and was dismantled in 1981. Designated NHS: 1982.

KICKING HORSE PASS
BANFF NATIONAL PARK, BC

Located in Banff and Yoho National Parks, Kicking Horse Pass is a major rail and highway transportation corridor through the Rocky Mountains surrounded by spectacular mountain scenery. The selection of Kicking Horse as the Canadian Pacific Railway's route instead of the more northerly Yellowhead Pass altered the location of the line and, in turn, the development of western Canada. Designated NHS: 1971.

KOOTENAE HOUSE
INVERMERE, BC

Located just north of Invermere, British Columbia, Kootenae House was built by explorer David Thompson in 1807. The house served as Thompson's base for exploration of the Columbia River and its tributaries, which led to contacts and trade with First Nations throughout the region. It was the first trading post in the area. Thompson's explorations and establishment of additional trading posts in the region helped establish British and, later, Canadian claims in the basin. Designated NHS: 1934.

ROCKIES

The Diverse Peoples of Canada

The Canadian population has often been likened to a mosaic. There have long been culturally diverse and thriving Indigenous populations who, 4,000 years ago, had settled all of Canada's ecosystems, including the Arctic. Archaeological sites across the country speak to ways of life that sustained peoples and their cultures for thousands of years. Indeed, except for the past 500 years, Canada's history is exclusively that of its Indigenous cultures.

Newcomers answer a series of questions in the Immigration Examination Hall, Pier 21, 1952.

The First Newcomers

The earliest non-Indigenous settlers were Norse who came from Greenland, followed several centuries later by whalers, fishers, and explorers from Europe. Archaeological evidence has confirmed and dated early Norse occupation to around A.D. 1000 at L'Anse aux Meadows National Historic Site (see pp. 72–75) in the province of Newfoundland and Labrador. By the late 1400s, Portuguese, Breton, Norman, and Basque fishers and whalers were an annual presence throughout Canada's east coast.

In the early 1600s, year-round English and French settlements had been established in eastern Newfoundland and in Québec, respectively. In the 17th and 18th centuries, the vast empires of France and Britain expanded to include extensive territories in North America. Competition for land and resources led to conflict and the construction of numerous military fortifications along coveted coastlines. Following the American War of Independence, Loyalists—including many people of African descent—sought refuge in British North America.

A Land of Hopes & Dreams

In the 19th and early 20th centuries, newcomers often sought to begin anew in North America. Famine drove thousands of Irish to Canada in the 1840s, and more than 15,000 Chinese workers arrived in the early 1880s to help build the transcontinental railway. By the turn of the 20th century, large numbers of Europeans and Americans flocked to Canada, attracted by the opening of arable western terrain and opportunities in the industrializing urban centres.

The vast majority of immigrants came from overseas. From 1832 to 1937, Québec City was the main port of entry for newcomers, with more than four million people passing through the Port of Québec and the quarantine station on nearby Grosse-Île (see pp. 40–44). Pier 21 in Halifax, Nova Scotia (see pp. 40–44), processed almost a million people who arrived between 1928 and 1971. Both places are now national historic sites. Immigrant experiences are further commemorated at sites like Kensington Market in Toronto, Ontario (see p. 217), and the Main in Montréal, Québec (see p. 141). The Historic Sites and Monuments Board of Canada has also recognized immigration history with other designations, such as Black Pioneers in British Columbia National Historic Event and Japanese Experience in Alberta National Historic Event.

Social, political, religious, and cultural barriers, not to mention difficulties adapting to an unfamiliar climate, were among the many challenges newcomers faced. However, the greatest barriers to entry into Canadian society were the restrictive immigration practices of the early 20th century, reflecting widespread prejudices, racial hatreds, and religious discrimination that often targeted visible minorities.

Xenophobic tendencies gradually gave way to greater inclusivity, based on a new sense of pride in the cultural diversity of Canadian society in the latter half of the 20th century. During hearings held by the Royal Commission on Bilingualism and Biculturalism in the 1960s, representatives speaking on behalf of ethnic minorities from across the country urged the government to recognize the heterogeneity of the Canadian peoples. Multiculturalism became official policy in 1971.

Canadians have since become more welcoming hosts, accepting refugees in the 1970s and '80s from Vietnam and more recently from Syria, for example. By 2011, one in five people residing in Canada were born elsewhere, and most immigrants cited Asia as their continent of origin. Today, diversity is a defining characteristic of the Canadian population, which gains economic strength and renewed cultural vibrancy with every wave of newcomers.

ROCKIES

ROCKIES SITES

JASPER PARK INFORMATION CENTRE
JASPER, AB

This 1913–14 building is one of the finest and most influential examples of the rustic design tradition in Canada's national parks. Its steeply pitched roof, various gables and porches, and use of natural materials such as fieldstone and timber helped define the character of Jasper's early development. It acted as a prominent landmark to greet park visitors upon their arrival by train. Originally a mixed residence and administrative space, it now serves as the park's information centre. Designated NHS: 1992. 500 Connaught Dr.

JASPER HOUSE
JASPER NATIONAL PARK, AB

Built by the North West Company in 1813, Jasper House was later moved by the Hudson's Bay Company to its current site on the Athabasca River. It was an important provisions point for people travelling through the Rockies over the Yellowhead and Athabasca Passes. No road access exists to the actual site, but a commemorative plaque is located 35 km (21.7 mi) east of Jasper on Trans-Canada 16; the site of Jasper House can be seen across the river from a viewing platform. Designated NHS: 1924.

ATHABASCA PASS
JASPER NATIONAL PARK, AB

In January 1811, David Thompson charted a path across the Rockies for the North West Company, with an Iroquois guide known only as Thomas. For nearly 50 years, the pass was part of the main fur trade route between Canada and the Oregon country because of its strategic location on the Continental Divide. Rivers to the west drain into the Pacific, those to the east into Hudson Bay. These mountains form the boundary between British Columbia and Alberta. Designated NHS: 1971.

YELLOWHEAD PASS
JASPER NATIONAL PARK, AB

First Nations peoples used Yellowhead Pass for centuries, and from the 1820s to the 1850s so too did the Hudson's Bay Company, followed by the Grand Trunk Pacific and the Canadian Northern Railways after 1906. One of the lowest elevation passes across the Continental Divide in the northern Rockies, Yellowhead was significant in the fur trade, rail and highway travel, and early tourism. Designated NHS: 1971. West of Jasper on Hwy. 16.

HOWSE PASS
BANFF NATIONAL PARK, AB

Howse Pass was part of the Kootenay Trail linking the eastern slope of the Rockies with the Columbia Valley and the North Saskatchewan and Columbia river systems. Ktunaxa First Nation people probably used this pass to gain access to the buffalo east of the mountains. Later, up to 1810, fur traders for both the North West and Hudson's Bay Companies used it to explore and establish trading posts west of the Rockies. Experienced backcountry travellers can reach the pass by trekking 26 km (16.2 mi) west from the Icefields Parkway (Hwy. 93N). Designated NHS: 1978.

ROCKIES

ABBOT PASS REFUGE CABIN
BANFF NATIONAL PARK, AB

Built in 1922, this high-alpine shelter is an enduring monument to the Swiss guides who first came to the Rocky Mountains in 1899. The hut's construction was a major undertaking—all materials were hauled by horse across the Victoria Glacier and then carried by guides the remainder of the way. The hut sits at an elevation of 2,925 m (9,596 ft) and continues to serve as a base for ascents. Designated NHS: 1992. Accessible from Lake Louise and the Lake O'Hara area.

ROCKIES SITES

SKOKI SKI LODGE
LAKE LOUISE, AB

Canada's first backcountry ski lodge, Skoki Lodge is a rare and well-preserved example of the rustic log-building tradition associated with Banff National Park and reflects the early days of ski tourism in the park. It was built in 1930–31 and enlarged to its current scale in 1935–36. Located at an elevation of 2,164 m (7,100 ft), the lodge is only accessible by hiking or skiing in. The 11-km (6.8 mi) trail begins at the Lake Louise Ski Resort. Designated NHS: 1992. (403) 522-1347 or (888) 997-5654.

BANFF SPRINGS HOTEL
BANFF, AB

One of the grandest and most renowned of the large-scale resort hotels built by the Canadian Pacific Railway during the late 19th and early 20th centuries, the Banff Springs continues to welcome visitors from around the world. The hotel is a tourism icon of the Canadian Rockies. When it was built, the hotel's breathtaking natural setting, château-style design, and lavish interior appealed to a wealthy clientele and those seeking a luxurious wilderness experience. Designated NHS: 1988. 405 Spray Ave.

FIRST OIL WELL IN WESTERN CANADA
WATERTON NATIONAL PARK, AB

In 1902, the Lineham Discovery Well No. 1 struck oil at a depth of 311 m (1,020 ft) just east of Waterton, Alberta. Although not the first attempt to drill for oil in western Canada, it was the first well to produce saleable quantities of oil. It was said to produce 300 barrels a day, but its success was short-lived. Early on, the well casing failed and the drilling tools became lodged in the well, and further attempts to exploit the well were unsuccessful. Designated NHS: 1965. Akamina Pkwy.

PRINCE OF WALES HOTEL
WATERTON PARK, AB

Built in 1926–27 by the U.S. company Great Northern Railway, the striking Prince of Wales Hotel, which features a Swiss chalet design, remains a landmark of Waterton Lakes National Park. Its construction took place during one of Waterton's windiest winters, when twice it was blown off its foundation. The Prince of Wales was the final stop in the Great Northern's chain of luxury hotels, backcountry chalets, and tent camps for affluent visitors travelling through the backcountry of Montana's Glacier National Park. Designated NHS: 1992. Off Alberta Rte. 5.

TWIN FALLS TEA HOUSE
YOHO NATIONAL PARK, BC

Located in Yoho National Park, Twin Falls is an unusual double waterfall reachable only by hiking in 8.5 km (5.3 mi) one way. The nearby tea-house, built to serve as a stopping place for recreationists, is a well-preserved example of rustic design in Canada's national parks. The Canadian Pacific Railway constructed the log teahouse in stages. It began as a one-storey cabin in 1908; years later, a two-storey chalet was added and linked to the earlier building. Designated NHS: 1992.

ROCKIES

FORT STEELE
FORT STEELE, BC

Established in 1887 as the first North West Mounted Police post in British Columbia by Superintendent "Sam" Steele, Fort Steele was strategically located on a bluff overlooking the Kootenay River. After Steele left the region, the citizens of Galbraith's Ferry renamed their town Fort Steele in appreciation of his work, and the town expanded to include the original post site. Designated NHS: 1925. Riverside Ave.

BRITISH COLUMBIA

Y U K O N

Chilkoot
Trail

CANADA
U.S.

B R I T I S H   C O

Gitwangak
Battle Hill

□   National Historic Site (NHS)
⊛   Province capital city

0 mi   200
0 km   200

SGang Gwaay
Llnagaay

BRITISH
COLUMBIA

Canada's westernmost province,
and the nation's third largest after
Québec and Ontario, has a geograph-
ical diversity unmatched in the
rest of the country. Two spectacular
mountain ranges dominate, the
Coast Mountains to the west and the
Rocky Mountains to the east, both
running north to south.

    Human settlement concentrated
in between on a plateau dotted by
small lakes, and along the Pacific
coast, where fjords and hundreds of
islands, left behind by melting glaciers some 7,000 to 13,000 years ago,
trace the water's edge. With more
than half of this region covered by
forest and little suitable for agriculture, the Coast Salish, Haida, and
other Indigenous Peoples who have
inhabited this region for 6,000 to

8,000 years developed
an economy based pri-
marily on fishing, hunting,
and forest products.

    European fur traders, who began
to arrive in the late 18th century,
depended heavily on the First Nations
and their well-established trade routes
for their success. European settlements sprang up along the Pacific
coast, but the interior remained relatively unexplored until the gold
rushes of the 1850s and 1860s, which
propelled the region's overall growth.

NORTHWEST
TERRITORIES

J M B I A

A L B E R T A

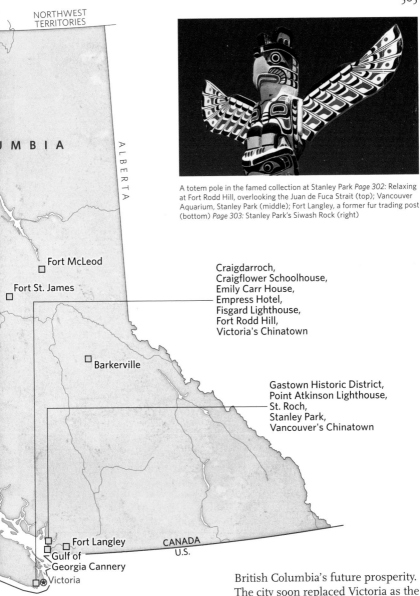

A totem pole in the famed collection at Stanley Park *Page 302:* Relaxing at Fort Rodd Hill, overlooking the Juan de Fuca Strait (top); Vancouver Aquarium, Stanley Park (middle); Fort Langley, a former fur trading post (bottom) *Page 303:* Stanley Park's Siwash Rock (right)

Fort McLeod

Fort St. James

Craigdarroch,
Craigflower Schoolhouse,
Emily Carr House,
Empress Hotel,
Fisgard Lighthouse,
Fort Rodd Hill,
Victoria's Chinatown

Barkerville

Gastown Historic District,
Point Atkinson Lighthouse,
St. Roch,
Stanley Park,
Vancouver's Chinatown

Fort Langley

Gulf of
Georgia Cannery

CANADA
U.S.

Victoria

BRITISH COLUMBIA

As the economy flourished, immigrant labourers flooded into the region. British Columbia, with Victoria as its capital city, became a province of Canada in 1871. By the mid-1880s, the Canadian Pacific Railway reached all the way to the port city of Vancouver, helping to ensure British Columbia's future prosperity. The city soon replaced Victoria as the centre of the province's economic activity and international trade.

The historic sites featured in this chapter cover the full range of British Columbia's history, from First Nations villages to gold rush sites, industrial centres, and the thriving urban neighbourhoods of Vancouver and Victoria.

Now protected from the elements, Stanley Park's Nine O'Clock Gun has sounded the 9 p.m. hour for more than 100 years.

WEST COAST

Long before the Fraser River gold rush drew prospectors by the thousands in the late 1850s, the west coast of Canada was inhabited by the Haida, Squamish, and other First Nations whose thriving trade routes helped shape western Canada's economy in the 19th and 20th centuries. First Nations people contributed to the success of the commercial activities at Fort Langley, an important trading post and provisions centre, and later worked the line at the Gulf of Georgia Cannery, which also drew labourers from Europe and Japan.

At strategic Fort Rodd Hill and neighbouring Fisgard Lighthouse, Canada's first permanent lighthouse, visitors can learn about the international contest for trade and territory and its impact on British Columbia's west coast, where Britain strove to remain sovereign. The region boasts the oldest surviving Chinatown in Canada and is also home to one of the world's greatest urban recreational spaces, Stanley Park, whose rain forest, collection of First Nations totem poles, and iconic seawall rank it among Vancouver's must-see sites.

British Columbia was declared a British Crown colony at Fort Langley, today rebuilt to its mid-1800s appearance.

▶ FORT LANGLEY

FORT LANGLEY, BC
Designated 1923

In strategic proximity to the Pacific Ocean and to the Indigenous Peoples who transported furs, food, and more along ancient trade routes, Fort Langley emerged as a key supply centre and lifeline for the many remote northern fur trading outposts across what is now British Columbia.

Here, too, the mainland of British Columbia was officially declared a British colony in 1858.

The Hudson's Bay Company (which had by 1821 merged with its rival, the North West Company) established the fort in the late 1820s to better compete with American fur traders, who by the early 19th century were undercutting their business. From Fort Langley, furs from points all over northern British Columbia were shipped to Europe via Cape Horn, produce was traded to the Russians in Alaska, local cranberries found their way to California, and Fraser River salmon was enjoyed as far away as Hawaii. As the local supply of furs was exhausted over time, Fort Langley shifted its business model to that of a provisioning centre—growing its farm output and salmon exporting businesses.

BRITISH COLUMBIA DECLARED BRITISH CROWN COLONY

A few decades later, in November 1858, Vancouver Island governor James Douglas sailed up the Fraser River by steam-powered paddle wheeler to Fort Langley, where he officially declared the mainland of British Columbia a colony of the British Empire. The birth of British Columbia, which occurred amid an immense downpour, was celebrated afterward with a great feast that included members of the Kwantlen First Nation, who at this point were key enabling business partners for the fort's fur trading and salmon-curing activities.

By this point, a now legendary rivalry had developed between Douglas and Fort Langley's chief trader, James Yale, the man who ran Fort Langley. In the mid-1820s, when both men worked at Fort St. James (see pp. 328–329), they had vied for the affections of the lovely Amelia, the daughter of a powerful European man, the local chief factor, William Connolly, and Miyo Nipiy, a Cree woman. Douglas prevailed. It is said that the powerfully built Douglas would drive Yale to distraction by deliberately positioning himself adjacent to the 152-cm-tall (almost 5 ft) Yale at official functions. And although Douglas enjoyed a meteoric career rise from fur trader to politician, Yale languished for nearly 30 years at Fort Langley without upward advancement (he retired in 1860), where to his credit, he developed the outpost into a significant business concern.

Douglas's presence that November at Fort Langley was motivated by fear. Earlier in 1858, news that gold had been discovered on the lower Fraser River prompted the unruly migration of about 30,000 American prospectors onto the mainland of what is now British Columbia. Prior to this event, the British had formally colonized only Vancouver Island. The lower Fraser River was the home of the Sto:lo First Nations people, a group of independent nations whose language had common roots. Fearful that the mainland would be swallowed by an expanding United States, Douglas not only declared the mainland a British colony, but also called for the Corps of Royal Engineers from Britain to construct and survey roads, clear townsites, and keep the peace in the gold-mining districts. From then on, Fort Langley took on new strategic importance as a bulwark against American territorial expansion.

Eventually, however, the fort began to decline in importance and fell into disrepair. Fort Langley stopped operating as a Hudson's Bay Company post in 1886.

FORT LANGLEY TODAY

Reconstructed 4.5-m (14.8 ft) sharpened wooden palisade walls ring the site, which is home to the oldest extant building in British Columbia's Lower Mainland, a wooden storehouse of post-on-sill construction that dates to the 1840s. From the visitor centre at the front gate, visitors walk into a reconstructed version of Fort Langley in the mid-1800s, much of which was built in the mid-20th century in time for the centennial of the Colony of British Columbia.

A trade window near the gate was where Chief Trader James Yale would have greeted Indigenous Peoples to buy their furs. The original storehouse is adjacent to a blacksmith station and cooperage (where wooden barrels were made)—the latter critical for the export of salmon, cranberries, and farm produce. The biggest and grandest building is the Big House, the 1958 reconstruction of the living quarters of the fort's managers, and the site from which Governor Douglas announced the British colony of British Columbia in 1858.

Year-round interpretive programs featuring staff in period dress allow visitors to experience life in Fort Langley as it existed in the early to mid-19th century.

WEST COAST

BRIGADE DAYS

Each August long weekend (a statutory BC holiday that falls on the first Monday in August), legions of local volunteer historical reenactors descend on Fort Langley to celebrate Brigade Days, the fort's annual event highlight. The event is a re-creation of the annual arrival of pack trains and canoes carrying furs to the fort from remote outposts in the north, made possible with the first spring melt. Historically, the fur brigades would have converged on Fort Langley from far-flung fur trade posts like Fort Kamloops and Fort St. James by the first thaw of late June, but this event has been moved to the peak of tourist season, during high summer.

The arrival of the brigades is reenacted with the arrival of a small

A visitor tries her hand at coopering.

Traditional fare cooked over a wood fire

fleet of large voyageur canoes and period-style boats and smaller canoes. Crowds cheer on the voyageurs, who were typically men of French-Canadian descent, as they carry bales of furs into the fort. Inside, the fort is transformed into an encampment populated with characters dressed in period costume—Hudson's Bay Company workers, trappers, traders, Indigenous Peoples, Métis, and more. Visitors are encouraged to interact with blacksmiths, fort workers preserving beaver pelts, and musicians playing period instruments and music. Visitors can try their hand at gold panning, and watch men fire period muskets from the palisade walls. The musket demonstration includes a description of the firing mechanisms of the flintlock muskets, common jargon ("lock, stock, and barrel"), and the differences between the various guns used at the fort. (The musket demonstration can be seen outside of Brigade Days too; it is offered June to Labour Day.)

At times, there is the opportunity to interact with descendants of the original Kwantlen First Nation at the fort, upon whose territory the fort was and remains built. (Their modern-day reserve land remains just across the river from the fort.) The influence of the Kwantlen on the fort cannot be overstated: The Hudson's Bay Company came wanting furs, but the commodities available here were plentiful salmon and cranberries. The Kwantlen not only became middlemen for the fur trade on their territory, but they were also master fishermen and thus became enablers of a lucrative salmon business that exported the fort-processed salmon across the western Pacific, including Hawaii, where barrel-salted salmon (known as "lomi lomi") remains a local traditional food to this day. In

FORT LANGLEY NATIONAL HISTORIC SITE
(Lieu historique national du Fort-Langley)

INFORMATION & ACTIVITIES

HOW TO REACH US
23433 Mavis Ave., Fort Langley, BC V1M 2R5. Phone (604) 513-4777. pc.gc.ca/eng /lhn-nhs/bc/langley/index.aspx.

ENTRANCE FEES
$7.80 per adult, $19.60 per family/group per day.

PETS
An on-leash area is located outside of the palisade walls, but pets are not permitted inside the visitor centre or the fort.

ACCESSIBLE SERVICES
All buildings have access ramps; the visitor centre and café have accessible washrooms.

THINGS TO DO
Explore the site of the 19th-century Hudson's Bay Company trading post, including a climb up the rustic bastion towers to stunning views of the Fraser River.

Hear the clang of an anvil at the blacksmith shop and the bang of black powder musket demonstrations, or watch a coopering demonstration.

Families can participate in the Parks Canada Xplorers program, packed with fun activities: Kids will receive a certificate and a souvenir for participating. Children can pan for gold, and at closing time, witness the lowering of the flag with song.

Activities and interpretive programs are always in flux, so check the website for current offerings and times.

CAMPGROUNDS
Fort Camping Brae Island Regional Park (604) 888-3678 or (866) 267-3678. fort camping.com. 156 camping sites, catering to single tents and RVs needing a 50-amp pull-through.

oTENTik accommodations Inside the fort, these are crosses between A-frame cabins and prospector tents built on a weatherproof, raised wooden floor, and themed to represent the heritage of the people who worked at the fort (for example, First Nations, Hawaiian, French voyageur). Available May 1 to Thanksgiving. Reservations begin early January (call 877-737-3783 or visit reservation.pc.gc.ca). 5 units (each sleeps six), $120.

HOTELS, MOTELS, & INNS
(Rates are for a 2-person double, high season, in Canadian dollars, unless otherwise noted.)

Langley Highway Hotel 20470 88 Ave., Langley, BC V1M 2Y6. (604) 888-4891. langleyhwyhotel.com. $89.
Sandman Signature Langley Hotel 8828 201 St., Langley, BC V2Y 0C8. (604) 455-7263. sandmansignature.ca /hotels/langley. $150.

WEST COAST

addition to interacting with Kwantlen interpreters, visitors can buy exquisite hand-carved jewellery, apparel, cedar bark baskets, traditional blankets, decorative housewares, and Fort Langley memorabilia from Šxwimələ Gifts (pronounced schwi-MAY-la, the shop's name means "store" in the Halq'eméylem language), a Kwantlen-run gift shop located in the visitor centre. The lelem' Café, also Kwantlen-run, offers visitors a taste of Fraser River salmon and other traditional and modern foods.

How to Get There
By car from Vancouver, take Trans-Canada 1 east 40 km (25 mi) to the 232nd Street exit. Follow the "beaver" signs north along 232nd Street to Glover Road; turn right and head into the village of Fort Langley. Turn right on Mavis Avenue at the flashing lights, just before the railway tracks. Park at the end of the street.

When to Go
The fort is open year-round, but high summer offers more activities.

Offshore from Fort Rodd Hill, the Fisgard Lighthouse served as a beacon of Britain's sovereignty.

▶ FORT RODD HILL AND FISGARD LIGHTHOUSE

COLWOOD, BC
Designated 1958

Built 30 years apart, Fisgard Lighthouse and Fort Rodd Hill were established on southern Vancouver Island to advance and strengthen British imperial control of the North Pacific while countering the real and imagined military threats faced by a large empire.

Perched above the turbulent Juan de Fuca Strait overlooking Esquimalt Harbour, the 1860 Fisgard Lighthouse was the first permanent lighthouse built on the west coast of what would become Canada. Immediately adjacent is the later built Fort Rodd Hill, a British artillery fort designed to defend the British Royal Navy base and the city of Victoria.

The lighthouse and the fort were declared independent national historic sites in 1958, but Parks Canada oversees them as a single location. The two sites, linked by a causeway, cover a collective area of 16 ha (39.5 acres).

■ FORT RODD HILL

Built in the 1890s, two decades after British Columbia joined the Confederation, Fort Rodd Hill was built under the joint oversight of both the British government and the fledgling Dominion of Canada. At the time, the British flag still flew over much of the world, and its Royal Navy, stationed in far-off colonial outposts like Vancouver Island, was the means by which it policed its vast empire. The fort was a small but strategically located station, equipped with state-of-the-art, scientifically sited coast artillery guns and an extensive system of electric searchlights and interlinked telephone communications.

By 1906, the British had left Esquimalt and the defence of the west coast to Canada, having reconsidered its strategic significance. By 1938 and the dawn of the Second World War, the Canadian government decided that the big guns had long been obsolete—newer, long-range guns mounted on enemy ships could bombard Esquimalt from far out to sea. New gun batteries were established west of the fort, and by wartime there were about 35 observation posts set up to locate enemy ships around Victoria, with the establishment of 18 new searchlights to replace the fort's original 1890 searchlights.

The guns of the fort were never fired in battle, but many warning shots were fired. During the Second World War, Esquimalt Harbour was protected by a log boom and submarine torpedo net, with a gate to let ships in and out. All ships entering were required to stop and wait to be recognized by naval patrol boats, but not everyone complied: In those cases, the battery at Fort Rodd Hill was authorized to fire live ammunition "across the bow" of these errant ships to stop them.

The fort was officially closed in 1956.

GEOPOLITICAL THREATS

By the time the fort was established, the threat of American annexation of western Canada was waning. Instead, the Russians—against whom the British waged a bitter war over possession of the Crimean Peninsula during the 1850s—posed the primary threat. As early as 1878, temporary gun batteries had been established in different parts of Victoria in response to fears of Russian expansionism. At the time, the British and Russians faced growing tensions over their respective colonial possessions in India and Afghanistan. Adding to fears was the fact that Russians were familiar with the British Columbia coast, having been active in the fur trade along this section of the Pacific since the 1600s. The Japanese annihilation of the Russian fleet in 1904 meant that for a time at least, the Russian threat to the North Pacific coast no longer existed.

During the First World War, Fort Rodd Hill became a naval repair facility for the British, but the fort was never tested by the Germans.

Imperial Japan had emerged as a potential enemy by the early 1930s, and definitively in the Second World War. By that war's end, the Soviet Union became the threat as the atomic stalemate of the Cold War era began. The fort's underground bunkers were turned into an air defence station, which was equipped to plot the flight paths of enemy Soviet aircraft invading Canadian airspace.

■ FISGARD LIGHTHOUSE

It is no coincidence that western Canada's first permanent lighthouse was built just as thousands of American prospectors were invading Victoria by sea on their way to the Fraser River goldfields. The influx badly spooked the British colonial leadership of Vancouver Island, which responded by establishing the lighthouse standing over Victoria's most important harbour as a beacon of British sovereignty. The lighthouse also made it easier for the British Navy to safely manoeuvre in and out of Esquimalt Harbour, another important counter to the threat of American annexation. It was a not-so-subtle expression to all visitors that Vancouver Island was British, and would remain so.

WEST COAST

Construction started in 1859 and was completed in 1860, which places it with some of the earliest buildings that still exist in Victoria. While the lighthouse and the keeper's residence were taking shape, George Davies, the first lighthouse keeper, was making his way from England by ship. Accompanying him were components for the lamp room at the top of the lighthouse—everything else used in the construction of the lighthouse, including the bricks and blacksmithed metallic components, were of local manufacture.

Once in operation, the lighthouse worked in concert with its sister lighthouse at nearby Race Rocks: The latter guided mariners along the Strait of Juan de Fuca; Fisgard helped them safely navigate the entrance of Esquimalt Harbour.

THE LIFE OF A KEEPER

About a dozen resident lighthouse keepers worked at Fisgard from 1860 to 1929, the year the site was automated and ceased to host a resident

Interpreter in period military costume at Fort Rodd Hill

employee. (The last keeper was hired to row out to the lighthouse at sunset, spend the night, and row back in the morning.) By all surviving accounts, it was a difficult, gruelling, and dangerous job.

The causeway that today connects the lighthouse to the coast is a modern construct: The keeper, his family, and an assistant lighthouse keeper were all expected to live on a tiny, ocean-battered island, in a house with two 3.5-m-by-3.5-m (11.5 by 11.5 ft) bedrooms.

Being a keeper was a trying occupation: The keeper by necessity had to be a jack of all trades, capable of fixing the lighthouse, boats, or anything else that broke. Surprise inspections from superiors were routine. A keeper was also not allowed to leave the station under any circumstances without written permission, which created life-and-death situations when spouses and children became injured or ill. And at least two keepers died on the job, one from a long-lingering illness, and a second who drowned when he fell out of his rowboat trying to retrieve a lost paddle in rough seas.

In the beginning, despite the danger and toil, the job of lighthouse keeper was a prestigious, relatively well-paid job, but this was not to last. By the time the lighthouse administration passed from the British to Canada after Confederation, the salary was cut in half, which meant the calibre of men willing to take the hardship and risk of the occupation plummeted.

How to Get There

The lighthouse and fort are located in the community of Colwood, just west of downtown Victoria. Car is the best way to get there. There is free parking and drive-through RV stalls.

From downtown Victoria, follow

FORT RODD HILL & FISGARD LIGHTHOUSE NATIONAL HISTORIC SITES
(Lieu historiques nationaux Fort Rodd Hill et du Phare-de-Fisgard)

INFORMATION & ACTIVITIES

HOW TO REACH US
603 Fort Rodd Hill Rd., Victoria, BC V9C 2W8. Phone (250) 478-5849. pc.gc.ca /eng/lhn-nhs/bc/fortroddhill/index.aspx.

SEASONS & ACCESSIBILITY
Open daily May 15 to October 15; reduced days and hours October 15 to February 28. Check the website for more details.

ENTRANCE FEES
$3.90 per adult, $9.80 per family/group per day.

PETS
None permitted.

ACCESSIBLE SERVICES
The lighthouse is wheelchair accessible. Fort batteries have stairs that cannot be accessed. Most washrooms are wheelchair accessible.

THINGS TO DO
Fort Rodd Hill Walk the original ramparts of three gun batteries, and explore underground magazines, command posts, guardhouses, barracks, and searchlight emplacements. There are numerous interpretive displays and information, including the firepower weapons demonstrations.
Fisgard Lighthouse Enjoy interactive video games (steer a 19th-century schooner or a present-day naval patrol vessel into Esquimalt Harbour, manoeuvring safely or crashing onto the rocky shore). Spy on the busy shipping lanes of Esquimalt Harbour using the free telescopes. Picnic amid wildlife and a stunning view of Washington's Olympic Mountains.

SPECIAL ADVISORIES
- There are no food providers on-site.
- The site is very large; bring good walking shoes.
- Be prepared for cool, windy conditions, even in summer.

CAMPGROUNDS
McDonald Campground Gulf Island National Park Reserve, near town of Sidney. Reservations can be made at reservation.pc.gc.ca or by calling (877) 737-3783. 43 vehicle sites and 6 walk-in sites.
oTENTik accommodations Inside Fort Rodd Hill, these are crosses between A-frame cabins and prospector tents built on a weatherproof, raised wooden floor. Available May 15 to September 30. Reservations begin early January (877-737-3783, reservation.pc.gc.ca). 5 units (each sleeps six); one of the units is wheelchair accessible. $120 + $13.50 reservation fee.

HOTELS, MOTELS, & INNS
(Rates are for a 2-person double, high season, in Canadian dollars, unless otherwise noted.)

Holiday Inn Express & Suites Victoria-Colwood 318 Wale Rd., Colwood, BC V9B 0J8. (250) 385-7829 or (877) 660-8550. ihg.com/holidayinnexpress/hotels/us/en /colwood/yyjcd/hoteldetail. $210.
Four Points by Sheraton Victoria Gateway 829 McCallum Rd., Victoria, BC V9B 6W6. (250) 474-6063 or (866) 716-8133. four pointsvictoriagateway.com. $200–$249.

WEST COAST

Douglas Street north onto Trans-Canada 1 and travel about 8 km (5 mi). Take exit 10 (Colwood), which becomes Hwy. 1A (Old Island Hwy.). Remain on Hwy. 1A for about 3 km (1.9 mi), turning left after passing the fifth traffic light, onto Ocean Boulevard. The sites are about 1.5 km (0.9 mi) down this road.

When to Go
July and August are when interpretive programs are at their peak; June and September also have a lot going on.

Work at the Gulf of Georgia Cannery lured hundreds of people to Steveston, both seasonally and permanently.

▶ GULF OF GEORGIA CANNERY

STEVESTON, BC
Designated 1976

Located in Canada's busiest fishing village of Steveston, this 1894 cannery has been preserved and transformed into an interactive museum dedicated to the West Coast fishing industry and the First Nations and immigrant fishermen and workers whose jobs were transformed over the decades by advances in industrial and transportation technology.

One constant at the cannery was the presence of First Nations people, who have fished these North Pacific waters from time immemorial and would form an important part of the seasonal fishing and processing workforce for more than 80 years.

The Gulf of Georgia Cannery was established in 1894 primarily to can and export the five species of Pacific salmon that returned in the millions each year to natal streams across the vast Fraser River watershed. Within a year, it was the second biggest salmon cannery in the province, eventually adding a herring canning and reduction plant. Today, the site comprises a cannery, an icehouse, and a vitamin oil shed, among other structures—a complex of buildings all built between 1894 and 1964.

After operations ceased in 1979, the community rallied to save the cannery site. It took a few years, but in 1994 a museum was opened to the public. The nonprofit Gulf of Georgia Cannery Society now runs the site on behalf of Parks Canada.

What to See & Do

Of the permanent exhibits, by far the most popular is the intact salmon canning line that operated until 1930. The cannery was a fresh fish plant in the 1930s, and herring canning and reduction were introduced during the Second World War. Herring reduction continued after the war, as did fresh fish and net loft operations. Guided and self-guided tours introduce visitors to jobs on the line: transferring whole fish from the boats, butchering, working the "sliming table," overseeing the vacuum sealer that closed the cans, and more. (Visitors do not touch the equipment.) When the line is not in use, motion detectors trigger sounds that give a sense of it in operation: a cacophony of tin clanging against iron and steel, the squeak and whirling of belts and engines.

The cannery line is a window into the social history of the many ethnic groups that made the annual migration to work here. The spring, summer, and fall runs of salmon initially attracted First Nations fishermen and families, followed shortly after by Japanese. While the men fished, wives and children worked at the cannery. (The First Nations workforce would later expand to replace Japanese workers interned during the Second World War.) Single Chinese men, many who had immigrated to build railways, began working here in the 1890s, specializing in tasks like butchering salmon, a dangerous job where losing fingers was common. By 1895, a Greek community was established on Deas Island, and the Finnish enclave of Finn Slough in south Richmond. The workforce included Scots, Britons, and other Europeans too. Most families were billeted at sites in the village, provided by the cannery's Scottish owners.

How to Get There

The cannery is located in Steveston, a seaside village in the suburb of Richmond, about 30 km (18.6 mi) southwest of downtown Vancouver, via Hwy. 99 and Steveston Hwy. Once in Steveston, turn left onto

No. 1 Road and then right onto Moncton Street to its end.

When to Go

The cannery is open year-round, but it lacks insulation and is built directly over the Fraser River so it becomes quite cool in winter. Daily guided tours are more frequent between Victoria Day and Labour Day.

WEST COAST

Tins of fish on the cannery line

A statue in Stanley Park honours hometown hero Harry Jerome, who competed in three Olympics in the 1960s.

▶ STANLEY PARK

VANCOUVER, BC
Designated 1988

Set on a peninsula jutting into Burrard Inlet adjacent to the downtown core of Vancouver, Stanley Park is more than one of the world's greatest urban parks: The land has been a home and sanctuary for local people for millennia. Established in 1888, the 404-ha (998 acres) park remains a beacon for visitors and residents alike.

The site of Stanley Park was occupied for more than 8,000 years by ancestors of the Musqueam, Squamish, and Tsleil-Waututh First Nations. It wasn't until the early 1790s that Spanish and British explorers first set eyes on the future park, including British explorer George Vancouver.

The influx of thousands of prospectors during the 1858 Fraser River gold rush changed the region forever. The British Columbia mainland was declared a colony (see pp. 304–307) soon after and the future parkland was set aside as a military reserve.

At the first meeting of the Vancouver City Council in May 1886, a resolution was passed to ask the Dominion government to convey the peninsula to the city "in order that it be used by the inhabitants of said City of Vancouver as a park." Despite the preexisting settlements within the new park boundary (see p. 319), Stanley Park was officially declared in September 1888, named for Governor General Sir Frederick Arthur Stanley.

The early history of the park had two competing visions: City elites prescribed to a romanticized 19th-century notion of "wilderness" and opposed most development, whereas primarily working-class Vancouverites pressed for the development of athletic amenities like pools and playing fields. Over the years, successive park administrators would walk a careful line between the two.

FIRST NATIONS PRESENCE & INFLUENCE

The three Coast Salish communities—the Musqueam, Tseil-Watuth, and Squamish Nations—who have lived in this region for millennia were prosperous fishermen, gatherers, and hunters.

Archaeologists have now documented nearly 20 separate sites that were home to Indigenous Peoples, including the Squamish villages of Chaythoos near Prospect Point and Xw'ay Xw'ay (Whoi Whoi) at Lumberman's Arch. (As recently as the 1880s, large potlatches involving thousands of Indigenous participants took place at the latter.) Not far from this site is a shell midden—a layered pile of crushed shells from generations of native shellfish harvesting—more than 2 m (6.6 ft) deep and covering 1.2 ha (3 acres). Much of its material was ground up and removed to build a park road. Another midden, believed to be three times this size, lies beneath Third Beach.

Even though the Coast Salish never relinquished their ownership of the land that includes the present-day park and Vancouver, sawmills were established in the 1860s to exploit the old-growth cedar and fir. First Nations intermingled and intermarried with settler cultures at Brockton Point, Lumberman's Arch, and at Prospect Point, where Portuguese, Hawaiian, and Scottish workers moved to work at the mills. After the park was created, the city branded these residents as "squatters," resulting in decades of conflict and court battles that stretched into the 1920s. Some residents successfully fought the city, but all the settlers eventually left.

At the same time that the park fathers were trying to evict Indigenous Peoples from the park, they were planning a reproduction First Nations village, inhabited by Indigenous Peoples, as a tourist attraction. The plan did not proceed, the result of its complexity, cost, and objections from local First Nations. In its place, it was decided to celebrate First Nations heritage by expanding the park's collection of totem poles, begun as early as 1903. In 1924, four totem poles from northern Vancouver Island were erected near the former Whoi Whoi village site. (By this time, newly amended Canadian laws enabled authorities to express greater ownership over totem poles and other cultural objects.) More poles from Haida Gwaii and Rivers Inlet would follow, and the entire display was moved to Brockton Point in 1960.

The totem display soon emerged as the most popular tourist site in British Columbia—more than three million people today visit each year. Among the oldest and most striking was the Skedans Mortuary Pole, the sole Haida mortuary pole of the collection, dating from pre-1878, which would have housed the remains of a chief in a cedar box positioned behind the frontal board on the top. It was purchased for 290 blankets, worth almost $600, from Chief

WEST COAST

Soaking up the sun and scenery at Stanley Park

Visitors sit back and enjoy the ride on a horse-drawn tour of Stanley Park.

The Seawall took more than 60 years to build.

Henry Moody in 1936, an enormous sum for the day. By 1962, the pole was showing its age; renowned Haida artist Bill Reid was hired to produce a replica, and the original was returned to Haida Gwaii.

Until 2008, this display of remote northern British Columbia coastal art had no connection to the culture of the First Nations peoples who lived in park's region. In that year, Coast Salish artist Susan Point unveiled three carved cedar welcome gates—a gateway welcoming visitors onto their territory never ceded—so that visitors now walk through traditional Musqueam and Squamish imagery to access the totem pole display. And a Squamish First Nation artist, Robert Yelton, created the most recent pole added to the site, in 2009.

Perhaps the most stunning First Nations site on the entire peninsula is not the work of human hands. Siwash Rock is an iconic landmark on the western edge of the seawall, a towering offshore stone monolith topped by a tangle of trees and shrubs. According to Squamish legend, it is the body of a great chief transformed into stone by supernatural giants who came upon the leader as he was swimming. So that he would not be alone, the Transformers turned his wife and child into smaller rocks found on the forest hillside above Siwash Rock.

STANLEY PARK SEAWALL

The Stanley Park Seawall (with a separated walking/biking trail) encircles the park's roughly 8.5-km (5.3 mi) site perimeter and took more than six

STANLEY PARK NATIONAL HISTORIC SITE
(Lieu historique national de parc Stanley)

INFORMATION & ACTIVITIES

HOW TO REACH US
Tourism Vancouver Visitor Centre 200 Burrard St., Vancouver, BC V6C 3L6. Phone (604) 683-2000. tourismvancouver.com.

ENTRANCE FEES
None (except for certain venues inside the park like the Vancouver Aquarium and Pitch and Putt Golf Course).

PETS
Dogs must be leashed, except in the Stanley Park off-leash area (open 7 a.m.–9 p.m.), located off Lagoon Drive (at the shuffleboard court).

ACCESSIBLE SERVICES
All washrooms have accessible stalls. The trail around Beaver Lake is wheelchair accessible.

THINGS TO DO
There is much to do here: the Pitch and Putt Golf Course, four playgrounds, multiple picnic areas, tennis courts, and swimming (sandy ocean beaches at Second and Third Beaches, a kids' water park at Lumberman's Arch, and a heated outdoor pool at Second Beach). The Vancouver Aquarium is a world-class facility, featuring sea life of the North Pacific and beyond.

There are multiple gardens: The Ted and Mary Greig Rhododendron Garden contains about 4,500 rhododendrons near the Pitch and Putt Golf Course; the Rose Garden (established 1920) has 3,500 rose bushes. The Shakespeare Garden is a diverse arboretum that includes many of the trees mentioned in the Bard's plays and poems.

SPECIAL ADVISORIES
• On weekends and holidays, parking can be difficult to find.
• If you drive to Stanley Park, consider a daily parking pass, which allows you to move your car and park at any location within the park.

HOTELS, MOTELS, & INNS
(Rates are for a 2-person double, high season, in Canadian dollars, unless otherwise noted.)

Sylvia Hotel 1154 Gilford St., Vancouver, BC V6G 2P6. (604) 681-9321 or (877) 681-9321. sylviahotel.com. $200–$229.
English Bay Hotel 1150 Denman St., Vancouver, BC V6G 2M9. (604) 685-2231. englishbayhotel.com. $130.

Additional visitor information:
For general inquiries (including all parks), call the City of Vancouver's information line at 311 from within Vancouver, and (604) 873-7000 from outside.

WEST COAST

---

decades and a massive mobilization of resources and labour to complete.

This wonder of masonry construction, over 3 m (9.8 ft) high at points, hugs the edges of cliffs and curving shoreline. The decision to begin construction in 1917 was motivated by practical concerns: Big ships generated enormous waves as they entered and departed from Vancouver, to the point that the immense sandstone shelf that underlies Stanley Park was in danger of eroding. What started as a bulwark against erosion would eventually become a continuous 22-km (13.7 mi) network of seawall protecting the scenic shoreline of English Bay and the entire False Creek inlet of Vancouver.

The seawall was built haphazardly over the years, with new additions coming as funds became available. In 1920, some 2,300 men were mobilized in its construction, and during the Great Depression, the job of breaking and hauling rocks became a relief make-work project for unemployed Vancouverites.

Scottish-born master stonemason Jimmy Cunningham emerged as the seawall's greatest champion. Not only did he oversee its construction for 32 years, but he also fought doggedly for funding to complete the project. After he retired, he came to the wall every day for coffee with his old mates. When he died in 1963 at the age of 85—17 years before the seawall would be completed—his ashes were mixed into the wall masonry. A granite plaque dedicated to Cunningham can be found near Siwash Rock.

How to Get There

By car, access the park from the main entrance at the west end of Georgia Street, west of downtown Vancouver, or alternately, enter from the English Bay side via Beach Avenue.

By foot or bike, access the west side of the park from the English Bay section of the seawall. Note: Bike travel on the seawall is one way.

When to Go

Late spring, summer, and early autumn are the best times to visit.

WEST COAST SITES

GITWANGAK BATTLE HILL
KITWANGA, BC

A self-guided trail leads to a small, fortified hilltop village of the Gitxsan, ancestors of today's Gitwangak First Nation, strategically located at the confluence of the Kitwanga and Skeena Rivers and on the Kitwankul Grease Trail, a trade route to the prairies. Built in the 18th century and occupied until 1835, it was used as a forward base for raids on nearby rivals. Remnants of former houses, defensive works, and other archaeological remains can be seen. Designated NHS: 1971. (250) 559-8818.

SGANG GWAAY LLNAGAAY
SGANG GWAAY, GWAII HAANAS NATIONAL PARK RESERVE, BC

SGang Gwaay Llnagaay is the best preserved example of a 19th-century Northwest Coast First Nations Haida village, including, most famously, some two dozen weathered mortuary and memorial poles. The Haida occupied the site until just after 1880. Because the remains of Haida ancestors are not always buried in caves, the presence of mortuary poles and the very earth here make the area sacred, and visitors are asked to respect the site. Designated NHS: 1981; Inscribed WH: 1981. SGang Gwaay (aka Anthony Island).

ST. ROCH
VANCOUVER, BC

Housed in the Vancouver Maritime Museum, the 31-m (101.7 ft) *St. Roch* (now fully restored) was the first ship to navigate the Northwest Passage from the Pacific Ocean to the Atlantic, in 1942. During this 28-month journey, the Royal Canadian Mounted Police schooner endured two winters frozen in the Arctic ice. This feat was followed by a second crossing via a more northerly route in just 86 days, making the *St. Roch* the first ship to make the crossing in both directions. Designated NHS: 1962. 1905 Ogden Ave. (604) 257-8300.

POINT ATKINSON LIGHTHOUSE
WEST VANCOUVER, BC

Set atop a rocky promontory with sweeping views of Vancouver's lower mainland, this roughly 18-m (59 ft) 1912 lighthouse still offers a beacon to ships entering Burrard Inlet. Built to replace a wooden lighthouse used since 1875, it was novel at the time for its hexagonal reinforced concrete construction, which includes a metal railing that encircles the lantern and winds down to the ground. It is now automated and unmanned. Designated NHS: 1974. Burrard Inlet.

VANCOUVER'S CHINATOWN
VANCOUVER, BC

Beginning in the late 19th century, Vancouver emerged as a major entry point for Chinese labourers and immigrants, who over the coming decades transformed this stretch of Pender Street between Taylor Street and Gore Avenue into one of North America's most vibrant Chinese expat communities. The extant early 20th-century buildings mix Western and regional Chinese styles, including deeply recessed balconies and winding staircases that lead to narrow alleys and back lanes. Designated NHS: 2011. Pender St.

WEST COAST

WEST COAST SITES

GASTOWN HISTORIC DISTRICT
VANCOUVER, BC

Laid out in a grid pattern, downtown Gastown is the result of a blooming western Canadian economy in the late 19th and early 20th centuries. Its more than 140 buildings, largely built between 1886 and 1914, form a district of stone and brick warehouses, commercial stores, hotels, and taverns harmonious in scale, material, and architectural detail. Gastown's existence as a protected area reflects the emergence around 1970 of a heritage movement that would spread across Canada. Designated NHS: 2009. South side of Burrard Inlet.

EMILY CARR HOUSE
VICTORIA, BC

This was the birthplace and childhood home of celebrated painter Emily Carr (1871–1945), located in a beautiful oceanside Victoria neighbourhood near Beacon Hill Park. The two-storey, three-bay house remains a well-preserved example of a picturesque Italianate villa, with a ground-floor veranda, round-headed paired windows on the upper storey, decorative wooden trim, and paired brick chimneys. Open year-round. Designated NHS: 1964. 207 Government St. (250) 383-5843.

CRAIGFLOWER SCHOOLHOUSE
VICTORIA, BC

Built in 1854–55, this two-storey, timber-framed structure is the oldest intact school building in western Canada. It was constructed to serve students from the nearby Hudson's Bay Company's Craigflower Farm and surrounding areas. The building was composed of a schoolroom, accommodation for the teacher, and several rooms for the boarders. The school deteriorated after it closed in 1911, until 1927 when it was acquired and restored. Designated NHS: 1964. 2765 Admirals Rd.

CRAIGDARROCH
VICTORIA, BC

Built for coal baron Robert Dunsmuir between 1887 and 1890 on a hill overlooking downtown Victoria, Craigdarroch was a deliberate display of conspicuous consumption. It borrowed from many architectural styles to evoke the romantic image of a castle in Dunsmuir's native Scotland. The use of imported materials (Italian marble, Vermont slate, and more) was unprecedented in western Canada at the time. Designated NHS: 1992. 1050 Joan Crescent. (250) 592-5323.

EMPRESS HOTEL
VICTORIA, BC

Among western Canada's most iconic and imposing hotels, the Empress was built between 1904 and 1908 for the Canadian Pacific Railway, which sought to attract train visitors to western Canada. This massive stone-constructed 470-room hotel—with steeply pitched copper roofs, ornate gables, and polygon turrets—is an example of what became a uniquely Canadian château style of architecture shared by a network of high-end, transcontinental railway-stop hotels. Designated NHS: 1981. 721 Government St. (250) 384-8111.

VICTORIA'S CHINATOWN
VICTORIA, BC

Within a three-block radius in downtown Victoria is Canada's oldest Chinatown, one of the few in North America to retain cohesive groupings of buildings of high heritage value. Chinese migrants first came to the area during the Fraser River gold rush in 1858, which turned Victoria into a transit point and supply hub for the goldfields. The neighbourhood was the largest urban centre of Chinese population in Canada through the first decade of the 20th century. Designated NHS: 1995. Pandora, Fisgard, Government, and Herald Sts.

WEST COAST

Living history at Fort St. James National Historic Site

NORTHERN BRITISH COLUMBIA

By the early 19th century, the competition for the lucrative fur trade between the North West Company and the Hudson's Bay Company finally reached across the Rocky Mountains to what is today inland British Columbia. In this region north of the Fraser River, dotted by lakes and forest, the North West Company established the first two permanent fur trading posts west of the Rockies: Fort McLeod (in 1805) and Fort St. James (1806). Situated on the shores of spectacular Stuart Lake, the latter boasts the largest

collection of 19th-century wooden buildings associated with the fur trade in Canada. Here visitors will also learn about the vital role played by the Dakelh First Nation, who had strong historical and spiritual ties to the land, in the success of the fort and the western fur trade.

Nearly 60 years after the first trading forts sprang up in the region, the Cariboo gold rush attracted large numbers of prospectors, who poured into the area, swelling the small town of Barkerville, the terminus of the Cariboo Wagon Road.

A costumed interpreter raises the Hudson's Bay Company standard over Fort St. James.

▶ FORT ST. JAMES

FORT ST. JAMES, BC
Designated 1948

For nearly 150 years, Fort St. James was an active fur trading post. Established in 1806 by explorer and fur trader Simon Fraser, it was the second one built by the North West Company west of the Rockies. It soon became an important regional trade centre.

Today, this 11.5-ha (28.4 acres) site retains the largest grouping of historic wooden buildings representing the fur trade in Canada. Most of the structures date from the late 1880s, when many of the fort's crumbling buildings were replaced.

The North West Company, which merged with rival Hudson's Bay Company in 1821, had come to the area to trade in furs. Local traplines worked by the Dakelh (or "Carrier") First Nations initially provided the beaver and other pelts to be transported eastward. The foreign traders were also dependent upon the Dakelh for their main food supply, salmon. It was vital for the fur traders to maintain good relations with the Dakelh because they emerged as the intermediaries through whom more distant First Nations traded furs at

the fort. Relations were mostly harmonious, except for a flashpoint in 1828, when James Douglas (much later, the first governor of the Colony of British Columbia) chased a Dakelh fugitive into Chief Kw'eh's lodge. Chief Kw'eh, who had accepted the role of fur trade chief and had single-handedly negotiated the new relationship between his people and the traders, violently confronted Douglas for the violation. Douglas left the fort soon after and the mutually beneficial trade relationship recovered.

What to See & Do

Learn about the influence of the Dakelh at Fort St. James through artefacts, Indigenous interpreters in period dress, as well as local elders who practice hide tanning and other traditional skills. An exhibit honours

Chief Kw'eh. There's also a 2-km (1.2 mi) interpretive trail. Chicken races, a re-creation of the horse races enjoyed by the fort staff, are held daily June through the third Sunday in September.

How to Get There

From the city of Prince George, head northwest on Hwy. 16. Past Vander-hoof, turn onto Hwy. 27, which leads to Fort St. James. Turn left on Kwah Road. It's about a two-hour drive.

When to Go

Open year-round, but June 1 to late September is the best time to go.

INFORMATION

HOW TO REACH US
280 Kwah Rd. W, Fort St. James, BC V0J 1P0. Phone (250) 996-7191. pc.gc.ca/stjames.

ENTRANCE FEES
$7.80 per adult, $19.60 per family/ group per day.

ACCESSIBLE SERVICES
All accessible but the fish cache.

HOTELS, MOTELS, & INNS
The View Hotel 309 Stuart Dr. W, Fort St. James, BC V0J 1P0. (855) 996-8737. theviewhotel.ca.

NORTHERN BRITISH COLUMBIA SITES

FORT MCLEOD
MCLEOD LAKE, BC

Established in 1805, Fort McLeod was the first fur trading fort to exist in what today is British Columbia. The outpost was founded by explorer Simon Fraser and his party, who were scouting out a strategic foothold west of the Rockies for the North West Company. Fort McLeod remained an active fur trading post into the 20th century. Four wood-sided buildings still stand from the 1920s–1940s, as do the remains of other features. Designated NHS: 1953. Carp Lake Rd.

BARKERVILLE
BARKERVILLE, BC

Named for an English prospector who struck gold in the Cariboo country in 1862, Barkerville is a restored gold rush boomtown. As the terminus of the 650-km (404 mi) Cariboo Wagon Road, it became the biggest town in the Colony of British Columbia virtu-ally overnight. It burned down in 1868 and was immediately rebuilt. About 100 original postfire structures still stand, and costumed interpreters bring the history to life. Designated NHS: 1924. (250) 994-3302.

Stewardship for the Future

Just as Canada has acknowledged the importance of conserving natural places, it has also counted historic places as worthy of conservation. But what was important to keep and why? Which buildings and landscapes? Who should decide? This is the story of historic conservation in Canada over the past 150 years.

Archaeological excavation at the Fortress of Louisbourg, Nova Scotia, 1964

When the Canadian government established the Hot Springs Reserve in 1885, laying the foundations for the country's first national park in Banff, Alberta, a movement to similarly preserve, protect, and present places of national historic significance was already gaining momentum. Historical societies and heritage conservationists were leading the way: Just a few years earlier, Governor General Lord Dufferin campaigned for the preservation of the Fortifications of Québec (see pp. 100–103), preventing their demolition.

The Historic Sites and Monuments Board

A national framework for the identification and acquisition of historic sites began to take shape after the establishment of the Dominion Parks Branch in 1911 and the Historic Sites and Monuments Board of Canada in 1919. The board served an advisory role, selecting sites, people, and events that merited commemoration. The Fortress of Louisbourg in Nova Scotia (see pp. 50–53) was among the earliest designations. During the Great Depression, the Parks Branch received funds for building projects that created employment at Louisbourg and other historic sites. The scope of development was limited to the stabilization of ruins and the construction of museums to house artefacts. In that era, ruins were believed to better evoke the past.

In the years that followed the Second World War, Canadian nationalism, especially around the time of Canada's centennial celebrations in 1967, generated widespread interest in places that bore witness to defining moments in the country's history and in landmark buildings in the history of Canadian architecture. Federal and provincial governments promoted the conservation of buildings, archaeological sites, and important objects with renewed energy and legislation in the 1960s and '70s. During this time, Parks Canada played a leading role with various partners, developing expertise in historical research and the conservation of buildings and objects. Innovative projects, such as the revitalization of Halifax's waterfront, garnered considerable attention and contributed to acceptance of the idea that urban renewal did not require the demolition of heritage buildings.

At the same time, the rise of the civil rights movement put pressure on all levels of government to consult more, to listen to local opinion, and to value the different uses and meanings prescribed to historic sites. Over the past 100 years, Indigenous advocacy and understandings of the land influenced the conservation movement, and traditional Indigenous knowledge has more recently been incorporated into land management planning.

Thinking Long Term

In the 2000s, the stewardship of Canada's national historic sites has become a collaborative effort between individuals and groups who value these places and wish to leave them unimpaired for future generations. To care for these places, Canada has made significant investments in maintenance and conservation. Through the decades, new questions have emerged as national historic sites age. How do we deal with major erosion? What conservation projects do we pursue? How do we deal with climate change? What stories do we tell? And how do we present national historic sites to new audiences and the millions of visitors from around the world, so that their historic value can be understood? Stewardship for the future continues to be a fundamental mission for Canada's national historic sites.

Acadian artefact from Beaubassin, Nova Scotia, 2008

FAR NORTH

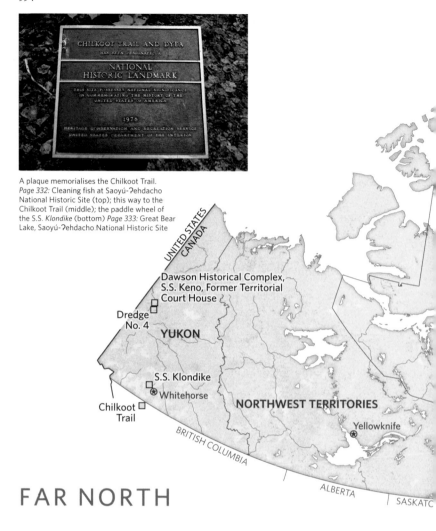

A plaque memorialises the Chilkoot Trail.
Page 332: Cleaning fish at Saoyú-ʔehdacho National Historic Site (top); this way to the Chilkoot Trail (middle); the paddle wheel of the S.S. *Klondike* (bottom) *Page 333:* Great Bear Lake, Saoyú-ʔehdacho National Historic Site

FAR NORTH

Encompassing Yukon, the Northwest Territories, and Nunavut, and extending above the Arctic Circle, the landscape of Canada's far north ranges from alpine peaks and plateaus to glacier-covered lowlands. Thousands of people flocked here during the short-lived Klondike gold rush of the late 1890s, spurred on by dreams of untold wealth in the Canadian goldfields. Many of those who made the arduous journey overland came via the Chilkoot Trail, which led from

Dyea, Alaska, up over the Chilkoot Pass and down to the Yukon River and once bustling Dawson City. Industry naturally followed the gold seekers to the Klondike, where mining eventually became a highly mechanized pursuit.

The historic sites in this region tell the history of the gold rush not only from the prospectors' perspective but also from the viewpoint of the Indigenous Peoples—like the Tlingit, Tagish, and other First Nations—who

National Historic Site (NHS)
Territory capital city

0 mi   250
0 km   250

N   U   N   A   V   U   T

Wrecks of HMS Erebus
and HMS Terror

Iqaluit

AN   MANITOBA

FAR NORTH

have inhabited the area around the trail for thousands of years and who constitute more than a quarter of the population of present-day Yukon. Today, visitors can relive the gold rush days: Hard-core hikers can traverse the full Chilkoot Trail in just a few days, and Dawson City offers visitors the chance to imagine daily life during the heady days at the height of the gold rush.

Other sites here commemorate the importance of the Yukon River as a major transportation artery in the first part of the 20th century, when hundreds of commercial paddle wheel steamboats plied this route, ferrying goods and people.

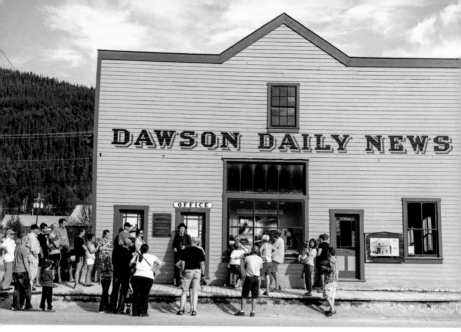

Many of Dawson's early 20th-century commercial buildings, like that of the *Dawson Daily News,* feature a false front.

▶ DAWSON HISTORICAL COMPLEX

DAWSON CITY, YT

Designated 1959

From the river-strewn, wild landscape to the artful vibrancy of the town to the creative resiliency of the Tr'ondëk Hwëch'in, there's so much more to Dawson City than the gold rush, though the boom following the discovery of gold at the end of the 19th century does account for much of the town's appearance today.

GOLD! GOLD! GOLD!

When news broke in 1897 that gold had been struck in the Klondike, around 100,000 people caught the fever, packed their suitcases, and headed north to Dawson City along the Yukon River, the last outpost before the goldfields.

Most of the prospectors journeyed by boat along the western shore of North America to Skagway (in Alaska), from where by foot they crossed the Chilkoot and White Passes and then floated down the Yukon River to Dawson City; other people travelled overland to Dawson the whole way. Only about a third of them actually completed the arduous journey to Dawson City. Promptly they transformed the region. Three hundred businesses were launched in 1898. Suddenly the makeshift tent settlement with one saloon became a thriving metropolis with many saloons. That same year, Yukon Territory was established as a way of bringing order to this so-called stampede. These "stampeders" established gold mining as the dominant economic driver, and it remains a mainstay in Dawson today.

For local Indigenous People, the Klondike gold rush meant a massive disruption to traditional ways of living, including the relocation of their fishing village at Tr'ochëk to Moosehide, 5 km (3 mi) downriver. The Tr'ondëk Hwëch'in had been living along the Yukon for hundreds of years. Although this Yukon First Nation adapted and negotiated creatively, the sudden arrival of 30,000 newcomers hurt. In 1911, Chief Isaac, a Tr'ondëk Hwëch'in leader celebrated for his effective diplomacy, reportedly told the *Dawson Daily News*, "All Yukon belong to my papas. All Klondike belong my people . . . White man come and take all my gold . . . Game is gone. White man kill all moose and caribou near Dawson."

Today, the First Nation continues to share its traditional territory with non-Indigenous people in the region. The Dänojà Zho Cultural Centre sits across the street from the Parks Canada Visitor Information Centre.

The architecture and natural environment of Dawson City are remarkable, but the town's most redeeming quality is its people. During the gold rush, it took considerable resolve for people to haul all of their gear over the Chilkoot Pass. When the gold rush fizzled in the early 1900s, locals in love with the land, as well as a shift toward large-scale corporate dredge mining, helped keep the town alive.

NOTABLE PEOPLE

Three people in particular represent the spirit of the people here. The first is Chief Isaac, a leader of the Tr'ondëk Hwëch'in of the Yukon River Valley during the gold rush. He led negotiations with the area's newcomers, making arrangements to move his people to Moosehide, away from Dawson. He helped bridge the cultural divide: mastering traditional technologies while exploring foreign ideas, attending church services and presiding over potlatch ceremonies, welcoming newcomers while reminding them that they prospered at the expense of his people by driving away game and taking over the land. Chief Isaac died of influenza in 1932 at age 85, but his legacy lives on in the renewal of songs and dances.

"Progressive" and "tough" would be good words to describe Martha Black. In 1898, a pregnant Black travelled with her brother to the Yukon in pursuit of golden adventure. (Her husband chose to go to Hawaii instead.) Arriving in Dawson City via the Chilkoot Pass in wintertime, she gave birth to her third son alone in a cabin, unable to afford a doctor despite her wealthy roots in Chicago. Eventually, however, she formed a gold-mining partnership and founded a successful sawmill. She remarried in 1904. Her new husband, George Black, would become commissioner of the Yukon Territory and a member of Parliament (MP). After her husband died, Black campaigned and was elected MP,

FAR NORTH

A costumed interpreter spins a yarn.

becoming the second woman ever to be elected to the Canadian House of Commons. At a time when women lacked many of the rights and freedoms they have today, Black proved women could lead a bold life beyond the domestic. Her story is told at the elegant Commissioner's Residence, which is open daily.

And finally, no Canadian post office should be without an inspirational poster of Percy Dewolfe—bundled from head to toe in fur, his dog sled loaded with 20 mailbags. For nearly 40 years, beginning in 1910, Dewolfe hauled mail through temperatures as low as minus 45°C (-49°F), from Dawson City to Eagle, Alaska. Dewolfe would make about four trips a month, and each trip usually took about four days. Today, an annual dog sled race dubbed "The Percy" pays tribute to the so-called "Iron Man of the North." The race begins in front of the grandiose historic post office, a building that symbolizes the determination, isolation, and connection that shaped Dawson City at the turn of the 20th century.

EXPLORING DAWSON

Start at the Parks Canada Visitor Information Centre (at the corner of Front and King Streets), to get information on the more than two dozen historic structures around town that compose the Dawson Historical Complex. Staff can explain the finer points of the many tours they offer, which are well worth joining.

From the centre, head across the street to the Dänojà Zho ("Long Ago House") Cultural Centre. This beautiful building on the banks of the Yukon River reminds visitors that human history in this region runs far deeper than 1898. Open year-round,

it is a gathering place for artists, business people, tourists, and community members. Take a river walk tour to learn how the Tr'ondëk Hwëch'in moved through the Yukon River Valley for hundreds of years, hunting moose and fishing for salmon. Ask the tour leader about the significance of the building's curious bar graph–like design feature, and hear how the Tr'ondëk Hwëch'in adapted their traditional ways of living when the miners rushed in. Inside the centre, the walls are filled with the wisdom and stories of Tr'ondëk Hwëch'in elders, such as the late renowned storyteller Mary McLeod. In addition, the centre often hosts film screenings and traditional dance performances.

From Dänojà Zho, walk to the cozy two-room cabin once home to Robert Service. Affectionately known as the "bard of the Yukon," Service was a rambling poet who liked crafting lines while trekking through woods full of willows and alders: "It grips you like some kinds of sinning; / It twists you from foe to a friend; / It seems it's been since the beginning; / It seems it will be to the end."

After checking out the poet's former set-up, follow a guide dressed as Service up a steep hill while he recites bits of poetry. At the top of the hike, a showstopping view of Dawson City unfolds from Crocus Bluff. Notice how the town sits close to where the Tr'ondëk Hwëch'in fishing camp once was—making this a great place from which to appreciate these overlapping histories. Ideally, visit this rocky bluff in spring when the crocuses are in full bloom.

Eat lunch the way a miner might have: Sit on a rock on the banks of Bonanza Creek at Discovery Site—where George Carmack, an American prospector, Keish (aka Skookum Jim) Mason, and Káa Goox (aka

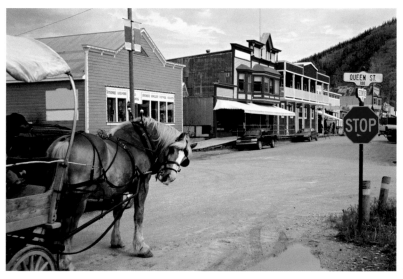

The corner of Second Avenue and Queen Street, in downtown Dawson City

Dawson Charlie) sparked the gold rush with their discovery. After lunch, walk along the short trail that features interpretive panels telling the history of the discovery and mining over the years, mining artefacts, and evocative life-size steel silhouettes of miners.

From the site, take a short drive up the road to Claim #6 to try panning for gold (the activity is free, but you must bring your own pan and shovel). On the way back to town, try to fit in a guided tour of Dredge No. 4 (see p. 341), an eight-storey mining machine that supplanted the pick-and-shovel miners.

How to Get There

From Whitehorse, Canada, the drive to Dawson City takes five or six hours, depending on the season, road conditions, and regional weather. The distance between Whitehorse and Dawson City is 525 km (326 mi), and there is limited cell and fuel service along the way. Alternatively, Air North (*flyairnorth.com*) flies between Whitehorse and Dawson City.

Period decor and dress bring the gold rush era to life.

When to Go

Try to visit Dawson City in mid- to late August. During this slightly off-peak season, there are fewer tourists than during the rest of summer (the high tourist season). It's also the time of year when the colours start to change in the higher-elevation areas around Dawson: Alpine willow, scrub birch, and berry bushes paint the hillsides with deep reds, purples, and golden hues. It can be warm enough to sport a T-shirt and shorts during daylight hours, and yet at night the air is crisp. It's also possible the northern lights will be visible after dark.

FAR NORTH

DAWSON HISTORICAL COMPLEX NATIONAL HISTORIC SITE
(Lieu historique national du Complexe-Historique-de-Dawson)

INFORMATION & ACTIVITIES

HOW TO REACH US
Box 390, Dawson City, YT Y0B 1G0. Phone (867) 993-7200. pc.gc.ca/eng/lhn-nhs/yt/klondike/natcul/dawson.aspx. **Visitor Information Centre** 102 Front St., Dawson City, YT Y0B 1G0. Phone (867) 993-7210 or (867) 993-5566.

SEASONS & ACCESSIBILITY
Summertime temperatures can reach 30°C to 35°C (86°F to 95°F); spring and fall are fairly chilly. The Visitor Information Centre is open daily from early May until the end of September.

ENTRANCE FEES
None. Guided tours are $6.30 per adult. If planning to take more than one tour, save money by buying a multitour pass.

PETS
Only service or guide dogs are permitted inside heritage buildings.

ACCESSIBLE SERVICES
Most buildings are accessible, but accessibility varies with each one. The wooden boardwalks and rough, unpaved roads throughout the town can be challenging to navigate. Call the Parks Canada Visitor Information Centre for more details.

THINGS TO DO
Take a walking tour, shop for Indigenous handicrafts, pan for gold, visit the elegant Commissioner's Residence, interact with a costumed interpreter in the streets, and practice reciting Robert Service's poetry.

CAMPGROUNDS
Dawson City RV Park and Campground Km 716 Klondike Hwy., Dawson City, YT Y0B 1G0. (867) 993-5142. dawsoncity rvpark.com. $18–$40 per night (incl. gold panning). Reservations recommended.

HOTELS, MOTELS, & INNS
(Rates are for a 2-person double, high season, in Canadian dollars, unless otherwise noted.)

Bombay Peggy's Inn & Pub 2nd Ave. and Princess St., Dawson City, YT Y0B 1G0. (867) 993-6969. bombaypeggys.com. 9 rooms, $114–$219.
Canada's Best Value Inn–Downtown Hotel 1026 2nd Ave., Dawson City, YT Y0B 1G0. (867) 993-5346. downtown hotel.ca. 59 rooms, U.S. $109.

FAR NORTH SITES

S.S. KENO
DAWSON CITY, YT

Moored on the Yukon River, the S.S. *Keno*, a 40-m (131 ft) sternwheeler steamer built in 1922, sounds her whistle daily at noon and 5 p.m. May through mid-September. The sound recalls the days when steam whistles meant the arrival of crucial supplies, longed-for love letters, or even the lovers themselves. On board, relive the paddle wheeler era or watch a documentary about the *Keno*'s last voyage in 1960. Designated NHS: 1962. Front St. (867) 993-7200.

FORMER TERRITORIAL COURT HOUSE
DAWSON CITY, YT

This classically styled wooden two-storey building (currently closed to the public) was built between 1900 and 1901. Its prominent position at the entrance to town was meant to convey the power and authority of the federal government to the people of the Yukon. After the court moved in 1910, the building was used by the North West Mounted Police and, later, by the Sisters of St. Anne. The courthouse is recognized for its exceptional craftsmanship. Designated NHS: 1981. Corner of Front and Turner Sts. (867) 993-7200.

DREDGE NO. 4
DAWSON CITY, YT

Shortly after gold seekers started flooding the Klondike, industry followed with huge mining machines like Dredge No. 4. Eight stories high, it is the largest dredge of its kind in North America. It was one of two dozen dredges working the Klondike, and it enjoyed an on-and-off digging career from 1913 until 1960. To tour the dredge's interior, call Goldbottom Mine Tours (867-993-5023). Designated NHS: 1997. Upper Bonanza Creek Rd. (867) 993-7200.

WRECKS OF THE HMS EREBUS AND HMS TERROR
QUEEN MAUD GULF, NU

These shipwrecks are associated with Sir John Franklin's tragic 1845 search for the Northwest Passage. HMS *Erebus* was found in September 2014 by Parks Canada and their public and private partners. Situated in Queen Maud Gulf, where 19th-century Inuit oral testimony identified a ship, the wreck is in excellent condition. This significant resource is in a restricted area, inaccessible without written authorization from Parks Canada's Nunavut Field Unit Superintendent. HMS *Terror* has yet to be located. Designated NHS: 1992. (867) 975-4673.

FAR NORTH

Finding Franklin's Ship: The Contributions of Inuit Traditional Knowledge

The vast Canadian Arctic today encompasses three territories—the Northwest Territories, Yukon, and Nunavut. The region has been occupied by Indigenous Peoples for thousands of years.

An artist's rendition of the HMS *Erebus* and HMS *Terror* with the HMS *Rattler* and HMS *Blazer* in June 1845

The Northwest Passage & Franklin

Five hundred years ago, Europeans began looking for a northern route to the riches of southern Asia. The first forays for the Northwest Passage did not penetrate the Arctic archipelago much farther west than Hudson Bay, but they did lead to the establishment of fur trading posts and entry points into the heart of the continent for the Hudson's Bay Company (established 1690) that are commemorated today at two national historic sites in Manitoba, Prince of Wales Fort (see pp. 248–249) and York Factory (see pp. 250–251).

European whalers, responding to the demand for whale oil and baleen, moved into the Lancaster Sound area from the bowhead whaling grounds near Greenland around 1820. Inevitably, both the whalers and explorers met members of the local population—Inuit who lived and travelled in small groups. Some of these Europeans wisely adopted Inuit methods for living in this environment.

The search for the Northwest Passage accelerated with the support of the British government after 1815. By 1845, expeditions had added to knowledge of Arctic geography, from the east and from the west, and many believed that the full passage could be established with one final expedition. Sir John Franklin, an experienced Arctic explorer, was chosen to lead this expedition in 1845 with two ships, the HMS *Erebus* and HMS *Terror*. The ships were reinforced and equipped with the latest technology and packed with supplies for three years. Franklin was to sail through the passage from the Atlantic to the Pacific, and return to England by sailing around the globe.

When no word had been received from Franklin by 1847, concern mounted in Britain. The ensuing search would become one of the largest manhunts in history, with more than 30 expeditions involving dozens of ships and hundreds of men over the next 12 years. Despite this effort, the two ships and 129 men appeared to have vanished. The first real clue was uncovered in 1850 with the discovery of three graves on Beechey Island (now a national historic site), southwest of Devon Island where the expedition party had spent its first winter. But the men were not found.

Then, in 1854, Inuit from the Pelly Bay region repeated stories to John Rae, a Hudson's Bay Company employee, of white men who had perished about four years previously. This led searchers to King William Island and evidence of tragedy—skeletons and objects scattered on the landscape. Francis McClintock's expedition found a rare surviving document in a cairn in 1859. It reported that Franklin died in June 1847, and that the following April, 105 survivors abandoned the ships after being trapped by ice for almost two years. The search continued, in the hope that survivors were living with Inuit groups, or that at least more documents existed to explain what had gone so wrong, but with no luck.

Mystery Solved

The mystery obsessed searchers throughout the 20th century. It was ultimately Parks Canada underwater archaeologists working with public and private partners who, in September 2014, located the *Erebus* west of the Adelaide Peninsula, hundreds of kilometres south of where it was first abandoned (commemorated as the Wrecks of HMS Erebus and HMS Terror National Historic Site).

The wreck's general position had been reported by Inuit in 1869 to Charles Francis Hall, an American explorer. Supported by additional Inuit information, concerning two ships at two separate locations, modern searches had been patiently scanning these waters for a number of years. In the end, a discovery on land of an iron ship's fitting informed the underwater team that the wreck was close by.

The wreck of the HMS *Erebus*, found in 2014

FAR NORTH

From Dyea, Alaska, the Chilkoot Trail passes through lush river-bottom forest before climbing to the Chilkoot Pass.

▶ CHILKOOT TRAIL

BENNETT, YT

Designated 1987

In 1897, word got out that people had struck it rich on the Yukon's Klondike River. And so it began: one of the last great gold rushes in the West. People poured north from Vancouver, Seattle, San Francisco, and beyond, with many using the Chilkoot Trail as their gateway to the Yukon.

During the winter of 1897–98, the Chilkoot Trail—covered with ice, mud, and snow—served as a super-highway for gold-hungry "stampeders." Beginning at sea level in Dyea, Alaska, thousands made the steep 53-km (33 mi) trek up to the Chilkoot Pass, many of them carrying their own food, supplies, and equipment. After descending through the sub-alpine boreal forest of British Columbia, they finally put their packs down at the headwaters of the Yukon River.

Before the gold rush, the Chilkoot Pass was one of five trade routes controlled by the Tlingit, who used it to carry eulachon grease, dried fish, and other trading goods to the interior, or to serve as middlemen in the fur trade. The gold rush was hugely disruptive for the Tlingit and Tagish people; however, they did find ways to benefit from the boom. Some Tlingit and Tagish acted as packers and guides on the trail, though they were soon undermined by non-Indigenous competition and high-tech alternatives. And others sold traditional clothes, taught survival skills, and built boats for use on the last leg of the journey: 800 km (497 mi) of lake and river travel from the Yukon headwaters to Dawson City.

Today, the Chilkoot Trail is jointly managed by Parks Canada and the U.S. National Park Service.

What to See & Do

On average, it takes three to five days to hike the full trail. The range of natural environments—from coastal rain forest to subalpine meadows to rocky alpine passes to sunlit boreal forest sprinkled with glacial lakes—

is spectacular. Day hikers doing a short out and back from either end of the trail can still enjoy walking in the footsteps of the stampeders. Note: Through-hikers must be well equipped and in good physical condition, as the terrain is rough and the weather often extreme.

How to Get There

Most people begin the trail in Skagway, Alaska, reached via cruise ship, or from Whitehorse, Yukon, via the South Klondike Hwy. In the summer, it is possible to combine bus service from Whitehorse with the historic White Pass & Yukon Route railway for a very scenic trip to Skagway. Tour companies (see the website for a current list of providers) offer transport to the Chilkoot trailhead in Dyea, 16 km (10 mi) from Skagway.

To start the trail in Canada, take a train from Carcross, Yukon, or Skagway, Alaska, to Bennett, Yukon. There is no road to Bennett.

When to Go

The trail is only patrolled June through early September.

INFORMATION

HOW TO REACH US
300 Main St., Suite 205, Whitehorse, YT Y1A 2B5. Phone (800) 661-0486 or (867) 667-3910. pc.gc.ca/chilkoot. **Trail Centre** 520 Broadway St., Skagway, AK 99840. Phone (907) 983-9234. nps.gov/klgo.

ENTRANCE FEES
$54.60 for full trail permit; $34.30 for Canadian side only (permit includes camping; see website for information and up-to-date list of licensed outfitters). Trail reservations are not required, but only 50 crossings of the Chilkoot Pass are permitted per day. All day hikers on the Canadian side of the trail, and overnighters on both sides, must have a permit; $11.70 to secure a reservation.

ACCESSIBLE SERVICES
The trail is not accessible.

HOTELS, MOTELS, & INNS
Historic Skagway Inn 655 Broadway St., Skagway, AK 99840. (907) 983-2289 or (888) 752-4929. skagwayinn.com. 10 rooms, $139–$239.

FAR NORTH SITES

S.S. KLONDIKE
WHITEHORSE, YT

During the first half of the 20th century, sternwheeler steamers were a transportation staple along the Yukon River. The S.S. *Klondike* was the biggest in the British Yukon Navigation Company's fleet. This wood-burning steamer carried freight and passengers along the river between 1937 and 1955—before roads came to supplant steamers. Today, the *Klondike* sits beside the Robert Campbell Bridge in Whitehorse, overlooking the Yukon River and restored to her 1937 appearance. Designated NHS: 1967. (800) 661-0486.

▶ NATIONAL PARKS OF CANADA

Parks Canada National Office
30 Victoria Street
Gatineau, Québec
Canada
J8X 0B3
General inquiries: 888-773-8888 or 819-420-9486 (international)

AKAMI-UAPISHKᵁ–KAKKASUAK–MEALY MOUNTAINS NATIONAL PARK RESERVE
(Réserve de parc national Akami-Uapishkᵁ–KakKasuak–Monts Mealy)
Newfoundland & Labrador
Established 2015
10,700 sq km/2,644,028 acres

AULAVIK NATIONAL PARK
(Parc national Aulavik)
Northwest Territories
Established 1992
12,200 sq km/3,014,686 acres

AUYUITTUQ NATIONAL PARK
(Parc national Auyuittuq)
Nunavut
Established 1972
19,089 sq km/4,716,995 acres

BANFF NATIONAL PARK
(Parc national Banff)
Alberta
Established 1885
6,641 sq km/1,641,027 acres

BRUCE PENINSULA NATIONAL PARK
(Parc national de la Péninsule-Bruce)
Ontario
Established 1987
125 sq km/30,888 acres

CAPE BRETON HIGHLANDS NATIONAL PARK
(Parc national des Hautes-Terres-du-Cap-Breton)
Nova Scotia
Established 1936
948 sq km/234,256 acres

ELK ISLAND NATIONAL PARK
(Parc national Elk Island)
Alberta

Established 1913
194 sq km/47,938 acres

FORILLON NATIONAL PARK
(Parc national Forillon)
Québec
Established 1970
217 sq km/53,622 acres

FUNDY NATIONAL PARK
(Parc national Fundy)
New Brunswick
Established 1948
206 sq km/50,904 acres

GEORGIAN BAY ISLANDS NATIONAL PARK
(Parc national des Îles-de-la-Baie-Georgienne)
Ontario
Established 1930
14 sq km/3,459 acres

GLACIER NATIONAL PARK
(Parc national des Glaciers)
British Columbia
Established 1886
1,349 sq km/333,345 acres

GRASSLANDS NATIONAL PARK
(Parc national des Prairies)
Saskatchewan
Established 1981
730 sq km/180,387 acres

GROS MORNE NATIONAL PARK
(Parc national du Gros-Morne)
Newfoundland & Labrador
Established 1973
1,805 sq km/446,025 acres

GULF ISLANDS NATIONAL PARK RESERVE
(Réserve de parc national des Îles-Gulf)
British Columbia
Established 2003
37 sq km/9,143 acres (land area: 31 sq km/7,660 acres; water area: 6 sq km/1,483 acres)

GWAII HAANAS NATIONAL PARK RESERVE & HAIDA HERITAGE SITE
(Réserve de parc national et site du patrimoine haïda Gwaii Haanas)
British Columbia
Established 1988
1,474 sq km/364,233 acres

IVVAVIK NATIONAL PARK
(Parc national Ivvavik)
Yukon
Established 1984
9,750 sq km/2,409,278 acres

JASPER NATIONAL PARK
(Parc national Jasper)
Alberta
Established 1907
11,228 sq km/2,774,499 acres

KEJIMKUJIK NATIONAL PARK
(Parc national Kejimkujik)
Nova Scotia
Established 1967
404 sq km/99,830 acres

KLUANE NATIONAL PARK & RESERVE
(Parc national et réserve de parc national Kluane)
Yukon
Established 1972
22,061 sq km/5,451,392 acres

KOOTENAY NATIONAL PARK
(Parc national Kootenay)
British Columbia
Established 1920
1,406 sq km/347,430 acres

KOUCHIBOUGUAC NATIONAL PARK
(Parc national Kouchibouguac)
New Brunswick
Established 1969
239 sq km/59,058 acres

LA MAURICIE NATIONAL PARK
(Parc national de la Mauricie)
Québec
Established 1970
536 sq km/132,448 acres

MINGAN ARCHIPELAGO NATIONAL PARK RESERVE
(Réserve de parc national de l'Archipel-de-Mingan)
Québec
Established 1984
151 sq km/37,313 acres

MOUNT REVELSTOKE NATIONAL PARK
(Parc national du Mont-Revelstoke)
British Columbia

Established 1914
262 sq km/64,742 acres

NÁÁTS'IHCH'OH NATIONAL PARK RESERVE
(Réserve de parc national Nááts'ihch'oh)
Between Northwest Territories and Yukon
Established 2012
4,850 sq km/1,198,461 acres

NAHANNI NATIONAL PARK RESERVE
(Réserve de parc national Nahanni)
Northwest Territories
Established 1972
30,000 sq km/7,413,161 acres

PACIFIC RIM NATIONAL PARK RESERVE
(Réserve de parc national Pacific Rim)
British Columbia
Established 1970
510 sq km/126,024 acres

POINT PELEE NATIONAL PARK
(Parc national de la Pointe-Pelée)
Ontario
Established 1918
15 sq km/3,707 acres

PRINCE ALBERT NATIONAL PARK
(Parc national de Prince Albert)
Saskatchewan
Established 1927
3,875 sq km/957,533 acres

PRINCE EDWARD ISLAND NATIONAL PARK
(Parc national de l'Île-du-Prince-Édouard)
Prince Edward Island
Established 1937
27 sq km/6,672 acres

PUKASKWA NATIONAL PARK
(Parc national Pukaskwa)
Ontario
Established 1971
1,878 sq km/464,064 acres

QAUSUITTUQ NATIONAL PARK
(Parc national Qausuittuq)
Nunavut
Established 2015

11,008 sq km/2,720,136
acres

QUTTINIRPAAQ
NATIONAL PARK
(Parc national
Quttinirpaaq)
Nunavut
Established 1986
37,775 sq km/9,334,406
acres

RIDING MOUNTAIN
NATIONAL PARK
(Parc national du
Mont-Riding)
Manitoba
Established 1929
2,968 sq km/733,409
acres

ROUGE NATIONAL
URBAN PARK
(Park urbain national de
la Rouge)
Ontario
Established 2015
79.1 sq km/19,546 acres
once fully established

SABLE ISLAND
NATIONAL PARK
RESERVE
(Réserve de parc national
de l'Île de Sable)
Nova Scotia
Established: 2013
30 sq km/7,413 acres

SIRMILIK NATIONAL
PARK
(Parc national Sirmilik)
Nunavut
Established 1999
22,200 sq km/5,485,740
acres

TERRA NOVA NATIONAL
PARK
(Parc national
Terra-Nova)
Newfoundland & Labrador
Established 1957
399 sq km/98,600 acres

THAIDENE NËNÉ
NATIONAL PARK
RESERVE
(Projet de réserve de parc
national Thaidene Nëné)
Northwest Territories
Proposed: 2015
14,000 sq km/3,459,475
acres

THOUSAND ISLANDS
NATIONAL PARK
(Parc national des
Mille-Îles)
Ontario

Established 1904
24 sq km/5,931 acres

TORNGAT MOUNTAINS
NATIONAL PARK
(Parc national des
Monts-Torngat)
Newfoundland & Labrador
Established 2005
9,700 sq km/2,396,922
acres

TUKTUT NOGAIT
NATIONAL PARK
(Parc national Tuktut
Nogait)
Northwest Territories
Established 1998
18,181 sq km/4,492,623
acres

UKKUSIKSALIK
NATIONAL PARK
(Parc national
Ukkusiksalik)
Nunavut
Established 2003
20,880 sq km/5,159,560
acres

VUNTUT NATIONAL
PARK
(Parc national Vuntut)
Yukon
Established 1993
4,345 sq km/1,073,673
acres

WAPUSK NATIONAL
PARK
(Parc national Wapusk)
Manitoba
Established 1996
11,475 sq km/2,835,534
acres

WATERTON LAKES
NATIONAL PARK
(Parc national des
Lacs-Waterton)
Alberta
Established 1895
505 sq km/124,788 acres

WOOD BUFFALO
NATIONAL PARK
(Parc national Wood
Buffalo)
Alberta and Northwest
Territories
Established 1922
44,792 sq km/11,069,344
acres

YOHO NATIONAL PARK
(Parc national Yoho)
British Columbia
Established 1886
1,313 sq km/324,449
acres

▶ NATIONAL MARINE CONSERVATION AREAS OF CANADA

FATHOM FIVE
NATIONAL MARINE
CONSERVATION AREA
(sister park to Bruce
Peninsula National Park)
(Parc marin national
Fathom Five)
Ontario
Established 1972
114 sq km/28,170 acres,
largely underwater

GWAII HAANAS
NATIONAL MARINE
CONSERVATION AREA
RESERVE
(Réserve d'aire marine
nationale de conservation
Gwaii Haanas)
British Columbia
Established 2010
3,500 sq km/864,869
acres

LAKE SUPERIOR
NATIONAL MARINE
CONSERVATION AREA
(Aire marine nationale
de conservation du
Lac-Supérieur)
Ontario
Established 2007
10,880 sq km/2,688,507
acres

SAGUENAY-ST.
LAWRENCE MARINE
CONSERVATION AREA
(Parc marin du
Saguenay–Saint-Laurent)
Québec
Established 1998
1,246 sq km/307,893
acres

▶ INDEX

Boldface indicates main entry.

ILLUSTRATIONS CREDITS

Cover, Bill Heinsohn/Alamy Stock Photo; back cover (UP), J.F. Bergeron/Envirofoto/Parks Canada; back cover (CT LE), Fritz Mueller/Parks Canada; back cover (CT RT), Justin + Lauren; back cover (LO), Jeff Bolingbroke/Parks Canada; 2-3, A. Cornellier/Parks Canada; 4, Aqnus/Adobe Stock; 6-7, Chris Reardon/Parks Canada; 8, Charles-Alexandre Paré/Parks Canada; 9, Scott Munn/Parks Canada; 12 (UP), Parks Canada; 12 (CTR), Dale Wilson/Parks Canada; 12 (LO), André Cornellier/Parks Canada; 13, M. Finkelstein/Parks Canada; 14, J. Steeves/Parks Canada; 16-17, © All Canada Photos/Alamy Stock Photo; 18-21, Chris Reardon/Parks Canada; 22 (UP), J. Butterill/Parks Canada; 22 (CTR), Wayne Barrett—Barrett and Mackay Photography/Parks Canada; 22 (LO), Confederation Centre of the Arts; 23 (UP), © Andre Jenny/Alamy; 23 (CTR), prosiaczeq/Shutterstock; 23 (LO), Megapress/Alamy; 24-5, Dale Wilson/Parks Canada; 26, Tourism Nova Scotia/Wally Hayes; 28-32, Chris Reardon/Parks Canada; 33 (UP), Éric Le Bel/Parks Canada; 33 (CTR), Parks Canada; 33 (LO), Rick Smith/Parks Canada; 34 (UP), Éric Le Bel/Parks Canada; 34 (CTR), Chris Reardon/Parks Canada; 34 (LO), Parks Canada; 35 (UP), Saffron Blaze at https://commons.wikimedia.org/wiki/File:York_Redoubt.jpg, Creative Commons license; 35 (CTR), Jocelin D'Entremont/Parks Canada; 35 (LO), Alan Deveau/Parks Canada; 36, Scott Tayler/Parks Canada; 37, Ron Garnett/Parks Canada; 38, Dale Wilson/Parks Canada; 40-43, Canadian Museum of Immigration at Pier 21; 45 (UP), Sandy McClearn, courtesy Canadian Naval Memorial Trust; 45 (CTR), Darryl Brooks/Shutterstock; 45 (LO), Andrew Pickett; 46 (UP), meunierd/Shutterstock; 46 (CTR), Louperivois, Wikimedia Commons at https://en.wikipedia.org/wiki/Province_House_(Nova_Scotia)#/media/File:Province_House_(Nova_Scotia).jpg, Creative Commons license; 46 (LO), meunierd/Shutterstock; 47 (UP), Courtesy of Old Burying Ground Foundation; 47 (CTR), SF photo/Shutterstock; 47 (LO), Peter S. Zwicker/Bacalao Photo; 48-9, J. Steeves/Parks Canada; 50, André Cornellier/Parks Canada; 52 (UP), Lauren Hardy/Parks Canada; 52 (LO), M. Powell/Parks Canada; 54, © Stock Connection Blue/Alamy; 55, Parks Canada; 57, Dale Wilson/Parks Canada; 58 (all), Parks Canada; 59 (UP), Parks Canada; 59 (CTR), Dennis Jarvis at https://commons.wikimedia.org/wiki/File:St._Peters_Canal_National_Historic_Site_of_Canada.jpg, Creative Commons license; 59 (LO), Parks Canada; 60-61, Geordon Harvey/Parks Canada; 62, Chris Reardon/Parks Canada; 63 (UP and LO LE), Chris Reardon/Parks Canada; 63 (LO RT), Geordon Harvey/Parks Canada; 64-5, Nigel Fearon/Parks Canada; 66 (UP), Brian Atkinson/Parks Canada; 66 (CTR), Fralambert, Wikimedia Commons at https://commons.wikimedia.org/wiki/File:Beaubears_Island.JPG, Creative Commons license; 66 (LO), © All Canada Photos/Alamy; 67 (UP), Chris Reardon/Parks Canada; 67 (CTR), Parks Canada; 67 (LO), Vibe Images/Adobe Stock; 68, Parks Canada; 69, Chris Reardon/Parks Canada; 70-71, Dale Wilson/Parks Canada; 72, D. Gordon E. Robertson, Wikimedia Commons at https://commons.wikimedia.org/wiki/File:L%27Anse_aux_Meadows,_recreated_long_house.jpg, Creative Commons license; 74 (both), Dale Wilson/Parks Canada; 76, E. Walsh/Parks Canada; 77, Dale Wilson/Parks Canada; 78 (UP), Dale Wilson/Parks Canada; 78 (LO), © Island Images/Alamy; 80, E. Walsh/Parks Canada; 81, Nate Gates/Parks Canada; 83-4, Chris Reardon/Parks Canada; 85, André Cornellier/Parks Canada; 86, Dale Wilson/Parks Canada; 87, J.F. Bergeron/ENVIROFOTO/Parks Canada; 88 (UP), © Cindy Hopkins/Alamy; 88 (CTR), Dale Wilson/Parks Canada; 88 (LO), Edith Cuerrier, CD; 89 (UP), Anglican Cathedral of St. John the Baptist in St. John's, NL; 89 (CTR), Nilfanion, Wikimedia Commons at https://commons.wikimedia.org/wiki/File:St_John%27s_Basilica.jpg, Creative Commons license; 89 (LO), Mo Laidlaw, Wikimedia Commons at https://commons.wikimedia.org/wiki/File:Commissariat_House,_St_John%27s,_NL.JPG, Creative Commons license; 90 (UP), Chris Reardon/Parks Canada; 90 (CTR), Charles-Alexandre Paré/Parks Canada; 90 (LO), Parks Canada; 91, Miguel Legault/Parks Canada; 93, Jacques Beardsell/Parks Canada; 94-6, Parks Canada; 97, © All Canada Photos/Alamy; 98-9, Nicolas Tondreau/iStockPhoto; 100, Ron Garnett/Parks Canada; 102 (LO), Peanutroaster/Dreamstime.com; 102 (UP), Musée Royal 22e Régiment; 104, Cpl. Olivier Lavigne-Ortiz, courtesy Musée Royal 22e Régiment; 105, John Stanton, Wikimedia Commons at http://fortwiki.com/File:Quebec_Dauphine_Redoubt_-_20.jpg, Creative Commons license; 107, Félix Genêt Laframboise; 109, Mathieu Dupuis/Parks Canada; 110, Parks Canada; 112, Canadian Tourism Commission/Parks Canada; 114 (UP LE and RT), Canadian Tourism Commission/Parks Canada; 114 (LO), N. Boisvert/Parks Canada; 115, Canadian Tourism Commission/Parks Canada; 116, Mathieu Dupuis/Parks Canada; 117 (UP and CTR), Mathieu Dupuis/Parks Canada; 117 (LO), Parks Canada; 118 (UP), Michel Roy/digitaldirect.ca; 118 (CTR), Patrick Matte; 118 (LO), Courtesy Mount Hermon Cemetery; 119 (UP), Archives Commission des champs de bataille nationaux; 119 (CTR), Luc-Antoine Couturier; 119 (LO), Musée des Ursulines de Trois-Rivières; 120-21, Miguel Legault/Parks Canada; 122, Charles-Alexandre Paré/Parks Canada; 123-4, Chris Reardon/Parks Canada; 125, Adqproductions at https://en.wikipedia.org/wiki/The_Fur_Trade_at_Lachine_National_Historic_Site#/media/File:Lachine_Poste_de_Traite.jpg, Creative Commons license; 126, Charles-Alexandre Paré/Parks Canada; 127, Chris Reardon/Parks Canada; 128, William James Topley/Library and Archives Canada/PA-010401; 129, Eugene M. Finn/National Film Board of Canada. Photothèque/Library and Archives Canada/PA-195432; 130, Chris Reardon/Parks Canada; 131-2, Fred Cattroll/Parks Canada; 133, Alexandre Choquette/Parks Canada; 134-7, Éli Michaud/Parks Canada; 139 (UP), Songquan Deng/Shutterstock; 139 (CTR), Yvan Dubé; 139 (LO), meunierd/Shutterstock; 140 (UP), The Montreal Museum of Fine Arts/Paul Boisvert; 140 (CTR), Jardin botanique de Montréal (Claude Lafond); 140 (LO), Martin New; 141 (CTR), Parks Canada; 141 (UP), UCSS/Pascale Bergeron; 141 (LO), Henrickson, English Wikipedia at https://en.wikipedia.org/wiki/Windsor_Station_(Montreal)#/media/File:Gare_Windsor_Station.jpg, Creative Commons license; 142-5, Éric Le Bel/Parks Canada; 146-7, Douglas Harvey/Parks Canada; 148, Alexandre Choquette/Parks Canada; 149-50, Parks Canada; 152, Gianni Dagli Orti/The Art Archive at Art Resource, NY; 153, Justin + Lauren; 154-7, Chris Reardon/Parks Canada; 159, Stéphane Lafrance/Parks Canada; 160, N. Rajotte/Parks Canada; 162 (UP), B. Morin/Parks Canada; 162 (CTR), AGF Srl/Alamy; 162 (LO), John McQuarrie/Parks Canada; 163, TonyIaniro/iStockPhoto; 164, Scott Munn/Parks Canada; 166-7, Adobe Stock; 168, Radius Images/Alamy; 170 (UP), S. Lunn/Parks Canada; 170 (LO), © John Sylvester/Alamy; 172-3, Madeleine Lahaie/Parks Canada; 174, John McQuarrie/Parks Canada; 176, Brian Morin/Parks Canada; 177, Robin Andrew/Parks Canada; 178, Museum of Health Care at Kingston; 179 (UP), Taxiarchos228 at https://en.wikipedia.org/wiki/Kingston_City_Hall_(Ontario)#/media/File:Kingston_City_Hall_(NHSC_chart).jpg, Free Art license; 179 (CTR), André Guindon/Parks Canada; 179 (LO), André Guindon/Parks Canada; 180, Adobe Stock; 182, jiawangkun/Shutterstock; 184 (UP), Courtesy City of Ottawa, Museums & Heritage Programs Unit; 184 (CTR), Agriculture and Agri-Food Canada; 184 (LO), Adobe Stock; 185 (UP), Courtesy National Capital Commission; 185 (CTR), Tracey Whitefoot/Alamy Stock Photo; 185 (LO), Martin Lipman © Canadian Museum of Nature; 186-8, Courtesy Diefenbunker: Canada's Cold War Museum; 190, David Joyner/Getty Images; 191, mikecphoto/Shutterstock; 192, Dwayne Brown Studio; 193, Courtesy St. Lawrence Parks Commission; 195 (both), All Canada Photos/Alamy; 196-7, Parks Canada; 198, Madeleine Lahaie/Parks Canada; 200 (UP), S. Howard/Parks Canada; 200 (LO), Madeleine Lahaie/Parks Canada; 202, J. Butterill/Parks Canada; 203 (UP), B. Morin/Parks Canada; 203 (LO), Parks Canada; 204-205, Scott Munn/Parks Canada; 206, Dale Wilson/Parks Canada; 207, B. Morin/Parks Canada; 208, Dale Wilson/Parks Canada; 210, Scott Munn/Parks Canada; 211 (UP), Scott Munn/Parks Canada; 211 (LO), Courtesy City of Hamilton, National Historic Dundurn & Hamilton Scourge; 212 (UP), Image © Ontario Heritage Trust; 212 (CTR), Greg's Southern Ontario (catching Up Slowly)/www.flickr.com/photos/57156785@N02/19411504978; 212 (LO), Courtesy City of Hamilton, National Historic Dundurn & Hamilton Scourge; 213 (UP), Royal Botanical Gardens/Mark Zelinski; 213 (CTR), Balcer/Public Domain at https://commons.wikimedia.org/wiki/File:Butler%27s_Barracks_NOTL_1.JPG; 213 (LO), Dale Wilson/Parks Canada; 214 (UP), G. Vandervlugt/Parks Canada; 214 (CTR), Image © Ontario Heritage Trust; 214 (LO), Kiev.Victor/Shutterstock.com; 215 (UP), B. Morin/Parks Canada; 215 (CTR), Cosmo Condina North America/Alamy Stock Photo; 215 (LO), Kurtis Bickell/Parks Canada; 216 (UP), Image © Ontario Heritage Trust; 216 (CTR), Image © Ontario Heritage Trust; 216 (LO), Kiev.Victor/Shutterstock.com; 217 (UP), rmnoa357/Shutterstock.com; 217 (CTR), lam_chihang, Wikimedia Commons at https://commons.wikimedia.org/wiki/File:Loblaws_at_Maple_Leaf_Gardens.jpg, Creative Commons license; 217 (LO), Christopher Dew; 218-21, Scott Munn/Parks Canada; 222, J. Butterill/Parks Canada; 223 (UP), Parks Canada; 223 (CTR), artcphotos/Shutterstock; 223 (LO), Deconstructhis, public domain at https://commons.wikimedia.org/wiki/File:Southwoldvillage.jpg; 224-6, Scott Munn/Parks Canada; 227 (UP and LO LE), Scott Munn/Parks Canada; 227 (LO RT), G. Vandervlugt/Parks Canada; 228-9, Scott Munn/Parks Canada; 230 (UP and CTR), Kevin Hogarth/Parks Canada; 230 (LO), © Bill McComish/Photoscanada.com; 231, Youth Ambassadors 2012/Parks Canada; 232, Kevin Hogarth/Parks Canada; 234-5, © All Canada Photos/Alamy; 236, D. Dealey/Parks Canada; 238 (UP), G. Kopelow/Parks Canada; 238 (LO), © Hemis/Alamy; 240, © Design Pics Inc/Alamy; 242 (UP), © All Canada Photos/Alamy; 242 (LO LE), © Ken Gillespie Photography/Alamy; 242 (LO RT), © Design Pics Inc/Alamy; 244, Hans-Jürgen Hübner, Wikimedia Commons at https://commons.wikimedia.org/wiki/File:Louis_Riel_Haus.JPG, Creative Commons license; 245, © John Elk III/Alamy; 246 (UP), © Paul Browne 2009; 246 (CTR and LO), Robyn Hanson at https://www.flickr.com/photos/travelmanitoba; 247 (UP), Dan McKay, Wikimedia Commons at https://commons.wikimedia.org/wiki/File:Dalnavert_Museum.jpg, Creative Commons license; 247 (CTR), Exchange District BIZ; 247 (LO), Claude Robidoux/Getty Images; 248, Jeff Bolingbroke/Parks Canada; 249-51, Parks Canada; 252-9, Kevin Hogarth/Parks Canada; 260, Greg Huszar Photography/Parks Canada; 261-2, Kevin Hogarth/Parks Canada; 263 (UP), Wayne Shiels/Lone Pine Photo; 263 (LO), Parks Canada; 264 (UP), Robin and Arlene Karpan; 264 (CTR and LO), Parks Canada; 265 (UP), Greg Huszar Photography/Parks Canada; 265 (CTR), Courtesy Colin Chatfield/Wanuskewin Heritage Park; 265 (LO), Saskatoon Forestry Farm Park & Zoo; 266, Photograph courtesy of the Chilliwack Museum and Archives, PP501976; 267, Parks Canada; 268 (UP), Courtesy Ministry of Parks, Culture and Sport, Government of Saskatchewan; 268 (CTR), All Canada Photos/Alamy Stock Photo; 268 (LO), Mrhyland, Wikimedia Commons at https://en.wikipedia.org/wiki/Fort_Carlton#/media/File:DC2_Stills-050807-043.jpg, Creative Commons license; 269 (UP), Courtesy Donna Choppe; 269 (CTR), Canadian2006, Wikimedia Commons at https://en.wikipedia.org/wiki/Seager_Wheeler%27s_Maple_Grove_Farm#/media/File:Seager_Wheeler_farm_2014.jpg, Creative Commons license; 269 (LO), TravelCollection/Alamy Stock Photo; 270-71, Witold Skrypczak/Getty Images; 272, Traveler100, Wikimedia Commons at https://commons.wikimedia.org/wiki/Category:Bar_U_Ranch#/media/File:BarURanch-02.jpg, Creative Commons license; 274 (LE), © All Canada Photos/Alamy; 274 (RT), Peter Carroll/Getty Images; 276, M. French/Parks Canada; 277, Grapher78, Wikimedia Commons at https://commons.wikimedia.org/wiki/File:Frog_Lake_National_Historic_Site.JPG, Creative Commons license; 278, © David Muenker/Alamy; 281 (UP), Historic Sites and Museums, Alberta Culture and Tourism; 281 (LO LE), © David Muenker/Alamy; 281 (LO RT), © Witold Skrypczak/Alamy; 282, Fort Whoop Up Interpretive Society, Wikimedia Commons at https://en.wikipedia.org/wiki/Fort_Whoop-Up#/media/File:Fortwhoopupnationalhistoricsite.jpg, Creative Commons license; 283 (UP), Lougheed House Conservation Society; 283 (CTR), Brenda Kean/Alamy Stock Photo; 283 (LO), Courtesy Epic Photography/Government House of Alberta Foundation; 284 (UP), Amar Athwal/Parks Canada; 284 (CTR), Graham Twoney/Parks Canada; 284 (LO), Parks Canada; 285, © Flirt/Alamy; 286, Parks Canada; 288, Graham Twoney/Parks Canada; 290, Amar Athwal/Parks Canada; 292, Jeff Bolingbroke/Parks Canada; 293, Amar Athwal/Parks Canada; 295 (UP), P. Kell/Parks Canada; 295 (CTR), Amy Krause/Parks Canada; 295 (LO), R. MacDonald/Parks Canada; 296, Chris Lund/National Film Board of Canada. Photothèque collection/Library and Archives Canada/PA-111579; 298 (UP), Ryan Bray/Parks Canada; 298 (CTR and LO), Rogier Gruys/BluePeak Travel Photography/Parks Canada; 299 (UP), R.D. Muir/Parks Canada; 299 (CTR), Parks Canada; 299 (LO), Michael Melford/Getty Images; 300 (UP), Stefanie Gignac/Parks Canada; 300w (CTR), Danita Delimont/Alamy Stock Photo; 300 (LO), Fort Steele Heritage Town; 301 (UP), Photo Courtesy of Glacier Park, Inc.; 301 (CTR), Paul Ruchlewicz; 301 (LO), Fort Steele Heritage Town; 302 (UP), Scott Munn/Parks Canada; 302 (CTR), Annie Griffiths/National Geographic Creative; 302 (LO), Bob Matheson/Parks Canada; 303, Michael Wheatley/Alamy Stock Photo; 305, ginevre/iStockphoto; 306-307, davemantel/iStockphoto; 308, Bob Matheson/Parks Canada; 310 (both), Scott Munn/Parks Canada; 312, John Butterill/Parks Canada; 314, Christian J. Stewart Photography/Parks Canada; 316-17, Kelly Jill/Parks Canada; 318, Michael Wheatley/Alamy Stock Photo; 319, iStockphoto; 320 (UP), Maurice Crooks/Alamy Stock Photo; 320 (LO), Jennifer Oehler/iStockPhoto; 322 (UP), redfishweb/iStockPhoto; 322 (LO), Tom Bean/Alamy Stock Photo; 323 (UP), John Mitchell/Alamy Stock Photo; 323 (CTR), Ferenc Cegledi/Shutterstock; 323 (LO), Sergei Bachlakov/Shutterstock.com; 324 (UP), cdrin/Shutterstock.com; 324 (CTR), Courtesy Sian James; 324 (LO), Hallmark Heritage Society; 325 (UP), CCHMS—Andrew Annuar; 325 (CTR), canadastock/Shutterstock; 325 (LO), Doug Schnurr/Shutterstock; 326-8, D. Houston/Parks Canada; 329 (UP), Courtesy Fort McLeod Historic Park; 329 (LO), Courtesy Barkerville Historic Town; 330, Ron Garnett/Parks Canada; 331, Parks Canada; 332 (UP), Fritz Mueller/Parks Canada; 332 (CTR), Sam DCruz/Shutterstock; 332 (LO), US Mission Canada, Wikimedia Commons at https://commons.wikimedia.org/wiki/Category:Klondike_(ship,_1937)#/media/File:Paddlewheel_of_the_SS_Klondike.jpg, Creative Commons license; 333, Fritz Mueller/Parks Canada; 334, Sam DCruz/Shutterstock; 336-7, Fritz Mueller/Parks Canada; 339 (UP), oksana.perkins/Shutterstock; 339 (LO), Fritz Mueller/Parks Canada; 340, Parks Canada; 341 (UP), Yukon Historic Sites, Wikimedia Commons at https://en.wikipedia.org/wiki/List_of_historic_places_in_Yukon#/media/File:Former_Territorial_Court_House.JPG, Creative Commons license; 341 (CTR), Fritz Mueller/Parks Canada; 341 (LO), Thierry Boyer/Parks Canada; 342, Scott Polar Research Institute, University of Cambridge; 343, Marc-André Bernier/Parks Canada; 344, Sam DCruz/Shutterstock; 345, Flickr/Gareth Sloan.

ACKNOWLEDGEMENTS

National Geographic thanks the authors for their contributions to the *National Geographic Guide to the National Historic Sites of Canada:* Amy Kenny (Atlantic Provinces, Ontario), Brielle Morgan (Québec, Far North), Colleen Seto (Prairie Provinces, Rockies), Christopher Pollon (British Columbia), John McCormick ("The First Peoples of Canada"), and Ken McGoogan ("Roots of Contemporary Canada"; "Urban Canada: Montreal, Vancouver, & Toronto").

National Geographic would like to thank all who generously gave time and talent to the creation of this book, especially John Thomson, Lori Bayne, Barbara Brownell Grogan, Bill O'Donnell, Marianne Koszorus, Charles Kogod, Jane Sunderland, Mary Stephanos, Uliana Bazaar, Andrew Campbell, George Green, Mike McNey, Heather McElwain, Marty Magne, Alexandra Mosquin, Mallory Schwartz, Marianne Stopp, Meg Stanley, Scott Stephen, Frieda Klippenstein, Dianne Dodd, Pascale Guindon, Brigitte Violette, Anne Marie Lane Jonah, Alain Gelly, Yvan Fortier, Christine Chartré, Meryl Oliver, Bob Garcia, Karen Routledge, Bill Perry, Cynthia Graham, Ariane Marin-Perreault, Ryan Harris, Geneviève Charrois, Marc-André Bernier, Norman Shields, Blythe MacInnis, Jennifer Cousineau, Camille Collinson, Jason Bouzanis, Julie Hahn, Joanne Huppe, Celine Corville, Celine Blanc, Francois Houle, Natalie-Anne Bussiere, Brock Fraser, Geordon Harvey, and Steve Duquette.

Thanks go to the following individuals at national historic sites for reviewing entries: Susan Kennard, Anne Frick, Melissa Banovich, Nancy Hildebrand, Sophie Lauro, Mimi Horita, Jacolyn Daniluck, Camille Girard-Ruel, Jessica Lambert, Terrie Dionne, Natalie Fournier, Elise Maltinsky, Carly Sims, Darlene Small, Kimberley Thompson, Isabelle Savoie, Simon Boiteau, Irene LeGatt, Doreen McGillis, Catherine Reynolds, Travis Weber, Danielle Hickey, Jeremy Roop, Jennifer Duff, Alannah Phillips, Coady Slaunwhite, Pamela Jalak, Kristy McKay, Lianne Roberts, David Lavallee, Neil Mcinnis, Bob Grill, Dale MacEachern, Meaghan Bradley, Natalie Austin, Martine Tousignant, Isabel Lariviere, Barbara MacDonald, Lindsay Oehlke, Michelle LeBlond, Kimberly Labar, Michael Queenton, Emilie Devoe, Julie Bastarache, Nadine Gauvin, Rachel Richardson, Lisa Curtis, Alex Dale, Elizabeth MacDonnell, Lorna Sierolawski, J. Paul Kennington, Kurt Hanson, Michael McAllister, Larry Ostola, Mathew Rosenblatt, John Hughes, Henriette Riegel, Dan Chevaldayoff, David MacKenzie, Rebecca Baker, Phil Townsend, Peter Haughn, Claude Grou, Barry McCullough, Gordon Kerr, Nathalie Bondil, Andre Delisle, Dr. James Low, Donald Lordly, Beth Hanna, Jens Jensen, Larry Pearson, Richard Linzey, Giles Bourque, Andrea O'Brien, Craig Beaton, Carlos Germann, Alex Reeves, Janice Penner, Francis Jacques, Reverend Father Floyd Gallant, David Sisley, Julian Smith, Yvonne MacNeil, RCMP Captain Ken Burton, Claude Pronovost, Lucie Rochette, and Andrew McDonald.

Since 1888, the National Geographic Society has funded more than 12,000 research, exploration, and preservation projects around the world. National Geographic Partners distributes a portion of the funds it receives from your purchase to National Geographic Society to support programs including the conservation of animals and their habitats.

National Geographic Partners
1145 17th Street NW
Washington, DC 20036-4688 USA

Become a member of National Geographic and activate your benefits today at natgeo.com/jointoday.

For information about special discounts for bulk purchases, please contact National Geographic Books Special Sales: specialsales@natgeo.com

For rights or permissions inquiries, please contact National Geographic Books Subsidiary Rights: bookrights@natgeo.com

All photographs and marks have been reproduced with the permission of the Parks Canada Agency, or as otherwise indicated in the credits on page 351.

All maps have been produced by National Geographic Partners based on data provided by the Parks Canada Agency or made available through Natural Earth. The incorporation of data sourced from the Parks Canada Agency or made available through Natural Earth within this book shall not be construed as constituting an endorsement by them of this book.

Parks Canada excludes all representations, warranties, obligations, and disclaims all liabilities in relation to the use of the maps included in this book.

The information in this book has been carefully checked and to the best of our knowledge is accurate. However, details are subject to change, and the publisher cannot be responsible for such changes, or for errors or omissions. Assessments of sites, hotels, and restaurants are based on the author's subjective opinions, which do not necessarily reflect the publisher's opinion.

ISBN: 978-1-4262-1755-5

Printed in Canada

16/FC/1